8.5.77

Urban Economics

An Introduction

Alan R. Winger

Federal Home Loan Bank of Cincinnati

University of Cincinnati

CHARLES E. MERRILL PUBLISHING COMPANY
A Bell & Howell Company
Columbus, Ohio

Published by
CHARLES E. MERRILL PUBLISHING COMPANY
A Bell & Howell Company
Columbus, Ohio 43216

This book was set in Times Roman.
The production editors were Laura Harder and Jo Ellen Diehl.
The cover was designed by Will Chenoweth.

International Standard Book Number: 0-675-08555-1

Library of Congress Catalog Card Number: 76-20179

1 2 3 4 5 6 7 8—81 80 79 78 77

Printed in the United States of America

Acknowledgments

p. 20, Table 2–7. Derived from Table 4–3 by Kevin Lancaster in *Introduction to Modern Micro Economics*. Chicago: Rand McNally and Company, 1969, p. 90. Used with permission of the author and publisher.

pp. 15, 16, 18, Tables 2–1, 2–2, and 2–3 by William Miernyk in *The Elements of Input-Output Analysis*. New York: Random House, 1965, pp. 9, 22, 26. Used with permission of author and publisher.

p. 190, Table 9–6. Data from Table 7–2 by Alan Batchelder, in *The Economics of Poverty*. New York: John Wiley and Sons, Inc., 1971, p. 146. Used with permission of author and publisher.

p. 191, Table 9–7. Data from Table 3–4 by Edward Fried, Alice Rivlin, Charles Schultze, and Nancy Teeters, in *Setting National Priorities: The 1974 Budget*. Washington, D.C., The Brookings Institution, 1973, p. 47. Used with permission of the Brookings Institution.

p. 204, Table 10–1. Derived from Table 41 in *American Housing Needs, 1970 to 1980*. Joint Center for Urban Studies of MIT and Harvard University, 1973. Used with permission of the Center.

p. 215, Table 10–2. Data from Table on Rental Housing (White-NonWhite) by Chester Rapkin in "Price Discrimination in the Rental Housing Market," in *Essays in Urban Land Economics,* Berkeley: University of California (1966).

p. 303, Figures 14–1 and 14–2. These figures are derived from Diagram 1 by James Ohls and Michelle White in "The Effect of Zoning on Land Value," in *Journal of Urban Economics,* 1 (1974), pp. 428–44. Used with permission of author and publisher.

Preface

This is a book about urban economics, written for those with limited exposure in economics, such as an introductory course in economics or its equivalent. The book's primary concern is to show how it is possible to make sensible statements about the economic aspects of urban facts, issues, and problems. To show this requires a theoretical framework.

In dealing with urban economic theory, this book differs from most other books on the subject in that the theory chapters come first consecutively. The reason for this is that most applications draw on more than one part of the theory. Considering the theory as one package to be taken up first provides more flexibility in considering the insights we gain from theory applications to particular urban facts, issues, and problems. It also provides a unity that, in my view, is missing when theory and applications are mixed.

Some may consider this part of the book to be too much theory at one time. It doesn't have to be. It is possible to rearrange the chapters to bring in certain applications immediately after the discussion of certain theoretical concepts. One alternative format is as follows:

1) Take up the concepts of economics of scale in chapter 2 and location theory and central place concepts in chapter 3 first. Then expose the student to some history and futurology—chapter 7, Urbanization and the Urban Hierarchy—and the issue of city size—chapter 13, City Size.

2) Take up the chapter on Macroeconomic Models and City Growth next, followed by chapter 15, Models of City Growth.

3) Chapter 5, Location Theory and City Structure, comes next, followed by some history and futurology in chapter 8, The Spreading Out of the American City, and urban modelling in chapter 16, Urban Simulation.

4) Finally, chapter 6, The Performance of the Urban Economy, is taken up, followed by parts III and IV.

The question of how to deal with applications is the real challenge in writing a book on urban economics. The possible topics are many; selections have to be made. The selections in this book reflect a concern with providing students with breadth in their exposure to these materials. There is some history, a sampling of urban problems, a concern with urban planning, and an elementary introduction to urban models and simulation.

After topics are selected, a decision must be made concerning how much detail should be incorporated into the discussion of these applications. In a book written for those with limited exposure to economics, the focus must be on applications that are easily understood. This is possible to do in considerable detail by using the case study method, in which a city or two could be selected, the facts assembled, and the applications developed. To approach the matter in this way is both strong and weak; strong, because details can be used in illustrating the applicability of some principle, but weak because the ability to apply the principles of the subject is restricted. While cities are alike in many respects, they also differ significantly in other respects. Conclusions that stem from applications to one city may not apply to others.

The other approach to how much detail to use is to work with more general data from the Bureau of the Census and other government agencies, as is done in this book. This leads to a general discussion of how the theory can be applied. The advantage of this approach is that the conclusions from such a discussion are applicable to a wide range of urban situations, touching upon situations found in most cities. Written in this way, this part of the book lends itself to supplementary materials. Some of the applications could be about a particular city of special interest to the class or instructor. Teaching in Cincinnati, for example, I would concentrate on developing material for metropolitan Cincinnati to be used in conjunction with the text.

As urban economics matures and our economic knowledge of the urban universe expands, books on urban economics begin to look more and more alike. This book looks like some others in a number of respects, but it is intended to differ in one significant respect. The primary emphasis is to show the student how economics, considered as scientific language, can be applied to help us understand the economic facts of urban life. The concern is with why people do what they do in cities; why they live where they do; why some live in slum housing; why most drive cars to work; why some live in poverty in ghettos. The objective is to show how we can, with the aid of urban economics, construct sensible responses to this type of question. There is, of course, much in the urban scene about which urban economists can say very little. If one has a reasonable grasp of the concepts of urban economics, however, there are a number of important questions that can be answered in a sensible way.

My intellectual debts are many, the most important of which are included in the references at the end of each chapter. I also owe a great debt to the late Professor Tiebout who stimulated my interest in the subject in a way that only Charlie could. Professor Bill Russell had much to do with my growing awareness of what economic analysis is all about. My education about this subject continues in my close association with my colleague Kirk Roberts. None of these are to be held responsible for what follows.

Accolades are also due to Louise Knapp and Margaret Thomas for the many contributions they made with tenderness and care in the preparation of the manuscript for publication.

Last but not least, I owe a debt of immense proportions to my wife Mary and daughter Lisa for their forbearance and understanding throughout the many months this project has been under way. You see, Mary and Lisa, I told you that one day it would be over.

A. R. W.

Contents

For Mary and Lisa

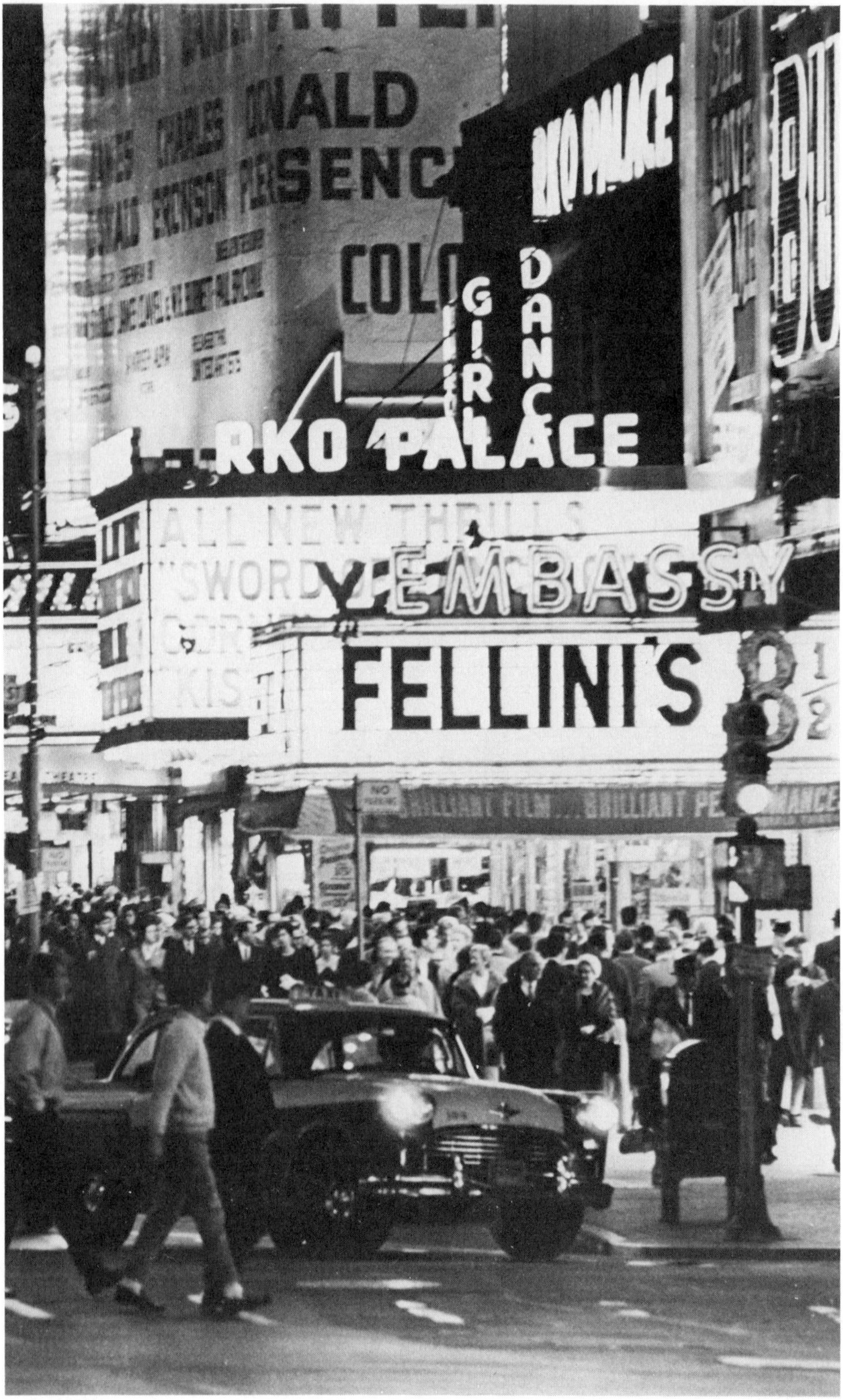
RKO PALACE
RKO PALACE
ALL NEW THRILLS
EMBASSY
FELLINI'S

Introduction

Most people today live in cities. Some live in affluence; some live in poverty. Some are happy; some uneasy. There are also people who would like to totally remove themselves from the city.

To many people, cities, of course, have always had problems. It is not difficult to find statements about the conditions of life in cities a hundred years ago parallelling statements being made about cities today. Still, cities have always been considered by most as where the action is. To many, cities are the places where excitement and the full life begins and ends. The numbers feeling this way, however, appear to be declining. But are people really disenchanted with the city?

Certainly the city has lost some of its appeal as a place to live and work. City residents have been buffeted recently with a seemingly endless succession of problems. In the 1950s it was the flight of the middle class to the suburbs and a massive movement of low-income whites and blacks from the south to the centers of many of our cities. Ghettos grew in number and size, and cities became sprawling megalopolises with what many considered to be unsightly and inefficient features.

Sprawl and the ghettoization of the central city continued as problems in the 1960s, with the problems of the latter building to a peak of intensity and erupting into urban riots of substantial force during the second half of the decade. Watts, Detroit, and Washington, D.C. are the most memorable, but there were many others.

Just as quickly and unexpectedly as they came, the riots disappeared as we entered the 1970s. City problems did not. Housing, poverty, urban renewal, congestion, pollution, crime, and excessive size were discussed as important problems of the city in the media, in universities, in places of business, and at home. But the public attention drawn to these problems diminished as the problems of inflation, recession, and energy came into the foreground. City problems received much less public attention during the middle part of the 1970s until the fiscal problems of New York City began to reach a climax. The public concern now, however, seems to be more with how cities can learn to live within their means rather than with how to cope with their problems. For whatever reasons, the public's perception of the problems of cities seems to have changed. While few are willing to argue that we have resolved the problems of urban poverty, urban housing, urban transportation, urban size, and urban pollution, the major concern now seems to be how can we keep what we have.

Certainly, this kind of attitude, if widespread, adds little to the appeal of living in cities; on the contrary, it greatly detracts from city living. Indeed, it suggests that we may be headed towards that day when cities are a thing of the past.

Care must be taken at this point. Attitudes, no matter how scientifically they are measured, are mercurial. Today we are pessimistic; tomorrow we may not be. To put this in perspective, we need only note that a pessimistic feeling about the fate of cities is nothing new. It was present during the riots of the sixties; it was probably also with us 100 years ago when our concerns were with slum housing, poverty, urban renewal, crime, congestion, and pollution, which then took the form of horse manure.

The significant question is: Does our current view of the city and its problems really reflect the "realities" of city life? Is New York City really "going down the tube"? Will it be followed by Baltimore, Detroit, and Los Angeles? What is happening in the ghettos? Do we still have urban housing problems? What ever happened to urban renewal? The congestion in some cities seems to be easing. What's going on? Are our cities too large? Have they spread out too much? What success have we had in dealing with city problems through urban planning?

It will not suffice to talk about the fate of cities in very general terms. Our judgments about the urban past, the urban present, and the urban future must be based on knowledge concerned with very specific facts about cities. It should be knowledge that will allow us to answer the questions just raised. This, moreover, is just a sample of questions that barely scratch the surface of any judgments we make about what is happening to our cities and what this implies with respect to the future.

URBAN ECONOMICS AND OUR VIEW OF CITIES

Urban economics is a body of knowledge concerned with the economic facts of urban areas. Urban areas are usually equated with cities, which, in turn, are thought of as groups of people clustered together in geographic space in their moments of work, rest, and play. When considered in this way, the spatial dimension becomes a central part of the meaning of *urban*. When this is so, the focus of urban discussions is on the pattern of urban settlements, and urban analysis concentrates on the task of constructing explanations of this pattern.

When urban society is considered in this way, urban economics becomes concerned with the explanation of the economic facts of a system of spatially delimited cities or urban areas. Economic facts, of course, are social facts; they are concerned with what people do as they function in groups, and their dealings with one another as they affect their common welfare. Conventional economic wisdom has it, however, that only activities directly related to the use of society's scarce resources constitute economic facts. Such facts are a reflection of optimizing behavior in the sense of seeking maximum benefit from activities involving scarce resources.

Obviously, in an urban economy of any size, there are a great many artifacts and much activity, too much to be grasped in any sense of the whole. As a practical matter, we look at parts of the whole and many who do so choose to focus on "issues" or problematic aspects of the facts of concern. Problem solving, however, requires understanding of the mechanism or process that generates the problem. If we choose to deal with the problem of rapidly rising housing costs for low-income families in central cities, for example, we stand a much better chance of taking constructive action if we can explain the reasons why these costs are rising.

What do we mean by an explanation of the facts? Explanations to some are to be found in terms of certain imagined personal entities. The "devil" theory of disease constitutes a well-known example of this form of explanation. Deadly disease is attributed to some personal entity that is equipped with a set of motives, e.g., the devil. These motives are construed as a concern with administering punishment for some "wrong" that has been done. Thus, deadly disease is to be attributed to a personal entity—the devil—and it is inflicted upon the person as punishment for something he or she has done.

Obviously, not many subscribe to this kind of an explanation of disease. Most people believe that much more insight is obtained through common sense. Such knowledge is, after all, practical and down to earth. Its application to the question of disease could take a number of forms. One of these might be to link death from a disease such as pneumonia to standing stark naked in a cold draft after taking a hot bath. Yet, one can contract pneumonia and not die, and it is by no means clear that the relation between body and external temperature is the "cause" of the disease. Common sense, contrary to popular belief, does not represent an explicitly systematic way of explaining particular facts.

If some facts cannot be explained by common sense, then how? Increasingly, we have come to believe that reliable explanations of facts are only forthcoming from the conclusions of scientific inquiry. Many who believe this, however, only have a vague and sometimes distorted view of what science is. In the mind of the nonscientist, for example, science tends to be viewed as a world of experience. It is filled with such concrete things as test tubes, instruments with pointers, strange looking chambers, computer print-outs, etc. But as we learn more about it, what goes on in the laboratory turns out to be only a small part of what's involved in scientific investigation. Science is in effect a filter through which experience is "purified," and this purification process relies heavily on inference or reasoning. Much is done prior to what goes on in the laboratory. Experiments or statistical testing of nonexperimental data are carefully thought-out events that are firmly rooted in certain basic concepts and principles. These experiments provide a foundation for inquiry into particular types of subject matter. Indeed, where success has been most notable, i.e., in the physical sciences, the corpus of statements that constitute scientific knowledge in these disciplines is theory laden. The successful scientist concentrates on matters that seem well removed from the facts of everyday life to the nonscientist. These are crucial matters; theory, in effect, provides the insights necessary to develop testable hypotheses about those facts which stand in a casual relation with the facts of concern.

Economic theory can be used as a means of illustrating what's involved in constructing a scientific explanation of some fact. Consider again the fact of an increase in the cost of housing for low-income families in the central city. Our concern is with explaining this fact. The question is: How can economic theory be used to help us do this?

Note that by asserting the housing costs of low-income families have risen, we are using language in a way that provides shape and form to the experience through which we come to know this fact. Costs, income, and families are linguistic representations of concepts on the basis of which we organize experimental data in ways that uncover the economic fact that the housing costs of low-income families in central cities have risen.

But why have these costs risen? According to the scientist, the answer is found in another fact or set of facts, e.g., an increase in urban renewal. Suppose we argue that urban renewal does explain the rise in housing costs of low-income families. To get anyone to believe us we must be able to show how and why these two sets of facts can be linked together in this way.

Linking facts requires that we be able to compare aspects of the facts to be linked. To make such comparisons, there must be characteristics that are common to the facts to be compared, no matter how diverse they appear. In economics, as in other sciences, attempts to discern these characteristics have resulted in the development of a language which allows the user to *abstract* facts from "extraneous" elements in particular situations. The subjects and predicates of that language are linguistic representations of concepts which embody distinctions that characterize abstract elements involved in most economic situations. Supply, demand, costs, and revenues are concepts in this sense, and they are characterized as theoretical in that they are abstract and hence are far-reaching or encompass many facts in the economic domain.

Theoretical concepts, however, do not provide a basis for linking sets of economic facts into cause-and-effect relationships. To know only what supply, demand, and price mean, for example, would contribute little to the explanation of why the price of low-income housing rose. These concepts have to be linked together in theories that denote the casual links between changes in demand or changes in supply and price. It is only theory in this sense that provides a basis for constructing models that assist us in the search for explanations.

Why have the housing costs of low-income families risen? Was it urban renewal?

Suppose we had a housing market model that had its roots in conventional microeconomic theory. Its functions should denote certain channels through which the price of housing will be influenced. At a very elementary level these channels might be construed as supply and demand. Even with a model as simple as this we can make statements about the direction of the price effects of particular kinds of change in demand and supply. This is important because, to the extent that links can be established between urban renewal and market demand or supply, this model provides a basis for making statements about the directional impact of urban renewal on the price or cost of housing in general, and low-income housing in particular.

In fact, our urban renewal programs appear to have been implemented in ways that had the effect of reducing the supply of housing units available to low-income families. According to a housing-market model, this should show up as a change which increases the price of low-income housing. Note that economic theory provides a basis for asserting that certain governmental programs, whether intended or not, have had the effect of increasing the costs of housing to low-income families.

How seriously such an assertion should be taken is another matter. To one who knows something about economics it will seem reasonable. But the question of whether it constitutes an explanation raises other questions. For one thing, there are many other kinds of change that affect the supply and demand for low-income housing, some of which may in fact have done so during the time interval under study. The point is that there are alternative hypotheses which have to be checked and the results collated with the investigation of the urban renewal. The outcome of such studies is by no means as certain as these few remarks imply. Moreover, the hypotheses that connect particular facts with changes in demand or supply and price are usually more involved than indicated above. Elemental economic models may not provide the means of generating suitable explanations of certain facts.

Still, this illustration should help to clarify the role of the theory of a discipline in the search for scientific explanations. If that theory has scope or power, it will provide the direction essential for the analysis of facts. We seek to explain facts in terms of other facts. But facts are infinite. Selections have to be made; and the theory of a discipline, if it is a good theory, provides clues which enable us to construct analysis models through which the links between facts can be established.

This view of scientific explanation makes clear the central element of any discipline that should form the core of a textbook about that discipline. The theories or theoretical frameworks are the first order of business. They should be sketched out systematically at the outset, for it is only after we have some grasp of the theories of the discipline that we can begin the task of explaining the facts and discussing the issues that constitute its subject mater. In urban economies, these are facts and issues concerned with cities.

SCOPE OF THE SUBJECT MATTER

The essential concern in this book is with urban areas construed as spatially delimited areas in which population densities are relatively high. When people talk about cities, this is what they usually have in mind.

But what of the fact that cities are also people? In fact, much of the interest in cities stems from a concern with problems that involve people. Shouldn't a concern with urbanism be a concern with the behavior of people in cities? Shouldn't we consider urbanism a concern with urban behavior?

In an earlier era, urbanism could be equated with what people did in cities. Back when the urban settlement pattern was one of a network of "compact" cities, i.e., densely settled areas, people in cities behaved in a way that was distinctive. They behaved in a way that set them apart from their "rural" counterparts. Now matters are more complicated. The settlement pattern is no longer properly characterized as one of a network of compact cities. Cities have grown and have done so by spreading out. From the relatively simple core-ring structures of an earlier era, most cities have become sprawling and polynucleated metropolitan areas. Moreover, an increasing number of cities are beginning to merge together, resulting in even larger areas of sprawling type multicentered urban developments often referred to as megalopolises.

This change in the settlement pattern has, in the view of some, made it difficult to equate urbanism with what people do in cities. The urban life style, it is argued, can no longer be equated with what goes on in places of high population density, for there is as much if not more "urbanity" in what is done in many "low" density suburbs. Nor has this movement of urban behavior away from the center of cities stopped at the perimeter of the metropolis. The activities of today's farmer in the developed nations of the world are just as urban as those who live in cities, and there are enclaves of artists, writers, and musicians nestled in rural areas, people whose activities have reached the peak of urbanity by most definitions. From such observations, it is just a short distance to the conclusion that the study of a contemporary urban population is, in effect, the study of society; that the prior equation of "urbaness" with "cityness" in the sense of a spatial entity is obsolete.

Such arguments, while not without merit, overstate the case. It is true that the activities of urban man now span greater distances. It is also true that some earlier behavioral distinctions between urban and rural people no longer hold. The market baskets of goods they consume, for example, are no longer so sharply differentiated from one another. Yet, there still are differences between what people do in cities and what they do in rural areas. Moreover, while the urban population has become much more dispersed in geographic space, spatial propinquity is still a significant attribute of such a population. Most people in developed countries still live in densely settled areas, e.g., cities or metropolitan areas. Such points of concentration are also the locus of some of society's major problems, e.g., substandard housing, transportation, poverty, and pollution. When talking about urban phenomenon and urban problems, we invariably have in mind human activities and institutions found somewhere within a system of spatially delimited cities and for good reason. The spatial dimension of urban society is still a crucial demarcation of that society, and cities are its hallmark.

If cities are the spatial entities of concern in this book, what about urban areas? Metropolitan areas? Megalopolises?

In this book, these terms are used interchangeably unless otherwise indicated. The reason for this has to do with style considerations in writing. Yet to treat these terms interchangeably could lead to confusion since they are not always synonymous in meaning as they are used in urban discourse. These differences warrant discussion.

While cities have a geographic dimension, they also have a legal dimension. Considered legally, cities are geographic clusters of people that have become incorporated as cities according to the laws of the state of which they are a part. The geographic scope of the legal city, however, may be too narrow. Cities in this sense are often surrounded by other cities and areas of some population density that are not incorporated. What we usually observe are clusters of people, the density peaks of which are found in some incorporated or legal city—the central city. This city, in turn, is surrounded by other cities and unincorporated areas with relatively high population densities, surroundings we often call *suburbs*. This overall conglomerate of both central city and its suburban environs has come to be called a *metropolitan area*. When, as a consequence of growth, what were once distinct and separate metropolitan areas began to converge, we have something often called *megalopolis*.

While we have all of these things now, the metropolitan area dominates. What exactly is it then that we mean by a metropolitan area? To raise this question is to become concerned with delineating urban boundaries in geographic space. It is to become concerned with the problem of separating urban from rural, which is essentially a problem of establishing the criteria against which decisions can be made about whether particular pieces of real estate do or do not belong within this or that urban or metropolitan area.

The Bureau of Census has, of course, been long engaged in the task of establishing these criteria, and in recent years the thrust of what it has done comes to focus on the urbanized area and standard metropolitan statistical area. In dealing with urbanized areas, Census has focused on the larger cities—the central cities—and attempted to determine which of those contiguous areas should be coupled with the larger area in delimiting the boundaries of the urbanized area. The criteria used in making these determinations include legal incorporation, levels of population density, and commuting patterns. The first two are particularly important. Cities for most purposes are considered to be the geographic equivalent of *local labor markets*. The important linkages are economic, and the most significant of these linkages are those involved in the purchase and sale of labor services. This means that cities are viewed as concentrations of jobs and people in geographic space where the extent of an area is delimited by the commuting radius to work. This is how cities are considered in this book unless otherwise indicated. They are, according to Census definitions, urbanized areas or standard metropolitan statistical areas.

Standard metropolitan statistical areas (SMSA) differ from urbanized areas in that the focus in the former is on counties within which the central city is located. If a city has a population above a certain specified minimum and that city and its environs are fully located within a county, the boundaries of the county are designated as a standard metropolitan statistical area. If, on the other hand, some of these environs or the city itself spills over into another county, that county will be included in the SMSA if it meets certain other criteria which are primarily concerned with commuting linkages.

So considered, cities or urban areas or metropolitan areas are depicted as units of area in which there is a point or points of peak population density—the central city. From these points density declines discontinuously, but nonetheless declines, as we move into the suburbs. It continues to decline until some minimum point of population density is reached on the periphery or rural area. (See Figure 1.1.)

Within these boundaries, there is no limit to our concerns. Anything that constitutes an urban economic fact or an urban problem that has economic content is something that can be put under the urban economic microscope. Not all of these facts or problems are considered in this book. Space and knowledge limitations mean that we must be selective. It is important nevertheless to recognize that anything that happens in our cities, if it has economic content, is potentially a part of the subject matter of urban economics. If we have a reasonable

Figure 1.1

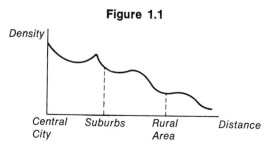

grasp of urban economic theory and a reasonable knowledge of the salient facts of our cities, we should be able to make reasonable interpretative statements about many of these facts.

URBAN ECONOMIC THEORY: WHAT IS IT?

The body of theory that provides the foundation of an economic analysis of urban facts has roots in both the macro and micro theories of the economist.

The Macro and Micro Theories of Economics   Macroeconomics is, of course, concerned with economic aggregates such as Gross National Product and price levels. Macro theory provides the framework that can be used as an aid in analyzing such economic problems as recession, inflation, and unemployment. *Microeconomics,* on the other hand, is concerned with individual units in the economy, such as the firm and households. The focus in micro theories is on explaining the economic behavior of these units, and how they interact in markets and in the public sector in allocating the nation's scarce resources. In fact, knowledge of macro- and microeconomics provides a basis for explaining a number of important urban economic facts. Yet, this theory is limited in the range of urban facts to which it can be applied. There is much in an urban setting that cannot be explained with a theory that does not explicitly incorporate the notion of space or distance as microeconomic theory does not. Nor is there enough in macroeconomic theory about certain aspects of the structure of the economy that have important bearing on the level and movement of income and employment in economies that are as open as cities.

The emerging interests of economists in regional and urban affairs led to research that has extended economic theory in ways that now provide theoretical frameworks better suited to the task of analyzing the salient facts of the urban economy. While it is unlikely that all urban economists share the same view with respect to the question of which of these frameworks should be included in the theory core of urban economics, certainly those concerning 1) the economic foundation of cities, 2) the system of cities, 3) city growth, 4) city structure or urban form, and 5) performance or welfare considerations in cities would be included by most. These are central features of urban society as we know it, and theories addressed to these features should be theories with scope, that is, they should help us to explain a wide range of urban phenomena.

The first part of this book is the theory portion. It is concerned with micro-economic theories as they have developed in research concerned with cities, systems of cities, city structure and the welfare aspects of cities, and macro-economic and growth theories that can be applied to the study of cities. These theories are developed in a very elemental way. All that is required is some understanding of economic concepts that are a part of an introductory course in basic economics.

Urban Applications: Which Ones?

Parts two, three, four, and five are concerned with an assortment of applications of these theories. In part two, the focus is on urban history. To ask about the lessons that can be learned from this history is to ask how history should be interpreted. Interpretations, in turn, require conceptual frameworks within which the facts can be fitted. Urban economic theory provides frameworks within which historical facts about cities can be fitted. The question is: Just how much do we profit by fitting these facts into those frameworks? Part two provides the reader with a sample of what can be done when economic theory is applied to the study of certain parts of urban history along with some indication of how both theory and history help in estimating the future.

Part three is concerned with urban problems. Factual settings are delineated and the problem or problems are defined in terms of economic criteria discussed in part one. Then the economic anatomy of the problem is developed along with possible solutions where appropriate. The list of problems selected for discussion—poverty, housing, transportation, problems in the urban public economy, and city size—is by no means complete. But it does represent a list of important problems about which a number of constructive things can be said on the basis of an application of the principles of urban economics.

Part four is a special section devoted to urban planning. Urban planning is a curious animal to many economists because planning is often taken as something that is done within the firm. If it is, markets that are working properly will do the rest. The problem is that markets apparently do not work as well as they should in some respects. Because of this, there is an urban planning profession, primarily concerned with directing certain activities in our cities into certain places.

While urban planning is considered important by many people, it has been the subject of comparatively few economic studies. Still, there are applications that can be made of urban economics theory notions which shed light on certain issues in urban planning.

Part five is concerned with a recent and important development in the study of urban areas, that is, urban modelling. Two sets of models are discussed. One set includes models of city growth, particularly those concerned with forecasting that growth. The second set includes models that focus more on urban structure or land use patterns. These are models that have been structured in ways that allow us to simulate the effects of particular kinds of change on that structure that can be initiated through policy actions taken by the local body politic. The discussion of these models is kept at a very elemental level. The primary concern is to convey the sense of what model builders are trying to accomplish, along with some very general statements about how they go about building models.

Scale Economics, Transportation Costs, and Cities

SUMMARY

We have cities for good economic reasons. Scale economies are involved, as are transportation costs.

If people as customers are dispersed geographically, production will be dispersed to minimize transportation costs. A technology entailing large scale methods of production can change this. Geographic concentrations of production may be necessary to realize the economies of scale inherent in this technology. Once the commitment to this technology is made and people and resources begin to concentrate in geographic space, transportation costs reinforce these pressures to move into the city.

Scale economies are a key to understanding why we have cities. Three kinds of economies of scale are distinguished. The first are those internal to the firm, stemming from a technology that fosters specialization in production. Their presence implies that unit or average costs decline with increased output. If, as production increases, technology is such that we can use more specialized methods of production, the productivity of the inputs used in production will increase. Productivity increases, in turn, mean falling average costs if input prices do not change.

Industry economies, the second of these economies, implies declining average costs for the firm as the output of the industry of which the firm is a part increases. The conditions giving rise to these economies, however, are much less evident than those that generate internal economies of scale.

The third set of scale economies are urbanization economies. These arise from conditions in which average costs of the firm fall as the scale of activity in the city in which it is located increases. Urbanization economies stem largely from a technology that promotes production on a scale that can only be achieved with firm specialization. Firm specialization, in turn, because of transportation costs, leads to geographic clustering and this clustering promotes further geographic specialization.

Diseconomies of scale are also possible. Conceivably, costs could rise with increases in the scale of output by the firm, the industry of which the firm is a part, or the city in which the firm is located. Whether diseconomies exist however, is less certain. The fact that costs rise in cities as they grow is more a consequence of the growing scarcity of some input such as land or management, rather than increases in the scale of activity in the city as a whole.

City building is construction activity that yields a physical plant, the individual units of which are in close geographic proximity to one another. It is a plant that houses the majority of the activities of a great many men and women and in doing so concentrates this activity in geographic space. The outcome is a city. But why cities? Scale economies are involved, as are transportation costs.

Before cities, when our society was mostly agrarian, the population was dispersed geographically. As long as there were no cost advantages in large-scale geographically concentrated production, production remained dispersed because of transportation costs. Concentrating production, given these conditions, would have increased the cost of getting the product from the producer to the consumer.

Suppose now that technology begins to generate methods of production that yield lower costs if the scale of production is increased. Now there are likely to be benefits from geographic concentration in the form of lower costs. With the new technology, geographic concentration yields both benefits and costs. In a sense, the economic arena becomes one in which economies of scale and transportation costs are pitted against one another. Transportation costs have dispersive effects when the population is dispersed.

Economies of scale, on the other hand, are concentrating in their effects. That we have cities suggests that the concentrating benefits of economies of scale outweigh the transportation costs that come with geographic concentration of production. Cities can thus be viewed as the outcome of a technology that gave us methods of production requiring large-scale production.

Precisely what is meant by economies of scale? What are transportation costs? Does it really make sense to view cities as the outcome of a contest in which economies of scale and transportation costs are pitted as opposing forces? These are the questions examined in this chapter. Before considering them, however, certain principles of economic costs as they relate to the output decisions of firms are reviewed briefly.

ECONOMIC COSTS AND OUTPUT DECISIONS

The Firm in Economic Theory

The *firm* in economic theory is the economic entity that combines scarce resources (inputs) and transforms them into the economic goods and services we consume (output). Decision makers within the firm are assumed to act on the basis of rational calculations made with relatively complete information. Their aim is to maximize profits. To view the world in this way abstracts from much that is a part of the day-to-day activities of the firm and, accordingly, is an incomplete view of what happens in the firm. Most economists argue, however, that the assumptions of rationality and restrictive goal-oriented behavior contribute much to economic analysis and economic understanding.

Ordinarily, in studying the firm, economists focus on nonspatial factors that affect costs and revenues. Given these costs and revenues and the assumptions of rationality and profit maximization, certain statements can be made about output decisions of the firm. The view of these decisions under competitive market conditions can be portrayed geometrically as follows in Figure 2.1.

Figure 2.1

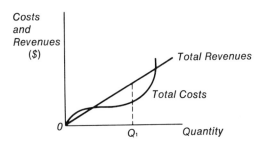

Quantity OQ_1 in Figure 2.1 assumes special significance. It is the level of output at which the spread between total revenue and total cost is at a maximum or profits are maximized. It is thus the output level a profit-maximizing firm will choose.

Costs in Economic Theory

Production is the process of transforming resources or inputs into output, and to produce is to incur costs. In economic theory, costs are construed as alternative outputs given up when inputs are used in a certain way. The economic cost of a luxury high-rise residential building in the city, for example, is the number of schools or bowling alleys that must be given up to produce that building. If we suppose the residential unit can be produced with 10,000 man days of labor (L) and $1 million in capital costs (K), the economic cost of that unit is the number of schools or bowling alleys we could produce with this amount of labor and capital.

Suppose economic resources are allocated among alternative users through markets, i.e., there is a labor market, a capital market and so forth. Market outcomes depend on the interaction of market demand and market supply. Market demand in economic theory is a schedule of quantities and prices. The quantities are quantities demanded at a price. As that price falls, the schedule shows quantity demanded increasing. Geometrically, the demand schedule is represented as a downward sloping line—see Figure 2.2.

Market supply in economic theory is also a schedule of quantities and prices. The quantities are quantities supplied at a price. As that price falls, the schedule shows quantity supplied decreasing. Geometrically, the supply schedule is represented as an upward sloping line—see Figure 2.3.

Figure 2.2

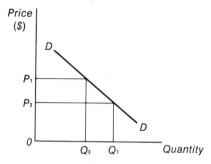

Figure 2.3

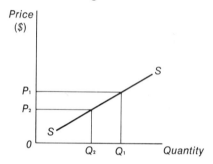

The interaction of demand and supply in markets determines price. In competitive markets that price will be the price at which quantity demanded equals quantity supplied—price OP_1 in Figure 2.4. At any other price, given demand (DD) and supply (SS), there will be excess demand or excess supply. In either case, competition will drive the price back to the level where quantity demanded equals quantity supplied.

Figure 2.4

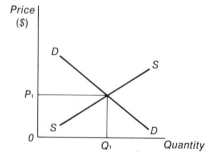

Given resource demands and supplies, markets determine resource prices, i.e., the price of labor, the price of capital, etc. These prices, along with the resource quantities required in production, determine the *money costs* of any given level of output. These relationships can be generalized as in Equation 2.1:

$$TC = LP_l + KP_k \tag{2.1}$$

where TC is money cost, P_l and P_k are the price of labor and capital respectively, and L and K are the quantities of labor and capital used.

If markets work properly, money costs should reflect economic costs. To illustrate, suppose the economic cost of that luxury high-rise residential building is high in the sense that the school buildings that must be given up to produce it are deemed important by society. If so, those who want to build school buildings should be in a position to bid resources away from their use in residential construction. By doing so, input prices will rise, which implies their use in residential construction will incur high money costs.

Economic theory is concerned with what happens to total money costs (TC) as output—(and hence input) requirements—vary. Much attention centers on the production function or the relationship between inputs and output in the production process. Given most technologies, it is possible to alter the *proportion* of inputs used in production. Instead of using a 1 to 1 ratio of labor to capital, for example, we might be able to use a 2 to 1 or 3 to 1 ratio. When we alter proportions, however, the relationship between inputs and output changes in ways captured in the celebrated economic law of diminishing returns.

The law of diminishing returns states that, as we alter the proportion of inputs used in production, the productivity of these inputs is changed. The standard example increases output by adding more of a variable input (labor) to a fixed input (capital) and shows how the amount of labor necessary to generate a constant increment in output changes as more and more labor is used with a given amount of capital. Table 2.1 provides a concrete illustration. Note, in column four,

Table 2.1

Diminishing Returns Example

(1) Output	(2) Capital	(3) Labor	(4) Add'l Units of Labor
0	16	0	6
1	16	6	4
2	16	10	3
3	16	13	4
4	16	17	7
5	16	24	12
6	16	36	19
7	16	55	28
8	16	83	

how the labor required to increase output by one unit changes as we use more and more labor. At first, the amount declines. Then it increases, which is taken to mean that we are in the stage of diminishing returns with respect to the use of labor.

The cost implications of the law are easy to show. Assume the price of capital and labor used in the production shown in Table 2.1 is $1.00. The total and average cost of producing these eight different levels of output can be easily calculated—see Table 2.2. Note the column for average costs (total costs divided by output), for the cost effects of the law of diminishing returns are clearly visible

Table 2.2

Cost Example

(1) *Output*	(2) *Total Costs*	(3) *Average Costs*
1	$22.00	$22.00
2	26.00	13.00
3	29.00	9.67
4	33.00	8.25
5	40.00	8.00
6	52.00	8.67
7	71.00	10.14
8	99.00	12.38

here. In the low range of output possibilities, average costs are declining. A point is reached, however, beyond which these costs begin to rise. They do so because at higher output levels relatively more labor must be used to increase output by one unit.

The law of diminishing returns occupies an important place in economic theories of cost and production because there are many real world situations in which output can only be varied by altering the proportion of inputs used in production. In the short run, e.g., a year, the capital or plant and equipment of the firm is fixed. If output is to be increased, more labor—and other inputs—must be applied to a given amount of capital which, in turn, results in a change in the mix or proportion of inputs used in production.

If input prices remain the same, average costs will change. They will fall initially if capital does not have enough labor to be utilized fully. Later on, with more and more additions of labor, each unit of labor will have too little capital to work with; hence average costs will rise.

This cost configuration—see Figure 2.5—is important. It lies at the bottom of explanations of a wide range of economic phenomena, including the size of the city. The emergence of cities, however, is more a consequence of changes in the scale of input use. Arguments that cities stem from cost advantages in concentrating economic activity in geographic space are arguments that most often have roots in the concept of scale economies.

SCALE ECONOMIES

The concept of scale economies refers to a set of conditions in which average costs of a firm decline as the scale of activity is increased. In specifying these conditions, a distinction is made between those that are internal and those that are external to the firm. The former are internal economies of scale. The external conditions are differentiated in the following way. First, there are those conditions that concern the industry of which the firm is a part, conditions that give rise to industry or localization economies. These are economies associated with industry expansion. The second set concerns the city in which the firm is located. These

Figure 2.5

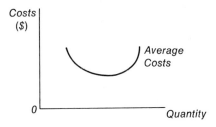

are the economies associated with the growth of cities, and they are called *urbaniza-tion economies*.

Internal Economies of Scale

The concept of internal economies of scale refers to a relationship between the average costs of the firm and the scale of production. Change in the scale of production means varying proportionately *all* inputs used in production—for example, doubling the quantity of all inputs. Such change alters total costs because it implies change in the amounts of all inputs used. Costs of production under these conditions are called long-run costs ($LRTC$); and if they are divided by output ($LRTC \div Q$), the quotient is the long-run average costs of a firm ($LRAC$).

Internal economies of scale denote a negative relationship between the long-run average costs of the firm and output. When there are economies, costs fall as the quantity of output increases—see Figure 2.6. Economists argue this happens when

Figure 2.6

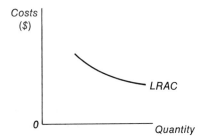

technology fosters increasing returns to scale, an economic concept that links change in the scale of input use to output. If we double the amount of all inputs used, for example, we have changed the scale of input use. The returns from such a change depend on what happens to output. If output is doubled or increases proportionately, the returns are constant. If output increases more than proportionately—more than doubles—there are increasing returns to scale.

To illustrate the point, consider a production process in which labor (L) is combined with capital (K) to yield output (O). If returns to scale refer to what happens to output as the scale of input use is increased and constant returns implies a proportionate increase, the constant returns case is illustrated in Table 2.3.

Table 2.3

Constant Returns Case

L	K	O
1	1	1
2	2	2
3	3	3
4	4	4

If the increasing returns case is denoted by a greater than proportionate increase in output, this might be reflected as follows:

Table 2.4

Increasing Returns Case

L	K	O
1	1	1
2	2	4
3	3	8
4	4	16

If the price of labor and capital is $1, total costs for selected levels of output can be calculated—see Table 2.5.

Table 2.5

Total Production Costs

Output	Total Costs Constant Returns Case	Total Costs Increasing Returns Case
1	$ 2	$2
4	8	4
8	16	6
16	32	8

Total costs for the constant returns case increase proportionately with increased output and increase less than proportionately with increasing returns to scale.

This difference is more dramatically reflected in the behavior of average costs— see Table 2.6.

Why increasing returns? Technology is involved. When the technical conditions of production give rise to both specialization and indivisibilities in production, increasing returns may arise.

Specialization refers to the division of labor in production. The fact that brick-layers, carpenters, hod carriers, plumbers, and electricians are a part of a team that builds houses denotes specialization. Each does something distinct and separate from the other even though their work is coordinated. They are specialists and their use means a division of labor in production.

Table 2.6

Average Costs

Output	Average Costs Constant Returns Case	Average Costs Increasing Returns Case
1	$2	$2.00
4	2	1.00
8	2	.75
16	2	.50

Indivisibilities stem from the fact that resources used in production are not perfectly divisible. To build more houses may require that we hire another electrician, plumber, hod carrier, carpenter, and bricklayer. Suppose we hire, fully utilize them and find we are able to build not one but four additional houses. Yet suppose we wanted to build just one more house. We would be confronted with a concrete illustration of an indivisibility.

Typically, production technology is such that there is more than one way to produce a product. These differences revolve around specialization and give rise to indivisibilities in production. The latter generally occurs when technology yields production processes whose minimum output levels are both relatively small and large, and the productivity of the inputs used in these alternative processes varies.

To illustrate, suppose technology is such that there are two ways of producing an automobile. Process 1 involves little specialization and hence is small scaled. Production is possible when one unit of labor is combined with one unit of capital, and one dose of each yields one automobile. Additional doses of both inputs with this process lead to proportionate increases in output. Production in process 2, on the other hand, is large scaled. Production is only possible when five units of labor are combined with five units of capital; but when this is done, because of specialization, ten autos are the result. Output can be increased using this process, but it cannot be reduced below ten automobiles.

A partial description of the outcome of using these two processes is shown in Table 2.7. Column four in this table, the index of returns to scale, requires some explanation. This index is the ratio of output to inputs for the production process "best" suited for production at given levels of output. Through output levels up to four units, this is process 1. The product cannot be produced with process 2 at these levels of output. At output levels of five and beyond, this is process 2 because it yields more output from given amounts of input.

That process 2 cannot be used in the production of output levels below five indicates the presence of an indivisibility in production. Significantly, associated with this indivisibility are increasing returns to scale in the sense that the output-input ratio increases as we shift from process 1 to process 2—the index of returns to scale rises from one to two. There are productivity benefits associated with process 2 at higher levels of output that stem from further specialization built into this process. Production technology is such that increasing returns to scale are realized.

Table 2.7

The Index of Returns to Scale

(1) Input Doses *	(2) Process 1 Output	(3) Process 2 Output	(4) Index of Return of Sale
1	1	—	1
2	2	—	1
3	3	—	1
4	4	—	1
5	5	10	2
6	6	12	2
7	7	14	2
8	8	16	2
9	9	18	2
10	10	20	2

* 1 denotes one unit of labor and one unit of capital, 2 denotes two units of labor and two units of capital and so forth.

Industry Economies

The concept of scale economies, as noted above, incorporates the possibility that long-run average costs fall as a consequence of increases in the scale of activity of the industry of which the firm is a part. Such a decline reflects the presence of industry economies. The essential concern is with what happens to the price of inputs. The concept of industry economies is taken to mean that input prices decline as industry output is increased; hence the long-run average costs of the firm are reduced.

How do we characterize industry economies? Suppose that before expansion, the output of the firm is OQ_1. We know from $LRAC_1$ in Figure 2.7 that the average cost of this level of output is OC_1. Assume now the industry expands. If there are industry economies, this expansion will lower input prices which, according to Equation 2.1, means a decline in total costs. It follows that the average costs of producing OQ_1 will now be less. Suppose they fall to OC_2. But if they are lower at OQ_1, they must be lower at every other level of output, since the reduction is due to lower input prices. Industry economies must therefore be reflected in a downward shift in the long-run average cost curve of the firm. $LRAC_2$ in Figure 2.7 can be taken as the long-run average cost curve in the firm after industry expansion.

The concept of industry economies is a part of the economics that is used to illustrate conceivable patterns of economic adjustments to certain kinds of change in the economy. If costs fall because of input price reductions, it is reasonable to ask why these prices fell. The question is not easily answered.

The inputs of most firms include not only primary inputs such as labor and capital, but also "intermediate" goods and services produced by other firms. The steel used by the automobile industry is an obvious example. When this fact is noted, the meaning of industry economy becomes blurred. The expansion of industry X means increased demand for the outputs of Y and Z if these industries

Figure 2.7

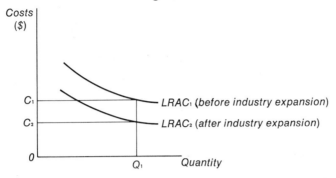

produce intermediate goods incorporated in the production processes of X. The price of such inputs will of course be influenced by what happens to costs as the scale of production of firms in industries Y and Z increases. If these firms experience increasing returns to scale, their costs will decline, and in competitive markets there will be a reduction in the price of what Y and Z sell to X.

Note in this illustration that what appear to be industry economies turn out to be internal economies whose effects are spreading throughout the economy because of industry linkages. Generally, these are not considered an industry economy.

Discussions of industry economies have generally focused on developments that occur in labor markets as industries expand. You can find arguments to the effect that as an industry expands, pools of qualified labor develop or the structural efficiency of its labor market is improved because of the increase in the number of workers. Such things, if they happen, lower the labor costs of the firms of an expanding industry. How a more qualified work force might develop as the industry expands, however, has never really been made very clear. Thus, the extent to which industry economies contribute to our understanding of the costs which confront the firm is debatable.

Urbanization Economies

The concept of urbanization economies refers to sets of conditions in which the long-run average costs of the firm fall as the scale of activity in the city in which it is located increases. The concept thus implies costs will be lower in larger cities—see Figure 2.8.

Figure 2.8

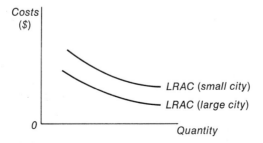

What reasons are there for believing that average costs will fall as city size increases? Urban economists point to three things.

One is statistical; it is an application of the law of large number. Firms operate under varying degrees of risk and uncertainty. Most experience fluctuations in demand and supply factors that are not easy to anticipate. Since the timing and magnitude of these ups and downs generally vary by industry, urban areas with their many industries provide firms with a setting in which the risks and uncertainties of operation are reduced.

When firms locate in the larger cities, they can sell to more customers and buy from more suppliers. This possibility is significant because if the number of customers—or suppliers—is larger, the probability of offsetting fluctuations in demand—or supply—is higher. Firms should find less variability in their operations, on the basis of which they can reduce costs. They may find themselves with smaller inventory requirements for example, and more smoothly flowing production scheduling routines, circumstances that are cost reducing in their effects.

A second set of conditions stems from production technology that fosters indivisibilities which in turn lead to firm specialization. Much of what can be said about such specialization has roots in an earlier discussion of internal economies. The concern now, however, is with a scale of activity in the urban community as a whole. The conclusion is that large-scale activity in this sense fosters firm specialization and the use of production processes within these firms that reduce costs, which through firm and industry linkages in the community are spread throughout the city.

Conceivably, there could be production with no intermediate products, that is, goods and services produced by other firms that are incorporated directly into production by other firms. Each firm would under such circumstances perform all functions in the production process. Seldom do we see this and for good reason. Production technology, as it has emerged, brought possibilities of specialization that cannot be realized when each firm performs all functions in the process of production. There are indivisibilities in production that generate opportunities that can only be fully exploited when output levels reached are well beyond the needs of any one firm. The emergent energy and communications technologies stand as a case in point. As technology has evolved in these areas, the required levels of output necessary to take full advantage of the benefits inherent in that technology have been beyond the needs of one or even several firms. The result has been a "spin-off" of this activity from firms and the development of an industry that provides these services to other firms as intermediate goods. So it has been with many other types of activity as well. What has emerged is an industrial system in which there is much firm specialization and hence a considerable amount of intermediate goods production.

What does all of this have to do with cities? Take the case of energy and communications functions. Changing technology and expanding markets caused these functions to spin off into the separate industries we generally call *utilities*. To realize the economies inherent in the new technologies, output levels had to be large. The investment requirements to achieve this scale of output were large and influenced by the spatial distribution of customers. Utilities selling in dispersed markets, for example, found their capital costs were higher than if they sold in markets where their customers were large in number and concentrated in space. Average costs of utilities were thus lower at sites of population concentration, which in turn attracted firms that consumed their services to these sites.

Business services were another class of activity that led to spatial agglomeration. Firms that were relatively small and confronted with more than the usual amount of uncertainty in demand could not support certain kinds of functions involving such things as law, economics, and printing and publishing. Since the provision of these things required relatively large markets and face-to-face communication, firms that provided them were attracted to relatively large urban centers. Once they located in these centers they, in turn, provided an attraction to those who used their services. The cost advantages of firm specialization of the sort were restricted to a certain class of firms. The number of these firms, however, was not small and the benefits they provided were not insignificant.

The final reason for firms locating in big cities has to do with the innovation and inventiveness that bigness spawns. Because of the diversity and richness of the activity in large cities, the probability of finding new ideas, products, and processes is higher in such cities. Since invention and innovation are important sources of economic vitality, the outcome will be a growing and viable economy. Such activity spawns new industries which probably function best in the earlier stages of their development in the places that provided the setting for their birth. These industries, of course, add to the economic base of that city.

DISECONOMIES OF SCALE

If we can conceive of average costs falling as the scale of production increases, we can just as easily conceive of average costs rising with increases in this scale. If there are economies of scale, it is not unreasonable to suppose there are diseconomies of scale.

The fact that firm size is finite suggests that costs must at some point begin to run up. That many firms operate with more than one plant is an even stronger indication. That they do could be a consequence of diseconomies of scale that come into play as certain size threshold levels are reached.

Typically, the long-run average costs of the plant are depicted as in Figure 2.9.

Figure 2.9

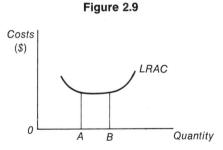

The technology applicable to most production gives rise to internal economies which lower average production costs over a certain range of output (OA).

Beyond *A,* returns to scale are relatively constant until *B* is reached. For many firms, this covers a wide range of production. After *B,* output is in a range where long-run average costs rise. No one denies that long-run average costs will begin to rise after a certain scale of production is reached. What is less clear is the reason why they begin to increase.

There are no compelling reasons for expecting returns to decrease as the scale of input use is increased. Some hold that returns decline because the entrepreneurial factor is indivisible and incapable of being augmented after a certain scale of output is reached. To argue this way, however, is to argue that costs increase because we are unable to increase the scale of the use of one input. In this case, what happens is that input proportions are changed; we experience diminishing returns rather than decreasing returns. Others believe problems arise from mounting difficulties of control and coordination when the scale of input use is increased. When we try to pin down precisely what is meant by coordination and control, however, the entrepreneurial or managerial factor creeps into the discussion; and the conclusion again seems to be that what is involved is more a matter of input proportions—the emerging scarcity of the managerial factor—rather than the scale of input use. The significance of the concept of internal diseconomies is uncertain.

What about industry diseconomies? Those diseconomies can be characterized in a general way. Their presence means the long-run average costs of firms will rise as the industry of which they are a part expands. This implies an upward shift in the long-term average cost curve of the firm—see Figure 2.10.

Figure 2.10

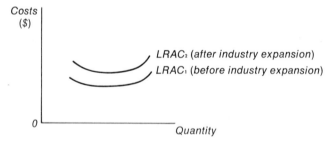

Why this might happen, however, is by no means clear. It could be a consequence of the impact of the increase in the industry's demand on the costs of industries which supply it with intermediate goods. Firms in the supplying industries could be experiencing diminishing returns as they respond to higher levels of demand, which raises their costs and, hence, prices of the goods they sell. Even so, this cannot be taken as something that is inherent in an industry that comes into play as the scale of activity within that industry is increased. Nor is there any indication of anything in the way in which labor and capital markets work that suggests that either labor and/or capital costs will rise as the industry being served by these markets expands beyond a certain point.

The concept of urbanization diseconomies also promises more than it delivers. The notion is one of rising long-run average costs as the scale of activity within the city increases or higher costs in larger cities—see Figure 2.11.

Figure 2.11

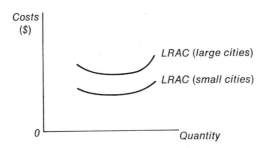

If Figure 2.11 holds, something has to happen within cities as they grow which causes long-run average costs of firms to rise.

Certainly things can happen that increase the average costs of firms in cities. What's involved, however, seems to be more a consequence of changes in the proportion rather than the scale of the inputs used.

Consider the matter of changing input proportions. If we take the geographic boundaries of the city as fixed, economic growth within these boundaries implies that the proportion of inputs used in production will change. Additional output obviously requires more of all inputs used in production. If one of these—land— is fixed, sooner or later efforts to expand output further will only be possible by expanding the use of inputs other than land. Input proportions will change and the land component of the costs of all firms operating in the city will rise.

When the supply of an input is fixed, any increase in demand will result in a price increase and hence an increase in the cost of its use. Ordinarily, if the price of an input rises, there will be market adjustments over the long run which add to the supply of that input in ways that lower its price. If supply is fixed, however, that price will not come back down. At this point economists talk about rents or those payments made to the owners of the fixed supply resource because of the way in which markets operate to allocate scarce resources among alternative users.

MARKET EXTERNALITIES

Costs for most firms are also alleged to be higher in larger cities because of the presence of problems such as congestion, pollution, and crime. The link between these problems and city size, however, is imperfect, which is not surprising in view of the fact that these problems have their origins in an economic system that is not working effectively. Markets often have external features that cause problems because they give rise to a divergence between marginal social and private costs or marginal social and private benefits. All of this is much less mysterious than it sounds. It is also subject matter best discussed at a later point when the subject of economic performance or welfare is taken up. For now it is enough to note that there are sets of economic conditions in which problems surface that add to the production costs of the firm in cities, and the magnitude of these problems appears to be greater in larger cities in some cases.

TRANSPORTATION COSTS

Transportation costs are the alternatives—the hamburgers and swimming pools—we give up by committing resources to the movement of people, goods, and information over geographic space. There are distance "frictions," meaning that movement over geographic space is not free. It requires scarce resources—transportation and communications inputs—which means economic costs. The magnitude of these costs depends on the technology that determines how things can be moved over geographic space and a milieu of social and physical facts that determine our need to move about in that space. The latter is the primary concern of location theory, and the nature of the transportation and communications technology occupies a prominent role in that theory. These are matters to be taken up in detail subsequently in chapters 3 and 5. For now, it is sufficient to talk about transportation costs in a more general way, that is, as costs incurred to overcome the frictions of distance.

For the profit-maximizing firm, there is incentive to minimize transportation costs just as there is incentive to minimize any other cost. Since transportation costs are positively correlated with geographic distance, their impact on economic decisions should be to minimize the geographic distances involved in our economic activities. Clearly this happens in production. Activities constituting production within a firm are not located indiscriminately in geographic space; rather they are spatially concentrated. Metal making is an obvious example of a production process that requires spatial proximity. The risks and costs of moving molten metals over great distances are substantial. Spatial proximity limiting these costs makes a good deal of sense. Moreover, even when there are no physical reasons for doing so, in many cases a rationale can be found in the organizational requirements of most firms. Nearness contributes to the resolution of control and coordinating problems that are a part of the production process. Face-to-face communications, given current technologies, contribute much to the development and maintenance of the sequence of efficient operations through which inputs are transformed into output. That production is concentrated in geographic space within a plant is no accident.

Nor is it an accident that firms that produce intermediate goods tend to be located near the firms to which they sell; or that employees live near their place of employment and firms which sell directly to these employees are near these places of residence. To locate away from markets or places of employment incurs a transportation cost which in some cases can be substantial. Proximity has a payoff that concentrates the activities of firms and households, an incentive that is intensified by the current technology. Our communication technology provides strong incentive for geographic clustering for that face-to-face contact necessary for many kinds of communication.

Current transportation technology and investments also provide strong incentive for a clustering of economic activity. The transportation industry consists of a network of routes that yields a high degree of access to only a limited portion of the geographic space it serves. Production at sites away from network routes can mean greatly increased transportation costs simply because of the difficulty of moving goods and people to and from these sites. Growth in the economy, of course, generates transportation investments that add new routes to the network. In the planning stages, a choice must be made with respect to what sites will be served by new routes. This implies that sites not now adequately served could become more accessible with future transportation investments, and this may have bearing on the location decisions of some firms. Most plant location decisions, however, are not made with this possibility in mind. In selecting sites, firms are strongly influenced by the existing transportation network, which means sites near the major connecting points in that network will be appealing because they are sites where substantial transportation costs savings may be realized.

ECONOMIC COSTS AND
CITY BUILDING

Why cities? Scale economies are involved as are transportation costs.

Consider a world in which people are dispersed. That a production technology that yields scale economies will lead to economic decisions which concentrate activity geographically is best illustrated by focusing on outcomes both with and without such economies. Consider first a production technology in which there are no economies of scale. Firms experience constant returns to scale as they expand output, and there is no warrant for firm specialization as output is expanded. Firms could, if they choose, concentrate production in space by increasing the scale of output within each firm and locating their plants in close geographic proximity to one another. Firms in pursuit of maximum profits would not choose to do so, however. There would be no advantage to it; only disadvantages. Scale economies are absent so that any large-scale geographic concentrations would yield no cost savings. It would merely add to the costs of firms that locate in such areas. If customers are dispersed, concentrating production will increase the distance between the site of production and the consumer. As a consequence, transportation costs will be higher. Spatially concentrated production will also lead to rising land costs for reasons noted above. Geographic concentration that leads to higher costs and lower profits is, of course, concentration that will not materialize in a market economy.

Consider now a technology that generates significant economies of scale in production. If customers are dispersed, concentrating production would again increase transportation and land costs. This time, however, such cost increases could be offset by cost savings stemming from economies of scale associated with higher and more spatially concentrated levels of output. These could be internal economies that stem from increasing returns in production within the firm—internal economies of scale. They could also be external economies that derive from, say, firm specialization made possible from higher levels of spatially concentrated output, that is, urbanization economies. Cities will emerge when technology is such that the cost savings associated with scale economies more than offset the rise in transportation and land costs that accompany spatially concentrated production.

Suppose the cost savings from scale economies are dominant and cities begin to emerge. When this happens, people who work in cities will live in cities. While employees, in principle, have freedom of choice with respect to where they can live, distance frictions give rise to the specter of commuting costs, which in the face of a limited budget severely limits the location options for most. Transportation costs also exert an important influence on the site decisions of firms that provide products or services to these firms and households. Concentration now begets more concentration because of transportation costs. At this point transportation costs begin to reinforce these pressures to move into the city.

As noted at the outset of this chapter, what's involved in city building can be considered in a scenario in which transportation costs and economies of scale are seen as opposing forces pitted against one another in an economic arena which, in the beginning, has its customers dispersed geographically. Transportation costs in this arena have dispersive effects. The force of economies of scale is, on the other hand, concentrating in its effect. The outcome depends largely on technology, as it has impact on production processes of both the transportation and non-transportation industries. This technology has been such that the city is the outcome. Urban society shows up, however, not as one but many cities which are linked together in ways that cannot be explained on the basis of scale economies and transportation costs. There are patterns in the urban configuration that some have characterized as hierarchical, the meaning and significance of which can only be understood in light of an understanding of certain of the rudiments of location theory.

REFERENCES

Chinitz, B. "Contrasts in Agglomeration: New York and Pittsburgh." *American Economic Review* 51 (1961): 279–89.

*Evans, A. "The Pure Theory of City Size in an Industrial Economy." *Urban Studies* 9 (1972): 49–77.

*Lancaster, K. *Introduction to Modern Microeconomics.* New York: Rand McNally and Company, 1969.

Losch, A. *The Economics of Location.* New York: John Wiley and Sons, 1967

Ogburn, W. and Duncan, O. "City Size as a Sociological Variable." In *Contributions to Urban Sociology,* edited by E. Burgess and D. Bogue. Chicago: Chicago University Press, 1964.

*Stigler, G. "The Division of Labor Is Limited by the Extent of the Market." *Journal of Political Economy* 59 (1951): 371–85.

Ullman, E. "The Nature of Cities Reconsidered." *Papers and Proceedings of the Regional Science Association* 9 (1962): 7–23.

Vernon, R. *Metropolis 1985.* Cambridge, Mass.: Harvard University Press, 1960.

* These sources were used extensively in preparing this chapter.

location Theory
and the Urban Hierarchy

SUMMARY

Urban America is made up of a great many cities scattered throughout the nation. The pattern takes the form of a hierarchy in the sense of a pyramidal distribution of cities by size. This pattern seems important because of its stability in the face of imposing changes in the urban population.

Location theory provides insights into the urban hierarchy. The location decisions of firms are crucial. Firms are concerned with the site of production because profits vary by site.

Site selection is a matter of choosing the location at which profits are at a maximum. For some firms this will be at the site where transportation costs are at a minimum—they have a transportation orientation. For others, this will be at a site where labor costs are at a minimum—they have a labor orientation. For still others, it will be at a site where their revenues are at a maximum—they have a market orientation.

Certain sets of conditions can be specified in which all firms will have a market orientation. When this is so, markets will organize and concentrate production into a system of central places. If we assume people live near their place of employment—a realistic assumption—we can consider these places in terms of people or as cities. By making certain assumptions about the size and shapes of the market areas that firms serve and that people live in, as well as the proportion of the population living in cities, a model of a system of cities can be constructed which has the pyramidal properties with respect to the size distribution of its cities that we characterize as an urban hierarchy.

The conclusions we can draw from such central place models have a limited scope. The conditions that must be fulfilled before the model is applicable are often not fulfilled. The nation's cities can be said to have a hierarchical structure, but that structure cannot be properly described with statements derived from models in which firms only search for sites at which revenues are maximized. To look at firms in this way helps us understand the geographic locations of some but not all firms. Cost factors have to be considered; and when they are, we find significant distortions from the outcomes expected on the basis of central place notions. In the real world, what we have is a "system of systems of cities." There is an

urban hierarchy, but it is a very complex structure. The differences between cities at various levels in the hierarchy are not as clear-cut as they
seem on the basis of a simple central place model.

Urban society, as noted above, is made up of a great many cities. The 1970
Census reported over 6,000 cities in the United States, cities that range in size
from the very small to the very large and all shapes and sizes in between—see
Table 3.1. While the concept of urbanism around which this book is organized

Table 3.1

Number of Cities 2,500 and Over
by Size Group 1790-1970

	All Cities	Cities 2,500 to 24,999	Cities 25,000 to 249,999	Cities 250,000 and Over
1790	24	22	2	—
1800	33	30	3	—
1810	46	42	4	—
1820	61	56	5	—
1830	90	83	7	—
1840	131	119	11	1
1850	236	210	25	1
1860	392	357	32	3
1870	663	611	45	7
1880	939	862	69	8
1890	1348	1224	113	11
1900	1737	1577	145	15
1910	2262	2034	209	19
1920	2722	2435	262	25
1930	3165	2789	339	37
1940	3464	3052	375	37
1950	4054	3534	479	41
1960	4996	4239	707	50
Current Definitions				
1950	4284	3800	443	41
1960	5445	4680	714	51
1970	6435	5519	860	56

Source: U.S. Bureau of the Census

emphasizes spatial concentration, Census data make clear that what we are
dealing with is "dispersed" concentration. There are many nodes or cluster points
dispersed widely throughout the nation. Despite the concentration of population
in urban centers in the northeastern part of the United States, Table 3.2 makes

Table 3.2

Urban Population by Region
1970

	Urban Population
Northeast	38,371,994
South	39,027,828
North Central	39,235,586
West	27,974,181

Source: U.S. Bureau of the Census

clear that our urban population is spread out over the nation. There are cities in every major region and the population of these regions are largely urban—see Table 3.3. What also comes through these numbers is a property of the urban configuration called *hierarchy*.

Table 3.3

Urbanization of Population in the U.S.
by Census Region, 1790–1970
(Proportion of Population Living in Urban Areas)

	Northeast	*South*	*North Central*	*West*
1790	8.1	2.1	—	—
1800	9.3	3.0	—	—
1810	10.9	4.1	0.9	—
1820	11.0	4.6	1.1	—
1830	14.2	5.3	2.6	—
1840	18.5	6.7	3.9	—
1850	26.5	8.3	9.2	6.4
1860	35.7	9.6	13.9	16.0
1870	44.3	12.2	20.8	25.8
1880	50.8	12.2	24.2	30.2
1890	59.0	16.3	33.1	37.0
1900	61.1	18.0	38.6	39.9
1910	71.8	22.5	45.1	47.9
1920	75.5	28.1	52.3	51.8
1930	77.6	34.1	57.9	58.4
1940	76.6	36.7	58.4	58.5
1950	75.4	44.6	61.1	59.9
1960	72.8	52.7	63.9	66.1
Current Definitions				
1950	79.5	48.6	64.1	69.5
1960	80.2	58.5	68.7	77.7
1970	80.5	64.0	71.3	82.6

Source: U.S. Bureau of Census

The concept of a hierarchy is generally taken to mean the interrelations between the component parts of some whole. When the concept is applied to organizations such as the firm or some unit of government, the concern is with the flow of something like control or authority throughout the organization, and a common interpretation of this flow is one that takes on a pyramidal form. A hierarchy in this sense comes through in data on the size distribution of the 6,000 American cities. For example, if the urban population is conceived of as one that breaks down into three major components—small cities, medium-size cities, and large cities—a hierarchy is exhibited in these figures. Table 3.1 clearly reveals a pyramid in the sense that the number of cities at the top is few, those at the bottom are many, and the number in the middle fall somewhere in between. What is significant about this is that the pattern shows up as being stable in the face of imposing changes in the size of the urban population.

These are phenomena that raise questions that cannot be fully answered on the basis of notions of scale economies and transfer costs. Geographers label them as having in mind something composed of entities that are interdependent parts of a whole. Much time and attention is devoted to this system in urban geography, as well it should be. Not only does the urban system concept constitute something that is close to what is meant by the whole urban society, it has the potential to make important contributions to significant urban policy questions, e.g., city size, new towns, etc.

There is a body of theory—location theory—that provides insights into the urban hierarchy. As such, this theory is a legitimate and important part of the body of urban economic theory. While location theory has roots in both geography and economics, an economic treatment of it must build on economic concepts. A discussion of the major elements of the economics of location is therefore the first order of business in this chapter.

THE ECONOMICS
OF LOCATION

The Firm as the Relevant Eonomic Unit

In an economic system, most people wear two hats; one as producer and the other as consumer. To be concerned with a system of cities is, in part, a concern with the question of where these people act out their roles as producers and consumers. Yet, must we be concerned with the location of both production and consumption?

When the concern is with urban hierarchies, emphasis on the location choices of producers is reasonable. Producer decisions are important because people tend to follow jobs and not the other way around. There are indications of this in survey data that show job-related motives as the dominant reason for moves from one urban community to another. While there are some who live where they do because of certain features of the area, e.g., climate, the number is still relatively small.

Location and the Firm

As noted in chapter 2, in economic theory, the firm is assumed to behave rationally in the pursuit of maximum profits. Given this behavioral assumption along with assumptions about market and production conditions, we can make statements about output and price decisions. A geometric representation of one set of these decisions was shown in Figure 2.1.

The usual interpretation of Figure 2.1 is one that takes the output to be independent of considerations of space. But the world is not spaceless. The firm has to locate production at some site in geographic space, and for most firms there are large numbers of possible production sites. This fact becomes important if costs and revenues vary by location. Such variation can be conceived of as differences in cost and revenue curves as shown in Figure 2.1. If costs were to vary by site, for example, there would be as many cost curves as there are sites, with each curve denoting cost conditions at a particular site. C_{s1}, C_{s2}, and C_{s3} in Figure 3.1 illustrate cost curves that show different levels of total costs at

Figure 3.1

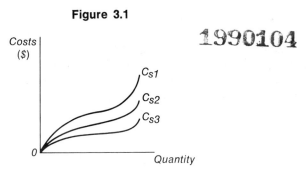

different locations, that is, at $s1$, $s2$, and $s3$. Correspondingly if there were revenue differences by site, there would be as many revenue curves as there are sites. R_{s1}, R_{s2}, and R_{s3} in Figure 3.2 are illustrative of revenue curves which show different levels of total revenue at locations $s1$, $s2$, and $s3$.

Figure 3.2

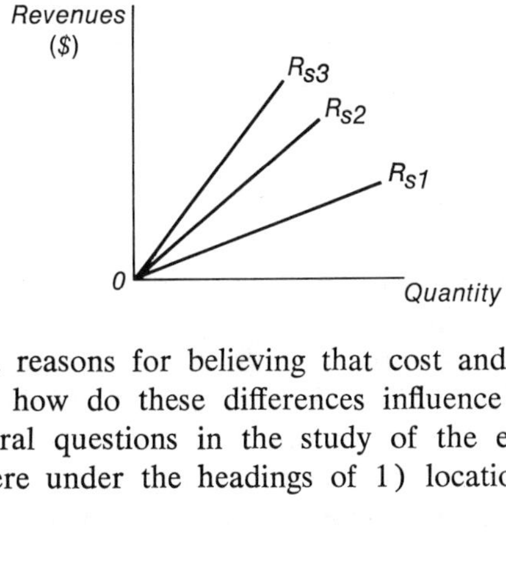

Are there any good reasons for believing that cost and revenue curves differ by location? Precisely how do these differences influence the site selections of firms? These are central questions in the study of the economics of location. They are taken up here under the headings of 1) location factors and 2) the location decision.

Location Factors

Location factors are elements that make particular geographic sites more or less attractive to firms. They influence profits either through the firm's costs and/or revenues. If present, they imply differences in costs and/or revenues at alternative sites.

Why might we expect to find spatial cost and revenue differences?

A fundamental element of location theory is the concept of distance frictions— the fact that movement over geographic space encounters resistance, entailing the use of scarce resources to overcome this resistance. This notion, combined with some reasonable assumptions about the spatial distribution of resources used in production, provides reason for believing there will be spatial cost and revenue differences.

Distance Frictions and Costs   If the resources used in production were available at every point in geographic space in equal amounts and technical conditions of production were the same everywhere, there would be no need to transport inputs from one site to another during production. The necessary ingredients would be available at any site. Costs would be the same at all sites.

Most inputs used in production, however, are not ubiquitous; rather they are found only at certain locations. Thus many inputs have to be transported to the plant unless the plant is located at the site of the inputs. Such movement, in turn, implies systematic cost variation over geographic space.

Consider a hypothetical illustration of a production process with only one input (I) which is found only at one location (S_1). If transportation costs are proportional with distance, the cost of the input will vary systematically with distance from the location of the input. If the plant is located at the site of the input (S_1) and the price of the input is P_1S_1, the cost per unit of input will be P_1S_1—see Figure 3.3. On the other hand, if the plant is located at S_2, the cost of per unit of input will be P_1S_1 plus the cost of transportation from S_1 to S_2— distance AB in Figure 3.3. Significantly, costs are at a minimum at site S_1, the point where transportation costs are at a minimum.

Figure 3.3

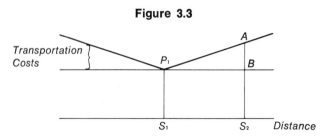

Figure 3.3 is, of course, an oversimplification. Transportation cost differences at alternative sites will probably not be proportionate with distance from the input location. As noted in chapter 2, not all sites are served equally well by the transportation network, and those closer to major routes have lower transportation costs. Also, the impact of transportation on production costs is not so easily discerned in commonplace production situations. Typically, there are a number of inputs used in production, some that may be found in only one place, some

in only several places, some in many places, and a few that may be found every-where. While one can very easily conceive of a location where transportation costs are at a minimum, this geographic point is often not immediately evident. Still, the presence of distance frictions and inputs that are not commonly found implies geographic variations in the cost of getting inputs to the plant. This means location will be important to profit-maximizing firms and suggests there will be firms looking for locations that minimize transportation costs.

Distance Frictions and Revenues   Distance frictions also give rise to trans-portation costs when production is located away from the consumer. This cost is usually considered, as it has impact on revenues and a distinction is made between a point and a dispersed market.

A *point market* is one in which customers are highly concentrated in geographic space. Put metaphorically, they are located on the head of a pin. If that market is perfectly competitive—that is, firms can sell all they produce at market price—the impact of location on revenues is evident.

Assume a market price exclusive of the cost of transporting the final goods from the site of production to the consumer. If *total revenue* is defined as market price less unit transportation costs times the number of units sold, it is clear that locations near the market generate the highest revenues. The point is dia-grammed in Figure 3.4. If TR_1 is the revenue line for a firm producing at the

Figure 3.4

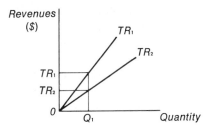

market, TR_2 must be the revenue line for a firm that has chosen a location away from the market. Revenues from that location are less at any level of output, e.g., OQ_1 in Figure 3.4, because of deductions for the cost of transporting the goods from the plant to the consumer.

Consider a spatial market and go to the other extreme. Assume customers that have the same tastes and incomes are spread evenly across the face of the map. Assume further that the actions of any one firm have no impact on others. Firms selling in this market will find that location has no influence on revenues.

Spatial markets are not purely competitive markets. Even though there may be many firms selling to many customers, each firm cannot sell all it produces at market price. When customers are dispersed, distance has impact on sales. Distance adds transportation costs to the cost of consumption, which in the normal case restricts purchases. The point warrants amplification.

With customers who are alike with respect to incomes and preferences, individual demands are the same. Consider three customers who live varying distances from the site of production. According to the law of demand, these demands can be represented by a downward-sloping line denoting a negative relation between price and quantity demanded—see Figure 3.5. The question of

Figure 3.5

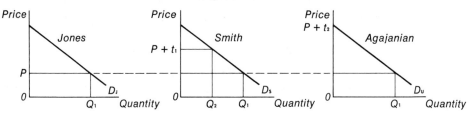

how much Jones will buy, given his demands represented by demand curve D_J, depends on price. Suppose that price, exclusive of the cost of getting the good to the customer, is $1.00. Measured off on the vertical axis, this turns out to be OP. At that price, the demand curve indicates Jones will buy OQ_1 units as will Smith and Agajanian if the consumption costs are OP. We cannot say however, exactly how much Jones, Smith, and Agajanian will buy in the absence of knowledge about *where* they live.

Suppose Jones lives in a location adjacent to the plant; Smith lives some distance away; and Agajanian lives even further way. The consumption cost is price (OP) plus transportation. Since the latter for Jones is zero, Jones will buy OQ_1 units. For Smith, on the other hand, consumption costs are OP plus transportation costs (t_1) or $OP + t_1$. With these costs, Smith will buy less than Jones even though Smith and Jones have the same tastes and incomes. For Agajanian, consumption costs are $OP + t_2$, which, as it turns out, are costs that preclude Agajanian from making purchases of the product. Agajanian is exactly like Jones and Smith, but buys nothing. Through its impact on consumption costs, distance is clearly seen to set a limit to the spatial extent of the market. Because of distance frictions, consumption costs can rise to a level where they effectively exclude some households from the market of any given firm. In Figure 3.5, Agajanian is one of these and there are others.

Market demand, of course, is the sum of the purchases of the individual consumer at some price. For Jones, given price OP, quantity demanded is OQ_1; for Smith it is OQ_2. Agajanian makes no purchases at all. With information on the residential locations of all those other monotonously similar households, statements could be made about their purchases. With these statements, market demand would be known and *total revenue*—price times quantity—could be calculated. The relationship between total revenues and price can be displayed geometrically as a "demand cone." A part of an illustrative demand cone is shown in Figure 3.6.

The vertical lines measure sales to particular households when price is OP. These sales are shown to decline as distance between the firm and household increases, a reflection of the impact of increasing transportation costs on consumption. Total sales at price OP is the sum of all vertical lines—which denotes sales to individuals—or, in effect, the volume of the cone that would appear if all sales appeared in Figure 3.6. The boundaries of this cone depict the market area of the firm, that is, the points in geographic space beyond which the firm can make no sales given the price OP.

Figure 3.6

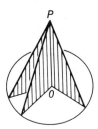

With knowledge of demand conditions—including the spatial dimensions—a demand cone can be calculated for each price which, in turn, allows us to calculate a total revenue curve. This curve shows the revenues associated with each price. The curve in Figure 3.7 represents the general shape of a revenue curve of the firm selling in a spatial market.

We are now in a position to address the question of what happens to revenues when a firm selling in a spatial market changes location. In markets where customers are evenly spaced and alike in all pertinent respects, the revenue curve is the same no matter where the firm locates, so long as there is no competitive interaction with other firms. The amounts sold to particular households will vary, of course, when the firm moves from one site to another. Households adjacent to the firm before the move will no longer be so after the move; hence they will buy less. But there will be households adjacent to the new site of production and households at varying distances from the site in precisely the same manner as they were before the move. If these households have the same income and tastes, as assumed, aggregate sales of the firm at a given price will be the same. Revenues associated with sales at each price will therefore be the same at all locations, which means the revenue curve—Figure 3.7—is the same all over.

Figure 3.7

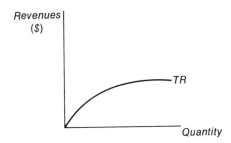

Firms, of course, neither sell in a spatial market in this sense nor in point markets in the sense indicated above. While all customers are not located on the head of a pin, neither are they distributed evenly in space, nor are they alike with respect to tastes and income. There are both dispersive and concentrative elements in the markets in which most firms sell. If so, the location of firms has impact on their revenues. Sites close to population concentrations yield higher revenues. How much higher depends on the spatial positioning of customers and their incomes and tastes.

Any attempt to evaluate the impact of location on the revenues of the firm raises tantalizing questions that do not have simple answers. It is nevertheless true that unless households are completely dispersed, which is unlikely, revenues will vary with the location of the firm. Some firms might, as a consequence, be expected to look for locations that maximize their revenues.

Other Location Factors   While transportation factors have been emphasized in studies of plant and industry location, there are other factors. Most of these influence costs.

In considering costs above, the price of inputs, exclusive of transportation costs, was assumed to be the same everywhere. This assumption was made to help clarify the role transportation plays in the location decision. There are, however, no compelling reasons to expect input prices to be the same all over. In fact, the evidence is to the contrary. There are indications of geographic differences in wage rates that cannot be explained in terms of productivity. Labor costs are lower in the South compared with the Northeast, North Central and West; and they are also higher in larger metropolitan areas than in small cities or rural areas. The notion of urbanization economies also implies geographic differences in the nontransportation cost components of a number of firms.

The locational significance of such cost differences, be it labor, agglomeration, power, communications, or capital, is the same as a cost differential attributed to transportation. The cost variations shown in Figure 3.1, for example, could be a consequence of labor cost differences at sites S_1, S_2, and S_3. In other words, where input prices, exclusive of transportation costs, are higher, production costs may be higher, and vice versa. It is thus conceivable that some firms will find certain sites more attractive than others because of lower input costs.

The Location Decision

The concern with economic aspects of the location decision means a concern with the logic of decisions designed to achieve profit maximization. The actual setting in which these decisions are made is complex and the outcomes are by no means obvious. This complexity is dealt with by first simplifying this setting and then gradually building up to more "realistic" situations. With location analysis this means an initial concern with transportation costs, which have long been considered the crucial locating force.

Costs: Transportation Orientation   Suppose input prices exclusive of transportation costs are the same all over, and there are no urbanization economies or diseconomies. Suppose further the inputs used in production are localized—found in one place—and the product is sold in a perfectly competitive point market located at C. Finally, assume the production process involves the use of only one input (I), which neither gains nor loses weight in production and which is found only at I_s—see Figure 3.8.

Figure 3.8

I_s •—————————————————————————————• C

In this setting, the location problem is one of finding the point of minimum transportation cost. What the firm has to do is get the input from I_s, process it, and ship the final product to customers at C. The costs of doing so, exclusive of transportation, are the same all over as are the revenues from operation exclusive of transportation. What does vary is the transportation bill (T), which in this case consists of two parts:

$$T = t_i + t_c \qquad (3.1)$$

where t_i is the cost of transporting the input to the site of the plant and t_c is the cost of transporting the output from the plant to the market. If transportation costs are movement costs that are proportional with distance and weight, these costs are at a minimum at any point on a straight line which connects I_s and C—see Figure 3.8. Transportation costs in this case are a mirror image of the distances involved in getting the input to the plant and output to the market. Hence they are at a minimum when shipping distance is at a minimum. With one localized input and one point market, this has to be a point which falls on the straight line connecting I_s and C.

Suppose we relax several assumptions. Let us recognize that transportation costs consist not only of movement costs but handling or terminal costs. The presence of terminal costs enhance the attractiveness of input and market location. Intermediate locations require handling operations for both inputs and outputs, whereas "end-point" locations require these operations for either inputs *or* outputs. Terminal costs are lower at input or market locations; hence total transportation costs tend to be lower there.

With terminal costs the conclusion is that the firm is "pulled" toward I_s or C. Will it be I_s or C? It cannot be both. Do we have a basis for choosing between these two?

More information is required, the most important of which concerns the nature of the production process. Suppose, for example, there is weight loss in production. If the transportation rate is influenced by the weight of the objects moved, weight loss means the cost per mile of shipping the finished product will be less than the input; the final product weighs less than the material. To minimize the transportation bill, the plant has to be located at the site of the input. Inputs thus exert a strong locational pull when they are localized and lose weight in the production.

The real world, of course, does not consist of simple production processes, of transportation surfaces with costs proportional with distances and weight, and of point markets. Generally, more than one material is used in production, and each material is often found in more than one location. Both possibilities could have impact on the pull of any one materials location. Also, the transportation system is not a surface but a network of routes, and the costs of movement over these routes may reflect long haul economies that have bearing on the transportation bill incurred at alternative sites.

The matter of evaluating the impact of the pull of inputs on location, given real world complexities, is difficult. Even so, the input component in production can, via transportation costs, pull production toward certain sites.

Costs: Other Input Orientations   As noted above, there is ample evidence of geographic differences in labor and other input costs, the locational significance of which is evident. Labor cost differences, for example, mean production costs will be lower for firms in some places than others. If the geography of these differences is not the same as that of transportation, e.g., labor costs are not lowest at locations where the transportation costs are at a minimum, labor costs could influence the location decision.

The question of the locational pull of labor versus transportation can be viewed as a trade-off. The firm can choose either the location at which the transportation bill is at a minimum or the one at which labor costs are lowest. The question is: How much higher will transportation costs be in relation to the savings in labor costs realized when locating at the point of minimum labor costs? Or how much higher will labor costs be in relation to the savings in transportation costs realized when locating at the point of minimum transportation costs?

The answer depends on the relative importance of labor and transportation costs as components of total cost. For firms whose production processes require large amounts of labor, and require material inputs that do not weigh very much and are available from a number of sources, e.g., textiles, the outcome is clear. Labor costs will loom large in their total cost structure; hence the cost savings associated with locations where labor costs are low will be large relative to the increase in transportation costs that stem from locating away from the minimum transportation cost point. These firms will be attracted to sites where labor costs are relatively low, and their mode of production will be said to be *labor-oriented*.

Suppose, on the other hand, labor is less important in production, the materials used are heavy and lose weight, and the final product is bulky and difficult to transport, e.g., steel. Labor costs will be low relative to the transportation bill. Firms facing these conditions will be attracted to sites where transportation costs are at a minimum. They have a *transportation orientation*.

This trade off, of course, need not be restricted to labor and transportation. Energy costs vary over space in ways that attract some firms to certain locations as do the costs of land. There are also the manmade enticements of subsidies and preferential tax treatments that vary over space and that are alleged to have impact on the locations of certain firms. Finally, there are those cost influences associated with urbanization. All of these things can exert strong locational pulls on firms whenever production requirements are such that these costs are important relative to all other costs.

Market Orientation   Revenues, as noted above, can vary by location. When these revenue variations are important and pull firms toward market locations, firms are said to have a market orientation.

Firms have a *market orientation* when spatial cost variations are less than the revenue variations. If we assume costs are the same all over, this is easy to see for firms operating in point markets—see Figure 3.4. It also holds for markets in which customers are dispersed. The outcome for spatial markets, however, is less evident. It stems from the competitive interactions of firms in these markets, interactions which can be best illustrated in the setting of the homogeneous customer dispersed evenly over a flat plain, blessed with a transportation surface and ubiquitous resources.

Suppose that wine can be produced with profit on this plain. Enter the little old winemaker (A) producing wine at a point picked out at random. With one firm it would make little difference where this production is located because revenues are the same no matter what the location. If the little old winemaker finds production profitable, however, and sells in a market area that is much smaller than the boundaries of that plain, more firms—B, for example—should appear. If it is profitable to produce wine at one location, it should be profitable to produce it elsewhere.

As other firms begin operations carving out their own market area, questions arise as to the configuration of market areas that will emerge. Since consumption costs are influenced by the distance from the site of production to the residential location of the consuming household, firms will find it advantageous to locate as far from one another as possible. Locating close to a competitor will reduce the firm's potential sales. The point is worth illustrating.

In Figure 3.9, CD denotes a line which divides the market between A and B when these two firms choose to produce wine at points P_1 and P_2 and charge the same price exclusive of the cost of transporting wine from the plant to the consumer. Customers to the left of CD will buy wine from A and those to the right of CD will buy from B. Were any to do otherwise, their consumption costs would be higher than necessary because they would be paying higher transportation costs than necessary.

Figure 3.9

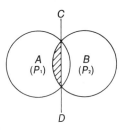

Suppose now that B chooses to locate further away from A. By doing so, it increases the number of customers by an amount equal to those found in the shaded area in Figure 3.9. Hence, B has incentive to move away from A. But as long as there are profits and freedom of entry, new firms will enter the industry; and all firms will, through the impact of competitive interaction, be forced into locations that abut one another. One possible pattern of market areas that could emerge is shown in Figure 3.10.

Figure 3.10

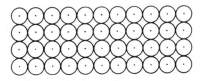

Yet, abutment of market areas that are circular in shape might not be a stable arrangement because it implies the presence of unserved areas. The pattern of market areas that emerges, of course, depends on the nature of the competition that develops among these firms, and much attention in economic studies of spatial competition centers on the pricing policies of the firms involved. This spatial competition can take a form called *monopolistic competition* in economics. Such a market setting assumes differentiation in what is being sold, which in this case is spatial differentiation—firms are located at different sites which gives them an advantage in selling to customers nearby. If we start out with excess profits being made, new firms will enter the industry. As they do, they take business away from existing firms, which is reflected in a shrinking demand and market area in which they sell. This process continues until the excess profits disappear, at which point some argue that the market areas of all firms in the industry will have become hexagonal in shape. While the issue of the shape of these market areas is more complicated than these few remarks suggest, the assumption of a hexagonal shape is appropriate for this discussion.

When the shape of these market areas is hexagonal, there is, for each product, a honeycomb of market areas that might cover the region as follows:

Figure 3.11

With the market organized in this way, production sites are fixed at points that are at the center of individual market areas. But precisely where will these sites be? How many of them will there be?

These are not unrelated questions. The number of sites depends on the size of the market area. This can be shown by simply altering the size of the market areas of the arrangement shown in Figure 3.11. If market areas are drawn to be large, production is shown to be concentrated at fewer sites, whereas if they are drawn to be small, the sites will be many in number, meaning the production will be dispersed throughout the region—see Figure 3.12.

Figure 3.12

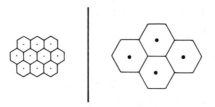

The question of market area size is a crucial one. The answer depends on transportation costs and economies of scale as they come in to play. As noted in chapter 2, transportation costs and economies of scale are opposing forces in an arena in which consumers are dispersed in geographic space and resources are common. In such a setting, transportation costs are additions to consumption costs and operate to restrict the size of a firm's market area. If transportation costs are high, the costs of consumption will be high except to those who live near to points of production. High transportation costs thus result in demand cones with a smaller circumference compared with a situation in which transportation costs are low. Small market areas, in turn, mean many production sites, thus the argument that transportation costs are dispersive in their effects on the spatial organization of economic resources.

Economies of scale have precisely the opposite effect. If the firm experiences significant internal economies of scale, increased levels of output mean lower costs, which implies a lower price for the product, thereby reducing consumption costs. As consumption costs fall, the market area of the firm is enlarged. Enlarged market areas in turn imply that production is more concentrated in space; that is, it takes place at fewer locations.

Suppose now the assumption that costs are not the same at all sites is relaxed. What does the firm do now? If the minimum production costs and maximum revenues are found at the same site, the answer is clear. Profits will be maximized at that site.

Suppose the site of maximum revenue and minimum costs are not the same. The firm must then weigh the trade off between costs and revenues at alternative sites. If revenue benefits of locations near the market exceed cost savings available at sites some distance from the market, the profit-maximizing firm will be pulled toward the market. This will generally happen when the inputs used in production are widely available and/or the cost of getting the product to the consumer is high relative to its price.

Efficient Locations

Profit-maximizing firms try to find sites at which profits are at a maximum. Since operating costs and revenues vary over space, firms find some sites better than others in the sense that profits are highest there. Firms seek such locations, and if they find them, the sites selected are designated as efficient locations in location theory.

Where will these sites be? Location theory does not provide an answer. What it provides is a framework that aids in the search for answer. It points to certain cost and revenue factors that can influence the attractiveness of alternative sites. How the firm responds to such cost and revenue cues depends on 1) the cues themselves and 2) location requirements of the firm. The cost and revenue cues are the outcome of factors that determine how costs and revenues are influenced by distance.

The most important of these is the transportation network and the configuration of costs it generates. When there is no transportation surface, for example, transportation routes and major connections become important. Sites near such routes and connections benefit greatly in terms of costs and revenues.

Population and resource geography are also important. The pull towards markets, for example, is obviously influenced by the spatial positioning of customers. The fact that there is a concentration of population in the corridor from Washington, D.C. on up through Boston is not unimportant to any study of new plant location in the United States. Nor is it unimportant to know something about the geography of the major minerals and other natural resources that are important inputs in production. The location of the wood-processing industry near the forests of the

Northwest and the South is no accident. Nor is the fact that the nation's "footloose" industries are found in abundance in states like California and Arizona.

Knowing something about transportation and communications networks and the population and resource geography of a nation, however, will not necessarily pinpoint efficient locations for particular firms. There is considerable variation in the location requirements of firms. For example, there is wide variation in production technology which is reflected in part in differences in input requirements. Some firms have large labor requirements; others have large materials requirements. Since inputs, for the most part, are not commonly found and oftentimes have different geographies, sites at which costs are at a minimum vary for certain classes of firms.

Nor will the revenue of each firm be the same at all locations. The output of each firm is not consumed by the same customers, nor do firms serve the same geographic area. Some sell nationwide, some sell locally, and some sell in regions that fall somewhere in between. There are production and market differences that generate revenue differences among firms at the same site. What is a maximum revenue site for one firm may not be so for another.

Clearly, before we can begin to make statements about the efficient locations of particular firms, we must have a good deal of factual knowledge of the processes of production and the characteristics of markets these processes serve. It is only with this information combined with factual knowledge of the spatial cost and revenue variations that we can say very much about efficient locations of certain classes of firms and the type of industry likely to be found at certain locations.

CENTRAL PLACE THEORY

Having covered some important territory in the domain of location theory, we are now in a position to consider another part of that domain—*central place theory*—an understanding of which is essential to any consideration of the urban hierarchy. While central place notions are discussed more frequently by geographers than economists, they have much economic content. The decisions made that locate firms in central places are decisions influenced by economic factors. We should therefore be able to make sensible statements about central place notions with the aid of the economic concepts just discussed.

To begin with, central place theory is a set of statements concerned with how markets organize production into a system of urban centers. The primary concern is with demand factors operating through markets. Simplifying assumptions are made. The concern is with a homogenous plain on which consumers are scattered evenly, consumers that have the same tastes and incomes. Firms in the same industry produce a homogenous product and the inputs and production technology are equally spread over the plain, i.e., industry costs of production are the same at any point on that plain.

All of this has a familiar ring. It is an unreal world, but we have already shown that to make it so serves a useful purpose in that it allows us to highlight important aspects of the way in which markets organize the production of individual commodities in geographic space. Now we simply wish to expand this discussion to show how markets can organize total production into a system of central places or urban centers. Three concepts play a key role in this discussion, namely, market areas, market nets, and networks of market nets.

The first two of these have already been discussed. To recapitulate briefly, market areas are areas delineated by the circumference of demand cones which denote the boundaries within which households that are served by particular firms are located —see Figure 3.6. Market nets are the configuration of market areas that emerge because of the competitive interaction of firms in the same industry—see Figures 3.10 and 3.11.

Consider now the people who are spread across that homogenous plain with its ubiquitous resources. Even in such a simplified setting, life consists of more than just the consumption of one good. In most economic situations, households are confronted with alternatives. They must make choices which producers respond to and by doing so make decisions which locate production in geographic space. There are many goods produced and hence there are many market nets. Each net considered individually denotes an arrangement of market areas with production sites in the center of each market area.

Consider these nets collectively—the network of nets. This has been considered by Losch and others as a question of ideal organization or regional structure. Losch, for example, worked with a homogenous plain that had a uniform distribution of households and resources as well as a transportation surface—that is, transportation costs that were proportional with distance throughout the region. For each commodity or service there was a market net composed of hexagonally shaped market areas. Given differences in commodity characteristics and production processes, differences could be postulated in the spatial extent of the market areas of firms in different industries. Firms in some industries had large market areas; for others these areas were not quite so large. In fact, the market areas of firms in this region were likely to range in size from the very small—market areas for the so-called convenience items such as barber shops, grocery stores, and the like—to markets that covered the entire nation—the automobile industry for example.

Suppose now that the market nets associated with total production—a net for each industry—were centered at the location of some household in the center of the region. When the nets were overlaid and centered in this way, central points of production, i.e., central places, would emerge. Initially, there would be points of convergence represented by commodities with nets composed of market areas of the same size. To the extent that barber shops, grocery stores, and drugstores had market areas of the same size, they would be found at the same location; and we would characterize those sites as central places.

Then the nets would be rotated further. If this rotation led to a cogwheel pattern of six sectors in which many points of production coincided, and six sectors in which there were only a few central places, Losch argued that we would have arranged production in a way that achieved an efficient arrangement of resources and hence central places. Such an arrangement was said to be efficient in the sense that the greatest number of production sites coincided, the sum of shipment distances between centers was least, and the shipment of goods was minimized.

What is important about all this is the general shape of the final outcome. Even though the consumers are dispersed space, it is shown that an efficient spatial arrangement will concentrate production in geographic space. Fundamentally, this concentration is a consequence of internal and external economies of scale in production. We can say more about the form it takes, however, when it is considered in the context of central place notions. Such production factors, considered in combination with transportation costs and the spatial positioning of customers, as it would be in a central place model, yield concentration in the form of a number of nodes, or cities, the spacing of which is systematic. Moreover, what emerges has a hierarchical property in the sense of a size distribution of urban centers that is pyramidal and in the kind of goods and services that are provided at different sized centers. In effect, from the notion of centrality, we can, with the aid of location theory, rationalize a pattern of urban settlement that has many of the characteristics of the system of cities described above.

What reason, if any, do we have to believe that markets, as they operate, will in fact organize production in this way? Is it reasonable to expect firms in different industries responding to a dispersed pattern of demand to choose production sites that are bunched together? There is little in this description of the Loschian conception of an ideal regional structure that indicates how markets generate such a model pattern. There are, however, reasons for believing that it will.

For example, there is reason to believe that firms with feasible production site possibilities that are not too far distant from one another will move toward one another. The fact that we have transportation networks rather than transportation surfaces pushes firms toward one another. Sites away from the major routes and connecting points in the transportation network could mean prohibitive transportation costs. It is in this sense that all firms tend to be pulled toward sites adjacent to or near connecting points in network routes. Urbanization economies would also come into play in ways that reinforce the pulling power of transportation networks.

CENTRAL PLACES AND THE URBAN HIERARCHY

To this point, only very general statements have been made about central place theory. We can, of course, become more specific and do so in ways that make the hierarchical character of the system of urban centers that can be generated by a central place model more visible.

First, note that market areas can be considered in terms of populations, that is, the population living within the boundaries of a market area. Second, these areas can be ranked in terms of orders. First order market areas are the smallest, second order areas the next smallest, and so forth. It follows that populations can be considered in terms of orders. Now restrict the concern to certain kinds of market nets and market areas. Let the focus be only on those market nets that fit together with others in the sense that the market area of one includes exactly s areas of the next smallest size. If s is set equal to four, for example, this would mean that second order market area populations will be four times larger than first order market area populations, third order market area populations will be four times larger than second order market area populations, and so forth.

Next assume that some fixed proportion (k) of the population in any market area is located in the urban center of that area, i.e., at the site of production in the center of the area. If k is set equal to 0.5, 50 percent of the first order popula-tion will be found living in the urban center of the smallest market area and 50 percent will be found living in a rural setting or hinterland of that area. With respect to second order populations, 50 percent will be living in urban center and 50 percent in the hinterland. In this case, because of the assumption made about s, the hinterland population will consist of four first order urban centers, in the second order market area along with the hinterlands of these smaller centers, i.e. rural areas. For third order market areas, 50 percent of the population will be found in third order urban centers—that is, at the site of production in the center of the third order market area. The other 50 percent will live in the hinterland, which in this case would consist of four second order urban centers in this third order market area, 16 first order market centers in the four second order market areas that are a part of the third order market area, and sixteen rural areas surrounding these first order centers.

This progression could be very easily extended to higher orders. By doing so, we further highlight the hierarchical character of this system, which takes the form of a size distribution of urban centers that is pyramidal in shape. Given the initial conditions, along with the value of four assigned to s, the system that emerges is one that has many small urban centers, a number of medium sized centers, and a few large centers. If we assume there are six orders in this hierarchy, the following distribution of cities would emerge:

Table 3.4

Order of the Urban Center	Number of Urban Centers
1	1024
2	256
3	64
4	16
5	4
6	1

If we now specify values for k and the rural population (r) of the first order populations, the populations of all urban centers and those served by these urban centers can be calculated. For example, if r is set at 1,000 and k at 0.5, the following hypothetical system of cities can be generated:

Table 3.5

Order of the Urban Center	Number of Urban Centers	Population of Urban Centers	Population Served by each Center
1	1024	1,000	2,000
2	256	8,000	16,000
3	64	64,000	128,000
4	16	512,000	1,024,000
5	4	4,096,000	8,192,000
6	1	32,768,000	65,536,000

The assumptions leading to these conclusions can be formalized in a way such that this discussion can be presented as a formal system of cities model. In the model underlying the calculations presented above, the population of a first order center is defined as $kr/(1 - k)$. That is, it is a function of the rural population (r) and the proportion of the population served by that center which lives in the center (k) standing in this relation to one another. The population of centers of the next order depends on the number of first order centers and their hinterlands which fit into the hinterlands of the second order center (s) and the proportion of the population served by that center which lives in the center (again k). It can in fact be shown that the population of a second order center is $s/1 - k)$ times the population of the first order center $kr/(1 - k)$. The expression $s/(1 - k)$ is, in effect, a population multiplier. If we know the value of $s, r,$ and $k,$ we can with the aid of this multiplier quickly calculate the population of the center of any order in the hierarchy.

What does all this have to do with the explanation of the facts of an urban hierarchy? It is possible to derive statements from such models that can be compared with certain facts. By making certain additional assumptions, we can derive the conclusion that, in a rank ordering of all centers, the rank of an urban center, when multiplied by its population, will equal a constant. This statement is a verbalization of the *rank-size rule,* a hypothesis that has been tested empirically. The results are inconclusive. In some cases, the rule has been found to fit the data well; in others it has not.

What does all of this mean? Suppose the rank-size rule did fit the data well and that elaborations of the model designed to predict, say, the distances between cities in the various classes of the hierarchy were equally promising. Successful empirical applications of a model suggest there is something here which should help explain the urban facts to which our model-building efforts are addressed. How would the hierarchy model presented above help us explain the facts of the urban hierarchy as we know them? We have to go back to the basic notions which provide the foundation of that model—the central place concepts. Fundamental to the emergence of the hypothetical system of cities constructed above were certain assumed facts. Dispersion of the population and its scarce resources, transportation costs that were not prohibitive, and a technology that generated scale economies both internal and external to the firm were the building blocks of the central place theory discussed here. On the basis of such facts, market areas and market nets were fitted together in ways that generated a configuration of urban centers that were ultimately summarized in the rank-size rule.

Certainly there is evidence of some dispersion of the population and its scarce resources. It is also the case that transportation costs cannot be considered as prohibitive, just as there is evidence of a technology that generates internal and external economies of scale. With these facts, you would expect markets to generate a system of cities, the size distributions of which would fit the rank-size rule. That the facts are consistent with this rule in some cases and not in others indicates one of two things. Either we are not making a proper test of the rule, or central place notions are not sufficiently powerful to provide the basis for explaining the many faces of the urban hierarchy. Both of these things probably help to account for the indifferent success in the empirical applications of central place models. The testing difficulties involve data problems, not discussed in this chapter. The scope of the applicability of central place notions, on the other hand, is something about which certain things can be said.

That central place notions provide the foundation for constructing a model that fits the facts for the state of Iowa yet not the facts of New York or Illinois should come as no surprise to those who have fully digested the earlier statements about location theory. Central place theory derives from certain assumptions made about the shape of the world, some of which are rather unrealistic. Consider the initial assumption of a uniform population distribution. The minute a central place emerges and we assume that some of the population served by industry in this center is itself located in such centers, the assumption of a uniform population is violated. There will no longer be uniform market areas for firms in the same industries, which raises questions about the outcomes that are generally a part of most expositions of the theory. It can be shown, however, that changes in the shapes and sizes of market areas that population concentration and other features of the market may bring about do not really disturb the hierarchical structure of the system.

A more fundamental difficulty is the assumption of constant costs over geographic space. This assumption does not hold for all industries. The resources of nature are not evenly distributed geographically, whether it is the mineral resources that stand as important material inputs in many industries or the amenity resources, such as mild climate, which influence costs in a growing number of industries. As a consequence many firms are confronted with costs that vary over geographic space. For some this is the crucial locating influence. The location behavior of these firms will not be explained by central place notions.

Urban settlement pattern in the nation can probably be best thought of as the outcome of several distinct sets of factors operating through markets. Our cities are, in effect, a composite of several systems of economic activity. One distinguishable system is found in much service-type activity and some small manufacturing. This is activity that requires productive inputs that are fairly widely distributed in geographic space. Costs are thus pretty much the same over space. We are dealing with industries that operate in a setting that is generally consistent with central place notions, which means activity in those industries tends to be distributed geographically in accordance with the logic of central place theory. The spatial characteristics of demand that are reflected through revenues is a crucially important locating influence to such firms. Since their number and the volume of business they generate is large, it should come as no surprise that the facts bear some resemblance to certain implications of central place theory, particularly when the focus is on settings in which this kind of activity is important—for example, the state of Iowa.

There is also a second distinguishing system reflected in much manufacturing activity. This activity requires the use of inputs, the cost of which vary widely geographically. Firms in such industries have production conditions that pull them locationally to sites where costs are at a minimum, which may or may not be at locations of maximum revenues. Their location decisions reflect more the logic of a cost-oriented location model than a central place model. Since the number of such firms and the volume of business they generate is also large, it comes as no surprise that the facts do not fit the certain implications of central place theory very well, particularly in places where there are concentrations of firms that are cost-oriented with respect to location—for example the state of New York.

THE URBAN HIERARCHY RECONSIDERED

If groups of cities reflect the operation of several distinct systems as they emerge through the urbanization process, the meaning of an urban hierarchy becomes less clear. On the basis of central place notions alone, it is possible to build a hypothetical system of cities that has a hierarchical structure. That structure was identified above in terms of the orders of urban centers; that is, each city in the system could be classified according to the order or size category into which it fitted. It is also possible to specify additional characteristics of those cities which fall into certain orders. If cities are what they are and where they are because of the response of firms to the market forces postulated in a central place model, we can make statements about the kind of output or industry structure likely to be found in particular cities. If the city were in a lower order center, for example, we would expect to find the production of commodities and services with the market areas that were quite small. In higher order centers, on the other hand, we would not only find this kind of production, but that which served populations of much broader market areas. Given the appropriate information about the market characteristics of particular products and services, we should be able to make some fairly specific statements about industry composition of an urban center if we know the order into which it fitted.

Economic activity, however, is organized in geographic space in ways that cannot be explained fully with the aid of central place theory. Cost factors come into play in ways that lead to significant distortions of central place outcomes. As a consequence, it is by no means clear that we can characterize lower order cities—or higher order cities—in the way indicated just above. With a system of systems of cities, we can still talk of an urban hierarchy. Such a system can be shown to generate cities of different orders, and the way in which cities are distributed as between these orders has hierarchical properties in the sense of a pyramidal shape with respect to size. But it is now more difficult to make statements about the kinds of activity we would expect to find in particular cities. If costs have impact on the location decisions of the firm, a dimension is added that could conceivably generate structural differences between cities of the same order that are greater than the differences that exist between cities in different orders.

The problems of classification in such a system of cities are difficult, and we have by no means developed a system of city classifications that provides a basis for making consistent and far-reaching statements about structural similarities and differences between cities that are a part of that system. Many attempts have been made to classify cities. One such classification distinguishes among cities that are national capitals, regional capitals, nodal centers, export specialization cities, and small cities. Another established the categories of national metropolis, diversified manufacturing with metropolitan functions, regional metropolises, diversified manufacturing with few metropolitan functions, regional capitals, specialized manufacturing, and special cases. Other classifications focus on still different features of the city. But careful inspection of classifications of this sort leads to the conclusion that we lack the knowledge on the basis of which detailed statements can be made about the salient differentiating characteristics of cities as they fit into an urban hierarchy. The notion of a hierarchy in a system of cities is potentially a productive one. But in its application to date, while it provides insights into the nation's system of cities, it does not really clarify aspects of that system in ways that many think it should. Nor does it provide us much insight into the dynamics of that system.

REFERENCES

Beckman, M. *Location Theory*. New York: Random House, 1968. Chapters 2, 3 and 5.

Christaller, W: *Central Places in Southern Germany*. Translated by C. Baskin. Engle-wood Cliffs, N.J.: Prentice-Hall, 1966.

Duncan, O., et al. *Metropolis and Region*. Baltimore: The Johns Hopkins Press, 1960.

Karaska, G. and Bramhall, D., eds. *Locational Analysis for Manufacturing*. Cambridge, Mass.: MIT Press, 1969.

Lampard, E. "The Evolving System of Cities in the United States: Urbanization and Economic Development." In *Issues in Urban Economics,* edited by H. Perloff and L. Wingo. Baltimore: The Johns Hopkins Press, 1968. Pp. 81–139.

*Losch, A. *The Economics of Location*. Translated by W. Woglom. New York: Science Editions, John Wiley and Sons, Inc., 1967.

*Weber, A. *The Theory of the Location of Industry*. Translated by C. Friedrich. Chi-cago: University of Chicago Press, 1929.

---

* This chapter draws heavily from the writings of Losch and Weber.

Macroeconomic Models
and City Growth

SUMMARY

Macroeconomic and economic growth concepts can be applied to the study of city growth. Demand-oriented models of macroeconomics have been frequently used in such studies. The most common application focuses on the city's links with other places. The notion of an economic base is introduced, which is to say that the exports from a city are taken to provide the impetus to growth. Urban base multipliers, an economic concept which describes the impact of increases in aggregate income on aggregate spending, provide insights into the overall impact of exports on the urban economy. Economic base models of this kind can contribute to the explanation of city growth. They also have important limitations.

Input-output analysis is used to expand our knowledge of the economic structure of cities, particularly as it has bearing on the impact of exports on city growth. Input-output is a way of looking at current production; it emphasizes the importance of intermediate production. Firms that produce goods that are sold to other firms and incorporated into their production are important because their presence or absence has important bearing on how much local spending remains in the local income stream. The amount of spending that remains in local income is important because it is a crucial determinant of the urban base multiplier.

Neither economic base nor input-output analysis has much to say about supply factors in the growth process. To be concerned with supply is to be concerned with resources such as labor and capital and the way they are combined in the production process. Supply factors are important in the study of city growth because resources are mobile geographically but do not always adjust quickly or completely to meet the requirements of a city experiencing significant demand-induced changes.

Studies of supply as a factor in city growth emphasize external movements of the population, filtering, and growth poles. External movements of the population are believed to be important because some people move from one urban area to another for reasons that have little to do with economic opportunities. Filtering theories of growth emphasize the way in which technological innovation comes into being and is diffused

57

throughout the nation. Growth occurs initially in the centers of innovation and at some later point filters on down to other cities. Growth poles is another theory with technological overtones. Innovation creates expanding industries and these industries, if they are "propulsive," stimulate expansion of other industries nearby.

The dynamics of the urban system is accounted for by population growth and urbanization. That population increases over time, as does the proportion of that population which lives in cities, means city building either in the sense of new cities and/or growth in existing ones. In fact, the urban system has grown over time through the emergence of new cities and the growth of existing ones. This growth has also been uneven in its distribution among cities. While measures of size distribution may show overall stability in the relative number of cities in different orders of the urban hierarchy, there has been movement between orders by individual cities. This, of course, implies differential growth among cities, a fact easy to verify. Most cities have grown over time, but they have grown at different rates; and the growth rate of most cities has changed over time. What is there about the dynamics of urban society that generates such patterns of urban change?

The answer to date is not found in analyses built around the concept of an urban hierarchy. More can be learned about the pact of city growth with the aid of the tools of macro and growth economics.

Economic growth, of course, is the outcome of factors that operate through both the supply and demand side of markets. Those on the supply side, the inputs of production such as labor and capital and the processes of production through which these inputs are combined into outputs, are the determinants of potential output. Whether actual output is equal to their potential depends on demand factors. A study of city growth therefore is also a concern with demand elements.

Aggregate demand and supply as determinants of the nation's output and income have been studied extensively. There is, in fact, an abundance of macro and growth models that can be applied to the study of aggregate economic change in the city. Care must be taken in such applications, however, because of special circumstances, the most important of which is the fact that the city is more open than the nation. Greater openness means that imports and exports play a more important role in determining aggregative economic outcomes. In cities that are a part of a system of cities, it also means a greater possibility of input movements among cities, e.g., labor migration, capital migration, etc.

The concern in this chapter is with macroeconomic and growth concepts applicable to the study of city growth. The presentation distinguishes between demand and supply factors. Demand models are taken up first, following a brief discussion of urban economic accounts. Supply concepts are then considered.

DEMAND ANALYSIS

Economic Accounts in an Urban Region

Making a substantive investigation of aggregate economic change requires pertinent facts. Most studies made to date have been demand-oriented. The emphasis in collecting facts has thus been on those relevant to the analysis of demand factors.

A coherent social accounting framework has developed which focuses on the concepts of income, production, and expenditures. The foundation of this framework is certain basic accounting relationships. The most important of these is

$$E \equiv Y \equiv O \qquad (4.1)$$

where E is total expenditure, Y is total income, and O is total production. While each refers to a different category of economic activity, they can also be considered as different ways of viewing the economic process as a whole. This is, in effect, denoted by $\equiv$, or the sign indicating the relationship is an identity. Taken together in this way, they make up the central elements of the notion of the circular flow of goods and money in an exchange economy. Production, of course, generates both the goods and the wherewithal—money income—necessary to acquire these goods. With actual acquisition giving rise to expenditures, the economic sense of equation 4.1 is evident. Goods and money flow in circular directions in an exchange economy because production is not consumed directly, but rather flows into markets and is cleared out of markets as a result of expenditures made out of incomes generated by production. This is essentially what equation 4.1 tells us.

This equation can, through division, be amplified in different ways. In elementary macroeconomics, expenditure distinctions are made. In the beginning, the world is taken to be one in which there is no government, and each nation is completely isolated. In such a world, expenditures are typically segmented into consumption (C) and investment (I). Hence

$$Y \equiv C + I \qquad (4.2)$$

Furthermore, if we define savings (S) as the abstinence from consumption, we know that

$$Y \equiv C + S \qquad (4.3)$$

Suppose we now take into account the rest of the world, something obviously important when the concern is with cities. Assume these contacts take the form of exports and imports. Exports (X) can be viewed as spending by outsiders on goods produced locally. Imports (M), correspondingly, can be viewed as expenditures by local residents on goods produced elsewhere. So considered, exports are seen adding to the spending stream of a nation or city and hence to its income and production streams. Imports, on the other hand, take away from the income stream. If there are exports and imports and the identity between income, production, and spending is to be maintained, it is clear that exports must be added to the spending stream and imports must be deducted or

$$Y \equiv C + I + (X - M) \tag{4.4}$$

The final extension takes into account the role of government in the economy. Government in its capacity as a fiscal agent both adds to and takes away from the spending stream. Government expenditures (G) are like any other expenditure and hence represent additions to that stream. Taxes (T), on the other hand, take away from the money that can be spent and hence stand as subtractions. Adding the government sector to equation 4.4 therefore means adding $(G - T)$ or

$$Y \equiv C + I + (X - M) + (G - T) \tag{4.5}$$

Equation 4.5 represents the core elements of a social accounting framework that provides the foundation for massive amounts of demand-oriented data collected on the national economy and to a lesser extent on regions and cities.

That we have collected less demand-oriented data on cities is a consequence of special data collection problems encountered. The basic problem with cities is that they are part of a system that has the same monetary system, tradition, and culture, which means there is less reason for enterprise, both public and private, to keep track of activities with others in other cities. These are, unfortunately, transactions that are crucially important in the analysis of aggregative change in open economies.

Still, certain income and employment numbers have been generated for many cities which provide a basis for investigating city growth in a demand-oriented macro framework.

Basic Elements in Macroeconomic Theory

Macroeconomic theory is a series of statements concerned with the determination of aggregate income (Y). The theory abstracts from commonplace everyday affairs. The focus is on aggregate demand. Aggregate income is taken to be a function of aggregate demand. What does this mean?

Consider this question in a world in which there is no government and no rest of the world, i.e., no exports and imports. According to equation 4.2, aggregate demand can be broken down into consumption and investment spending categories. In macroeconomic theory, these are taken as meaningful categories; consumption and investment spending are treated as "causes." The critical questions are: What are the determinants of consumption and investment and how do they interact in determining income?

At the most elemental level, macro theory treats consumption as a fixed proportion of income, e.g., $C = bY$, and investment as exogenous or determined by forces external to the economic system, e.g., $I = \bar{I}$. Given these assumptions, the following three equations can be taken as a model of the macroeconomic system

$$Y = C + I \tag{4.6}$$
$$C = bY \tag{4.7}$$
$$I = \bar{I} \tag{4.8}$$

where b is propensity to consume out of income.

This model can be solved for Y. By substitution, Y can be shown to equal

$$Y = \frac{1}{1-b}\bar{I} \qquad (4.9)$$

where $1/(1-b)$ is the income multiplier. What this equation says in effect is that if we know the level of aggregate business investment and the propensity of households to consume out of income—and hence the income multiplier—we can estimate the level of aggregate income. For example, if we assign the values of 10 and 0.5 to $\bar{I}$ and b respectively, Y can be shown to equal 20. If $\bar{I}$ and b are assigned the values of 100 and 0.8, the level of income will be 500.

If these equations adequately describe the macroeconomic world, they tell us that income is determined by business investment spending and the propensity to consume. Given the signs in the equations, we also note that income varies positively with these two factors.

The geometry of these relationships provides further insights into the model and hence the economy. The basic accounting relation $(Y \equiv S)$ can be shown as a line—the guideline—which bisects a quadrant in which spending is shown on the vertical axis and income on the horizontal axis—see Figure 4.1. The

Figure 4.1

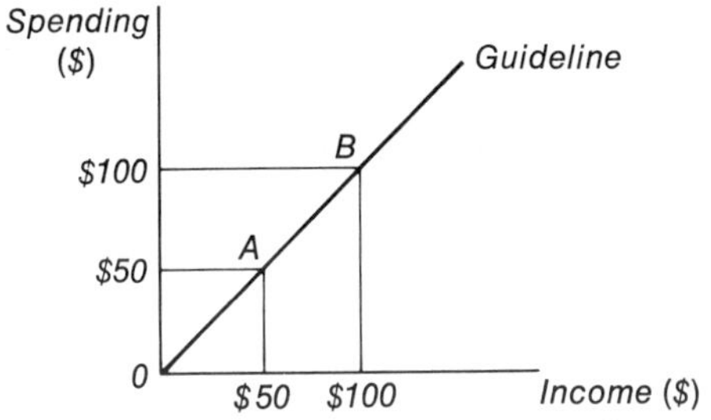

identity comes through in that point A on this line denotes an income and/or expenditure level of $50; point B signifies an income and/or expenditure level of $100.

Consider now the determinants of income. If consumption is a function of income in the way denoted by equation 4.7, consumption spending at alternative levels of income is shown by line OC in Figure 4.2. Any point on this line denotes a level of income and consumption spending at that income. What consumption is at any income level in this model depends on the propensity to consume (b)—see equation 4.7.

Figure 4.2

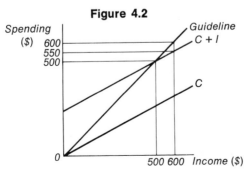

Investment in this model is given—see equation 4.8—or, in effect, is taken as a constant amount. If this amount is added to the consumption line, the $C + I$ line is derived—see Figure 4.2. This line denotes total spending in the economy at alternative levels of income. Investment at any income is shown as the difference between the C and $C + I$ lines at that income.

Figure 4.2 displays geometrically the solution to the problem of income determination, given the $C + I$ line. To illustrate, suppose that $b = 0.8$ and $\bar{I} = \$100$. Geometrically, b is the slope of the C line and $\bar{I}$ is the difference between the C and $C + I$ line. Given these values, we know from equation 4.9 that Y must equal \$500. But why?

With Figure 4.2, it is easy to show why income must be \$500. Given demand, this is the only income at which all goods flowing into the market from production are cleared out of the market by purchases of consumers and business firms. Were production and hence income at \$600, the amount of spending would, according to the $C + I$ line, be only \$550. All the income earned as a consequence of participation in production would not be spent; hence all goods flowing from production into the market would not be cleared out of the market. Business inventories would accumulate and production would be cut back with a resulting decline in income. These adjustments would continue until production and hence income are at the \$500 level. If we suppose that production and income were below \$500, we could argue analogously, only in this case inventories would decline and there would be upward pressure on production and income. Given the "behavioral" assumptions implicit in the $C + I$ line, this model indicates income will be \$500.

Obviously, equations 4.6 through 4.9 and Figure 4.2 are oversimplified representations of the economy. Not only do they exclude important segments of the economy, i.e., government and connections with the rest of the world, they present a simplistic view of the determinants of the major components of spending. Still, they provide a base from which extensions can be made which are appropriate to the study of macro change in cities. One of these is the concept of the urban base multiplier.

Urban Income Multipliers   The city, as noted above, is an open economy, which means its relation with the rest of the world must be taken into account. In a macro model, this means the inclusion of imports (M) and exports (X). The expenditures equation thus becomes

$$Y = C + I + (X - M) \tag{4.10}$$

If we treat C and I as above, suppose that exports are determined by factors outside the economy, i.e., $X = \bar{X}$, and assume imports are a simple function of income, e.g., $M = mY$, we have the following:

$$C = bY \tag{4.11}$$
$$I = \bar{I} \tag{4.12}$$
$$M = mY \tag{4.13}$$
$$X = \bar{X} \tag{4.14}$$

By substituting equations 4.11 through 4.14 into equation 4.10, we can solve for Y or

$$Y = \frac{1}{1 - b + m} (\bar{I} + \bar{X}) \tag{4.15}$$

The expression $1/(1 - b + m)$ is the urban base multiplier. It differs from the income multiplier $1/(1 - b)$ in that it includes m, the propensity to import out of income. That the community's population buys goods and services produced elsewhere is significant. Imports cause dollars to leak out of the local income stream, which has important bearing on the impact of spending on local income.

In a closed economy when the propensity to consume (b) is 0.6, the multiplier $1/(1 - b)$ is 2.5. Suppose the economy is opened up in the sense that households can buy elsewhere. Suppose further that 10 cents of each income dollar is spent on imported goods, i.e., $m = 0.1$. The multiplying effect of exogenous spending in the economy is now reduced to 2, i.e., $k = 1/(1 - 0.6 + 0.1) = 2$. If we suppose investment and exports are $100, the level of income in the economy when there is no importing is $250. When there are imports, the equilibrium level of income is $200. This reduction in the economic power of a dollar spent locally is, of course, attributable to the fact that some of these dollars leave the area as a consequence of imports.

The impact of imports on local income generation shows up as a reduction in overall spending on local production. Given consumption with no imports—line OC in Figure 4.3—and specified amounts of investment and exports, the total spending line shows up as $C + I + X$. With the spending behavior implicit in this line, which intersects the guideline at point A, equilibrium income is $250.

Consider now the possibility of imports. With imports, consumption spending on local goods becomes $(C - M)$. If imports are a constant proportion of income, e.g., $M = mY$, $(C - M)$ at each level of income will be represented by a line such as $(C - M)$ in Figure 4.3. Adding on investment and export

Figure 4.3

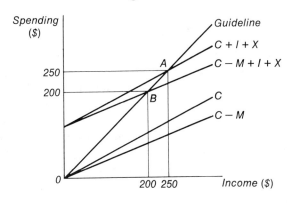

spending, the total spending line now becomes $C - M + I + X$. This line intersects the guideline at point B, a lower level of income—see Figure 4.3. It does so because of the leakage from the local income stream when households use local income to buy goods and services produced outside the community.

How much will the community import at each income level? The tastes and preferences of local households are involved. As these preferences have bearing on decisions made with respect to the allocation of income among consumption alternatives, so do they have bearing on whether these choices favor locally or foreign produced goods. More important, however, are factors that influence the amount of consumption goods produced locally.

The majority of imports in most communities stem from inventory purchases of distributive industries, i.e., retailing and wholesaling. If households spend 80 cents out of every income dollar, the bulk of these expenditures in most urban communities will be made locally. On the surface, these income dollars appear to remain in the local income stream. If all that is purchased from the local retailer is in fact produced locally, there will be no income leakage as the retailers replenish their inventories. In most urban communities, however, much of what is bought locally is not produced locally. There is, for reasons discussed in chapter 3, spatial specialization in the production of many commodities. We find it to our advantage to produce certain things in certain places and to take advantage of the productivity benefits of this specialization through interregional trade or exchange. This implies that the purchase of food, clothing, and the means of transportation in most urban communities will often mean the purchase of something that is imported by the retailer who sells it to the consumer. When this happens, many of the dollars spent locally leak out of the local income stream. Moreover, even when we purchase locally produced goods and services, some of these dollars may still leave the area. If the clothing we buy locally is produced locally, much of the material used in its manufacture may have been produced elsewhere. Some of the money spent locally for hamburgers and milk shakes at McDonalds or Burger King may also leave the local income stream. The meat and dairy products used in providing the food service may have come from other places, as the napkins and straws that are used.

The import propensity of an urban community—and hence its urban base multiplier—is thus importantly influenced by what is produced locally or the industry structure of that community.

Economic Base Theory and City Growth

Economic growth refers to an increase in some economic quantity, e.g., income, over a relatively long time period, e.g., five years or more. The income model just discussed provides a framework for analyzing such growth. Economic growth in such a model is viewed as movement from one equilibrium position to another. In the simple system denoted by equations 4.6 through 4.9, the economy is sectored into external and internal elements. Investment is assumed to be determined by external forces, and consumption by the internal workings of the economy. Movement from one equilibrium position to another originates from a change in investment. Growth is a consequence of change in investments spending, but equation 4.9 shows that such change will have multiplying effects on the level of income. The size of the multiplier, in turn, depends on the propensity of households to spend out of current income or (b) in equation 4.9.

The basic structure of this model has been used frequently in the study of urban areas. Exports rather than investments, however, have been the driving force in these urban applications, and the substitution of exports for investment means, in urban economics, a concern with the economic base of the city.

Economic base is a concept that assigns exports the critical role in the growth of an urban economy. Exports are taken to be important because of the scope of their market. Goods and services sold to local residents are limited by the size of the local market. There are no such restrictions on production that is exported. The market for exports may be national or even international, which means the possibilities for expanding output are much greater.

Economic base notions can be incorporated into a macro model of the urban economy. Start with equation 4.10:

$$Y \equiv C + I + (X - M) \qquad \text{(4.10)}$$

This becomes an economic base model if we assume there is only one exogenous variable—exports.

$$X = \overline{X} \qquad \text{(4.14)}$$

All other components of spending are tied to income. If we assume proportional relationships, the behavior of households and business firms is described as follows:

$$C = bY \qquad \text{(4.16)}$$
$$M = mY \qquad \text{(4.17)}$$
$$I = wY \qquad \text{(4.18)}$$

Consumption, imports, and investment spending are shown to depend on income in ways denoted by coefficients b, m, and w.

Substitution of equations 4.16 through 4.18 into equation 4.10 and solving for Y yields:

$$Y = \frac{1}{1 - b - w + m} X_e \qquad \text{(4.19)}$$

where $1/(1 - b - w + m)$ is the urban base multiplier.

This equation is easy to interpret. If the spending propensities denoted by b, m, and w are stable, as base theorists assume, growth in the economy is a consequence of changes in exports. How much growth is associated with given increases in exports depends on the urban base multiplier $1/(1 - b - w + m)$. This, in turn, is determined by the pattern of community spending reflected in the propensity of local households and businesses to spend out of income and the extent to which this spending is on goods and services produced locally.

The application of base theory to the study of urban growth is clear enough. The immediate concern is with structuring the economy into its basic and nonbasic components. Having done this, the ingredients are there from which the urban base multiplier can be calculated. With this multiplier and knowledge of how the economic base of the community has grown, interpretative statements can be made about that growth.

Most who have used base theory in this way have been concerned not so much with the explanation of historical change but with forecasting future growth. Certainly base models provide a forecasting framework. They say in effect that we must independently forecast the future output of the local exporting industry. Once we have this quantity, we can apply the local urban base multiplier, which gives us a forecasted value for total income or output.

Economic base models have been used extensively in the analysis of city growth. The model is not without shortcomings, however. One problem is that the urban base multiplier is not always stable. An unstable urban base multiplier causes problems because the internal mechanism postulated in a base model takes the multiplier as a constant. The problem is that there is plenty of evidence that shows the urban base multiplier changes over longer periods of time when there is growth.

Urban economic base models are in fact more appropriately applied to the study of short-term aggregate change. Urban and regional economists have, as a consequence, explored other ways of looking at the structure of the urban economy to come to understand better the forces of growth in an urban region. Input-output applications in the study of the urban economy can be looked at in this light.

Input-Output Analysis of the City

Input-output is a term that refers to a way of looking at current production. The concern is with total sales and purchases. It is distinguished from gross national or urban products in that the focus is on all sales and purchases, not just those involving final products. This distinction is important because of intermediate production. As noted in chapter 2, production technology and industry organization have created "intermediate" steps in the production process. Not all output produced by any one firm is sold to final customers. Much is sold to other firms and incorporated in the production of these firms. These are matters of little concern in conventional income analyses and accounting. They are matters of central concern in input-output analysis and accounting.

The heart of input-output analysis is an input-output transaction table. Such a table is an accounting scheme, the columns and rows of which denote both industries and sectors. In Table 4.1, local industries are shown in the processing sector. Those that buy the final output of industry fall under the heading of final demand sector; those who provide the inputs used in production other than intermediate products show up in the payments sector.

If the cells in Table 4.1 were filled, we would have information that tells us much about the structure of an urban economy. Reading across this table, for example, provides information about the markets of the products of local industry, the markets of the productive resources of local residents, and the local markets for imports. Reading down this table provides information about the purchase requirements of local industry with respect to intermediate goods, imports, and other inputs, as well as those requirements by final demand sectors in the local economy.

The initial concern with such information ordinarily focuses on interindustry purchases and sales or the processing sector in Table 4.1. To the extent that technology and market organization ordain intermediate production that is produced locally, there will be numbers filling up the processing sector in an input-output table. This information allows us to make statements about inter-industry relationships.

Statements about the processing sector are generally made with reference to technical or input-output coefficients. Strictly speaking, an input-output coefficient

Table 4.1

Illustrative Transaction Table
Industry Purchasing*

	Processing Sector						Final Demand					Total Gross Output
INDUSTRY PRODUCING — Processing Sector / Payments Sector	A	B	C	D	E	F	Gross Industry Accumulation	Exports	Local Government Purchases	Gross Private Capital Formation	Households	
Industry A	100	150	10	20	50	60	20	50	10	30	140	640
Industry B	50	40	70	10	30	80	10	60	30	40	170	590
Industry C	70	20	80	10	50	30	20	30	10	30	50	400
Industry D	110	10	20	80	60	40	—	—	10	20	40	390
Industry E	40	—	10	140	30	20	10	20	10	30	90	400
Industry F	20	60	70	60	20	60	20	40	20	10	80	460
Gross Inventory Depletion	10	20	10	—	20	10	—	10	—	—	—	80
Imports	20	10	30	—	30	20	—	—	—	—	20	130
Payments to Government	20	30	20	20	10	20	30	20	10	20	120	320
Depreciation Allowances	10	20	10	—	10	—	—	—	—	—	10	50
Households	190	230	70	50	90	120	10	—	80	—	10	850
Total Gross Outlay	640	590	400	390	400	460	120	230	180	180	720	4310

*William H. Miernyk, *The Elements of Input-Output Analysis* (New York: Random House, 1965) p. 9.

indicates the amount of an input required from an industry (the ith industry) to produce a dollar's worth of output for another industry (the jth industry). For example, if industry A, in order to produce a dollar's worth of output, must use and therefore purchase six cents' worth of product from B, the input-output coefficient —a_{ij} where B is the ith industry and A is the jth industry—is 0.06.

These coefficients are calculated from the information in an input-output transaction table. Information on interindustry purchases and sales, along with information on the gross sales of these industries, is all that is necessary to calculate the "direct" coefficients for each industry.

Table 4.2 exhibits the direct coefficients calculated from Table 4.1. Reading

Table 4.2

Technical Coefficients
(Direct Purchases per Dollar of Output)*

INDUSTRY PURCHASING

		A	B	C	D	E	F
Industry purchasing	A	$0.16	$0.26	$0.03	$0.05	$0.13	$0.13
	B	0.08	0.07	0.18	0.03	0.08	0.18
	C	0.11	0.04	0.21	0.03	0.13	0.07
	D	0.17	0.02	0.05	0.21	0.16	0.09
	E	0.06	—	0.03	0.36	0.08	0.04
	F	0.03	0.11	0.18	0.15	0.05	0.13

*William H. Miernyk, *The Elements of Input-Output Analysis* (New York: Random House, 1965) p. 22.

down each column, the coefficients indicate the amount of output required from each industry to produce a dollar's worth of output of the industry denoted at the top of the column. Industry A, in producing a dollar's worth of output, for example, requires eight cents worth of output from B, eleven cents from C, and so on.

The direct effects of a dollar's worth of output by A are not an end to the story. Industry B, in order to produce and hence supply eight cents worth of output, must purchase outputs from other industries, as must C, D, and so forth. Once this round is over, there will be the requirement of another round and so on, with each round of requirements becoming progressively smaller and ultimately converging to zero. The point is there are indirect effects associated with supplying a given "bill of goods," which have to be taken into account in estimating the technical relations between industries.

With the aid of matrix algebra, it is possible to calculate with dispatch a set of technical coefficients that indicate both the direct and indirect requirements of each dollar of output from any industry delivered outside the processing sector, e.g. to a final demand sector. Table 4.3 shows such a set of coefficients calculated from the data in Table 4.1. Reading across any row, these coefficients show the direct and indirect output requirements from each industry at the top for

Table 4.3

*Direct and Indirect Requirements
per Dollar of Final Demand**

	A	B	C	D	E	F
A	$1.38	$0.25	$0.28	$0.41	$0.27	$0.23
B	0.45	1.21	0.16	0.19	0.12	0.24
C	0.27	0.38	1.38	0.23	0.17	0.39
D	0.35	0.25	0.25	1.53	0.65	0.41
E	0.35	0.26	0.31	0.39	1.28	0.25
F	0.35	0.35	0.22	0.30	0.21	1.32

*William H. Miernyk, *The Elements of Input-Output Analysis* (New York: Random House, 1965) p. 26.

each dollar of output delivered by the industry at the left. For example, the requirements of industry *A* when it produces and sells a dollar's worth of output to some final demand sector is twenty-five cents from industry *B*, twenty-eight cents from industry *C*, forty-one cents from industry *D*, twenty-seven cents from industry *E*, and twenty-three cents from industry *F*.

Input-output coefficients can, of course, be used as a means of estimating industry requirements—both direct and indirect—of a given "bill of goods," that is, the sale of a given dollar amount of goods and services to some final demand sector or sectors. If the dollar amount of this shipment is known and can be specified by industry source, the coefficients in Table 4.3 provide a basis of calculating total gross output required from each industry to meet this bill of goods.

How this might contribute to the process of economic growth in an urban setting is less evident. A concern with growth in a demand-oriented framework is a concern with the determinants of spending on final output. In input-output applications such as these, this spending is taken as a constant.

Input-output nevertheless has much to contribute to the study of city growth. If the size of the urban base multiplier is linked to industry structure, for example, input-output information will contribute much to our understanding of that multiplier and hence the process of urban growth. Industry or economic structure, as pointed out above, can tell us much about the nature of income leakages from imports. If that structure is such that much of what is consumed locally is produced locally, there will be little leakage from imports; hence the urban base multiplier will have a relatively high value. If the reverse is true, much income will leak out through imports, which means the base multiplier will have a relatively low value.

Communities that have large urban base multipliers are generally thought to be communities that have diversity and richness in what they produce. To put it this way, however, is not very enlightening. What do diversity and richness mean? Input-output information can help us answer this question. It both highlights the importance of intermediate goods production in the structure that reflects this richness and diversity and provides specific information about the importance and composition of such production in the community being studied. It thus provides us with much relevant information about the process through demand factors operating to generate growth in an urban community.

All of this, of course, is a concern with inquiry that has a demand orientation. Supply factors are either ignored or taken into account in some ad hoc fashion. What this implies about the knowledge we acquire of the urban growth process with the aid of demand-oriented models, raises questions that can only be answered in light of knowledge of supply as a factor in urban growth.

SUPPLY ANALYSIS

Urban Production Processes or Functions

To be concerned with supply factors is to be concerned with inputs such as labor and capital, and the ways they are combined to produce output. Obviously, consumption is limited by production, and production limitations and possibilities are the core of supply analysis. The actual analysis is focused on the production process or what is usually called a *production function*. This function is nothing more than an equation specifying the relationship between quantities of inputs and quantities of output obtained from these inputs. The simplest of these functions relates capital and labor to output in the following way:

$$O_t = A_t L_t C_t{}^{1-k} \qquad (4.20)$$

where O_t is an index of output at time t, and L_t and C_t are indexes of labor and capital respectively. A_t is an index of total factor productivity or a factor which denotes the productiveness of the inputs used in existing production processes. The more productive they are, the higher the value we assign to O_t and conversely.

This function can be expressed in a form that assumes constant returns to scale. With constant returns to scale and the assumption that k is a constant, equation 4.20 can be written as follows:

$$\Delta O/O = \Delta A/A + k\,(\Delta L/L) + 1 - k\,(\Delta G/C) \qquad (4.21)$$

This equation, in effect, tells us that change in potential output—economic growth—depends on the rate of change in labor supply, stock of capital, and factor productivity.

Equation 4.21 obviously oversimplifies the process by which productive capacity is expanded. Even so, it has served as the basis for the development of a growth theory—neoclassical growth theory in economies. This theory assumes labor force and one of the primary components of factor productivity—technology—grow smoothly at rates determined by noneconomic factors and that the stock of capital grows at a rate determined by the thrift of the community. Much attention centers on a "steady state" model in which the rate of growth of output, labor, capital, and technology are assumed to be equal.

Applied to economies that are relatively closed, e.g., the U.S. economy, such models have been shown to fit observable growth trends reasonably well. Their applications to open economies is another question. While it may be reasonable to assume steady state growth for a closed economy, in an open economy there are difficulties. Not only must we account for indigenous variables which influence the supplies of labor and capital and the force of technology, but in an open economy, input mobility must be considered. In cities, the supply of labor and capital can be augmented or reduced by migration. The determinants of this mobility thus become important elements in the analysis of potential output in the city.

Input Mobility

There are clear indications of geographic mobility of productive inputs. The migration of labor is well documented with certain broad overall trends noted. One of these was the rural to urban migration which accompanied urbanization, one aspect of which was the movement of blacks from the rural South to the urban North. Another was the movement of people to the West. Less publicized but also important are migratory flows of people in and out of particular cities throughout our history. While some of this was due to urbanization and the westward movement of people, there are also cities in regions losing population that have experienced population gains and cities in regions gaining population that have suffered population losses.

The geographic mobility of capital has been at least equal if not more pronounced, although the indications of such movement are less visible. Geographic interest rate differentials are found from time to time and then disappear, which implies movements of capital, as does the fact that banks in some regions or cities gain reserves at the expense of others.

Technology also moves geographically. Technical innovation usually emerges at a particular site and then through various communications channels becomes diffused over geographic space. While we do not have direct measures of this diffusion process, the fact that the production processes of firms in the same industry tend to be alike all over strongly suggests production technology is geographically mobile.

How do we explain the geographic mobility of inputs? Economic theory offers one explanation. Labor, capital, and technology move from one place to another in response to economic differentials, that is, the differences in income earned for doing the same thing at different sites. If wage rates and interest rates are higher in Lexington, Kentucky, than in Pikeville, Kentucky, for example, owners of labor and capital resources have the incentive to provide the services of their labor and capital in Lexington rather than in Pikeville.

Suppose there is movement of labor and capital from Pikeville to Lexington. As a consequence, the supply of both labor and capital will increase in Lexington and be reduced in Pikeville. Given the normal operation of labor and capital markets, this will generate downward pressure on wages and interest rates in Lexington and upward pressure in Pikeville. Presumably, the migration of labor and capital from Pikeville to Lexington will continue until wage and interest rates are equalized.

This, of course, is an oversimplified statement of what can become a very elaborate economic statement of the conditions under which inputs will move in geographic space. There is sufficient empirical evidence to conclude that economic factors operate in this way. There is also evidence, however, that says this argument, even in its more elaborate form, does not say enough.

In most, though not all cases, geographic wage differential is a necessary condition for the movement of people. It may not be a sufficient condition, however. Nor do such differentials always indicate the ultimate destinations of movers. Other things enter into the decision to move, such as information, movement costs, inertia, and location preferences.

Some people are willing to accept lower *money* income to live where they want to live. Some people may wish to move but do not want to incur the psychological costs associated with a move. These are the kinds of things that help to explain the fact that money income differences persist between some regions for long periods of time.

Differences in the information system also have impact on migration. This system is reasonably good for those coming out of universities and colleges or those who already have responsible positions in industry or government. It is less so for those who have little education and/or who are currently working at the lower end of the hierarchy in public and private enterprise. Friends who have migrated earlier often provide the primary source of information to these people, and such information may not be a proper basis for reasonable assessment of actual market conditions. This dichotomy in the information system helps explain the fact that not all people movement is to high-wage regions.

Capital tends to be both more and less mobile geographically than labor. This apparent contradiction is a consequence of a distinction that has to be made between the stock of existing capital, most of which is fixed, as at a site, and additions to the stock of capital through the capital formation process. That which is fixed at a site is not very movable. That which is currently accumulating through the savings and investment process is highly mobile, for it is possible to direct these savings in ways that will result in the construction of a plant anywhere just as it is possible to secure new equipment at a plant anywhere.

The location of new capital is indeed more sensitive to geographic income differentials than labor and is so partly because its use at alternative locations is largely divorced from personal considerations. This sensitivity also stems from the fact that movement costs of the funds that give rise to the new physical capital are less. If strong economic opportunities for capital are found in California, for example, money and capital markets will generate a flow of funds to the Golden State. The cost of moving funds is slight. These funds, in turn, will be quickly converted into plants and equipment. The resources used to build the plants and produce the equipment are very responsive to money demands in a market economy.

Supply Factors in Demand-Oriented Models

The failure to account explicitly for supply factors in demand-oriented models implies the supply of labor, capital, and other inputs is perfectly elastic; that is, the firm in any urban community can get all of the labor and other inputs it wants at the prevailing national market price. Is this a reasonable assumption?

Consider the following set of hypothetical circumstances. Suppose a comparative cost study concludes that the bill of export goods for, say, Lexington, Kentucky, will reach a certain level at some future date. Assume this level implies a substantial increase in total production which requires a scale of input use that cannot be met locally. There will be excess demand for inputs, which should drive up their price. Upward moving wage and interest rates will, in turn, mean geographic differentials which should lead to in-migration of labor and capital inputs. Augmenting supply in this way should lower wage and interest rates in Lexington. Conceivably they could fall back to their original levels. If they did, input supplies in Lexington would be characterized as *perfectly elastic*. These are the circumstances in which supply factors can be ignored in studies of city growth. The question is: Are they the circumstances we find in cities?

Certainly, there is room for doubt. Not only do we have the legacy of poor economic forecasts for regions and urban areas with demand-oriented models, but studies of input mobility, as noted above, do not show movements that equalize wage and interest rates over geographic space. Input supplies do not necessarily adjust quickly and completely.

There is reason enough to argue that supply factors should be introduced explicitly in studies of the economic growth of cities. How this should be done is another question. What is known about the influence of supply factors is ordinarily discussed under the heading of supply-oriented theories of urban growth.

Supply-Oriented Theories of Urban Growth

Exogenous Population Movements   Much emphasis in some studies of rapidly growing regions is given to exogenous movements of population into these areas. California, some believe, has grown rapidly because of its climate and certain other reasons that have little to do with economic advantage. People live there because they want to. They are also said to live in Florida and Arizona for the same reasons. These reasons are potentially important in the analysis of urban growth because they have little to do with opportunities stemming from comparative economic advantage; hence the talk about exogenous population movements as a source of regional or urban growth.

How reasonable is this argument? While it raises issues that fall beyond the scope of this discussion, earlier remarks about the determinants of input mobility suggest it is not unreasonable. Recall how it was indicated earlier that studies that show both labor and capital to be sensitive to geographic income differentials suggest that newly formed capital is more sensitive than labor. The funds that initiate capital formation apparently flow more freely over geographic space than does labor. If so, this fact lends credence to the argument. If people who move to Florida, Arizona, and California are willing to live there with incomes that are less than they could earn elsewhere, their presence will generate investment opportunities which might not be accommodated out of local savings. Hence, there will be opportunities for outside funds which will be forthcoming since financial capital is income sensitive. The ultimate cause of growth, if it happens this way, will be the exogenous shift in the population.

How important this kind of movement is, relative to population movement in response to economic differentials, is unknown. While its significance can be very easily exaggerated, it is apparently of some consequence. The fact that it is suggests that local labor market developments warrant special attention in studies of community economic growth. Indeed, recent studies of the growth of regions suggest what happens to labor supply does have bearing on the economic growth of regions—and by inference urban regions—and does so in a way that implies some of this movement is a consequence of events external to the urban economy.

Filtering Theories   Some believe that developments that reflect through total factor productivity—A_t, in equation 4.20—bear special attention. What is important is spatial diffusion of basic or seminal technological innovations. They are the innovations that stem from new and fundamental ideas, ideas believed to be most often hatched in the heart of some of our larger cities, such as New York, Chicago, or San Francisco. In the earlier stages of their development, the manpower and other requirements are apparently best met in the setting in which the area initially emerged, that is, in the larger cities. As the process of production is further developed and refined, however, this often involves operations that are repetitive and have lower skilled-labor requirements. At this point, the activity moves away from the major center to some smaller urban center where the labor and land costs are lower. As it is often put, production begins to filter down through the various levels of the urban hierarchy. What happens in any urban center is thus influenced by technology, its initial location point, and the process through which it filters throughout the entire urban hierarchy.

The argument is broad and sweeping. It is also attractive because of its applicability to the entire system of cities. Its validity, on the other hand, is difficult to judge because of problems associated with expressing the argument in ways that can be confronted with facts. No one denies that technology has impact on the growth path of individual cities. Moreover, the notion of a filtering process is not an unreasonable one, if only because there are visible illustrations of the movement of some activities from larger urban centers to smaller ones, at points in the evolution of their technology where the production requirements changed. But evidence of the sort is anecdotal and really provides no real basis for judging exactly how important and under what sets of conditions the filtering process is applicable to cities in the various parts of the urban hierarchy. The idea has promise. How much promise remains to be seen.

Growth Poles   Another supply-oriented theory with technological overtones is the *growth pole theory*. These poles are defined as a set of expanding industries located in an urban area, industries that induce further development of economic activity in that area. The origins of the concept are traceable to notions of agglomeration discussed earlier. But there is a significant difference. The expansion that takes place in growth pole theory is not equated with the cost reductions associated with urbanization economies; rather the emphasis in this theory is on the interaction of key industries and others at the pole. The key industries are the so-called "propulsive" industries. They are not necessarily the largest, but they are industries that have the greatest direct and indirect impact on economic activity in the urban region in which they are located. These industries have strong multiplier and strong polarizing effects, and they have these effects because they draw much of their inputs from within the city—and its hinterland—in which they are located.

The propelling force of such industries is often attributed to the technical change they induce elsewhere. The key industries are advanced technologically, and the effect of their technological efficiency tends to be transmitted to other nearby industries, often by the force of their example, and sometimes by requirements imposed upon those industries that deal directly with them. All of these things in fact tend to create a growth mentality which further reinforces the activities and actions which foster more growth.

While there are many questions that can be raised about the exact meaning of propulsive industries and the kinds of interindustry linkages they spawn, it is not unreasonable to suppose that agglomerating tendencies found in cities can generate the conditions which foster further polarizing growth. Knowledge of the nature of these tendencies as they permeate particular urban communities then constitutes knowledge that should help us to understand urban growth patterns. Just how much they contribute to our understanding of these patterns is unknown.

REFERENCES

Artle, R. *The Structure of the Stockholm Economy.* Ithaca, N.Y.: Cornell University Press, 1965.

Borts, G. and Stein, J. *Economic Growth in a Free Market.* New York: Columbia University Press, 1964.

Hansen, N. "Development Pole Theory in a Regional Context." *Kyklos* 20 (1967): 709–27.

*Miernyk, W. *The Elements of Input-Output Analysis.* New York: Random House, Inc., 1965.

Shaw, P. *Migration: Theory and Fact.* Bibliography Series No. 5, Regional Science Research Institute (1975).

Siebert, H. *Regional Economic Growth: Theory and Policy.* New York: International Textbook Company, 1969.

Thompson, W. "Internal and External Factors in the Development of Urban Economics." In *Issues in Urban Economics.* Edited by H. Perloff and L. Wingo. Baltimore: The Johns Hopkins Press, 1968.

*Tiebout, C. *The Community Economic Base Study.* Supplementary Paper No. 16, Committee for Economic Development (1962).

---

* This chapter draws heavily from the writings of Tiebout and Miernyk.

location Theory
and City Structure

SUMMARY

In addressing the question of what goes where in our cities, it is helpful to consider a world in which there is only land and users of land. The study of the urban land market throws into sharp focus the importance of accessibility as a determinant of location in the city.

People locate their activities in the city according to the outcome of the competitive bidding process in the urban land market. Those who make the highest price bids for particular sites win the competition, which is to say that they acquire these sites. Who wins out at what sites and why? These are the essential concerns in this chapter.

In considering the price or rent bids of residential users, accessibility to place of work is emphasized. To live near a place of work is to minimize the commuting cost. Since these costs are positively associated with distance, it can be easily shown that the locations that minimize commuting costs are locations at which satisfactions from consumption are maximized. If accessibility is important to residential users, and there are reasons for believing that it is, the bid rent or bid price curves of residential users will show higher bids at central locations.

Suppose accessibility is also important to firms. They too will make higher bids for land at central points in the city. The importance of accessibility to the firm should reflect through costs and revenues and hence profits. Movement away from central locations should add to costs and reduce revenues. For some firms, this happens; for others, it does not. The most notable case where a central location does not seem to make much difference is the firm that exports. Those that sell locally in a widely dispersed market, on the other hand, tend to be attracted to central locations.

While important, these conclusions have to be modified when improvements on the land—particularly buildings—are taken into account. The durability and differentiation of these structures means that even if accessibility is important, the accessibility of particular sites may not be rated very highly. This could happen because structures may be erected on these sites which are inappropriate to the uses in demand. Or some sites may be ranked highly even though they don't have the best accessibility because of some feature of the structures on that site.

Structures can be altered or replaced, which suggests these qualifica-
tions may be less important over the long run. Still, there are site attributes
other than accessibility that have bearing on what goes where. The concepts of residential filtering and neighborhood effects combined with what
we know about upkeep and maintenance decisions provide insights into
what some of these other things are and how they interact with accessibility
in influencing site decisions.

City structure refers to the spatial dimensions of our activities in cities, or the
matter of what goes where. Knowledge of this structure is important; it contributes
much to our understanding urban history and urban problems. Indeed, to many,
the study of city structure is the heart of an investigation of the anatomy of cities.

Most studies of city structure focus on density and use features of the urban
landscape. *Density* refers to the number of people or amount of activity found
at various geographic points in the city. The concept is significant because of the
systematic variation found in measures of density, e.g., population per square mile.
In earlier times, this density pattern was pronounced and easy to describe. There
was one place—in the core or center of the city—of extreme concentration of
people or activity. From that point, density declined, reaching its lowest value at the
perimeter of the city. A cross-section view of such a density "function" is shown
in Figure 5.1.

Figure 5.1

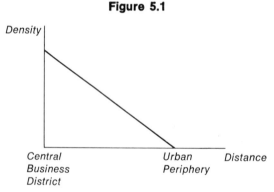

More recently, as our cities have grown, they have spread out. Activity is less
concentrated and there is now more than one point of extreme concentration—
see Figure 5.2. The central business district remains, but there are other points
of concentration around shopping centers, industrial parks, and airports.

Studies have also uncovered systematic spatial variation in the uses to which
land is put in cities. While there are different ways of classifying the use of land,
one important distinction is between residential and nonresidential use. This
distinction is important. That we call the center of the city the central business
district is no accident. In earlier cities, business, government, and industry located
in and around the core area. Residents, on the other hand, were in outlying areas,

Figure 5.2

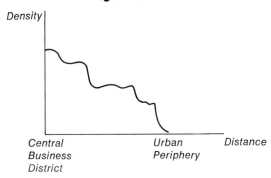

ringing the central business district. Today there is less residential and nonresidential segregation in the city. Yet, nonresidential uses still predominate in areas of
high density and residential neighborhoods remain.

Facts about density and land use configurations are facts about city structure.
Urban economic theory concerns with city structure are concerns with theory
concepts pertinent to the economic explanation of these facts. Such theory has,
as its focus, economic aspects of decisions that locate people in cities. These
decisions are considered as they mesh through the competitive bidding process
of the urban real estate market.

The initial focus in the discussion of these decisions is on the urban land market.
The emphasis is on delineating the facts which determine the prices or rents
particular users bid for land at alternative sites. While such a concern neglects
important aspects of urban real estate, it does throw into sharp focus the key
role of the accessibility of sites in the urban real estate market. After accessibility
has been discussed, the improvements to urban land, e.g., buildings, are added
to the analysis. It is at this point that notions of market filtering, neighborhood
effects, and upkeep expenditures are introduced.

A THEORY OF THE
URBAN LAND MARKET

The question addressed in this chapter is: What goes where in the city? This
question is considered initially in a world that is oversimplified, where there is only
land and users of land. It is also a world in which markets allocate land space to
alternative users.

Consider the land market of a city that has fixed boundaries within which there
is a flat homogeneous plain. Land in this city can be represented by two dimensions,
as in Figure 5.3. Now subdivide that land into points of spatial extension, as in
Figure 5.4, and consider each point as parcel of urban land in use. The "assignment" of each of these parcels through the operations of the urban land market
comes about through competitive bidding of owners and users or demanders.
The concern with this market is initially restricted to the competition between
demanders.

Figure 5.3

Figure 5.4

In a competitive market, price is the primary instrument of competition. If Smith wishes to compete with Jones for land at site S_1, Smith does so through the price he offers for that site. Figure 5.5 indicates the price bids of both

Figure 5.5

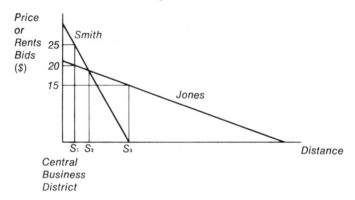

Smith and Jones for land at sites that stretch from the central business district out to the edge of the boundaries of the city.

This figure is highly revealing. For whatever reasons, Smith is both willing and able to pay more for certain sites and Jones is both willing and able to pay more for other sites. At site S_1, for example, Smith is willing to pay $25, whereas Jones is willing to pay only $20. On the other hand, Jones is willing to pay $15 for site S_3, while Smith apparently has no interest in land at S_3.

This hypothetical information provides important insight into the outcome of the competitive bidding process in the urban land market. Apparently, those who use land space in the city are willing and able to pay more for land space at some sites than others. Since we know that those who make the highest bids win out, we expect to find some winning at certain locations, others winning at other locations.

Suppose the world consisted only of Smith and Jones. Suppose further that the bid price or rent curves shown in Figure 5.5 adequately represent their behavior in the urban land market. The outcome of the competitive bidding process between demanders in this market would have Smith located somewhere between the *CBD* and S_2 and Jones somewhere beyond site S_2. This statement seemingly provides insights into the question of what goes where within the city.

Just how much do we learn from this statement? Do we really have good reasons for believing that these price or rent bid curves properly characterize the behavior of Smith and Jones? These are the questions of primary concern in the theory of urban land. The emphasis is on the accessibility of the site. Transportation and communication costs are key elements in the theory. Distance friction means the movement of goods, people, and messages requires the use of economic resources. Because the cost of that movement is correlated with distance, accessibility to sites where these costs are at a minimum becomes important. Since some sites have better accessibility than others, they are more desirable locations.

But are these sites more desirable? If so, to whom? For what purpose? How does all of this help account for the existence of a central business district and residential neighborhood?

To answer these questions, we must look more carefully at accessibility in decisions people make with respect to where they live and work in cities.

The Residential Location Decision

Housing expenditure stands as the most important element in the budget of most households. One important aspect of the housing choice most people make is its location. If we consider location in the sense of nearness to places of work, schooling, and shopping, we become concerned with matters in which accessibility is important. Society is organized in ways that require face-to-face contact in many activities. But these activities have, at the same time, a spatial dimension—we cannot act out our roles in society on the head of a pin. Thus, the movement or circulation of people is an integral part of our activities. In the face of distance frictions this means transportation costs. A concern with the accessibility of residential sites is a concern with something that has economic overtones. The site we choose has impact on our budget, via transportation or commuting costs. The residential location decision can thus be studied as an economic decision.

The accessibility of a site is not a simple matter. Accessibility to what? Place of work? Good schools? Shopping centers? Playgrounds? Adequate fire protection?

All of these things and more are involved. Some aspects of accessibility, however, are more important than others. Since the most important of these is accessibility to place of work, the residential location decision has been most often studied in a framework in which journey to work is the primary element in that decision. If it is assumed that there is only one central point of employment, i.e., the central business district, demand theory in economics can be used effectively to analyze that decision. To look at the question of residential location in this way is to exclude some important elements in the location decision. But to do so clarifies and puts the crucial aspects of that decision into perspective.

Journey to Work and Residential Location   Demand theory in economics postulates behavior that is rational, calculating, and goal-oriented. The goal is maximum satisfaction. It is achieved through consumption that is the outcome of a series of rational choices which reflect the tastes and preferences of the household, subject to the constraint of not consuming more than it can afford, i.e., the budget constraint.

Housing is an item of consumption, and the location of the site of the dwelling is one aspect of that consumption. The residential site decision is thus a part of the housing decision. An economic analysis of the residential site decision is simply an application of consumer theory to an item that competes with others for the limited dollars in the household's budget. Posing the question of why Smith lives at site S_1 has the economist considering such prosaic matters as tastes or preferences, income, and prices.

To highlight the way in which demand theory in economics is applied to the study of the question of why Smith lives where he does, certain simplifying assumptions are necessary. The first assumption is to assume the site is only important because of its location in relation to the household's place of employment. The second assumption is to assume there is one central place of employment, which is located in the center of the city. The third is to assume that commuting costs are money outlays proportional with distance traveled. Finally, the site decision made is assumed to reflect economic behavior.

The way in which households divide their limited income dollars among alternative goods and services is influenced by the satisfactions from consumption, the costs of the alternatives, and the income of the consumer. Satisfactions in demand theory are taken as a constant. The nature of what is given is described by the household's "utility function." This is simply a function that denotes the household's satisfaction from the consumption of alternatives, which in its most general form is

$$U = f(X_1, X_2 \ldots\ldots\ldots X_n) \tag{5.1}$$

where U is total satisfaction and the X's are quantities of the consumption goods alternatives. What this equation says, in effect, is that total satisfaction depends on the amount of each good consumed.

The costs of consumption and income denote the budget restriction. In demand theory, the household is not permitted to spend more than it has, a restriction that, in a simple situation, depends upon its income and the price of the things consumed. Or

$$Y = p_1 X_1 + p_2 X_2 \ldots\ldots\ldots p_n X_n \tag{5.2}$$

where Y is the household's income, p is the price of the good, and X is the quantity of the good consumed.

Consider now the impact of residential selection on the consumption decision. If the site is one whose sole virtue is its accessibility to places of employment located in the central business district, its impact on the household's budget and utility function is apparent. Consider the budget impact first.

Residential locations at distances away from places of work mean commuting costs, and if commuting costs are considered as money outlays, they reduce the amount of income available for consumption. Equation 5.2 thus becomes

$$Y = p_1 X_1 + p_2 X_2 \ldots\ldots\ldots p_n X_n - k \tag{5.3}$$

where k is commuting costs.

Consider now the impact of commuting on the household's utility function. Commuting from locations away from the central business district not only costs money; for many households it generates psychic costs as well. To most commuters, the travel to and from work is a nuisance. Considered as such, it subtracts from the satisfactions of consumption and can therefore be treated as a factor of negative utility.

The consumption implications of these two facts are evident. If the household has to commute, there will be money costs, which means income for consumption will be less by an amount equal to those costs. In addition, there will be psychic costs for most households, which means satisfactions from a given level of consumption expenditures will be less by an amount equal to the negative satisfactions these costs imply.

If we suppose that both the money and psychic costs associated with commuting are correlated with distance, the location of the site becomes important. The household will have reason to consider some locations better than others. If that correlation is positive, as it is in most cases, sites with accessibility to the CBD— such as S_1 in Figure 5.6, will be favored over those with less accessibility, such as S_2 in Figure 5.6. Living at accessible sites entails lower money outlays for commuting, which means more consumption for given amounts of income. Accessibility also means lower psychic costs from commuting, which implies more satisfaction from a given amount of consumption spending. Consumption at accessible locations thus yields more satisfaction than it does at inaccessible locations.

The necessity of commuting, with commuting costs that are positively correlated with distance, implies that households will pay for sites that are accessible and will pay more for the more accessible sites, such as site S_1 in Figure 5.6 as compared with S_2. Put the other way around, the price or rent households will pay for sites is less for those that are inaccessible. This rent, in effect, declines with distance from the center. If we consider it as a demand price, household residential site

Figure 5.6

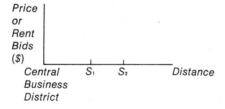

demands can be represented by the curve in Figure 5.7—sometimes called the *bid rent* or *bid price curve*. With a slope that is negative, this demand curve clearly indicates that households assign a greater value to sites that are near to places of work.

Relaxing Some Assumptions

Commuting Costs Redefined   The visible budget effects of commuting are the money outlays incurred in getting to and from work. For those commuting by car, this means operating and capital costs (e.g., gasoline, repairs, and deprecia-

Figure 5.7

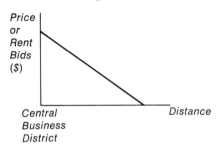

tion) and parking costs. For those who use public transportation, it means the money costs of the fare. There are also other, less visible, effects. There is the time spent in transit. This might not only be considered as a nuisance, but as time spent that could be otherwise devoted to earning income. This time has an opportunity cost in the sense of lost income that should be included as a part of the cost of commuting.

Note what happens if commuting costs are considered to include both money outlays and the time or opportunity costs of travel. Distance becomes more painful to those with high incomes, since their time is more valuable.

The actual importance of the time costs of travel in the site decision is uncertain. Apart from the obstacles to measuring what households consider these costs to be, there are differences in the way in which the time is used. Some, in fact, work during the time spent in transit and those who do are likely to come from the upper end of the income scale. The opportunity cost of travel to some upper-income families may thus be less than it appears at first sight. Yet, most urban economists argue that time costs do have impact on the residential locations decisions of urban households.

Other Aspects of Accessibility   While distance from the place of work of the household head may be a primary factor in the evaluation of the accessibility of a residential site, there are other dimensions to accessibility. For example, in many families both husband and wife work and usually not at the same place. In such cases, must we not take into account the location of both places?

For most families, the answer is probably no. When both work, this employment typically yields an income that is higher for the male member of the household. If income weighs heavily in the site decision, it is not unreasonable to argue that the heaviest weight will be assigned to the accessibility needs of those who contribute the most to family income. This means families should, in most cases, prefer sites closer to the place of work of the husband. The current earnings pattern, however, could change.

More important is the fact that families are concerned with more than accessibility to places of work. Surveys indicate a concern with accessibility to schools and places to shop. Let's consider first accessibility to schools, or other public services, for that matter.

For families with children, nearness to a school is said to be important, but what is really important is accessibility to a "good" school. School facilities are usually distributed throughout most cities, so that most sites are provided with reasonable access to some set of physical facilities. What can differ is the "quality" of the education at these neighborhood schools. Given qualitative differences, the spatial distribution of schools within a city can influence residential location decisions. Locations with ready access to good schools have appeal to many families precisely because of the importance they assign to quality education. How these differences influence that decision, however, remains in doubt. Clearly, in the short run, the location of good schools has impact on the residential location decisions of many families. Over the long run, causation may run in the opposite direction.

Education, as it is made available in most places, is a public good. This implies the caliber of services found in particular neighborhoods depends on the ability and willingness of people, acting collectively, to bear the cost of providing the service. If our concern is with the long run, this must be taken into account.

How the relevant political and economic factors operate to determine the caliber of education provided in particular schools is not fully known. What we do know is that people tend to move to places within the city where they get the most for their tax dollars. For many, this has meant movement to unincorporated suburbs away from the central city. Some economists believe this constitutes an explanation of why local governments appear to us in a highly fragmented form in most metropolitan areas. See chapter 12. If so, it can be argued that the quality of education found in the neighborhood schools of a city is more a function of where people choose to live rather than the other way around.

Access to shopping facilities—though not too close—is also an interest factor to many families. How important such access is to the actual decision, however, is questionable. Shopping facilities are usually dispersed throughout the city, which implies most residential sites in most cities will have reasonable access to such facilities. The causation here is generally believed to run more in the other direction, that is, the sites that households choose exert strong influence on the locational choices of firms that provide this kind of service to households.

Transportation Networks   Up to this point, we have considered families choosing residential sites in cities that are flat homogeneous plains with transportation surfaces. Moves have been possible between any two points for a cost that is proportional with distance. Obviously, these conditions are not likely to be fulfilled. Cities are not usually located on flat homogeneous plains; nor is there a transportation surface. Rather there is a transportation network, the focal point of which, in most cities, is a system of streets and highways. The nature of this configuration can have bearing on the time and money cost involved in moving from one point to another within the city and hence influence the attractiveness of particular sites. To illustrate, suppose the automobile were king and the terrain is such that an axial pattern of arterial highways is established—see Figure 5.8. Such a configuration will, in a journey-to-work model, lead to an axial pattern of residential development because sites near the major arterials provide residents with best access to places of work. Commuting costs will be lower at locations near the highways, which means locations near highways will be found attractive.

The transportation network itself is a function of many things, some of which are indigenous to the city being studied. Knowledge of local conditions, such as terrain and political structures, as they come to bear on transportation investment decisions is essential to any study of commuting or movement costs in the city.

Figure 5.8

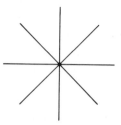

Yet the general shape of the transportation network also depends on where people want to live. Hopefully, transportation investment decisions are made with a view toward satisfying transportation needs in the community. But what are these needs?

Presumably, the transportation needs of the community reflect the needs of individual families subject to the constraint of their budget. According to journey-to-work notions, these needs would emphazise providing adequate transportation service from the place of residence to the place of work of the head of the household. Given this and whatever other factors influence these needs, a set of transportation demands emerges. While local factors such as terrain and political structure have important impact on the network of transportation facilities that are built, the structure of the community's transportation demands is certainly not ignored. In considering these demands, it is not unreasonable to emphasize factors which underlie the residential site demands of families in the community.

The notion of a transportation surface is a simplification that has to be qualified when looking at outcomes in particular communities. But it certainly is not an unreasonable one to use in studying residential choice.

Quantity or Lot Size Considerations   While journey to work has important bearing on residential site demands, the way in which accessibility influences the choice is related to the quantity or lot size demands of the family. Demand theory and casual observation indicate households are concerned with quantity or lot size. The lot is a normal good, that is, more of it is purchased if price falls. Suppose the price of land declines with distance from the center of the city—as it does. Since land is a normal good, people will demand larger lots away from the center of the city.

What do people want? Location? Or a large spacious lot? Most cannot have both. To get a large lot, they must be willing to trade some location benefits and vice versa.

This trade-off possibility implies that the price people are willing to pay for a site is influenced by the quantity of space they wish to consume. Sites with access are worth something to most households, but the consumption of large quantities of space at such sites is expensive. If households want sites that are large enough to give them "elbow" room, they are likely to find the cost of this space at the most accessible locations too high. To get a larger lot, the family will have to trade access for size. Those with a strong taste for large lots are therefore likely to offer less for sites with accessibility than those who find space less important even though their needs for accessibility may be roughly the same.

Producer Site Demands

Firms require land space, and if they choose an urban location, they become competitors for space within the city. The question of how firms go about making this decision must be treated separately from households because of differences in the nature of their activities. The firm is concerned with costs, revenues, and profit maximization, not with the selection of some set of product alternatives, which when consumed will maximize satisfactions.

The language appropriate to the study of the use of space by the firm is that discussed earlier when the concern was with the urban hierarchy. There, the emphasis was on site selection from a set that encompassed all available sites. Little was said about the impact of competition for any given site on that decision. Now we are concerned with a more limited set of sites—those available within the city—so that competition for those sites becomes important. The site demands of the firm must then be reconsidered in a way that will allow us to consider how firms compete for space within the city.

The firm is considered in much the same way as it was earlier. It is assumed to be concerned with costs, revenues, and profit maximization, and the focus is on the question of how location has impact on profits through its impact on the firm's costs and revenues. But now the concern is not so much with the problem of finding a particular site; rather it is a concern with the maximum price firms are willing to pay for alternative sites within the city. In investigating the way in which accessibility and certain other factors have impact on that price, it is useful to distinguish between two classes of firm discussed in chapter 4, basic and nonbasic firms.

Urban Site Demands of Basic Firms   The modus operandi of the firm in economics, to review earlier statements, are depicted in equations or geometry concerned with what happens to the costs and revenues of the firm as output varies. For firms operating in competitive markets, that behavior was described previously in a figure which depicted total revenues and total costs in the following way:

Figure 5.9

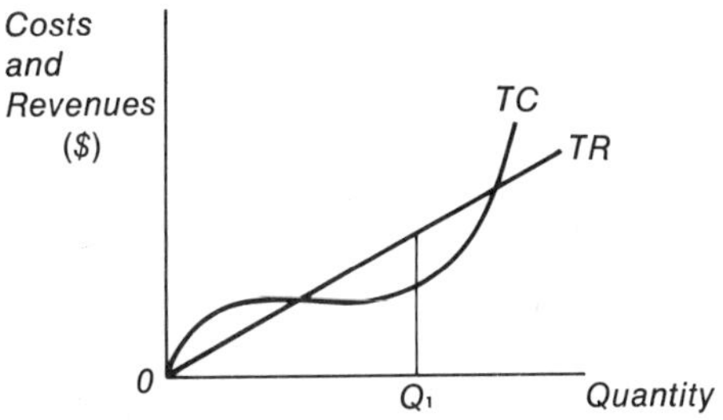

Output OQ_1 was denoted as the operating point at which the economic goals of the firm are fulfilled.

The impact of location of those operations was shown through these cost and revenue curves. Conditions were specified under which it was reasonable to expect revenues and cost to be higher (or lower) at some locations. The trick was to find the location at which the spread between revenues and costs was at a maximum.

Looking at the location decision of the firm within the city, the objective is still the same, but it may be that what is best for one, is also best for another. As a consequence of competitive interaction in the urban land market, some firms may have to settle for second best. Where the firm locates, however, depends, in the first instance, on the shape of its bids for alternative sites in the city.

The rent bids of the firm are, of course, related to its profitability at alternative sites. If revenues and costs vary by location, profits will be greater at some locations than others. To illustrate, consider two sites—S_1 and S_2—and assume revenues are higher and costs are lower at S_1 than S_2—see Figure 5.10.

Figure 5.10

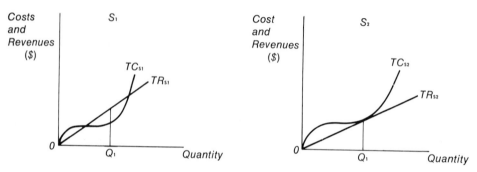

Profits are clearly higher at S_1 than S_2. Thus, this firm should be willing to pay a rent for the use of land at S_1, equal to an amount up to the difference in profits it would make at sites 1 and 2. If S_1 is closer to the center of the city, the bid price or bid rent curve of this firm would have a negative slope as in Figure 5.11. The prices or rents offered for sites closer to the center will be higher because profits made there are higher.

Figure 5.11

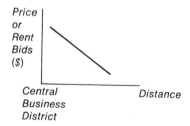

Is it reasonable to expect revenue and cost variations by location? Is it reasonable to expect variations of the kind shown in Figure 5.10 with the outcome shown in Figure 5.11? First consider firms that are a part of the economic base of the urban community.

Basic firms, as noted earlier, export what they produce in the city. One might expect to find firms that make up a city's economic base in the center of the city if only because they provided the center of activity around which most cities have been built. Moreover, in terms of revenues, if they start out in the center, there is little reason for them to move away. Since their customers are often located far away, the distance from plant to those customers is unlikely to be affected very much by where within the city the firm locates. Whether the firm chooses a location in the central city or in the outer ring probably has little impact on the transportation bill incurred by moving the product to the final customer. Location within the city thus has little impact on consumption costs and therefore the sales of such firms.

Yet, it is easy to show that many basic firms are located outside of the central city. If the explanation is not to be found in revenue factors, it must be in costs. In other words, there must be cost variations in the city that make some locations more attractive to basic firms than others.

Certainly there is reason to believe that intracity cost variations exist. The labor costs of a basic firm could vary by location. If the firm draws labor from residential locations spread randomly throughout the city, the selection of a site that is away from the center could lead to a higher wage bill. Since the commuting costs of such a work force would, on the average, be higher at locations further from the center of the city, wage payments would have to be higher to attract the necessary labor.

Land costs also vary with location. While the theory is not yet well enough developed to warrant the assertion that land rents will be higher in the center of the city than away from it, enough has been said so that such a conclusion should come as no surprise. Such a rent configuration, of course, makes locations away from the center attractive to the firm simply because land costs are lower there.

Capital costs probably have no influence on the intracity location of basic firms, since these costs tend to be the same throughout the city.

The impact of all other input costs is an iffy matter. If they are materials or intermediate goods imported into the city, they will probably have little impact on where within the city the firm locates because location will have only marginal impact on the cost of transporting the goods to the firm. If these materials are made available from within the city, on the other hand, transportation costs could vary significantly. The locational impact of such variation depends on where within the city the suppliers are and the relative importance of transportation costs to the firm.

For some firms, the links to output of other firms are important. In the case where the service involved requires face-to-face contact, the location pull of its source, as reflected in costs, is likely to be strong. But for others—e.g., laundry service provided to motels that provide food and lodging service to those who live outside the city—the transit costs of distance in relation to total costs are probably minimal. In fact, it is the location of the motels that is likely to influence the site of the laundry rather than the other way around.

Most economic studies of urban land markets take the site of the exporting firm as given and try to explain land rents or prices and land use patterns in terms of decisions by households and nonbasic firms that are assumed to be strongly influenced by the location of the basic firms. This assumption is not a frivolous one. The importance of accessibility to the basic firm within the city is by no means clear on the basis of theory alone. Urban economic theory does not allow us to say in advance whether the rent or price the basic firm is willing to pay for urban land will decline with distance from the center of the city. It could decline for the firms that rely heavily on services that require face-to-face contact if these services are provided by firms located in the center of the city. It might also decline for firms that have important labor requirements that must be drawn from a work force that is randomly distributed in the city. Whether it is for basic firms that have a sizeable requirement for space is questionable, however. These firms will be more influenced by the pattern of land costs which tend to decline with distance from the center of the city.

Urban Site Demands of Nonbasic Firms   Urban site demands made of firms that sell to local residents and businesses can be considered in the same way as those of basic firms. The impact of location on costs is much the same for the nonbasic firm as it is for the basic firm. Labor requirements and where workers live, for example, can generate cost differences at alternative sites for the nonbasic firm. These differences could be reflected in lower labor costs in the center of the city, and higher costs away from the center for reasons just discussed. It could also be, however, that labor requirements are more cheaply met at locations in the outer ring. This would happen if the requirements could be fully met by drawing from residents in certain parts of that ring. The probability that the firms will be able to satisfy their labor requirements in a less costly way at some distance from the central city seems higher for nonbasic firms, partly because such firms tend to be smaller than exporting firms.

Land requirements of nonbasic firms can also influence the cost of operations at alternative sites in the same way these requirements do for the basic firm. Its links with inputs supplied by other locally based firms can also affect costs in similar ways.

The impact of this assortment of cost influences on the attractiveness of urban sites to the nonbasic firm is uncertain, just as it is with the basic firm. The cost influences could pull the firm toward the center of the city, push it out to the fringe of urban development, or shove it somewhere inbetween. The outcome depends partly on the relative importance of the transportation costs associated with input use and the spatial distribution of those inputs. Urban economics theory does not enable us to say in advance whether these things work themselves out to cause the rent or price bids of the nonbasic firm to fall with distance from the center. For some it may; for others it might not.

There is reason to believe, however, that nonbasic firms are attracted to the center of the city, or other points of centrality in the city. The nonbasic firm, in sharp contrast with the basic firm, finds its revenues are affected by its location in the city. Its customers are residents of the city. The customers are close enough to the firm that movement towards or away from these firms can significantly alter the distance from the site of the firm's operation to the customer. For example, if these customers live in residences located in rings surrounding the center of the city, movement away from the center could substantially increase the cost of getting the product to the customer. If these demands are responsive to price, such transportation cost additions to consumption costs will lower sales and may reduce revenues. If this happens, firms selling in local markets will find central locations attractive. This, in turn, will be reflected in their rent or price bids for locations near the center. But are these firms, in fact, attracted to such locations?

The best answer seems to be that some are and others are not. How location affects the revenues of the nonbasic firm is influenced by the characteristics of its customers, economies of scale possible in its operation, and the centrality of the good or service it sells. As to the characteristics of its customers, an important distinction can be made between households and business firms. When the firm sells to households, central locations may be attractive. Households are numerous, and more likely to be randomly distributed throughout the city. If the goods and services these firms provide have a high degree of centrality, and are produced under conditions in which there are sizable internal economies of scale, the firm is likely to choose a location somewhere near the center of the city. These are, according to central-place notions, the revenue-maximizing locations. But are they realizable conditions?

Certainly firms that are producing and distributing—or just distributing— "big ticket" items such as refrigerators, automobiles, or television sets, or more specialized items such as riding or ski equipment, are providing goods and/or services that have a relatively high degree of centrality. If the buying population for such items is widely dispersed, distribution operations are likely to be found most profitable at central locations because of the impact of such locations on revenues. They will be in excess of what they are at other locations. There are also some services found "downtown" that people are willing to travel distances to consume. These are services that also have high revenue requirements for a profitable scale of operation, e.g., the theatre and sporting events. The bid rent or price curve of firms serving these consumer needs under these conditions of production will show bids that decline with distance from the center.

There is also much local consumption of goods and services with less centrality that are provided to customers in ways not subject to significant economies of scale, e.g., food, haircuts, and nonprescription drugs. Revenue conditions dictate a smaller geographic sphere of operation. To some this will mean location in the central city. To others, competitive interaction will lead to locating in outlying locations. In all cases the matter of finding a correct location is influenced by the impact of location on the revenues of firms selling to the city's household population. Revenues fall off as firms move away from central locations, one of which is the central business district. If costs do not fall proportionately, this implies that rent or price bids will fall off as the firms move away from these central points. These firms will be dispersed, but found on locations that are central to certain parts of the population.

The revenue effects of location to firms that sell to other firms are less certain. Central-place notions can assist in making statements about these effects if the local firms sell to a number of firms dispersed throughout the city. With dispersion, the revenue impact of location depends on the centrality of the good or service being provided and the possibility of realizing economies of scale in the operation. Firms that sell to only a few others are less influenced by the impact of location on revenues. The question now becomes one of propinquity. Nearness to the firms that are the primary customer will lower transportation costs. How important this is depends on the relative importance of that transportation cost and/or the nature of the service.

Precisely what can we say about the site demands of the nonbasic firm? There is reason to believe that not all nonbasic firms will make the same rent offer for sites in the center of the city, or sites away from the center for that matter. In general, central sites seem to be preferred. In some cases, that center will be in the heart of the city. But cost and revenue factors could also exert a dispersive influence.

Central locations will be sought, but in many cases these will not be in the center of the city. There will be other points in the city that are central with respect to parts of the population or points that are near clusters of activity that may be composed of basic firms.

URBAN LAND MARKET OUTCOMES

While the outcome of the operation of the urban land market has many dimensions, one important one is price or rents. In commodity markets, price plays a key role in the way in which these markets mesh demand and supply influences together. The same holds true in the urban land market. Demand and supply factors in this market interact in ways that determine land rents which, in turn, have important bearing on the way in which land is used or allocated among alternative users.

Since land as it is used in cities is a highly differentiated product, if only because of differences in the accessibility of sites of available parcels, what is important is the configuration of land rents. When accessibility is emphasized, as it should be, the market focus is not on some rent level but a configuration of land rents which is sometimes called a *rent or price gradient*. Any concern with market outcomes in the urban land market thus becomes a concern with the way in which this market generates rent gradients.

We are now back to where we were in the beginning of this chapter. The question of concern is the assignment of those parcels of land to alternative uses through the competitive bidding of owners and users. If we assume that basic industries are in the center of the city, that all other activities are assigned to remaining points on a random basis, and we open up the possibility of exchange, the question is: Will there be exchange?

If journey to work is important, if basic employment is in the center of the city, if there are commuting costs, if the community experiences dissatisfaction during the time spent in transit, and if households exhibit economic behavior, there will be exchange. Households seek to locate at sites that minimize both the budget and psychic impact of journey-to-work costs. With employment in the center, these are sites in and around that center. Note now that if households seek to locate in or near the center of the city, the firms that produce goods and services sold to local residents will seek locations there as well, for these are the locations at which revenues will be at a maximum and labor costs may be at a minimum.

If we assume that households and nonbasic firms have been randomly assigned to locations throughout the city, those located some distance away from the city should enter the market, to get a site closer to the core. Will they get what they want?

Ordinarily, market participants who are willing and able to pay the most, wind up with what they want. Those who have the ability and willingness to pay should thus get the sites that are closest to the center. They will, by their market activity, also generate a configuration of rents or prices that decline with distance from the center of the city.

By way of illustrating how this comes about, consider a market with three participants—a business firm, a household, and a farmer—the behavior of which is depicted by the following bid rent curves.

It is clear that competitive bidding among these participants would generate rings of land use with the business firm located closest in and the farmer farthest out. Figure 5.12 indicates the business firm winning the battle for those sites from CBD to t_1, households from t_1 to t_2, and the farmer from t_2 on away from the city.

Figure 5.12

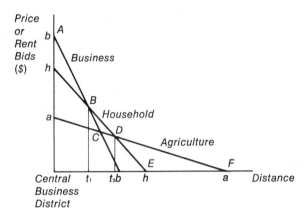

Note that for sites close in, rents fall within a range defined by the rent bids of the users in active competition for those sites—the business firm and the household. The business firm in this case must pay a rent at least equal to the rent the household is willing to pay, as denoted by hB, and will not pay anything that is in excess of the rents shown by the relevant portion of its bid rent curve, denoted by AB. Sites that fall between t_1 and t_2 command a rent no greater than that the household will pay—BD—and no less than that shown by BCD— the rents the business firm and the farmer will pay. For sites beyond t_2, the maximum price is given by DF, the rent the farmer is willing to pay, and the minimum price is shown by DEF.

No matter where actual rents fall within these ranges, one thing is clear. The rents paid for land between CBD and t_1 are higher than those paid for land between t_1 and t_2. The latter, in turn, are higher than those paid for land beyond t_2. If the rent paid is equal to the rent each winner is willing to pay, $ABDF$ would trace out the rent gradient that would emerge. Significantly, this is a curve that has a negative slope, denoting a negative relationship between rent and distance from the center of the city.

Note what has been done. Starting with simplified notions about what's important in the location decisions of households and firms, and applying these notions to the behavior of both in the urban land market, a rent gradient has been derived. That it shows rent to be negatively related to distance is a logical consequence of economic behavior of both firms and households as they deal with the "frictions" of distance in the city.

URBAN REAL ESTATE MARKETS

The discussion thus far has been stripped of any consideration of urban land improvements, the most obvious and important of which are buildings or structures put-in-place on the site. When such improvements are considered, our concern is with the urban real estate market. Much of what was said about city structure, with the aid of a theory that abstracted from such improvements, can be expressed in a conceptual framework that takes these improvements into account. This need not be done here. What must be done now is to show how these improvements alter the environment in ways that influence city structure not captured by an analysis of the urban land market.

To take improvements into account means that we must reckon with the durability and nonaccessibility features of the dwelling and other structures, and indicate how these things add another dimension to supply, which exerts influence on the market assignment of values to sites. In considering the nature of this influence, the concepts of market filtering and neighborhood effects can be appropriately introduced. Primitive though they may be, these concepts do contribute to our understanding of how a stock of differentiated dwellings influence residential location decisions. Household behavior with respect to upkeep and improvements also has impact on these decisions.

The Differentiated and Long-lasting Dwelling

Fixed site dwelling units are a highly durable asset which, with proper maintenance and care, can last almost forever. Because of this, the household population in each urban community is fitted into a stock of dwellings that has been accumulating over a relatively long period of time. In most communities, this is a stock that has reached its present size as a consequence of diverse forces manifested in residential mobility. These are circumstances that engender "spin-offs" from established households, which result in new households. Such household formations mean moves, and there are usually many new households being formed in most urban communities all of the time. Many established households also move because their current residence becomes unsuitable and they have the ability to do something about it. The housing desicions of established families are also influenced by developments on the supply side. In most urban communities, for example, housing units are frequently removed from stock, both intentionally and unintentionally, which forces the resident families to live elsewhere. New construction might also induce some families to move by making a set of highly attractive housing alternatives available.

Mobility of the sort leads to new construction and the diversity of these demands results in dwelling additions that are not only differentiated with respect to accessibility, but in structural characteristics of the dwellings as well. Not all units are the same size, nor do they reflect the same quality of construction. There are also architectural differences and differences in current condition. Census data make abundantly clear the magnitude of such differences in the spread of the distribution of the housing units in virtually all metropolitan areas over the classes established for the characteristics the Bureau considers.

Differentiation of a sort is important because it could constrain residential site choice in ways not envisioned in the above discussion of the urban land market. Accessibility can still be important to the family. But the efficiency apartments found in abundance near the center of the city where the employment opportunities are will not meet the housing needs of a husband-wife family with five children.

Certainly, the structural characteristics of the existing stock of dwellings can have impact on the demand price of particular households for the real estate lying along a line that goes from the center of the city to its periphery. Even if journey to work is important to the family, certain sites with accessibility may not be rated very highly because the dwellings erected on them are not suited to the housing needs of these families. Correspondingly, some inaccessible sites may nonetheless be valued highly by some households because of the structural characteristics of the dwelling units at those sites. It appears that the nonaccessibility characteristics of the stock require a modification of the conclusions about residential location derived from a journey-to-work model. To suggest this modification is to fail to take into account the possibility of changes in the stock accommodating the housing needs of those who want accessibility. Existing units can be demolished and replaced via new construction with other units more appropriate to the housing needs of these families. Rehabilitation, including the merger or conversion of existing units, is another means of providing such units. In the long run then, might we not expect the stock to be adjusted in ways that make the outcome consistent with the expectations of a journey-to-work model?

The question is not easily answered. But we get insights from the concepts of filtering and neighborhood effects, and by considering the upkeep decisions of the owners of residential property.

Residential Filtering   Where people live within the city is not a matter resolved by exchange in an auction-type setting similar to the setting we discussed above when we were attempting to illustrate outcomes in the urban land market. This theory helps bring into sharp focus certain important elements of the market process through which urban land is allocated among residential users. It does not, however, help us explain all urban real estate market outcomes. To come to understand these markets more fully requires other frameworks. One of these frequently used in the study of these markets, revolves around the concept of filtering.

The basic idea in filtering is movement through a structure. In the housing market that structure is the housing stock.

What moves? The dwelling?

As noted above, because of the lasting power of the dwelling, the household stock of dwellings has been accumulating over a long period of time. It is possible to conceive of this stock as an *equilibrium stock*. Consider, for a moment, one implication of doing so. An equilibrium stock implies that individual population units are living in the "best" housing possible, given their preferences, budget constraint, and the cost of housing. Consequently, it implies there will be no transactions in the housing market, since the housing adjustments these transactions would entail cannot result in anything better for any household, given existing conditions. There is, however, continuous activity in our urban housing markets, which implies that the equilibrium "conditions" in housing are seldom, if ever, fulfilled. There are market influences that produce disequilibria, which lead to household moves, that generate the movement through the structure of housing.

The movement of what? The answer to this question requires understanding of the nature of the transaction when families move. Many involve units in the existing stock; some involve newly constructed units. These existing units come onto the market when households established within the community move. Those in this set of families who move to another location within the same urban community are families who come onto the market both as demanders and suppliers. They can be households who presently live in owner-occupied housing and want to move into another home, those who now rent but want to become homeowners, and those who now own but want to move into a rental unit. It is conceivable, although not very likely, that moves could be accomplished simply by a multilateral exchange of units in the standing stock—that is, those units brought into the market by those who are moving. In fact, much activity in our urban housing market takes this form. But, it is also the case that a significant proportion of housing transactions in most communities involve the newly constructed unit. Such new construction is generally associated with the demographic and replacement pressures created by additions to the household population, both from within and from outside (in-migration) and demolitions. These pressures generate "excess" demand in the market in the sense that they result in more families entering the market as demanders and then suppliers. Excess demand, in turn, leads to a decline in the vacancy rate, putting upward pressure on price, which makes construction more profitable.

What general statements can be made about who moves into what kind of units, and where? Notions of filtering, as they were initially developed, focused on the release of dwelling units to low income households by middle and upper-income families who moved into better dwellings. As found in earlier statements of the sector theory of residential development, it was the rich who led the way, moving out into expensive dwellings found in the spacious places of natural beauty, away from the central city. The units they left behind came to be occupied by middle-income families who, in turn, would vacate units that were made available to those with still lower incomes. One set of moves would, in effect, generate a chain of moves in which a number of units in the standing stock filtered down the quality scale and became available to families with lower incomes.

While this form of the argument is naive, leaving much housing phenomena unexplained, it is consistent with several significant market facts. One is that the construction industry has been selective in the way in which it responds to demand.

The characteristics of the newly constructed dwelling indicate that the industry is much more sensitive to the moves of white families in the middle and upper income categories. When there are subsidies, housing for low-income families may be built. Without such subsidies, the industry will concentrate on the other portions of the market. The acquisition of housing by the low-income family tends to involve units in the standing stock, which have filtered down. New construction for middle and upper-income groups can thus give rise to filtering, which actually comes about partly as a result of the chain of moves this new construction precipitates.

Filtering in this sense, however, may have its origins in the demands of the poor. To the extent that their number increases and their housing demands are not accommodated by new construction, excess demand in this market strata could lead owned units in the next higher income strata to do things that add standing stock units to the supplies available to the low-income families. This could come about as a consequence of adjustments made in maintenance and upkeep expenditures, which lowered the quality and hence the costs of these units. This possibility will be discussed in more detail below. But if it happens, disequilibrium will develop in other housing strata, which will be brought into balance by filtering or downward adjustments in the quality, and hence costs of units in the standing stock. Some of these imbalances will disappear as a consequence of additions to the stock through new construction, an adjustment, as noted above, that is more probable in strata where households have relatively high incomes.

This concept of filtering emphasizes the downward movement of dwelling units to meet the housing needs of those with low incomes. Stated in this way, the concept suggests housing markets work in a way that can be described in understandable terms. Yet that description leaves out much that is involved, as these markets adjust the stock of housing units to the changing requirements of the tenant population. When we try to become more specific about these details, controversy arises as to what filtering really means.

No one denies that certain sets of housing adjustments can be properly described as a chain of moves, the outcome of which is filtering in the above sense. Even in these cases, however, the outcomes are not nearly as precise as those implied by the earlier theories. There are, for reasons that will be discussed in detail in a later chapter, market constraints (e.g., discrimination) which influence the way in which available units are reallocated to the different households entering the market. Low income blacks, for example, have been shown to be less fortunate than their white counterparts in becoming a part of the chain of moves through which filtering takes place. It is also the case that many units do not move down the quality ladder very quickly with the passage of time, and that some, through rehabilitation, move up the quality scale. Finally, Census data indicate some of the new units put up are low quality substandard units, although most of this construction occurs in rural areas.

There is filtering in our urban housing markets, a good deal of which involves the movement of units down the quality scale. That movement is by no means unidirectional, however, when it occurs, nor does it alter the housing opportunities of all households in different income strata in the same way. The process is complex and not easily described. But to understand filtering, we have to conceive of it as a process through which the qualitative characteristics of housing units in the existing stock are adjusted to make this stock conform more to the structure of housing demands.

Neighborhood Effects   *Demand* in economics is the study of the likes, dislikes, and incomes of households as they influence consumption. Prices are also an important part of the subject. In the model of behavior constructed, attention centers on the household's response to the price of the good being consumed, e.g., housing. Some attention is also paid to the price of other goods, particularly those that can be conceived of as substitutes (international travel services) or complements (household furnishings).

All these things clearly have important bearing on consumption decisions. But with housing, there is another dimension. To most, the neighborhood within which the dwelling is situated is important in the evaluations they make. Residential housing in our cities is such that individual dwelling units tend to fit into particular neighborhoods, and certain characteristics of that neighborhood have bearing on the way in which the individual dwelling is rated. Neighborhoods that are made up of well-kept, attractive and in some cases expensive homes, for example, are often considered to be desirable, as are those with special terrain features, such as a spectacular view. The presence of good neighborhood schools is also appealing. Many families find neighborhood features of this sort very attractive and are willing to pay for them. Put another way, such features—the amenities of a neighborhood—are quite often reflected in the rent or price bids of the households seeking to locate there.

The features of the neighborhood which influence household site demands need not always be attractive. The site may be next door to a huge shopping center which, while convenient, is extremely noisy and generates much congestion. Such conditions are likely to be considered as disamenities which exert a downward influence on the bid price of many households. Or to some, neighborhoods that are populated with low-income families are not rated very highly as places to live, even though they may be highly accessible.

Nobody denies the presence of neighborhood effects. What is less clear are those combinations of conditions which influence households in certain specified ways. While many families may be favorably impressed with a well maintained and orderly group of houses in a particular subdivision, others may be less so. Who is and who is not favorably impressed by these and other neighborhood conditions are questions that do not have clear-cut answers. Only very general statements can be made about the links between the scale of valuations of individual households and the dwelling and occupant characteristics of neighborhoods. Many argue that there is reason to believe neighborhoods populated with high-income professional people, living in expensive homes, are neighborhoods that have special appeal to some households, which will be reflected in the prices they bid for homes in these neighborhoods. However, how much higher these prices are because of neighborhood effects is uncertain.

Upkeep and Maintenance   The condition of a dwelling, which has bearing on its attractiveness to potential users, depends largely on upkeep decisions of landlords and homeowners. *Upkeep* can be viewed as a means by which owners alter their housing investment. This investment declines through physical depreciation; yet owners can at least partially offset the effect of depreciation through upkeep expenditures. Upkeep can thus be construed as an investment decision and analyzed as such.

When looked at in this way, the focus is on the profitability of upkeep, which, in an investment framework, is evaluated in terms of expected income streams, prices or costs, and the market rate of interest. Income for the landlord is income from rentals. For the homeowner, it refers to implicit rents which cover the value of the housing services received. With the application of some level of upkeep spending, the level of housing consumption should be higher than in its absence. Upkeep expenditures influence the condition of the dwelling which, in turn, controls the volume of services provided over the life of the dwelling. Higher levels of upkeep spending should, through their impact on condition, mean more services over that life span or, in effect, more housing consumption. Since higher consumption should mean higher levels of rent, upkeep has income effects. But to get these benefits imposes a cost—the expenditure itself. When expected benefits and expected costs are discounted, a comparison of present values will provide profitability indications. The owner has wide latitude in this choice. At one extreme, he can choose a level of upkeep spending so high as to minimize depreciation, or he can spend nothing on upkeep, thereby permitting maximum depreciation. As economic beings analyzed in an investment framework, they choose upkeep levels which maximize the present value of their investment.

What now of the determinants of upkeep spending? When upkeep is considered as investment, a concern with determinants is a concern with factors which affect the rate of return on this type of investment. There are factors that are internal to the dwelling and occupant. These factors influence the benefits from upkeep spending. One set of these operates through the dwelling to which these expenditures are being applied. The impact of $100 in maintenance spent each year on a poorly engineered structure, for example, is less than the same amount spent on one that is structurally superior. The condition of the dwelling at the time of the expenditure also influences the amount of the benefit. $100 spent on a dwelling that is in poor condition, for example, yields less benefit than if that money were spent on a dwelling which, though structurally the same, is in better condition.

How benefits per dollar of expenditure influence the decision depends on how the beneficiary views the future. The benefits could be high, for example, yet upkeep might be kept at relatively low levels because the owner has a low regard for the future.

There are differences in the time preferences of owners that could have impact on their views about the present worth of upkeep benefits. Consider homeowners by way of example. The old and the young who own homes could be expected to emphasize the present more than middle-age households do. The income and education of these owners could also have bearing on their views with respect to the future. The time horizons of those with higher incomes and more education, for example, are probably longer than those at the other end of the income and education scale. Hence it can be argued that the middle-aged homeowner and those who have relatively high incomes and are "well educated" would value upkeep investment more than those who are young or old, have low incomes and little formal education. Consequently, they are likely to spend more to maintain their homes.

Factors external to the dwelling and the occupant can also influence upkeep spending. The ones most frequently discussed are neighborhood effects. Given significant neighborhood effects, it has been argued that any owner of property can maximize the present value of his property if that property is "under-maintained" relative to all others in the neighborhood. If my neighbors do more in keeping up their residence than I do, I benefit from their actions, if neighborhood appearance has impact on the valuation of individual dwellings in the neighbor-hood. If this holds for me, however, it holds for my neighbors as well. Thus, it can be argued that each of us has incentive to minimize the upkeep of our property which leads to urban residential decay.

This argument provides insights and is persuasive. But it by no means explains all the facts about urban residential depreciation. The most important of these is that in all communities there are neighborhoods that are deteriorating, some that are well maintained, and some that are "mixed bags." If we are to account for maintenance in terms of neighborhood effects, such facts imply that these effects are strong in some neighborhoods, less so in others, and perhaps absent in still others. Under what conditions do neighborhood effects give rise to rapid deterioration? Under what conditions will a more "normal" depreciation take place?

These are questions not easily answered unless we combine what we know about neighborhood effects with our knowledge of internal factors as they influence upkeep and maintenance decisions of property owners. Even so, there are limits to what can be said about upkeep spending in different parts of the city, and how this has bearing on residential location decisions as these things have been discussed in this chapter. To extend these limits requires understanding of the basic elements of welfare economics as they are applied to evaluating the per-formance of the urban economy. This, as it turns out, is also knowledge that will serve us well as we consider many other questions about cities.

REFERENCES

*Alonso, W. *Location and Land Use*. Cambridge, Mass.: Harvard University Press, 1964.

Bailey, M. "Note on Economics of Residential Zoning and Urban Renewal." *Land Economics* 35 (1959): 225–34.

Davis, O., and Whinston, A. "Economics of Urban Renewal." *Law and Contemporary Problems* 26 (1961): 106–17.

Hoover, E. *The Location of Economic Activity*. New York: McGraw-Hill, Inc., 1948.

Lansing, J.; Clifton, C.; and Morgan, J. *New Homes and Poor People*. Institute for Social Research (1969).

Lowry, I. "Filtering and Housing Standards; A Conceptual Analysis." *Land Economics* 36 (1960): 362–70.

*Muth, R. *Cities and Housing*. Chicago: University of Chicago Press, 1969.

von Thunen, J. *Der Isolierte in Beziehung auf Landwirtschaft und Nationalokonomie*. Hamburg, Germany: Hamburg and Rostock, 1826.

---

* This chapter draws heavily from the writings of Alonso and Muth.

The Performance of
the Urban Economy

SUMMARY

Understanding how the urban economy works is important. Just as important is the question of the quality of life this economy helps to generate as it works. To address the question of quality or performance, we must have *normative knowledge,* that is, standards or norms against which this performance can be judged.

The study of welfare economics provides two sets of criteria against which quality or performance can be measured. These criteria are the primary subject matter in this chapter.

The criterion of efficiency is examined first. This is a concern with the allocation of resources between alternative uses. The focus is on allocations in which no change is possible that will make anyone better off without making someone else worse off. The criterion for economic efficiency can be expressed either in terms of cost and benefits, or substitution and transformation rates of goods between consumers and producers. Conditions can be specified in which efficiency in the allocation of resources is achieved, conditions that can be shown to be realized in a system of competitive markets.

Because of this conclusion about the efficiency of competitive markets, welfare problems in economics are usually viewed as departures from competitive market norms. The primary sources of market failure in this sense are *ownership spillovers or externalities,* which in their extreme form involve goods we call *public goods.* Ownership spillovers arise when the use of some scarce resource—owned by someone—spills over on parties not directly involved with that activity. These spillovers can either be costs or benefits. When present, markets will generate either too much or too little output. In the case of a public good, the market mechanism does not work at all.

If we were able to diagnose the areas of inefficiency in the economy and prescribe the appropriate remedies, problems might remain. It could be that we might not like the results because we are unhappy with the distribution of the product among consumers. Equity considerations enter in the judgments we make about economic outcomes. Unfortunately, economic analysis provides less help in establishing the criteria against which equity judgments can be made.

As a practical matter, most evaluations of the quality of life in cities centers on individual projects and whether they generate any real improvements. Such evaluations usually involve some form of cost-benefit analysis. The significant aspects of such analyses are discussed. Concrete illustrations of the rudiments of a cost benefit analysis, both in the public and private sectors of the economy, are given.

Our concern to this point has been with urban economic theory as it contributes to an understanding of how the urban economy works. This is important subject matter. Equally important, however, is the quality of life we find in cities. This raises the question of how well the urban economy works. While, with the aid of the tools in chapter 5, we may come to understand why our cities have spread out, we won't be able to decide whether this is *good* or *bad* on the basis of these tools. The economic analysis discussed to this point is often called *positive economics*. Its concern is with the explanation of facts, irrespective of whether we think those facts are good or bad. If we want to evaluate performance, we must have "normative" knowledge, that is, we must have standards or norms against which such an assessment can be made. If we want to evaluate the performance of urban housing markets, for example, we must be able to make statements about the adequacy of housing. To do this, we must have something against which the current housing can be compared. The conclusions of positive economic analysis do not supply us with these criteria. We need a normative analysis, which in economics is commonly called *welfare economics*.

In welfare economics there are two propositions, ethical in nature, that are central to the analysis. The first of these is: The purpose of economic activity is to produce goods and services for use and to do it in a way, given the constraints operating through supply, that maximizes total production. The second proposition is: What should be produced? The alternatives are many and choices have to be made. Questions can be raised about who should make these choices. In welfare economics, it is generally assumed that individuals are best able to make judgments about what is best for them. In other words, in our judgments about the performance of the economy, we must reckon with an economic system in which the individuals who are a part of that system have a good deal of freedom with respect to what they do and what they consume.

Given these two general propositions, there are two sets of criteria against which judgments can be made about the performance of the economy. One of these is allocative efficiency. The other is equity.

ALLOCATIVE EFFICIENCY

When the focus is on allocative efficiency, the concern is with the assignment of resources to alternative uses in a way that achieves the "best" or most efficient use of those resources. A concern with efficiency in this sense stems from the first of the two general propositions noted above—to produce as much as is possible with our stocks of resources. Is this a legitimate concern? Are resources really scarce? Do people really want more than they can currently get from the productive use of their resources?

To most economists, the evidence of scarcity is overwhelming; consequently there is reason to be concerned with how resources are used. What is involved in allocative efficiency, however, is more than a concern with using resources in ways that yield maximum output from a given set of inputs. This is engineering efficiency, which is important; yet there is more. Output composition is also important. It is possible, for example, to produce efficiently in an engineering sense, but to produce the wrong things. This is inefficiency in an economic sense.

The point is easy to illustrate. Suppose we were able to produce automobiles more efficiently than dwellings, in an engineering sense, that is, we get more output per dose of inputs in the production of automobiles. Suppose further that all resources were used in producing automobiles. Is this efficiency in an economic sense? It could be; yet we must remember that to get automobiles we must give up housing. Suppose housing ranks high in the ordering of our preferences. Overall benefits from consumption would increase if resources were shifted from automobiles to housing. To produce nothing but automobiles in the face of these preferences would be an economically inefficient use of resources.

What constitutes an economically efficient allocation of resources? Looked at in a very general way, resources can be said to be efficiently allocated if they cannot be rearranged in their use in production in a way that makes the population better off. To say this, however, is to say very little. Under what conditions will this arrangement be achieved? What criteria do we use as a basis of making this judgment?

One criterion was put forth by Vilfredo Pareto at the turn of the century. The so-called Pareto Optimum is that this arrangement should be such that no change is possible which will make anyone better off without making someone else worse off. What kind of an arrangement is this? To answer this question, we must indicate the conditions under which a Pareto Optimum is realized. We can do this best by focusing on the costs and benefits associated with production.

Costs and Benefits

As noted just above, the cost of building a home can be viewed as the benefits foregone because of the reduced level of automobile production. Benefits, on the other hand, refer to satisfactions from consumption of some commodity, such as housing or automobiles.

If resources are allocated through a system of markets, costs and benefits can be expressed in terms of money. In a market setting, firms must purchase inputs which involve a money outlay, and households cast dollar votes in purchasing the goods they consume. For firms, these outlays can be construed as costs in the sense that they are required to bid resources away from alternative uses. For consumers, these payments can be taken as an index of anticipated benefits from consumption; otherwise there would be no reason for a willingness to make such payments.

Suppose we consider the costs and benefits from the production and consumption of automobiles. One representation of these costs and benefits is shown in Figure 6.1, which denotes increasing total costs and benefits with increased production

Figure 6.1

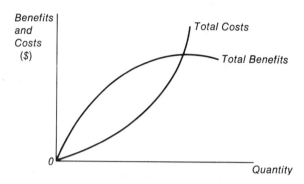

and consumption. It also depicts total benefits as increasing at a decreasing rate with increased consumption and total costs increasing at an increasing rate with increased production. Allocative efficiency criteria can be defined in terms of these cost and benefit curves. Resources can be said to be efficiently allocated to automobiles when the difference between total benefits and total costs is positive and at a maximum. Put somewhat differently, efficient production occurs at the point where net benefits from production—total benefits less total costs—are at a maximum. Why is this the case? Consider the argument as it is expressed in terms of what is gained and given up by producing more or less cars, that is, in terms of marginal benefits and marginal costs.

To consider costs and benefits out on the margin is to consider the change in total costs and total benefits as we produce more or less. If consumption is increased, say, by one unit and total benefits rise by $4,000, the marginal benefits from consumption would be $4,000. If production is increased by one unit and total costs rise by $3,000, the marginal costs of production would be $3,000. Obviously, given information on the total costs and benefits of different levels of production and consumption, marginal benefit and marginal cost curves can be derived. Figure 6.2 represents the marginal curves derived from Figure 6.1.

Consider now the question of economic efficiency with respect to the production of automobiles. We have the option of not producing. We also have the option of producing OQ_1 which is, say, one automobile. Suppose we produce that unit. Do we have any basis for saying that we are better off as a result?

Clearly we do if the cost and benefit curves shown in Figure 6.2 really represent the marginal costs and benefits of production and consumption. Society is better off with production and consumption at OQ_1, for at this point marginal benefits (OB_1) are well in excess of marginal costs (OC_1). The satisfaction of consumption is greater than the satisfaction from the consumption possible if the resources required to produce OQ_1 were put to other uses.

It is clear that it would also be to our advantage to produce and consume OQ_2, OQ_3, and all the way up to OQ_b. More production would lead to more benefits

Figure 6.2

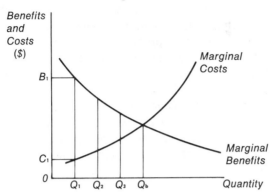

than costs—or the benefits foregone. Note beyond OQ_b the reverse is true. To extend production beyond OQ_b would require that we forego benefits which were larger than those derived from their use in the production of automobiles. Why? Simply because marginal costs exceed marginal benefits at these output levels.

What can we conclude from this? If we want as much as we can get from our resources, we should not produce more than OQ_b automobiles. We should also produce at least that much. Output, in other words, should be adjusted to the point of *equality* between *marginal benefits* and *marginal costs*.

Competitive Markets and Efficiency

Suppose our economic resources were allocated so that marginal costs and marginal benefits were equal in all directions. There would be, under the circumstances, no other possible arrangement of resource use which would make one person better off without making another worse. Were the arrangement otherwise to begin with, it could be easily shown that a rearrangement bringing marginal costs and benefits into equality would be a rearrangement of resources that would make somebody better off without making anyone else worse off. These consequences are implicit in the remarks above. Once we reach the point of equality, we cannot improve upon what we have, unless we choose to redistribute the product among consumers. The welfare implications of redistribution are discussed below; the concern here is with efficiency and the allocation of resources.

While important, this view of the criteria of allocative efficiency tells us little about precisely how much labor and/or capital should be used in the production of alternatives. Much supplementary information is required before we can even begin to answer this question. Yet, this is not really one of the purposes served by these concepts. They abstract from particulars and, because they do, are in a form that serves us in other important ways. One of these is to provide a basis for making statements that apply to a wide range of situations.

One important set of these applications concerns the type of markets within which efficiency is likely to be achieved. It can be shown on the basis of these notions that for any given distribution of income, a system of purely competitive markets will generate an efficient allocation of resources. The argument is involved and covers materials that have not been touched upon above. It can be expressed in several different ways. One has to do with the fact that there is only one price for each commodity, to which producers and consumers adjust and only one price for each input, to which producers adjust. When this is the case and markets are the means through which resource allocation takes place, firms and households will adjust their purchases and other activities in ways that generate the equality in the relevant costs and benefits.

In light of this argument, many economists view welfare problems as departures or derivations from competitive market outcomes, which, in turn, are viewed as "norms." Considered in this way, the welfare problem is taken to mean the problem of market failure and the central point of inquiry is one of identifying the kinds of conditions that give rise to such failure.

Sources of Market Failure

As the issue of market failure has been studied, a distinction has emerged among three sets of contributing conditions. One is technical; another stems from ownership "spillovers"; the third is sometimes called the case of public goods.

Technical Difficulties   Market problems can arise from production technologies that reward large or mass scale levels of output. When output within the firm has to be taken to very high levels to get full advantage of the benefits possible from current technology, competition breaks down. Firm adjustments to such a set of technical conditions leads to fewness in number within these markets. When there is monopoly in the market, it can be easily shown through positive economic analysis that production will not be taken to the point where marginal benefits are equal to marginal costs. Thus, the market fails or there is market inefficiency, which in this case usually takes the form of less production than what the market indicates to be socially desirable.

Ownership Spillovers or Externalities   Ownership externalities also constitute conditions that give rise to allocative efficiency problems. When economic activities associated with the use of some scarce resource, which is owned by someone, has impact or spills over on parties that are not directly involved with that activity, there are externalities in the sense of costs or benefits imposed on persons not directly involved in the activity. When these externalities are present, the cost and benefits that people respond to in markets, that is, *private* costs and benefits, do not equal *social* costs or benefits. Ownership spillovers thus mean a divergence between private and social costs and/or benefits.

Generally, ownership externalities fall into one of two general categories. First there are those which stem from production, which either bestow uncompensated advantage on someone, or impose uncompensated costs on someone. As to benefits, there are many things firms do which could provide others with uncompensated advantages. For example, they might train workers that eventually go to work for others who do not have to pay the training costs. Or they could house their activities in attractively landscaped and creatively designed plants that lie along major throughways. In doing so, they might bestow benefits on those who commute, even though the landscaping and design features may not have been intended for this purpose.

Examples of uncompensated costs that firms impose on others are even easier to come by. There is, of course, the old widow who takes in laundry and hangs it out to dry in an atmosphere polluted with the smoke and soot belching from the stacks of a factory located down the street. Here the spillover is a cost imposed by one—the factory—on another—the widow—who has no way of collecting from the first. Or there are those firms that pump waste materials into our rivers and bays and in doing so impose a number of uncompensated costs on others. Chesapeake Bay's oyster beds and Long Island's clam beds are just two of many kinds of resources along our water ways that are being threatened by water pollution because of our penchant for disposing of waste in our rivers and streams.

The second class of ownership externalities stems from consumption. The neighborhood effects discussed above are ownership externalities. Families who maintain their house and lawn provide uncompensated benefits to their neighbors just as those who do not impose uncompensated costs on theirs. But the property involved in consumption need not be a house. Expenditures on educating one's children can also bestow benefits on the neighbors if the children become responsible neighbors as a result. Conspicuous consumption, say, on cars and dress might also impose uncompensated costs on neighbors, who are not in a financial position to purchase the same things.

What now of the economic implications of ownership spillovers? What does it mean to say that they give rise to a divergence between social costs and benefits and private costs and benefits?

Consider the case of costs first. Go back to the factors with smoke stacks that belch soot that spills over into the yard of the woman that takes in and hangs out laundry. Suppose the firm does not include the pollution it imposes on this woman in its costs. The costs the firm responds to in making output decisions are private costs. In this case, they do not equal the social costs of production because they do not include adequate provision for dealing with the pollution the firm creates. To cope with this problem requires the use of resources and hence means incurring costs. The social costs of production in this instance are the private costs confronting the firm plus the costs incurred in dealing with the pollution problem. In this case, social costs exceed private costs.

That private and social costs diverge is important. It means that the profit-maximizing firm, in responding to market forces, will adjust output to an inefficient level. How can this be?

Recall that the output of the firm is taken to the point where the marginal costs and marginal benefits are equal. Suppose the costs that confront the firm—its private costs—do not reflect command over the resources required to deal with pollution spillovers stemming from production. This means a divergence between the marginal private and marginal social costs of production; the latter will be higher than the former at all levels of output—see Figure 6.3. Suppose now that there are no benefit spillovers, that is, the marginal social and private benefits from production are the same—see Figure 6.3.

The profit - maximizing firm operating under these conditions will adjust production to the point where marginal private costs and marginal private benefits are equal. This is output OQ_2 in Figure 6.3. Suppose now that the firm, in making this decision, is confronted with total social costs. Profit-maximizing behavior

Figure 6.3

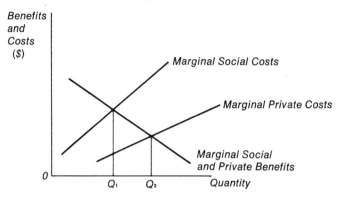

will take output to the point of equality between marginal costs—which in this case are marginal social costs—and benefits, or to point OQ_1. Significantly, OQ_1 is less than OQ_2. Profit-maximizing behavior when the firm is not confronted with full social costs results in too much production from the viewpoint of society.

Similarly, when there are positive benefits that spill over to those who are not a party to the activity, the output decisions of a profit-maximizing firm may also be wrong. In this case, output may fall short of the point at which marginal social benefits and marginal social costs are equal. When there are positive spillovers, marginal social benefits are greater than the market or private benefits which confront the firm. Suppose this difference is equal to the difference between the marginal social benefit and the marginal private benefit curves, as in Figure 6.4. Firms responding to private costs and benefits will adjust output to OQ_1.

Figure 6.4

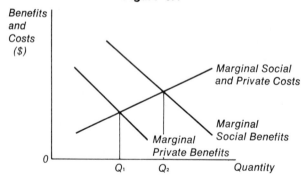

This is the output level at which private benefits and costs are equal. It is also an output level that is below what it would have been if the firm responded to a benefit curve which reflected total or social benefits—OQ_2 in Figure 6.4. Firms that produce where there is a divergence between marginal social and marginal private benefits will not produce enough from the viewpoint of society.

Public Goods   A pure public good is an extreme case of an externality. It involves transactions from which others cannot be excluded. Such externalities arise when we produce goods that can be consumed by one person without diminishing the good's consumption by others. National defense is, of course, the time-honored example. No one has any incentive to buy national defense because they can get all they want free of any charge if someone else buys it. This is the "free rider" problem. When one buys, others share in the benefits at no charge. As a result, no one has any incentive to buy the good. The market in such cases will not provide a mechanism through which individual preferences can be expressed.

The point is typically illustrated in the following way. The demand for any good can be construed as the sum of individual demands, which, according to economic theory, are the outcome of decisions which reflect the preferences of individuals, the constraining influence of their income and price tags which attach to the things they consume. In the case of a private good, these individual demand curves are summed horizontally. To illustrate the point, assume consumers X, Y, and Z constitute the market for product A. Given their individual demand curves as shown in Figure 6.5, the market demand curve for A can be derived by

Figure 6.5

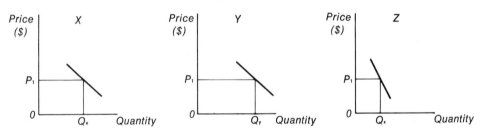

simply summing across individual demand curves. Total quantity demanded when the price is OP_1, for example, is the sum of the demands of X, Y, and Z or OQ_x, OQ_y, and OQ_z.

Suppose now our concern is with a public good, that is, the consumption of which by any one individual does not diminish the consumption of others. It is no longer true that aggregate demand is the horizontal summation of the demands of individuals. The reason is evident. If X consumes OQ_x, for example, that quantity is still available for consumption by Y and Z.

In the case of public goods, aggregate demand is the vertical summation of individual demands. If we specify a quantity—say OQ_1 in Figure 6.6—and find

Figure 6.6

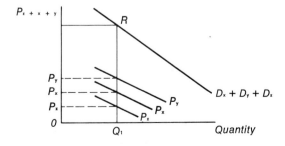

that customers X, Y, and Z are willing to pay a different price, e.g., P_x, P_y, and P_z for OQ_1, these prices when summed up constitute a price (P_{x+y+z}) the public would be willing to pay for that quantity of good A, which we assume is consumed simultaneously.

What Figure 6.6 really shows is the amount (the rectangle OQ_1RP_{x+y+z}) the public is willing to pay for OQ_1. That amount will not be forthcoming if the good is offered in the market. There is no incentive to make individual purchases, since a free ride is possible from the purchases of others. Very little or perhaps even nothing will be produced if the matter is left to the market. But there are obviously benefits associated with production, as clearly indicated by the amount people are willing to pay for OQ_1 in Figure 6.6. What is needed is a mechanism through which each person can pay for a portion of the cost. If such a mechanism is provided, we will have provided the basis for a vertical summation of these demand curves to which there can be a response, a collective response. We shall be providing the public with a public good.

EQUITY CONSIDERATIONS

Suppose we were able to diagnose correctly the areas of inefficiency in the economy and prescribe the appropriate remedies. The application of these remedies should lead us to the best of all possible worlds. Or will it?

To this point, income distribution, or, in effect, the distribution of production among consumers, has been taken as given. If this assumption is relaxed, another dimension is added to the problem. With different income distributions, there are different patterns of resource use which can achieve efficiency in the allocation of resources. The point warrants elaboration.

If we suppose a very simple economy consisting of consumers Smith, Jones, and Agajanian, who spend all of their money income on bread and wine, it can be easily shown that there is more than one possible combination of resource use in the production of bread and wine which would be considered as efficient.

Assume the cost of a loaf of bread and bottle of wine is $1 each, that the tastes and preferences of Smith, Jones, and Agajanian differ, and that there is a money income of $1,000 which is initially distributed among the three, such that Smith gets $500, Jones gets $250, and Agajanian gets $250. With these incomes, assume the following expenditures are made:

Table 6.1

	Income	Expenditures	
		Bread	Wine
Smith	$500	$400	$100
Jones	250	125	125
Agajanian	250	50	200
	$1,000	$575	$425

With the $1 price of a loaf of bread and a bottle of wine, the efficient allocation of resources is one in which 575 loaves of bread and 425 bottles of wine are produced. The best allocation of resources is one in which more bread than wine is produced.

Suppose now we redistribute income in a way such that Agajanian has $500, and Smith and Jones have $250. Suppose further that Smith, Jones, and Agajanian spend the same proportion of their incomes on bread and wine as before. The distribution of these expenditures would now appear as follows:

Table 6.2

| | Income | Expenditures | |
		Bread	Wine
Smith	$ 250	$200	50
Jones	250	125	125
Agajanian	500	100	400
	$1,000	$425	$575

The efficient allocation of resources implicit in these figures is now one in which 425 loaves of bread and 575 bottles of wine are produced. The best allocation of resources is now one in which more wine than bread is produced. Why is this the case?

It obviously has to do with the fact that Agajanian's expenditures now weigh more heavily than they did and Agajanian prefers wine to bread. Agajanian, of course, assumes a more prominent role in the scheme of things because income in the economy has been redistributed in a way that benefits Agajanian.

Which of these two allocations constitutes the best use of the community's resources? No unambiguous answer can be given unless society could agree on the relative deservingness of the three individuals. When we alter the distribution of income in the community, we effectively take something from somebody—Smith in the illustration above—and give it to someone else—Agajanian above. We inflict pain on one and bring pleasure to another. Are we better off as a result? This is not an easy question to answer. There is little in economics analogous to the conditions of allocative efficiency that can be used as a means of making statements about the best distribution of income. The difficulties arise because of the virtual impossibility of comparing the satisfactions from consumption of two or more persons—the problem of interpersonal utility comparisons. If it is not possible to compare the pain and pleasure of members of society, and we consider that society as one in which considerable conflict is generated by altering the distribution of income, it is not clear how one can begin to make statements about which distribution will generate the most happiness.

Many have argued that we could make statements about what is best for society if we were able to specify the conditions that maximize the social welfare of the community. But there are problems with the notion of social welfare. To specify the conditions that maximize the social welfare of the community means to specify a function that indicates the conditions in society that have bearing on that thing we call *social welfare*. This is not easy in a world in which the individual is assigned a prominent role. In such a society, social welfare has to mean the aggregate of the welfare of individuals that make up that society. The construction of a social welfare function in such a setting is a task that involves finding the circumstances in which this aggregate is at a maximum. The problem, of course, is that for this to be done, we must be able to aggregate and hence compare the welfare of individuals. We are back to the problems of interpersonal utility comparisons, which become especially troublesome when there are conflicting interests among those who make up the community.

If a social welfare function cannot be objectively determined, how then are we to deal with the question of equity? Some have argued that there is no need for anyone to try to determine this function objectively, since it is, in fact, overtly erxpessed when people vote or cast ballots in the ballot box. If we do not have what we want through the operation of markets, collective action is possible. Indeed, government as it operates through its fiscal and other policies does redistribute some of the nation's real product among individuals. But do we get the kind of redistributions we want through the activities of government? Both political scientists and economists have devoted much time in recent years researching the question of whether the decision rules of a democracy lead to a consistent transitive ranking of social alternatives. If it did, there are valid arguments which hold that the ballot box could be used as a means of dealing with the equity question. But apparently it doesn't, or at least early research raises some doubts.

What is involved here is intimately tied in with a set of "norms" or ethical propositions that represent irreducible elements in what is taken as the common good. To say this, really moves us away from the subject matter economists are equipped to deal with, that is, the matter of value judgments. These kinds of judgments do not really lend themselves to analysis with the aid of the current tools of a positivistic science. Most economists and other scientists do, in fact, have personal views about equity which reflect certain judgments they have made about what constitutes the common good. As they are publicly reported, economists seem to come out overwhelmingly in favor of more rather than less equality in consumption and the ownership of economic wealth. But the question of how much is enough is never really answered.

Equity in economics is generally considered a matter of ascertaining the impact of particular types of activity on the distribution of income. What is fair or equitable is taken as given; it is something that is determined by the community through its political representatives. Given the established standards, attention then centers on the distribution of the costs and benefits of governmental programs among individuals, with notions of horizontal and vertical equity often providing some explicit criteria against which these programs are judged. *Horizontal equity* is the requirement that equals receive equal treatment. *Vertical equity* is the requirement that unequals receive unequal treatment. Taken together, these two criteria are often invoked in discussions of the role of government in society in arguments that emphasize the benefits principle. Very generally stated, the argument is that the costs of government to the individual should be related to the benefits received. Yet there are other principles that can be invoked such as ability-to-pay.

Many questions can be raised about the way in which economists handle the equity criterion, the answers to which are not forthcoming on the basis of analysis to be found in welfare economics. Perhaps the greatest contribution economics can make to the issue of equity—and it is not unimportant in its application to the task of evaluating the performance of the urban economy—is through positive economic analysis, which denotes the efficiency consequences of particular activities and programs.

COST-BENEFIT ANALYSIS

Some Conceptual Problems in the Measurement of Costs and Benefits

Measuring the costs and benefits associated with a project seems, on the surface, to be a straightforward task. By committing resources to produce automobiles or to build urban highways, we incur costs and generate benefits. All we have to do in making a decision about the project is to add up the costs, add up the benefits, and compare the two. But what costs? And what benefits?

Consider costs first. The real costs of building that highway are, according to an earlier discussion, the low-cost housing, medical-care services, and/or automobiles we give up by using our resources in a certain way. In a competitive market economy, costs in this sense are reflected in the money costs incurred in purchasing the inputs used in production, *plus* an amount to cover the profits necessary for production.

Profit, of course, is an elusive element in economics. The general conception of profit is something that is necessary to keep owners from withdrawing their resources from the business. Looked at in this way, the difficulties with the concept become apparent. First, owners commit a number of resources to their businesses. Many provide labor inputs; all commit capital resources. The incomes they earn from their businesses must thus be considered, in part, as wage and interest payments for the labor and capital resources they commit to the business. Yet, there is something over and beyond this that goes to the owners of a business, something which we call a *profit*. What then is profit?

In economics, profit is associated with the entrepreneurial function, which in turn, means taking full responsibility for the operation of the enterprise and assuming the risks associated with that enterprise. These tasks are integral parts of any successful business, and in a free market system profit provides people with the incentive to do these tasks.

What the profits of a firm should be, of course, varies because of variations in the degree of risk assumed. But how much of the variation in observed profits is attributable to risk differences is not easily ascertained, in part because of the difficulty we have in measuring risk. Even more important is the fact that the issue is obscured by data that reflect the presence of monopoly profits for some firms.

Be that as it may, the question is an important one which must be addressed in any attempt to estimate the costs of a particular action or project. When it is addressed, it is usually called the *problem of calculating a rate of return on investment*.

Money expenditures on inputs purchased and used in production are not so easily estimated in some cases either. The cost of labor, for example, would seem to be the money price of labor times the quantity used. Yet the project itself, by increasing the demand for labor could push up the price for labor. This could happen very easily in the short-run. In the long-run, if markets are working properly, there should be a supply adjustment which brings the wage back down to its "long-term equilibrium level." If people are responsive to wage rates in their job decisions, they should move towards those jobs where wages are highest. Yet, there are circumstances in which labor demands increase and wage rates rise and stay above their earlier level over the long-run; or, as the economist would put it, economic rents arise.

Consider, for example, a labor input that is highly specialized and, as a consequence, is limited in supply. Or go further and assume the supply of this type of labor is fixed. If its demand is increased as a consequence of our project, its price will be bid up and will remain at the new higher level. When supply is fixed, a rise in price is inevitable and the difference between the price before and after is generally called *rent*.

Short-run adjustment in input prices and the realization of economic rents can make a difference. If we seek to estimate the labor costs of a project, for example, we might be tempted to use current wage rate information as a basis for estimating future labor costs. Yet, by doing so, we could be underestimating these costs. This would happen if the wage rate rose and rents emerged as a consequence of the project. The probability of this happening for most projects, however, is not believed to be very high. Inputs are more substitutable for one another than are products. Granted this, a project that increases the demand for a particular product and hence the demand for the inputs used in production, will have a greater impact on the price of the final product than on the price of the inputs. Costs may thus be reasonably estimated in many cases by use of current market information on the prices of inputs, adjusted, of course, for inflation.

If product prices fluctuate substantially in response to a change in demand or supply, there can be problems in estimating the benefits from a proposed project. Benefits are, in the final analysis, satisfactions from consumption which could be measured in terms of utility. Yet, if our concern is with the satisfactions derived from consumption by more than one, the difficulties in making interpersonal comparisons of utility preclude the use of utility measure as a means of estimating these satisfactions. We must rely instead on information about the willingness and ability to pay provided by the market.

Some indication of willingness and ability of individuals to pay is given by dollars spent. Yet, the benefits from consumption cannot be fully equated with dollars spent for reasons that warrant discussion.

Market demand, as noted earlier, can be represented as a straight line which slopes downward and to the right—see Figure 6.7.

Given knowledge of this demand and a market price, we can make statements about quantity demanded and total dollars spent. If the market price is *OP,* for example, quantity purchased will be *OQ*—see Figure 6.7—and dollars spent will be price times quantity, or *OPRQ*—see Figure 6.7. Note, however, that the

Figure 6.7

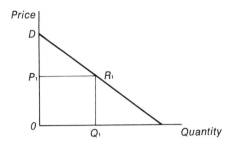

people who purchase OQ at price OP, and hence spend $OPRQ$ dollars, would have been willing to spend $ODRQ$ dollars in making this purchase.

In the normal case, there is a difference between the maximum amount people are willing to pay for a given quantity of a product and the amount they actually pay. That difference shows up in Figure 6.7 as the areas of the triangle PDR. That difference is also known as *consumers' surplus* in economics.

The concept of consumers' surplus is an important one in welfare economics and provides the conceptual foundation for benefit calculations in cost-benefit studies. The reason is easy to illustrate. Suppose our concern is with an investment project, such as a new highway. The benefits can be reflected in price, either directly in the form of a lower cost journey to work, or indirectly in terms of time saved in that journey. Suppose for the sake of simplicity that all projected benefits are reflected in price. Specifically, the proposed project lowers journey-to-work costs from OP to OP_1—see Figure 6.8.

Figure 6.8

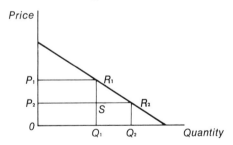

It is clear from Figure 6.8 that knowledge of what happens to the price or cost of the journey to work will not tell the full story about the benefits of the new highway to the community. Consumers' surplus obviously increases. If the price is reduced, the difference between the amount now paid for quantity OQ and the maximum amount consumers are willing to pay for this quantity increases by P_1PRS. Yet because the price is lower, quantity demanded increases, which gives rise to a further difference between the maximum amount consumers are willing to pay and what they actually pay. This additional difference is denoted by RR_1S in Figure 6.8.

What this implies, of course, is that price information alone will not suffice in making estimates of the benefits from economic projects. We rely on market information because it provides us with the best index of the benefits to the community, stemming from particular kinds of economic activity. But we cannot rely solely on historical and projected price information. Our concern must be with what happens to consumer surplus, and this implies knowledge of the response of demanders to the change in price we bring about by particular investments, that is, knowledge of the demand curve.

Cost Benefit Calculations: Some Numerical Examples

Investment Project in the Private Sector of the Economy   Business firms are constantly engaged in making cost-benefit calculations concerned with investment decisions that are fundamental to the growth and survival of the firm. As noted previously, these calculations are considered by businessmen to provide the firm with estimates of the expected profitability of proposed investments. That profitability, in turn, is a function of the cost and benefit factors associated with the proposed projects.

Consider, by way of illustration, the investment in a new drill press. The analysis of the potential profitability of such a press would typically focus on expected income flows from use, its costs and the market rate of interest. Expected income flows are, of course, additions to the net income of the firm, stemming from the use of the drill press in production. To get these figures, estimates must first be made of the physical productivity of the drill press over its expected life. Suppose the engineers of the firm estimate that this press will add 100 units per year to total output for a period of five years and that the market researchers forecast these units will be sold for $5 each—their current price. Gross income stemming from the use of the drill press will thus be $500 per year for five years— see Table 6.3.

Table 6.3

Net Income from the Use of X

Year	Gross Income	Production Costs	Net Income
1	$500	$400	$100
2	500	400	100
3	500	400	100
4	500	400	100
5	500	400	100

Of course, all of this income cannot be attributed to the drill press. Capital is combined with labor and other inputs in production, the cost of which must be covered by the revenues from the sale of the added output. All such expenditures must be deducted from gross income, leaving a total we call *net income*. Suppose the only input is labor and the annual production requirement is 100 units at $4 per unit. With labor costs of $400 per year, the net income stemming from the use of this press is $100 per year for five years—see Table 6.3.

Much has been assumed to this point. Certainty of outcome is one assumption. Prices of the product and the labor inputs that are unaffected by the investment itself are two more. Questions can be raised about these assumptions, for their inclusion—as should be evident from the discussion above—can have bearing on the answers we get from this part of the calculations. Uncertainty is, of course, difficult to deal with. The price assumptions, on the other hand, might not be too far off the market if the firm is only a relatively small part of the total structure of industry.

Suppose we set aside these questions and take these estimates of net income as being reasonable. Suppose further that the cost of the drill press is $425. It appears that the firm should purchase the press, since the estimated benefits—expected net income—exceed the costs by $75. Yet to argue this way ignores the influence of time on business decisions.

While decision-makers in the private sector may not bring their time preference to bear directly on the investment decision, if they are rational, time will be taken into account in that decision. If there are loan funds or financial markets, there will be opportunities to take the $425 required to purchase the drill press and "put it to work elsewhere." Invested in some financial asset, for example, it will return more than the original amount with the passage of time. If these funds were invested for a period of five years at an interest rate of six percent, for example, they would build up to over $500 by the end of that time.

What the decision maker must do at this point is usually expressed as *discounting that net income stream to arrive at its present value.* Discounting in this sense means adjusting that income stream to reflect the fact that most of it will be received in the future and hence, because of impatience, is not worth as much as it would be were it all available today.

To discount the future, of course, implies discount rate. Suppose that rate were 6 percent. Following standard calculation procedures, the present value of the net income stream of the drill press would be $421.24—see Table 6.4. If the cost of the drill press is $425 and the firm is in business to make money, the press would not be purchased. The decision rule involved, if profit maximization is the aim of the firm, is that

$$PV \geq C \qquad\qquad (6.1)$$

where PV is the present value of the estimated net income stream and C is the cost of the drill press. Since the cost exceeds present value, the acquisition of the press is not consistent with profit maximization.

Yet is this a proper decision? It can easily be shown to depend on the discount rate applied. Suppose, for example, that we applied a 5 percent rate? Or, a 4 percent rate? The standard calculation with these rates yields $432.94 and $445.18 respectively, amounts that exceed the cost of the drill press. A rational decision is now one of purchasing that press.

What should we do? Purchase or forget about that drill press? Obviously, the choice of a discount is important and this decision is generally viewed as a matter of choosing an interest rate. Since the funds used in purchasing the press—if they are internally generated—can earn interest, the rate they can earn might seem appropriate. But what rate should that be? There are a great many interest rates; there is no one interest rate, rather there is a structure of rates.

Table 6.4

Present Value of Net Income Stream
at Different Rates of Discount

Estimate of Income	Discounted at 4%	5%	6%
$100 at end of year 1	$ 96.15	$ 95.24	$ 94.34
$100 at end of year 2	92.46	90.70	89.00
$100 at end of year 3	88.90	86.35	83.90
$100 at end of year 4	85.48	82.27	79.21
$100 at end of year 5	82.19	78.35	74.73
Total of Present Values	$445.18	$432.94	$421.24

One answer would be to use the "pure" rate of interest, or a rate that is free from any considerations of risk. Rates on government securities are usually taken to approximate the pure rate. Yet it might be that the drill press, if purchased, would be used in a setting in which there was a good deal of risk. Risk in earnings capacity is generally reflected in our financial markets in higher rates of return or interest. If a high risk firm, for example, seeks to borrow funds in the money and capital markets, it will have to pay more for the funds than the low risk firm.

What this implies, of course, is that in selecting a discount rate, the firm has to be mindful of the risks that are inherent in the operations of the business. If there is much risk in those operations, the use of the pure rate of interest as the discounting factor is wrong. There should be some kind of risk premium added to that rate. Suppose, for example, that the pure rate of interest were 4 percent and the firm considering the purchase of the drill press operates in a very risky setting. Suppose further this firm decided to add a 2 percent premium to the pure rate to arrive at a discount factor. When the discount factor—now 6 percent —is applied to the expected net income stream as it is in Table 6.6, the present value of that press is shown to be less than it cost. As a consequence, it is not acquired; its costs exceed the benefits from use. If, on the other hand, the firm is exposed to very little risk, the pure rate of interest might be appropriate as a discount factor and, if applied, would yield a decision to purchase.

While that matter of calculating the expected profitability of investment is more involved and complicated than these few remarks imply, the basic elements of that decision are here. These elements, in turn, can be easily fitted into a cost-benefit framework and the project can be evaluated in terms of its impact on the welfare of the community, if that welfare is viewed according to the economic criteria discussed earlier. Whether firms in the private sector make decisions that are consistent with these criteria, particularly in an urban setting, is an important part of the subject matter of urban problems and cost-benefit calculations can provide useful inputs into the judgments we make. How this is so, however, can be best illustrated by considering an example of a cost benefit calculation involving a project that is more public in character.

Urban Redevelopment and Cost-Benefit Analysis　　Most American cities have a long history, and with time go depreciation, obsolescence, and oftentimes deterioration. When buildings in a city wear out or become obsolete, so long as the city lives, the possibility of redevelopment exists.

Redevelopment, of course, can be defined in various ways to include all or parts of a process that can encompass land acquisition and razing on through new construction and maintenance. It goes on continuously in many parts of most cities. It apparently does not go on enough in the private sector of the economy, however, because for over twenty-five years we have had a public program concerned with renewal and redevelopment in our cities. Since the public program has been concerned primarily with land acquisition and demolition activity, it is here where the private sector has apparently failed.

Consider first, redevelopment in the sense of land acquisition and razing activity as it might be initiated by a private developer, and assume all benefits and costs are incurred during a one-year period. The latter assumption says, in effect, that we do not have to worry about discounting the results.

The costs of redevelopment as the term is used here are land acquisition and razing costs. Suppose these costs for a central city site covering a city block are $40 million. For what reason, if any, might some developer be willing to incur these costs? In other words, what is the nature of the benefits?

Presumably, if the land is prepared for redevelopment in this way, its value is enhanced. The act of redevelopment should put the land into its highest and best use, which implies it will be worth more. With markets as the means of allocating land use within the city, this means the price of that land should rise.

Will there be private redevelopment? If the developer's aim is profit maximization, there will be redevelopment only if it is anticipated that the price of the land after it is redeveloped will increase by $40 million plus an amount equal to the profit necessary to get the developer to commit himself, his energies, and his resources to the project.

These kind of decisions are made continuously and sometimes they are positive in that the private developer decides to initiate the project. But apparently too many times in the past the decision was no, particularly in the central city of many metropolitan areas.

A federal government program designed to subsidize this part of the redevelopment process was initiated in 1949. Cities were provided with the opportunity to facilitate urban redevelopment with the assistance of federal money. Whether redevelopment is done through the private sector or the public sector, however, the concern in evaluating the project remains with its potential costs and benefits.

Let us suppose that land acquisition and razing costs of this project remain at $40 million, but that the land value after redevelopment only increases by $20 million. Now there is no incentive for the private developer.

Might there nevertheless be some reason for bothering with the property and the project? The answer, of course, is yes, if there are market externalities which take the form of positive "spillover" effects. But will there be these spillover effects that make this a worthwhile venture? There could be. The redevelopment of the land in question could, if it is strategically located, alter the land values of adjacent areas. It could do this in any number of ways. It might, for example, increase the traffic flows through these areas in ways that increased their commercial potential. Or redevelopment might work in ways to improve social conditions, say by reducing the crime rate in these areas. These are external benefits of redevelopment of value to the community and would not be realized in the absence of some kind of collective action such as a subsidy.

Spillovers of the sort, since they are benefits accruing from the project, must be considered as project benefits. They must be measured and added to the direct benefits reflected in the increase in the value of the redeveloped land.

It is, of course, one thing to say that spillover benefits must be included in our estimate of the total benefits of a project. It is quite another to make estimates of them. Suppose, however, that these estimates can be made and they reveal the spillover benefits to be $25 million. The balance sheet of the project would thus look something like:

Table 6.5

Redevelopment Costs	Redevelopment Benefits	
	Direct	*Spillover*
$40 million	$20 million	$25 million

If we assume that $45 million in total benefits are sufficient to induce private redevelopment, one could argue that the government should subsidize this project by an amount equal to the spillover benefits and thus make the land available to private developers who should be willing to pay $15 million for it.

Clearly, when considering a public project, special attention must be paid to spillovers that can be reflected on both the cost and benefit side. This is not to say that they should not be considered in the cost-benefit calculations, although there is no incentive for the private developer to do so. They are, however, likely to be the core of the calculations made for a public project. If the major economic warrant for a public program is the presence of market externalities, those externalities or spillovers should form an important part of any cost-benefit calculations made to answer the all-important question of whether that project represents an efficient use of the community's resources.

REFERENCES

Buchanan, J. and Stubblebine, W. "Externality." *Economica.* 29 (1962): 371–84.

Feldstein, M. "The Social Time Preference Discount Rate in Cost-Benefit Analysis." *Economic Journal.* 74 (1964): 360–79.

*Graaf, J. *Theoretical Welfare Economics.* New York: Cambridge University Press, 1967.

Lipsey, R. and Lancaster, K. "The General Theory of Second Best." *Review of Economic Studies.* 24 (1956): 11–37.

Little, I. *A Critique of Welfare Economics.* New York: Oxford University Press, 1960.

*Mishan, E. "The Postwar Literature on Externalities: An Interpretative Essay." *The Journal of Economic Literature.* 9 (1971): 1–28.

*Prest, A. and Turvey, R. "Cost-Benefit Analysis: A Survey." *Economic Journal.* 75 (1965): 683–735.

Rothenburg, J. *The Measurement of Social Welfare.* Englewood Cliffs, N.J.: Prentice-Hall, 1961.

---

*This chapter draws heavily from the writings of Graaf, Mishan and Prest.

Urbanization and the Urban Hierarchy

SUMMARY

Urbanization in the sense of an increasing proportion of the nation's population living in cities is a pervasive fact throughout our history. American cities have grown in number and size for reasons that can be best investigated with the aid of the scale economy and transportation cost concepts discussed in chapters 2 and 3.

In its earlier stages of urbanization, the nation's city-building activity was concentrated in and around transshipment points on the Eastern seaboard, and, to a lesser extent, in central points for exchange further inland. The industrial revolution accelerated the urbanization process. New methods of production dramatically increased and concentrated geographically the scale of operations of many firms. Much of this occurred in the United States' Midwest, which ultimately became known as the industrial heartland. Minerals of certain kinds that were found in abundance in heartland states became important inputs in the production process, and firms were pulled to these locations.

In more recent times, the movement toward cities has continued, although for different reasons. Urbanization economies account for some of these recent moves. That many people were living in cities was also a factor. The economy has been shifting toward the production and consumption of services, which means a shift towards items that have a market orientation with respect to location. Manufacturing, while declining in relative importance, continued to attract people to cities, although the new higher technology forms of manufacturing began pulling people toward the West and Southwest rather than to cities in the industrial heartland.

What the future holds in store for the nation's cities is uncertain. Impending technical change in transportation, communications, and materials use suggests a technology that will harbor strong dispersive forces. This technology could work itself out in ways such that cities, as we know them today, will disappear. This is not likely to happen in the foreseeable future, however. Urban history strongly suggests that cities do not come and go in a whimsical fashion. There are also reasons in the fixed site character of investment, our energy problems, and future population growth for believing that it will not happen for some time, if indeed it happens at all.

If urbanism is equated with cityness in the sense of population density, urbanization is the process through which proportionately more of the nation's population comes to live in cities or areas of high population density. So understood, urbanization is a process that has been underway in the United States since its inception. Census data, shown earlier and reproduced below—see Table 7.1—

Table 7.1

*Proportion of Population
Living in Urban Areas
1790–1970*

1790	5.1
1800	6.1
1810	7.3
1820	7.2
1830	8.8
1840	10.8
1850	15.3
1860	19.8
1870	25.7
1880	28.2
1890	35.1
1900	39.7
1910	45.7
1920	51.2
1930	56.2
1940	56.5
1950	59.6
1960	63.1
Current Definitions	
1950	64.0
1960	69.9
1970	73.5

Source: U.S. Bureau of Census

reveal the persistence and pervasiveness of this movement into cities. This is a fact worth pondering. It is also a fact that is losing its force as the nation approaches the upper limit of urbanization.

The subject matter in this chapter is the urbanization of the United States. The principal concern is with the history of that process, including its hierarchical aspects. A secondary concern is with the question of urbanization as a future dynamic force in the United States. Just what can be said about these matters if we try to fit the available facts into a framework fashioned from the theory discussed above? What economic facts best help account for the facts of urbanization here? And what light, if any, do these facts shed on the future course of urbanization here? These are the concerns of this chapter.

HISTORY

Urbanization and the Hierarchy of Cities in the United States

Historical analysis implies a concern with facts. But what facts? There is much in chapters 2 and 3 that helps in answering this question.

A concern with urbanization or city building is, according to chapter 2, a concern with cost advantages and disadvantages associated with being located in close geographic proximity to one another. These advantages stem from an assortment of scale economies which were discussed in chapter 2 under the heading of internal, industry, and urbanization economies. Historical facts about these economies are thus relevant to an historical analysis of urbanization in America, as are those which concern diseconomies of scale.

The way in which scale economies contributed to urbanization and the development of our urban hierarchy, however, was closely linked to the transportation and communications technology and investments of the time. Scale economies and distance frictions, as discussed in chapters 2 and 3, are countervailing forces whose interaction has important bearing on the shape and form of a nation's system of cities. Thus, historical facts about the nation's transportation and communication system are important.

Finally, although cities may be largely the outcome of decisions of profit-maximizing firms responding to cost advantages associated with concentrating production geographically, that these firms choose to locate in cities is dependent on the likes and dislikes of those who consume their output. Living and consuming the menu of goods and services produced in cities implies certain things about consumer demands. Facts which tell us something about these demands should contribute to an historical analysis of urbanization and the evolution of the urban hierarchy in the United States.

Urbanization in the United States: Historical Patterns and Causes   Urbanization in the United States, according to the notions set forth in chapter 2, was the consequence of a set of facts or events that fostered economies of scale in production which, given the transportation and communication facilities of the time, could best be realized by firms in close geographic proximity to one another. What facts were these?

The question cannot be answered with precision. The history of urbanization in the United States is a reflection of events that occurred in a diverse and complex milieu. Unambiguous facts are not easy to garner in such a setting. Nor is it clear that those identified can be linked together as neatly as these few remarks imply. Sensible statements, however, can be made about historical patterns and causes of urbanization in America.

It is clear from Table 7.1 that the nation was far from urbanized at the time of the first census. Only about 5 percent of its population lived in what the Census Bureau classified as urban. These were, for the most part, people living in cities along the eastern seaboard, such as New York, Boston, Philadelphia, Charleston, and Baltimore—see Table 7.2. The agglomerations at these locations were a reflection of the economic forces of the times. The nation, as it was developing economically, specialized in certain agricultural commodities it shipped

Table 7.2

Urbanization of Population in the U.S.
by Census Region: 1790–1970
(Proportion of Population Living in Urban Areas)

	Northeast	South	North Central	West
1790	8.1	2.1	—	—
1800	9.3	3.0	—	—
1810	10.9	4.1	0.9	—
1820	11.0	4.6	1.1	—
1830	14.2	5.3	2.6	—
1840	18.5	6.7	3.9	—
1850	26.5	8.3	9.2	6.4
1860	35.7	9.6	13.9	16.0
1870	44.3	12.2	20.8	25.8
1880	50.8	12.2	24.2	30.2
1890	59.0	16.3	33.1	37.0
1900	61.1	18.0	38.6	39.9
1910	71.8	22.5	45.1	47.9
1920	75.5	28.1	52.3	51.8
1930	77.6	34.1	57.9	58.4
1940	76.6	36.7	58.4	58.5
1950	75.4	44.6	61.1	59.9
1960	72.8	52.7	63.9	66.1
Current Definitions				
1950	79.5	48.6	64.1	69.5
1960	80.2	58.5	68.7	77.7
1970	80.5	64.0	71.3	82.6

Source: U.S. Bureau of the Census

abroad to European nations in exchange for a relatively wide range of goods. Significantly, these shipments from the American farmer to the European consumer required movement over land and/or inland waterways and then on to vessels capable of moving over the high seas. Because of the transportation technology and the terrain over which these goods moved, there were transshipment points in the journey and these points—that is, where the transfers were made—ultimately became the nation's New Yorks, Philadelphias, and Charlestons.

Since specialization was involved in the work of transferring exports from one means of transportation to the other, there was a basis for spatial agglomeration, given the relatively high communication and transportation costs of the time. Handling and distributing the imports that came in at these points also required specialized activity and hence a basis for the spatial concentration of economic activity. Moreover, the people involved in these exporting and importing activities were compelled to live near where they worked, which meant further clustering around these activity points. The seeds of urbanization were there. Still, the great bulk of economic activity, at the time, was located outside these cities.

Rapid population growth, largely through in-migration from abroad, helped spur the initial westward movement of the nation's population. While contained initially by natural barriers such as the Appalachian Mountains, the extension of inland waterway transportation routes helped the population push into the heartland of the continent. The opening up of the West to the economic exploitation of its natural resources gave rise to specialized activities and exchange which, in turn, fostered geographic concentrations of activity in places like St. Louis, New Orleans, and Cincinnati. Significantly, each of these cities was strategically located on important inland waterways. These developments explain most of the gradual urbanization which occurred up to 1840—see Table 7.1. Following 1840, the nation began urbanizing much more rapidly.

The initial burst was associated with the industrial revolution. While the transition from an agrarian to an industrial society did not happen overnight, the biggest part of the change occurred during the last half of the 19th century and got its start in the decade of the 1840s. The revolution, itself, consisted of innovations that reflected in the nation's agriculture and transportation industries, as well as in the birth of its manufacturing activities.

The advances in agriculture, that is, the application of certain important new techniques of farming, brought the necessary increases in farm output per worker to allow people to shift into nonfarm pursuits. The opportunities to do so were there with the rapid growth of new industry. The core of this development was the implementation of mass production methods which incorporated power-driven machinery, a dramatic departure from the "hand-tool" methods that had been the central mode of nonfarm production for literally centuries on end.

These new production methods had important implications with respect to both the scale and spatial aspects of production. For reasons discussed at length in chapter 2, the specialization inherent in this new technology dramatically increased the scale of operations of the firm. The many parts of what was now a substantially lengthened production process also had to be in close geographic proximity to one another. The alternative was a process that had prohibitive transportation and/or communication costs. The introduction of mass production techniques thus concentrated production in geographic space.

Manufacturing cities began to appear at various points, cities that in their earlier stages of development were properly characterized as "company" towns. This initial clustering of economic activity and people, concentrated as it was on the production of manufactured goods that were exported, generated incomes that began to have multiplying effects on the economy of the city. Nonbasic or service-type activity began to develop in and around this core of activity when certain threshold levels with respect to city size were reached. The appearance of such industry, in turn, added layers of activity onto the city, reinforcing its growth trend. In some cases, further impetus to growth was provided by the cost advantages some firms experienced when those in the same industry located near one another. While the exact set of circumstances in which they flourished is not well known, industry economies of scale are generally believed to have stimulated the growth of certain cities.

All this took place in a national setting in which there were significant transportation developments taking place. A part of the transportation revolution consisted of improvements in waterborne transportation associated with the development of canals and the invention of the steamship. More important was the emergence of the steam railroads which dramatically enhanced our ability to move both people and goods over land.

How goods and people moved over water was largely determined by the geography of the inland water system. The development of more effective overland routes of transportation, on the other hand, provided more flexibility, at least until the investments into the fixed path land routes were made. While the layout of these routes was the outcome of a great many conflicting forces, the most important of these were economic and stemmed from the requirements of the new technology in manufacturing. Manufacturing activity at that time required certain inputs—e.g., minerals—which were not evenly distributed in geographic space and were costly to move. This fact provided real impetus for spatial concentrations in economic activity at input locations.

Transportation developments, along with the development of mass production methods, in effect, provided the impetus for the development of the mideastern and midwestern parts of the nation, the so-called industrial heartland. This, among other things, helped spawn the nation's Pittsburghs, Clevelands, and Buffalos, and provided impetus for continued growth of its New Yorks, Bostons, St. Louises, and Chicagos. The growth of these cities accounted for much of the urbanization of the nation during the last half of the 19th century, which was substantial—see Table 7.1.

The urbanization of America continued to be dominated by industrialization as the nation entered the twentieth century, on through to the Great Depression of the 1930s. Much city building during these years was associated with the construction of plants to house some new manufacturing activity, increasingly more of which was located in the western and southwestern part of the nation. Many cities in the Midwest and East continued to grow, but for reasons that had more to do with urbanization economies than industrialization.

The process of urbanization virtually stopped in the depression years of the 1930s—see Table 7.1. It began anew during World War II and continued on in the postwar period at a modest pace. By the time we reached the post-World War II era, industrialization was no longer the major reason for movement into our cities. The U.S. economy, in fact, was beginning to move into the postindustrial world, that is, a world in which services dominate the economy.

Some growth in the nation's urban population following World II was a consequence of the migration of low-income blacks and whites from the South to industrial cities in the North. Technical change which displaced much black farm labor in the South and the decline in the demand for coal mined in the Appalachians created severe unemployment problems in these places. Unemployment, combined with the circulation of information about the economic promise of the North, underlie the movement of a significant number of southerners to northern cities in the 1940s and the 1950s, particularly to those cities in the nation's industrial heartland. This movement continued in the 1960s, only now more of the migrants seemed to head toward the eastern seaboard cities.

While this happened, a number of cities in the states of California, Arizona, Texas, and Florida virtually exploded with growth. More recently, there have been signs of a growth explosion in a number of southern cities, such as Atlanta. While these southern developments are partly a consequence of a regional redistribution of manufacturing, some of it had to do with amenities. Amenities also had much to do with the rapid growth of western and southwestern cities. Phoenix, Los Angeles, and San Jose grew as rapidly as they did, in part, because they were pleasant places to live. They had an abundance of amenities.

Discussions of amenities as a locating force, as noted in chapter 3, usually focus on physical features of the site, such as climate, topography, and propinquity to water. While such a view may be too restrictive for in-depth analysis, many of our most rapidly growing cities in recent years have been in places where the climate is pleasant, the topography is generally attractive and/or water is at hand.

This correlation is informative. Most would accept the argument that the geographic distribution of the nation's amenity resources explains much of the interregional migration pattern of the elderly. The movement to Florida, Arizona, and California has been a move away from what many consider to be the uninviting climates of the Midwest and East. It is less evident that amenity notions help explain the recent plant locations of a profit-maximizing firm in California or Arizona. Yet, these notions can contribute to the explanation of what happened in the Southwest and West over the past twenty-five years, if, in addition, we recognize the growth in importance of "footloose" industries.

The character of many production processes has changed over the years. One important aspect of this change recently has been the emergence of the so-called "high" technology operations; for example, operations in the aerospace industry. An important characteristic of such operations is that labor—particularly professional and highly skilled labor—is a crucial input. Since labor of this kind is, in general, highly mobile, the location options of the firm are many. The importance of the labor component in production combined with the mobility of that labor, in effect, loosens the attachment of these firms from sites where the markets and/or materials are. Such firms are footloose in their operations, and many of them have apparently chosen locations blessed with an abundance of amenity resources.

Was this a reasonable choice for a profit-maximizing firm? It could have been because of the impact of amenity resources on operating costs. Aerospace firms, of course, could have chosen to concentrate their investment in the northern tip of the state of Minnesota or in the upper reaches of the state of Maine. The wage bill incurred to attract professional people to such places, however, would probably have been much higher than was necessary to get them to come to San Jose, San Diego, or Phoenix. With the wage bill as the dominant cost component, it is easy to see how operating costs would be lower and profit higher in sunny California, if professional people really do prefer sunshine to rain and snow. While not all high technology activity is found in places with temperate climates, beautiful beaches, and desert sunsets, a good deal of it is. This, no doubt, is partly a consequence of these amenities which, in turn, were reflected in operating costs.

Significantly, most high technology investment is in or near some city. While people may prefer the West and Southwest to the East and Midwest, they also prefer living in cities to living in rural areas. The high technology firms which provided the employment opportunities, required propinquity to certain kinds of resources found in cities, e.g., universities, libraries, and business service firms. Transportation costs, along with prevailing patterns of consumption, continued to make the probability of finding the good life highest in the city. It was just that these new forms of industry pulled people into different cities from those that had grown and prospered in the past.

At the time high technology firms began to flourish, the service sector was expanding rapidly. We began our entry into the postindustrial era. Services such as automobile servicing, personal care services, food services, and medical care services became important items of consumption, as did the consumption of a wide assortment of governmental services. These are, significantly, items of consumption that can be supplied at most sites without real cost differences. They are also items that customers are usually not willing to travel great distances to consume. Thus, they are items with a market orientation with respect to location which, according to central place notions discussed in chapter 3, would reinforce the existing urban settlement pattern.

The growth of the service sector in the economy did reinforce the trend of urbanization in the United States, although not by as much as these few remarks imply. Not all of the services we consume can be produced with inputs that are ubiquitous. Some recreational services, for example, require inputs that are localized. Interesting topography and temperate climate are what many seek in their moments of recreation. These are not common elements in nature. While we may be able, through public power projects, to alter the topography in ways that enhance the recreational attributes of certain places, the bodies of water we create will not be at our doorstep; nor do they really rival many of those found in nature. Some public and private investment in recreation has, of course, been made with a view toward serving certain regional populations, meeting with considerable success in many instances. In the process, they have helped to develop links between the metropolitan areas they are designed to serve and the inter-metropolitan area periphery in which the recreation facility is located. Much recreation investment, however, is in places with "natural" advantages, and growth in the demand for recreational services provided by these places has altered urban settlement patterns in ways consistent with notions of amenity.

Finally, we must consider the impact of those much talked-about diseconomies and negative market externalities in our cities, particularly in the larger ones. Diseconomies, of course, add to private costs; negative externalities can also add to private costs and make the city an unpleasant place in which to work and play in other respects. Diseconomies and negative externalities are thus conditions which could cause movement away from the city. If operating costs are increased because of diseconomies and negative externalities that come with increased city size, some firms might find profits at a maximum at other locations. Profit-maximizing behavior implies movement to these locations.

There is evidence that firms, in addition to moving away from the central cities into the metropolitan periphery, have been moving away from the nation's larger metropolitan areas. Growth in recent years has been concentrated in some of the nation's medium-sized and smaller cities. The interstate highway system has also made it feasible to locate plant facilities away from cities, in rural settings, and some firms have built plants in these places. The location of most of these plants, however, is not really very far away from some urban center. It is possible, for example, for employees of these plants to maintain urban links by living in some urban center and many apparently choose to do so.

How much of this movement can be explained by newly emerging diseconomies and negative externalities in the nation's largest cities is a question not easily answered. It is also a question best addressed in chapter 14 when the issue of city size is taken up.

How all of this affects urbanization depends on how we choose to delineate our urban areas. By most definitions, much of this movement is from one urban setting to another; some of it is not. To the extent that it isn't, such movement might be considered as symptomatic of a levelling off of the urbanization process. But is it levelling off?

This is another question with no easy answer. Clearly, we approach a point of urban maturity as the proportion of the population living in cities approaches 100 percent. When that point might be reached is, in fact, a question more appropriately considered below when the future is discussed.

The American Urban Hierarchy as a System of Systems of Cities   The urban hierarchy, as discussed in chapter 3, is a system of systems of cities. Groups of cities, as they emerge through the urbanization process, are the outcome of the functioning of several distinct systems. One of these is a system much like the one described in central place theory. Given dispersion of the population, ubiquitous resources, transportation costs that are not prohibitive, and a technology that generates scale economies, firms responding to market forces will locate in ways consistent with central place notions. Such a pattern or hierarchy of cities can be described in terms of such characteristics as number, city size groups, distance from one another, and industry composition.

American cities cannot be neatly fitted into simple categories derived from any one or a combination of these characteristics. There are many reasons for this, not the least of which is the fact that per unit costs of production are not the same all over. Still, if we look at the broad sweep of American urban history and try to make general statements about the emerging urban hierarchy, central place notions are helpful.

While the New Yorks, Bostons, and Baltimores were located along the Atlantic seaboard and grew as large as they did in part because of our trade with Europe and the available transportation network, there were other cities. Cities were, in fact, springing up all over the East and Midwest as the population pushed westward. The economy at the time was primarily agrarian; hence the population was spread out. While people were more self-sufficient then, there was agricultural specialization and exchange; and such exchange, according to central place notions, implied concentration in the form of trading centers. Furthermore, there was also some nonfarm specialization and therefore the exchange of nonfarm goods. The spatial dimensions of the demand for these goods also implied central points of production and exchange. All this points to an urban settlement pattern with some of the features that characterize a hypothetical system of central places.

Many cities which sprang up during our early history were central places in this sense. To say this leaves many facts known about these cities unexplained, but does go to the core of some important matters, which, if understood, provide a reasonable starting point for any in-depth study of the nation's urban hierarchy at this point in its history.

Then came the industrial revolution which overlaid another system on the first. As noted above, the most significant feature of this revolution was the emergence of a production process that required the use of inputs—minerals—which were unevenly distributed in geographic space and costly to move. This added another dimension to the location decision. Costs, particularly the costs of transporting material inputs from their source to the plant, became important. Decisions concerning the location of new investment now became, for many firms, a matter of evaluating the pull of the market in relation to the pull of materials used in production. Since many of these materials lost weight in production and were costly in transport, firms using them—growing in number—built plants near the materials location.

The regional implications of these developments are clear. Much economic activity was attracted to regions with the sites of minimum transportation cost. This is not to say that all manufacturing firms located at these sites. Still, most of them could not be too far away if they had a transportation orientation and aimed to maximize profits. While the exact location of Detroit may have been an "accident," the fact that the automobile industry found a site in the heart of the nation's industrial heartland, rather than the Black Hills of South Dakota, was not.

Industrialization in this sense led to more geographic concentration in production, which meant the building of new cities or the growth of existing ones. Since the focal point of the locational pull was the industrial heartland, it spawned the nation's Pittsburghs Clevelands, and Buffalos and provided impetus for the continued growth of its Chicagos and New Yorks.

The industrial revolution, in effect, superimposed a different system on the earlier one. Rather than following the market, industrial firms often found it necessary to locate at sites considerable distances away from their customers. The industrial revolution thus distorted the earlier settlement patterns. No longer could the nation's system of cities be characterized as one that had the nodal and hierarchical properties of a hypothetical system derivable from central place notions. This is not to say that the spatial dimension of demand had no impact on the urban hierarchy. But market demands became less important relative to newly emerging cost factors. The nation's system of cities at mid-nineteenth century was constituted by two major subsystems with the one that had cost elements at its core exerting the dominant influence.

Again, note that making these statements provides background that will not serve us very well in answering a number of questions that can be raised about the hierarchy of cities that was evolving in the latter part of the nineteenth century and the early part of the twentieth century. What making these statements does is suggest a framework within which an in-depth study of urban history during this period might be carried out, and from which answers to these questions might be forthcoming.

The more recent dimensions of change in the economy that had impact on the urban hierarchy are those technical changes that gave us high technology industry and the sociotechnical changes that increased the importance of the consumption of services.

High technology industries, in their search for production sites as noted above tend to choose locations that have an abundance of amenity resources. In the recent past this has often meant locations in regions with warmer climates. The regional dimension of the urban hierarchy has changed as a consequence. It has done so because of factors, as discussed above, that operated largely through the cost side of the market. Many high technology firms chose to locate in California, for example, because this was a minimum cost location in terms of the most important of its input, i.e., highly skilled labor. Traditional notions of location, as discussed in chapter 3, thus provide insights into the recent urbanization of the West, Southwest, and South, just as they helped explain the urbanization of the nation's industrial heartland earlier. The urbanization of California, Texas, Arizona, and Florida, however, was not a consequence of accessibility to mineral resources that were important in production. More important to the explanation of the spatial distribution of high technology industry were the attributes of the site that related to the tastes and preferences of those who provided the important human inputs into this kind of production.

The recent growth in the importance of services in the economy, on the other hand, added layers onto the urban hierarchy in ways that were more consistent with central place notions. While some recreation expenditures took people to sites where there were special amenities that were a part of the natural setting, a large part of this increase in the consumption of services occurred at sites not too far distant from existing residential locations, e.g., fast food services. Since the costs of most of these services tend to be the same everywhere, the location of consumers became the dominant locating force. All this reinforced the pattern of the existing urban hierarchy and helps explain why most cities have grown over the past twenty-five to fifty years. The changing patterns of consumption reflected in the movement into the postindustrial era thus set into motion forces that affected the nation's urban hierarchy in ways that are best understood with the aid of central place notions.

As in the more distant past, there are many particular recent historical facts about cities in this hierarchy that cannot be explained with the aid of either traditional or central place notions about the location decisions of firms in the private sector of the economy. Considered as starting points for in-depth historical analyses, however, these notions could contribute much to any investigation made.

THE FUTURE

Forces of Change: Technology

While technological forecasting is, at best, a hazardous art, it is much more widely practiced now and is carried out increasingly within scientific frameworks. The forecasts which have most bearing on the likely future shape and form of the nation's hierarchy of cities are those made for transportation and communications and for materials used in production. From most forecasts made of the future technology in these areas, it is tempting to paint a picture in which the technical environment will harbor strong dispersive forces. Technology seems to be heading in directions that will result in larger cities shrinking in size and smaller ones becoming more numerous. Urbanization as we know it today may disappear.

Consider first the technical prospects for transportation. While changes in transportation will not be restricted to air travel, there could be important developments in this form of travel that will loosen the ties to sites near the routes and connecting points of the nation's network of transportation investment. The technology to do so is already here in the form of short take-off and landing and vertical take-off and landing vehicles which are with us now in the form of Twin Otters and helicopters. These are transportation forms that require less "embedded" investments than do cars, which require highways, and the supersonic jet, which requires large terminal facilities. Any substantial increase in the use of such aircraft will make many sites now off the "beaten path" potentially more accessible and therefore more competitive with sites on or near the currently embedded network of transportation routes and connecting points. The locational ties to points along that network, now quite strong, could thus be weakened and dispersal encouraged.

Ground movement could, through innovation, also become more dispersive. The hovercraft represents a step in this direction since it requires little investment embedded in the earth. The dispersing potential of such transportation forms, were they to become economically feasible and generally acceptable, might rival that of the automobile as it came to the center of the stage fifty years ago.

A more important impetus for dispersal could come through future technical developments expected in telecommunications. The impact of the communications network of urban life is recognized, if not fully understood. The payoffs from the current networks are greatest when interaction occurs in a setting in which people are in close geographic proximity to one another. Communications efficiency is thus a part of what's involved in economies of scale realized when production is concentrated in cities.

Technical developments on the communications horizon seem destined to reduce the advantage of such proximity. The technical know-how is developing that will provide the basis for the "generalization" of communications over geographic space. Much communication in our day-to-day activities now requires face-to-face contact. The development of relatively cheap broadband transmission mechanisms, however, combined with the hoped-for emergence of inexpensive, flexible, and mobile terminal equipment, suggests that we may soon be able to communicate with one another at greater distances in ways that do not lose much of what is now considered of value in face-to-face contact. While it overstates the case, much futuristic writing about communications leaves the impression that it may come to living and working where we please and traveling only for pleasure.

Future materials expected to be used in production also appear to be dispersive in their impact. Traditional basic materials such as steel, glass, ceramics, and timber are generally thought of as substances coming from one resource and being used for certain purposes. The use of such materials tends to "pull" firms to locations near sources that are unevenly distributed geographically and does so because of the weight of these materials and the fact that some of this weight is lost in production. In the past, such locations have become sites of a number of major cities.

The emerging materials technology may be changing all of this. We now consider materials as composites or structures and, by design, alter the structural elements in ways that provide materials which serve different purposes. The starting point now is a microstructure of atoms and molecules, and we think of what emerges as something that has certain structural properties governed by physical laws. The end result of this new materials technology is and will continue to be materials that serve us better by being lighter, stronger, more durable, and less bulky. It also means firms are, and will continue to become, less dependent on the location of particular natural resources since their materials needs will be increasingly satisfied by the outcome of processes that can start with any natural resource. Nature's resources, as they will be used in production, are becoming increasingly ubiquitous, which means the location options of manufacturing firms are expanding and will continue to do so in the future.

One interesting implication of the new materials technology is the possibility that it will lead to more "flexible" buildings or structures which house our various urban activities. Construction materials, have and will continue to become, lighter in weight, less bulky, and more durable. That this is so has and will continue to facilitate the movement toward industrialized construction—off-site processes of production. The productivity increases implicit in the use of such processes could reduce the impact of sunk costs on the capital replacement decisions of firms, accelerate such investments, and thus loosen the ties of production to existing locations. Equally important is the fact that these developments seem to be providing a foundation for the construction of structures that have weaker links to any given site. It may be that the mobile home of today stands as a preview of things to come in the construction industry generally. The physical plant, which is now something embedded in the earth at a particular site, may be less so over time. If so, it will enhance the ability of the system to respond to the dispersing force of technical change operating through the transportation and communications.

Forces of Stability: Technology, Energy Problems, and Future Population Growth

While urban society may, for reasons just discussed, become much less concentrated than it is today, there are reasons for doubting that it will happen in the foreseeable future. First, there is our history, which, as noted above, indicates stability in important aspects of the urban hierarchy in the face of substantial change. The force of change has impinged upon this system for years and our cities have changed. Yet, the system of cities has been quite stable in some respects, e.g., the size distribution of our cities still takes the form of a pyramid as it has for some time.

What this stability implies is that cities as we now know them do not emerge and disappear in a whimsical way. While there are ghost towns and towns that have seemingly been built overnight, any dispassionate examination of the facts will reveal most cities have a history that, for most periods, records a relatively slow but sustained path of growth and development. Revolutionary change is possible. The nation may indeed shortly become what Buckminster Fuller and others envisaged—a nation transformed into a scattered but still united village in which all knowledge is instantly available and in which work and play are detached from reliance on space. Yet, there are several reasons for believing that it is improbable, at least in the foreseeable future, that metropolitan areas like New York, Chicago, and Philadelphia will begin to lose significant amounts of population to smaller cities cropping up throughout the nation.

First, despite recent technical change and that which is seen to be in the offing, there is no compelling reason to believe that the system is fast approaching a point where it is free from the restraints that have vested important advantages to the sites of existing urban plants. That plant still represents a sunk cost which must be reckoned with in current location decisions, simply because our technology still does not generate the productivity increases in construction necessary to get us to turn our backs on existing structures. All of the socioeconomic and political factors which have constrained the force of change in construction have not disappeared. Nor do they seem about to vanish.

Second, even if important incentives for change were to appear in the construction industry, the force they would have in the future is clouded by a declining birth rate, which some believe will lead to a steady state or no population growth in the not too distant future. Currently, there is much urban expansion and it will continue on through the early 1990s. Beyond this point, if the current trend continues, the impact of population on urban society will change. Demand for additional urban plants will be less, which, in a market economy, does not represent the economic environment in which radical innovation flourishes. Profits to be made from the new products depends not only on possible price reductions and/or quality improvements, but also on the response of the buyers to such change. That response in the past has been strongest in a setting in which there have been strong demand pressures. As we move into the 1990s, the force of the demographic impetus will lessen, which will mean sagging demand pressures. The incentive for innovations will thus be reduced.

Third, the recent signs that we are beginning to undergo the transition from a society whose energy needs are largely satisfied with a base of fossil fuels, to one in which these needs will be satisfied with what are now still undetermined means, could provide the contemporary urban hierarchy with strong elements of stability. Currently, there appears to be a high probability that relative energy costs, which have increased substantially over the past several years, will continue to increase in the foreseeable future. This, of course, implies rising transportation costs.

Increases in our transportation costs could cut one of two ways. According to central place notions, an increase in transportation costs could be dispersive in its impact on the hierarchy. This would happen if the population were dispersed and consumption became much more costly because of higher transportation costs. Dispersing production facilities further would be one means of reducing these costs.

Suppose population were not dispersed; rather, it was concentrated in a hierarchy of cities. Dispersion or movement away from the cities that are a part of this hierarchy could increase the required movement of people, materials, and goods in the production process. If this happened in the face of higher transportation costs generated by our energy problems, overall costs would increase. Increasing costs would, in turn, act as a restraining influence on movement away from cities.

Since most people now live in cities, our emerging energy problems, through their impact on transportation costs, should operate in ways that restrain future movement away from cities.

Finally, it is possible that the new technology will be used in ways that reinforce existing urban spatial patterns. The urban ramifications of emerging technologies are many, only some of which were discussed above. One possibility not discussed is the application of "space-age" technology to the problem of the cities that are a part of the existing system. If that technology can be brought to bear successfully on the problems of urban poverty, housing, pollution, and education, the existing system will benefit and the incentives for radical change will be reduced.

Social Values

Suppose further technology does generate dispersive forces which have the potential to bring about radical change in our existing urban settlement patterns. Suppose, further, that the obstacles to change are reduced and that innovation can flourish in a steady state of economy. It is still by no means assured that urban America will turn out to be anything like the futuristic views of a Buckminster Fuller. There remains the question of whether people want such a world, a question which, in a free society, will have bearing on the outcome. What people want, in turn, is influenced by their values. When we look at the system as a whole, the values that are important are social values.

The question of social values must be addressed because of the possibility that they might change. Historically, there have been perceptible shifts in these values. One of the more important of these was the shift from other-worldly ideals to a more secular, pragmatic, and utilitarian view of the world. One rough application of this is the distinction between the Middle Ages and more recent times in Western culture. Life in earlier years in European countries, for example, was other-worldly in the sense that a good deal of emphasis was put on the spiritual and communistic aims of life, in sharp contrast to the most worldly aims of the contemporary European. Perhaps Communism has revived a culture concerned with more than worldly things as they are ordinarily viewed. Then too, there is the recent emergence of the so-called "counter-culture" in noncommunist states, a culture that features people who indulge in nihilistic, disillusioned, and alienated forms of social expression and behavior, with antimaterialistic overtones. Still, it seems fair to assert that the social values which currently guide the actions of the great majority of people in the noncommunist countries in the West are oriented toward this world and what it has to offer.

If this is a reasonable characterization of the primary goals of the majority of the U.S. population, the impact of future technology on urban America might well turn out to be that envisaged by Buckminster Fuller and others. If our aim is to take full advantage of what life has to offer, we will move apart if the technology of tomorrow offers opportunities for dispersal that have benefits which substantially exceed their costs. If the new transportation, communication, and material technologies turn out as expected, we could see urban settlement changes that dwarf those which materialized when the automobile and telephone substantially broadened the spatial extent of movement and communication.

Is it really reasonable to assert that many will respond to the coming gadgets of transportation and telecommunications in much the same way they did to the automobile and telephone fifty years earlier? Are people much the same as they were fifty years ago? There is room for doubt. The counter-culture, while its force has diminished, has by no means disappeared. This is important because if the values expressed by this group over the past ten years were to take hold, our collective view toward technology would change perceptibly in ways that would diminish the force of the change it precipitates. In fact, some of these notions seem to be catching on a bit as technology appears to be viewed increasingly as a mixed blessing. Still, there appears to be nothing very radical in the viewpoint of the majority about technological progress. Moreover, even if a more radical viewpoint does emerge, it is by no means clear what such a change implies with respect to the issue of dispersion or concentration in urban America. What the possibility of change in our social values does, is to add to the uncertainty which envelops our view of the future.

A Scenario of the Future

People who speculate about the future tend to take positions that stand at one of two ends of a continuum. Their conclusions tend to express the probabilities in favor of either radical change or little change. When one looks for statements that have the most scientific warrant, the conservative viewpoint generally comes through. The view is generally that the world twenty-five years from now will look more alike than different from what we have now. In light of our knowledge of urban history and what we know about the restraints to change that are built into the urban system, this would seem to be an eminently sensible view about the nation's system of cities at the turn of the century. As we look to the measures of various aspects of our system of cities, it seems highly probable that many will remain pretty much as they have been. The New Yorks, San Franciscos, and Bostons will not disappear and the urban village will not become the primary setting for our economic and other activities. The fixed site characteristics of investment will be with us for a while and will, along with our energy problems, provide the inertia that will help make it so.

Yet, it is also possible that these probabilities are changing. We are adding to our stock of knowledge in ways that could provide the basis for a radical transformation of aspects of the spatial dimensions of urban society. Impending technical change certainly suggests that strong incentives for dispersal could be there. If we suppose this technology is not held in contempt by the majority of its cities, we could be moving closer to the day when there are radical alterations in the nation's system of cities. So long as society is receptive, our body of technical knowledge will expand more rapidly than it has in the past, and the scope of the impact of that even more powerful technology on location decisions will increase. If that technology, as it emerges, generates real advantages for dispersal, these dispersing forces could eventually take hold. While the probabilities that this will happen seem very slight, they are probably increasing a bit.

REFERENCES

Bell, D. *The Coming of the Post-Industrial Society.* New York: Basic Books, Inc., 1973.

Bright, J., and Schoeman, M. *A Guide to Practical Technological Forecasting.* Englewood Cliffs, N.J.: Prentice-Hall, Inc., 1973.

Drucker, P. *The Age of Discontinuity.* New York: Harper and Row, Publishers, 1969.

Fuller, B. R. *Comprehensive Thinking.* Carbondale, Ill.: Southern Illinois University Press, 1965.

Lampard, E. E. "The Evolving System of Cities in the United States: Urbanization and Economic Development." In *Issues in Urban Economics,* edited by H. S. Perloff and L. Wingo. Baltimore: The Johns Hopkins Press, 1968, 81–139.

McKelvey, B. *The Urbanization of America: 1860–1915.* New Brunswick, N.J.: Rutgers University Press, 1963.

———. *The Emergence of Metropolitan America.* New Brunswick, N.J.: Rutgers University Press, 1968.

Perloff, H. S.; Dunn, E. S.; Lampard, E. E.; and Muth, R. *Regions, Resources, and Economic Growth.* Baltimore: The Johns Hopkins Press, 1960.

The Spreading Out
of the American City

SUMMARY

Spread city is a term meaning the contemporary city. Today's city differs from the compact city of times past in that it encompasses much more territory and has less "centrality." The day-to-day activities of people in today's city are literally much more spread out than they were. Some people take a dim view of this change, which they characterize as urban sprawl.

Certain kinds of population and technological change lie at the bottom of the spreading out of the city. Population growth is one change; the migration of southern blacks to northern cities is another. Change in our transportation technology is still another factor, as is the technical change that has given rise to productivity increases and hence real income gains. There is also the technical change that increased the operating space requirements of many businesses.

An understanding of why our cities have spread out provides useful perspective in considering the issue of urban sprawl. Much of what we observe in today's spread city can be construed as the outcome of a market response to certain basic forces of change, e.g., population growth, the automobile, etc. Urban sprawl can thus be considered an outcome of decisions that reflected economic behavior. Stated in this way, the nature of the problem of urban sprawl becomes clear. If there is a problem, it must stem from the fact that our markets are not in good working order.

Economic knowledge of historical changes in the structure of cities provides a reasonable base for speculating about the future shape of the city. To do so, we must focus initially on probable future technical and population developments and the social values that population is likely to have. What appears likely are developments that could be both dispersive and concentrative in their impact on city structure. It is not difficult to develop a scenario in which the city becomes much more spread out than it is now. Nor is it difficult to develop a scenario in which the end result is a "skyscraper" city. A more realistic view takes both dispersive and concentrative elements into account. What this view implies is that the American city will continue on that path leading to megalopolis. The metropolis of the future will be large in size, highly diverse in its make-up and constituted of many nodes or points of high density, interspersed with zones of low density. Our cities of tomorrow will, in certain respects, look much the same as some of them do today.

Spread city is a term taken to designate a city with certain features that sharply differentiate it from the compact city of the nineteenth century. Figure 8.1 depicts

Figure 8.1

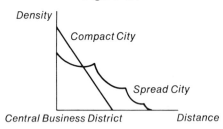

the most important of these. Consider the population of the two cities represented by the density gradients, shown in this figure, to be the same. The differences between the two are apparent. One is in the areal extent of the two cities. The spread city encompasses much more territory than does the other. Second, there are differences with respect to density of population; the spread city does not reach the peak attained in the compact city. The central portion is less visible and there are other nodes around which much activity is found.

The spread city is, obviously, the contemporary American city. It is the outcome of an urbanization process that has transformed cities from their compacted form of 50 to 100 years ago into sprawling and seemingly disjointed centers of activity. This is an important fact of American urban history. Rather than growing upward, American cities—as have cities in most other parts of the world—have grown by spreading out. It shows up in the numbers in Tables 8.1, 8.2, and 8.3 which indicate proportionately less and less of both the residential and nonresidential urban populations living in central cities as we move through the twentieth century.

That the city has grown by spreading out rather than building upward has pejorative implications to some. The spread city is ugly and depressing. The spread city is urban sprawl. It is a way of life that falls below a minimum acceptable standard of aesthetics. It is also inefficient, in that the pattern of land use it entails is associated with higher living costs. Who needs it?

The question is an important one. Yet, we do not really address it by asserting that urban sprawl is the problem of ugliness and inefficiency in the use of urban land. Such a use of language provides categories that are too vague and ambiguous. What is ugliness? Ugliness to whom? In what way is sprawl involved? What inefficiencies? Are these inefficiencies we find in our cities to be explained by sprawl?

Questions of this sort come flowing in endless quantities. As a consequence, it is not immediately clear what the issue is, if indeed there can be said to be one that arises exclusively out of the fact that our cities have spread out. To answer

Table 8.1

Percent of Population of SMSA in Control City
Selected SMSA's *

	Percent of SMSA Population in Central City		
	1950	1960	1970
Baltimore	67.6%	52.0%	43.8%
Boston	33.2	24.2	23.0
Buffalo	53.3	40.8	34.0
Chicago	70.0	57.0	48.2
Cleveland	59.7	48.7	36.2
Detroit	61.3	44.3	35.9
Houston	73.9	75.5	62.0
Los Angeles	53.5	46.7	44.9
Milwaukee	73.1	62.0	51.0
New York	82.6	72.8	68.1
Philadelphia	56.4	46.1	40.4
Pittsburgh	30.6	25.1	21.5
San Francisco	34.6	26.6	22.9
St. Louis	48.8	35.6	26.0
Washington	54.8	37.0	26.9

* Standard Metropolitan Statistical Area

Source: U.S. Bureau of the Census

Table 8.2

Central Cities Percentage of Manufacturing Employment
in Selected SMSA's

	1929	1947	1963
Baltimore	85.5%	70.4%	56.7%
Boston	40.6	40.5	29.5
Buffalo	59.8	47.9	34.7
Chicago	73.6	70.4	59.0
Cincinnati	67.7	71.3	47.6
Cleveland	89.1	83.0	59.3
Detroit	75.2	60.3	42.7
Los Angeles	66.6	46.9	37.8
New York	69.8	66.3	68.9
Philadelphia	65.7	61.3	49.6
Pittsburgh	27.1	23.0	21.9
St. Louis	69.0	70.6	49.7
San Francisco– Oakland	68.2	55.9	26.9

Source: U.S. Bureau of the Census

Table 8.3

Central Cities Percentage of Retail Trade
by Selected SMSA's

	1929	1948	1963
Baltimore	94.8%	88.3%	60.4%
Boston	61.3	52.4	35.6
Buffalo	78.9	70.3	43.2
Chicago	81.7	75.6	55.3
Cincinnati	79.8	73.8	52.8
Cleveland	87.7	80.6	49.6
Detroit	82.2	72.6	43.3
Los Angeles	70.0	54.4	42.2
New York	79.8	74.6	65.7
Philadelphia	79.2	67.8	46.5
Pittsburgh	61.0	52.5	39.2
St. Louis	79.9	67.6	43.0
San Francisco–			
Oakland	85.2	72.3	36.7

Source: U.S. Bureau of the Census

questions of this type, we need knowledge of the forces and processes of change that give rise to urban sprawl. Only if we satisfy our curiosity about the causes of urban sprawl, will we be in a position to comment on the question of its significance.

CITY STRUCTURE AND THE
SPREADING OUT OF THE CITY

Obviously, if the city has spread out, certain things have happened which gave rise to decisions by firms, government, and households to locate farther away from the center of the city. What things were these?

As studied by urban economists, certain kinds of population and technical change surface as important facts. Population growth is one; the migration of southern blacks to northern cities is another. Change in our transportation technology is still another, as is the technical change which has given rise to productivity increases and hence real income gains. There is also the technical change which altered the operating space requirements of business.

While this by no means ends the list, it includes what are believed to be the important sources of change. But are they important? Do they really help explain the spreading out of American cities?

If these kinds of population and technical change were the cause of the movement of people away from our central cities, they should show up as factors affecting the location decisions of firms and households. Do we have any basis for asserting that these things had something to do with these decisions? It is at this point the theory of city structure discussed in chapter 5 comes into the picture.

If the automobile or rising real incomes caused people to move away from the central city, this should be implied in location decisions, as they are considered in the context of theory of city structure. The question of the significance or importance of these things must be addressed on the basis of what we have learned from empirical studies that have investigated these implications.

FACTORS IN CHANGING RESIDENTIAL LOCATIONS

Technology

Technical Change and Transportation Costs   The importance of transportation costs as a determinant of residential location was noted earlier. The importance of the transportation network as a force organizing the city's population over geographic space was also noted.

What that network is, and hence what the level and pattern of transportation costs are within the city, depends on a great many things, not the least of which is transportation technology. No one disputes that transportation systems are strongly influenced by the knowledge of what's involved in transporting goods and people over geographic space. There is less agreement about the nature and extent of that influence. There have been transportation "breakthroughs," however, whose impact is clear. The "breakthrough" pertinent to a discussion of the spreading out of the city is the automobile and its commercial counterpart, the truck.

Prior to the automobile and the truck, movement in the city was largely by rail modes—trolley and street railway systems—and modes involving horse and wagons. Significantly, the trolley and electric railway system moved people while the horse and wagons moved the goods. Since the former was much less expensive than the latter, the cost of moving people was less than the cost of moving goods. As a consequence, households placed a lower value on sites at the center of the city than firms. Put in the language of chapter 5, the bid rent curve of the firm was more steeply sloped than that of the household—see Figure 8.2. Given these bid rent curves and a competitive land market, you would expect to find business in the center of the city, ringed by residences of various kinds.

Figure 8.2

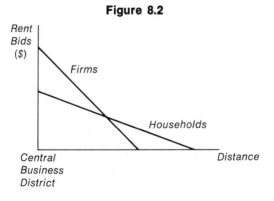

Now superimpose the automobile on this system. Prior to its coming, families were largely restricted to sites within a perimeter that was defined by both the length and direction of the trolley and street railway system in the city. Setting aside the question of movement costs in the interstices, anything beyond the end of the lines required the use of time-consuming modes of transportation, e.g., walking, horse and buggy, etc. In other words, the end of the rail lines constituted a break in the transportation cost curve—see Figure 8.3.

Figure 8.3

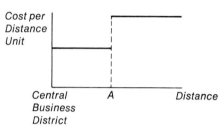

Point *A* in Figure 8.3 represents the end of the rail line, beyond which the cost per distance unit was substantially higher. The budget impact of this commuting cost increase was apparently sufficient to rule out most sites that fell beyond that point.

Enter now the automobile, along with the necessary street and highway investment, and the cost of movement beyond the end of the rail lines is sharply reduced. What happened to these costs between the center of the city and the end of the rail lines is less certain. Households now had alternative modes. The fact of two or more modes of transportation raises complications best considered at a later point when urban transportation is taken up. For now, it is enough to note that the automobile extended the locational options of households beyond the ends of the existing rail lines.

Expressed in this way, the full significance of the automobile to the question of city structure fails to come through. The location options of the households are extended. So what? Is there any reason to believe that there will be households taking advantage of this fact?

The theory of residential choice, discussed in chapter 5, provides a reason for believing so. Since commuting costs are now less beyond the end of the rail lines, *k* in the budget constraint, that is:

$$Y = P_1X_1 + P_2X_2 \text{———} P_nX_n - k \tag{8.1}$$

is less at these locations than before. This means households should now be willing to pay more for these locations, which has the effect of "flattening out" the bid rent curves of the residential user—see Figure 8.4. If so, more households in competition with others in the urban land market would find what was best for them farther away from the central business district.

Most students of the city believe the automobile was a key reason why many households moved away from central cities, and there are empirical tests of formal hypotheses that provide support for this view.

Figure 8.4

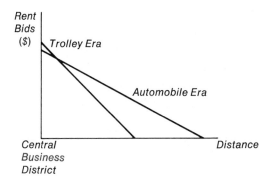

Technology and Real Income Gains   Technical change is a pervasive feature of American society that has had important income implications. Real income in the nation has increased substantially and can be easily documented. Much of this is attributable to new technology, manifested both in new capital goods and in the organizational structures within which production takes place. Rising real income, in turn, has important economic implications, for as our real incomes increase, we are freed from restraints that necessitated our spending money in certain ways. Rising real incomes may thus generate changes in the way dollar votes are cast and in doing so induce certain kinds of change in the economic system. One of these changes could be residential movements away from the central business district.

Certainly, income has impact on residential site selection. If commuting costs are considered as money outlays and we assume there is only one mode of transportation, k for specified distances will be the same for all families. But if this be so, commuting costs impose a greater burden on those with low incomes. In turn, this implies that low-income families will bid very little for sites away from the center of the city. They will concentrate their bids on sites close in. The bid rent curves of low-income families will thus be more steeply sloped than those with higher incomes—see Figure 8.5.

With bid rent curves like this, one would expect the urban land market to work to concentrate low-income families in the central city and high-income families in the suburban rings. In fact, there is evidence of this kind of concentration in many cities, even though there are high-income families living in the central cities and low-income families living in the suburban ring. Family income can, by no means, be used to explain fully residential spatial distributions within the city; but it does count for something.

Consider now a community in which real income is rising—a very realistic presumption. We know that as incomes rise, the constraining influence of commuting costs is reduced. Hence, households will be able to bid more for all sites, including those that were once excluded from the set of feasible alternatives because they were too far away. Stated in this way, what appears to happen is that the bid rent curve of the family whose income increases shifts to the right—see Figure 8.6. But if this is so, it is not clear why rising incomes lead families to

Figure 8.5

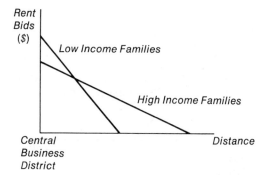

seek housing farther away from the center of the city. Only if the bid rent curve flattens out as income rises will the family have gained the incentive to move away from the central city.

Figure 8.6

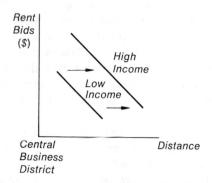

Is there any reason to expect bid rent curves to flatten out as real incomes rise? There is, if commuting costs per distance unit do not change as incomes increase. Families with low incomes are, of course, limited in the trade-offs they can make between access and space. Because of the importance of commuting costs in the family budget, they are attracted to locations with accessibility; space is secondary. After their incomes increase, more income is left over for expenditures on space. What was once only a vision or an unreal possibility—more land space— may now fall within the range of feasible alternatives. The quest for more space might begin in earnest and the trade-offs are best at locations away from the central business district, where the cost of space is less. The benefits from increased space consumption could begin to outweigh the added costs of commuting from the more distant locations. If so, the bid rent curve of the family will have flattened out and it will be pulled toward the suburbs in competition with others for a place to live.

Based on empirical studies made to date, the importance of rising real incomes —the extent to which they flattened out bid rent curves—is uncertain. It is still a reasonable possibility, however, in that it happened to a number of households.

Population Dynamics

Population Growth   Growth in the nation's urban population was documented in the previous chapter. This is growth that stemmed both from an increase in the overall population and process of urbanization. It was also growth that reflected in most of the nation's cities, although with varying degrees of intensity at various points in time. What was not discussed was the impact of this growth on the structure of the city.

Start with the compact city with densities and rents that are at a peak in the center, falling off gradually, and reaching a low point on the periphery of urban development. Now, assume an increase in the overall population of that city as a consequence of natural growth and/or in-migration. The question is: What will these additional people mean in terms of the boundaries of that city?

If those who are added to the population are to be adequately housed, more housing will be added, one important input of which is land space. Space for newly constructed dwellings is, of course, available on the periphery of the city. But will this development take place there? Will the boundaries of the city be extended to meet its housing needs?

Much depends on the availability of vacant land space within the city. If we suppose there is none, it might appear that the new housing will have to be put up on the periphery. But to assert this neglects the fact that units within the existing stock could be torn down and new high-rise structures which housed more families could be put up. Which is the more likely of these outcomes?

The theory of city structure points to several factors that could have bearing on the outcome. One set of these would work in the direction of extending the boundaries of the city. Housing costs in the city will, in the face of a population increase, rise. More people bidding for the same amount of land space will, in a market setting, increase land costs, which adds to the cost of housing. There will also be those added costs associated with the acquisition of certain properties and the demolition of the structures on those properties. If more people are to be housed on the same land space, some structures will have to be torn down and replaced with ones that house more people.

The overall effect of accommodating a larger population within the existing boundaries of the city will thus be higher housing costs. To the extent that costs influence consumption decisions, as they do, there is reason to believe that an increasing urban population will give rise to market pressures that extend the boundaries of the city.

But movement away from the center, to sites outside the existing city boundaries, may not really lower overall consumption costs very much. Life at the outlying sites will add to the family's commuting costs. Moreover, when votes in the market are cast in a way that fosters new construction out on the periphery of the city, land costs there will be bid up.

The point is evident. As cities grow, families are confronted with the prospect of higher living costs both within and on the outer edges of the city. The question of what happens to city structure as the city grows, then hinges on what happens to housing costs both within and on the periphery of urban development and the pattern of commuting costs. About these matters we can say very little in the absence of a great deal of specific information about the level and pattern of transportation costs and construction and demolition costs.

Suppose, however, that this growth in population took place when the urban transportation network was being revolutionized by the automobile. As the housing cost pressures from population growth surfaced in the central city, transportation costs on the periphery were being reduced by a rapidly developing network of streets and highways which facilitated automobile travel in the city. Urban populations would thus be growing rapidly at a time when consumption costs on the periphery were declining, relative to those in the central city. Obviously, these are the kinds of conditions in which extensive growth would be highly probable. Population growth would be reinforcing the outward movement precipitated by the automobile.

These two sets of historical developments, in the judgment of some urban investigators, help explain much of the movement away from the central city, and there is empirical evidence that provides limited support for this belief.

Migration: Southern Blacks to Northern Cities   Interregional migration is a well-established fact. It has a number of dimensions, one of which has relevance to the explanation of the spread city. Until recently, there has been a massive movement of southern rural blacks and poor whites to northern cities. While these movements had many ramifications, the concern here is limited to its impact on neighborhoods in cities into which these people moved—particularly the blacks.

Southern blacks came in great numbers to many northern cities during the middle of the twentieth century and settled for the most part in and around the central business district of those cities. In most cases, they brought with them little in the way of money and human capital. What they brought were personal needs which, in some cases, were apparently best satisfied with some form of public assistance. They also brought with them modes of behavior that were substantially different from the masses or those who formed the middle class, most of whom were white.

How these blacks were assimilated into the culture of these cities is a question that goes far beyond the scope of the remarks made here. The concern here is restricted to a consideration of the effects that their presence had on white households living in central cities. Apparently, that presence precipitated the movement of a number of white households to the suburbs.

Political scientists and sociologists talk about the flight of middle-class whites from the central city to the suburbs, apparently for good reason. The movement of blacks into some city neighborhoods probably generated neighborhood effects. If the neighborhood was white to begin with, and the people living there much preferred to live among their own, the movement of blacks into the neighborhood probably affected the valuations whites made of their neighborhoods. This didn't have to be a matter of race. Anyone who was different who moved into the neighborhood could have had the same impact. Much of this movement was, however, movement of southern blacks into northern cities, and it apparently did generate neighborhood effects in some central city neighborhoods. These were effects that, in the whites' eyes, reduced the value of the neighborhoods in which they lived. These effects also increased the valuations of these whites of locations well away from the central cities. This implies that they had the effect of flattening out the bid rent curves of these households, who, as a consequence, were attracted to suburban locations when making a housing adjustment.

How many whites actually fled central city neighborhoods because of the movement of southern blacks into central cities is uncertain. The fact that there are such strong patterns of residential segregation by race in our central cities suggests that the number may be less than some believe. If there are to be neighborhood effects which flatten out bid rent curves of households, there must be nearness to those who generate these effects. If the blacks live largely among themselves in a highly segregated residential housing pattern, however, they cannot be near too many whites. Thus, it is difficult to see how one could argue that most of the movement of whites away from central cities to the suburbs during the 1940s, 1950s and early part of the 1960s, when this movement was at its heaviest, can be attributed to the movement of blacks into the center of our cities. Certainly some of it was, but not as much as some would have us believe.

FACTORS IN CHANGING BUSINESS LOCATIONS

Technological Change

The Coming of the Truck   As noted above, earlier in our history, people moved about in the city in electric railway systems and goods in the horse and wagon. The pattern of movement costs was such that business found profits at a maximum in the center of the city and households found satisfactions at a maximum in residences that ringed the center. When the truck, along with a network of streets and highways, were superimposed on this layout, the cost of moving goods in the city was substantially reduced. With business located in the center of the city, this reduction bestowed greater net benefits on locations in the suburban rings. Nearness to the center was no longer so important, with lower transportation costs throughout the entire metropolitan area. The technology that gave us the truck thus had the effect of flattening out the bid rent curves of firms whose operations involved the movement of physical goods—see Figure 8.7.

Basic or exporting industries that processed certain materials shipped in from outside rail, for example, were, prior to the truck, tied closely to sites near the major railway junctions in the city simply because of transportation costs. Truck transportation, in effect, expanded the locational options within the city, and did so in a way that flattened out bid rent curves.

The Changing Space Requirements of Business: Manufacturing   There are clear indications that the amount of land "consumed" by manufacturing firms in most of our cities has increased over the past thirty years. Increased land use, of course, can be construed as the outcome of a movement of business to the suburbs, since it is only out in the wide-open spaces that such consumption is possible. But profit-maximizing firms do not necessarily come to occupy larger

Figure 8.7

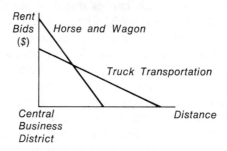

sites simply because these sites are there. They only do so if there is some economic advantage.

Certainly, there is reason to believe that manufacturing firms came to locate on large sites because it was to their advantage to do so. For many, there was technical change which substantially altered their production processes. The emergence of continuous materials-flow systems, with an abundance of automatic controls, substantially increased the internal space requirements for many. Some of these processes called for straight-line runs of several hundred feet or more, a requirement which made the typical city block obsolete as a site for production. No longer could production take place in the earlier mill-style buildings of five or six stories which fit comfortably within a city block; much more space was required. The practice of building a new plant became one of designing the production process first and then "wrapping" the building around it. More important, these processes often required generous amounts of space.

The fact that more space was required had important implications with respect to the bid rent curves of these firms because land costs were cheaper away from the central business district. The space needs of such firms were thus met with less expense at suburban locations, which meant that profits were greater there than they were before the change. This implies a flatter bid rent curve. If more money is now to be made away from the center of the city, profit-maximizing firms should be willing to offer more for land at these more distant sites than they did before. If more money is to be made on the periphery than in the center, the probability that firms will locate in the suburbs is increased.

Empirical studies, other than case studies, that test these notions are scarce. Still, few doubt that technology, in this sense, had important bearing on the location of many manufacturing firms in our cities and was responsible for much of the outward movement of industry. Indeed, the changing space requirements of manufacturing firms are almost universally believed to be an important reason for the spreading-out of the American city.

Changing Space Requirements of Business: Service Industries   The internal space requirements of service industries—including the retailing industry—have been less affected by technological change than manufacturing, even though we now find many retail establishments consuming more space in shopping centers than their counterparts in the central business districts. For most, however, there appears to be no great advantage to operating in a larger plant facility. Yet, many service establishments have moved away from the central business district because of the automobile.

The automobile, of course, not only expanded the location options of the household in terms of journey to work considerations, it also provided a more flexible, and hence to many a more desirable, means of travel to shopping places. Automobile use in shopping trips, however, meant the need for parking space at destination points. The parking problems in the central business district of American cities are well-known and highly publicized. They have also been a constant source of difficulty to the "downtown" merchant for which there was no quick and inexpensive solution. Solutions were to be found, however, in the suburbs where land was more plentiful. But were they?

The theory of city structure implies that there is every reason to believe that outlying locations became more attractive to these firms. When the provision of parking space for customers with automobiles becomes a part of the service provided by retailers, the bid rent curves of many retailers should flatten out. If the cost of land declines from the center of the city, as it did, the cost of providing for the parking needs of customers will be less at sites away from the center. This could mean that profits at these locations will be higher than they were prior to the growth in the parking needs of these firms. If so, this should increase their willingness to pay for land at outlying locations, which implies a flattening of their bid rent curves.

While there are few, if any, empirical studies of this hypothesis, most urban economists argue that the growing parking needs of retail firms were partly responsible for their movement away from the center of the city.

Population Factors

The Residential Flight to the Suburbs   If there was reason for families to move away from the center of the city, there was also reason for some firms to follow after them. As noted in chapter 5, firms that provide services or sell products to local residents find their revenues affected by location. Propinquity to customers increases revenues, which, all other things being equal, increases profits.

The residential flight to the suburbs meant the movement of customers away from many firms, which reduced their revenues and hence profits. The way to recoup these profits was to move out near to their customers, and move they did. The rapid growth in the importance of the suburban shopping center in most American cities was no accident.

All this can be cast in terms of what happened to the bid rent curves of a certain class of firms. When revenues and profits decline as a consequence of customers moving out of a firm's market area, it will reevaluate its present location. In doing so, the firm may find profits are now maximized at suburban locations. This will be true if costs are unaffected by the move or are lower because of it. If costs are higher, profits may or may not be higher in outlying locations. It depends on how much costs increase in relation to the increase in revenues that come with the move. If profits, in fact, turned out to be higher at outlying locations, this meant firms were able and should have been willing to pay more for these locations; hence their bid rent curves should have flattened out.

There is some empirical evidence that the flight of households to the suburbs had the effect of flattening out the bid rent curves of many nonbasic firms. The firms most affected were those who served customers in relatively small market areas—those that provided the so-called convenience goods. Given the new market conditions, profit maximization by many retailing firms meant a multiplant operation with locations scattered judiciously throughout the entire metropolitan area.

WHAT'S REALLY IMPORTANT?

In light of the theory of city structure, all that has been discussed to this point stands as reasonable parts of an explanation of the spread city. As also noted, empirical studies do provide varying degrees of support for each part. The problem is that few, if any, of the empirical tests made to date really address the issue of relative importance.

Perhaps the most comprehensive empirical inquiry made of residential decentralization to date was by Muth. On the basis of his studies, he argues that increases in population and improvements in automobile transportation largely account for the suburbanization of the residential population that has taken place in American cities. Yet, there are questions that can be raised about the specifications in the model which lie at the heart of his analysis. Whether the notion of the "flight of whites to the suburbs" was adequately dealt with, for example, is an open question. While Muth has conducted what, in my view, is one of the strongest tests of the hypotheses of economists concerning the decentralization of residential households, what he has done by no means closes the issue.

Empirical investigations of hypotheses concerning the movement of business firms out to the suburbs, as noted above, have been made, but they consist, for the most part, of case studies of such metropolitan areas as New York and Pittsburgh. The conclusions from these studies are generally consistent with the notions discussed above, indicating as they do the importance of technology and the movement of households to the suburbs. The question of relative importance, however, is rarely addressed.

In summary, there is empirical support or arguments to the effect that the spread city is a consequence of the automobile, the truck, rising real incomes, changing space requirements for firms, increasing population and the flight of white households to the suburbs. That evidence, however, does not provide a basis for assigning degrees of importance to each of these. What this suggests is that we would not go too far wrong, when considering future prospects for city structure, to focus on prospective transportation, population, income, and production developments. Since our view of the future is importantly conditioned by our understanding of the past, that view will be closer to the mark if it reflects what it is that we know about the past. But, it could also turn out to be wrong in some respects because we are unable to specify in advance the probable relative importance of impending developments in each of these areas.

URBAN SPRAWL
RECONSIDERED

Urban sprawl, as noted above, is a characterization of cities that has pejorative overtones. It conveys such notions as ugliness and inefficiency, things that no one wants. But is this really a useful way to characterize the city?

A discussion of the reasons why our cities have spread out casts doubt on the usefulness of this conception of urban sprawl. Much of what we observe in today's spread city can be construed as the outcome of a market response to certain basic forces of change in society. Our cities have spread out because of population and technical developments that enhanced the attractiveness of sites away from the urban center, for a relatively large range of urban activities. To the extent that location in the city was a consequence of the operation of markets and market decisions that reflected economic behavior, as it did in many instances, the spreading out of cities was an inevitability.

In the face of this conclusion, it is difficult to see how one could argue that urban sprawl is necessarily bad. Obviously, there are not many cities that measure up to our conception of the city beautiful. Yet, if what we have is the outcome of hard economic choices made in markets that were working properly, that outcome can be construed as a reflection of what people wanted. Stated in this way, the nature of the problem begins to emerge. Was our urban land market in good working order? Or is what we observe a consequence of the market meshing of decisions of people who were not very well informed, who did not take into account certain economic facts that should have had bearing on our use of scarce resources, or who had what may be considered as excessive market power? If any or all of these were the case, there is reason for concern.

The issue of urban sprawl, as it is generally discussed, is phoney. Not that a concern with certain aesthetic and engineering efficiency features of the emerging urban form is not cause for thought. Yet if we are to deal with the troublesome features of the city implicit in this notion, we have to address the particular features that are the source of concern. If we believe, for example, that urban sprawl is bad because of the transportation inefficiencies it causes, we would be in a better position to evaluate and suggest a solution if we were able to show how and in what sense there are economic inefficiencies in the urban transportation system. Of if we argue that the urban decay now in the center of our cities is largely a consequence of the sprawl development in these cities, our arguments would be more convincing if we were able to show the connection between these two. In fact, we can only do so if we have some understanding of the urban renewal process.

In dealing with the issues implicit in the pejorative use of urban sprawl, it is clear that we are better off if we try to become as specific as possible. We must delineate precisely what is wrong and why. It may be that in doing so, we shall find features in the contemporary urban landscape that represent problems to be dealt with. It could also be that some of what we see is the best of all possible worlds, given the economic constraints that were imposed on those making the decisions which lead to this outcome.

FORCES OF CHANGE
IN THE FUTURE

What of the city tomorrow? What will it look like? Will city structure be more alike or different from that of the contemporary city?

These are questions that have fascinated students of the city for years and have provided a focal point around which there has been a great deal of speculation. Given imperfect knowledge, any remarks one might choose to make about the future shape of the city are speculative. Those that have roots in our economic knowledge of city structure, however, are likely to be more sensible than those which ignore these economic "realities."

If we suppose that the technological and population factors discussed above provide the foundation of today's city, what we expect to happen to technology and population should tell much about what the city of tomorrow will look like.

Technology

While technological forecasting is a hazardous art, there are a number of sensible statements that can be made about prospective developments in transportation and communications, which will have important bearing on the question of where people will live and work within cities.

Transportation Possibilities   As noted in the previous chapter, technology in transportation appears to be heading in directions that will further loosen man's ties to particular points in geographic space. Over the long run, we appear to be moving toward a world in which the role of fixed path forms of transportation—the automobile, the train and the like—will diminish. We already have the technology to move in this direction. The short take-off and landing and vertical take-off and landing aircraft will move us about in this way. The application of the air-cushion principle of travel, as now exemplified in the hovercraft, could also provide ground vehicles that move much more freely than do automobiles and trains.

The practicality of such transportation to movement *within* the city, however, seems doubtful at this point. As these vehicles are in use now, their bulk and cost work against their supplanting existing modes of transportation. Moreover, technical developments are currently taking place that enhance the attractiveness of fixed path vehicles. The application of the computer and computer models to the problem of traffic flows on both our streets and highways and railways, for example, should help to generate more efficiency in the use of facilities and thereby increase the attractiveness of their use.

As between the automobile and mass transit, the technology of both today and tomorrow could work more in favor of the latter. The technical know-how that is developing to deal with the problem of pollution emanating from the automobile is adding to the cost of its use relative to other forms of transportation. On the other hand, new techniques of tunnel construction, such as those involving the laser beam, could lower substantially the cost of constructing underground transportation channels, particularly for those transportation systems that involve some form of mass transit. Technology may thus provide us with a means of more effectively resolving the matter of right-of-way acquisitions, a problem that has been so troublesome in developing mass transit systems. Any lowering in the cost of tunneling might also give rise to the development of underground means of moving goods through such mass models as underground belt conveyors and pipe systems through which solid materials might move.

Communication Possibilities   As noted in the previous chapter, actual and impending communications technology contains seeds that could have revolutionary implications with respect to where people live. The possibility of technical know-how that leads to a "generalization" of communications over geographic space has obvious implications with respect to where people live within cities. The development of a relatively cheap broadband transmission mechanism combined with inexpensive, flexible, and mobile terminal equipment could, as indicated earlier, provide for a further substantial dispersal of the population. If it *did* come to living and working where we pleased and traveling for pleasure, the distinction between choosing a city within which to live and choosing a site within that city would disappear.

While the world will not evolve in this way in the foreseeable future, two specific communication innovations could come into play in dispersive ways. One of these is the video-phone. Although the telephone has reduced the need for face-to-face contact in communicating with one another, face-to-face contact is still necessary, in part, because of the importance of nonverbal signs in our communications with one another. To consummate many transactions properly, some people must be able to look at one another eyeball-to-eyeball. This implies that the addition of a visual dimension to our communications with the telephone could reduce the need for face-to-face contact in our business dealings. This reduced need would not only hold for communications between businesses, but between households and businesses. The technology is developing that might enable households to do much of their shopping from home. At least you can imagine a large share of the routine purchases being made by visually scanning some merchandise displays, selecting alternatives, and making payments without even leaving home.

It is also possible that more work will be done from locations further distant from the physical structures that now house our work-related activities. Information retrieval systems with low-cost remote terminals are not only a possibility but a reality. To the extent that the work revolves around activities that require access to some kind of centrally located information, remote terminals that have quick access to that information might keep many people at home while they work.

Population

Growth in the nation's urban population, along with the automobile, as noted above, accounts for much of the spreading of the American city. This fact is significant when considering future forces of change because of the recent change in the rate of population growth.

The historic growth of the nation's population is well known and easily documented. The data make clear that, with the exception of certain periods, the rate of population growth in the nation has been declining.

Prior to the baby boom of the 1940s and 1950s, both in-migration and the birth rate fell off to a point that population stability was anticipated by the 1960s or 1970s. But the extraordinary rise in the birth rate immediately following World War II and on through most of the 1950s changed all of that. Then, just as suddenly, the birth rate began to decline and has been lowered to a point now where the population is expected to stabilize over the next twenty to thirty years.

Much has been written about the earlier decline and the subsequent rise and fall in the fertility rate of the American woman. For purposes of this discussion it is enough to simply note that recent trends portend a dramatic decline in the rate of growth of the households populating our cities. If we are approaching a peak in the urbanization of the population, the rate of growth in the household population of most of our cities will slow down, and in some cases population will begin to decline. This will not happen immediately, but will indeed happen if current demographic trends continue.

Social and Private Values

While social and private values are seldom found as subject matter in economic discussions, they are important to any concern with the future shape of our cities. Taking a broad view and looking at humans as we evolved over relatively long periods of time, there are indications of change in our goals and aspirations. One of these, noted earlier, was a shift from other world ideas to a more secular, pragmatic, and utilitarian view of the world, a change that corresponds roughly to what happened between the Middle Ages and the beginning of the industrial revolution.

More recently, there have been rumblings that some have interpreted as indications of a lessening of our concern with material things. Some of the openly expressed concerns of communist nations, for example, can be given this interpretation, as can some of the behavior of those who make up the so-called "counter-culture" in noncommunist states.

Yet, the recent inflationary binge in the noncommunist world strongly suggests that the world is not becoming increasingly populated with ascetics. To the contrary, it denotes a high consumptive world, one in which people are very much concerned with material things. Nor do the communist nations of the world seem any less preoccupied with the material, as indicated by their continual search for formulas which will improve the efficiency of their economic systems and, by implication, increase per capita output. It seems fair to assert that the social values that currently guide the actions of the great majority of people in the world are "oriented toward this world and what it has to offer."

But this does not mean the tastes and preferences of the American household are not changing. Even if we remain a high consumption society, there are opportunities for change in the sense of the mix of things we consume and where we consume them.

What we do as consumers usually revolves heavily around the mind activities of perceiving, comparing, thinking, and judging. While the view of what's involved in these activities varies considerably, most agree that consumption involves behavior that incorporates some habitual elements, involves learning, and is to a considerable extent, rational and maximizing in its thrust.

The outcome of the consumption decision is something that is rich in variety in terms of individuals. But there are also patterns, one of which is that, in the aggregate, the consumer stands willing to adjust his or her living standard upward in the face of an increase in the ability to do so. And as he or she does, the market basket of goods consumed tends to change a bit. In the United States, for example, over the past fifty years, these changes have been reflected in increased purchases of durable goods and services and a decline in the relative importance of nondurable goods. More recently, the proportion of consumption dollars spent on durable goods has levelled off, with the offset found in a sharp increase in the purchase of a number of services, the most important of which are medical services and recreation.

The significant thing about these changes is that they have been very gradual. Historically, the American consumers have not been revolutionary. They have adapted to change in ways that suggest some stability in behavior. While the market basket of goods consumed today differs in many respects from what it was fifty years ago, there is nevertheless historical evidence of stability.

The paradox here is apparent. The explanation is to be found in technology and how that technology has been manifested in the goods we consume. What has happened is that households are, for the most part, now consuming the same general kinds of goods, although in somewhat different proportions, but certain specific characteristics of these goods differ substantially from what they were earlier. Households still have transportation needs, but they are now largely satisfied with modes of transportation that differ dramatically from their counterparts of 100 years ago. Our technology has, for the most part, been providing goods gradually improved over time but not fundamentally different. History indeed suggests the American consumer is not whimsical, but rather predictable and, in the eyes of some, a bit stodgy and dull.

More recently, some consumers have behaved in ways that suggest the possibility of dramatic changes in life styles. The "freaked-out" activities of many of the young and some of the old during the latter part of the 1960s and the early 1970s was taken by some to be forerunners of what is seen to be dramatic changes in life styles. Yet, most of what appeared to be coming into vogue then, now seems to have receded into the background. The revolution in life styles, portended by the events of five to ten years ago, seems now to have been greatly exaggerated.

Some argue, however, that there are certain more basic societal changes taking place that hint at a much more volatile consumer in the future. One of these changes is the fact that the mass media has replaced tradition as an arbiter of tastes and styles, the implication being that consumers are now more easily manipulated. If so, they could become more volatile in the consumption behavior. Second, there are those who argue that income has become less of a constraint on what we do, and more of a variable. The argument focuses on the point that people now exercise more discretion in the decisions they make about work and income. If they want to consume more, they will work more to get the income to do it. If so, what this does is to add a volatile element to the spending equation, which, when combined with the former, would seem to give rise to a set of circumstances in which there is more uncertainty in what the consumer does.

How seriously are we to take such arguments and their conclusions? There is no easy answer. But it does seem difficult to take them too seriously at this point. Social critics have belittled American consumers for years and noted with glee the ease with which they can be manipulated by the producer. Yet, consumers have behaved in ways that are stable enough to raise serious questions about their manipulability. Whether we are closer to such a point now is by no means clear in terms of the available evidence. Nor is it really clear just how many people are becoming much more concerned with consumption and leisure rather than occupation. Statements of this kind are not new. What we lack, however, are concrete indications of the fact of such change. What appears to be most reasonable at this juncture is a conservative view of what the consumers will do in the future. The structure of their values is likely to be such that personal tastes and preferences will come into play in the future much as they have in the past, which implies no dramatic change in consumer behavior in the foreseeable future. There will be change, but not as much as some foresee.

SOME SCENARIOS OF
THE FUTURE

Density Patterns

Much long-term prognostication about the city is concerned with the question of whether the city will continue to grow out or—as some wags would have it —start to grow up. The issue of dispersion versus concentration is a big one and there are sharply divergent views among the "experts" about which will be the dominant force in the future. Some foresee a continuing decline in the centrality of the city, along much the same lines that have been taken over the past fifty years. Others believe that these dispersing trends will be reversed. Still others take a middle of the road position, arguing, in effect, that the future will materialize in ways that encompass the best—or worst—of our dispersed and concentrated ways. While a world in which cities contain both elements of concentration and dispersion is probably the most reasonable model of what the future will look like, before considering that model, it is helpful first to consider the arguments for expecting more dispersion and/or more concentration.

Much More Dispersion?   Certainly, the preceding discussion about technology that is either here or on the horizon provides reason for believing that cities will spread out even further in the years ahead. The spreading out in the past was, as noted above, in good measure attributable to technical change. Technology, however, has many ramifications, not all of which implied dispersions in the make-up of our cities. In fact, the implications of the automobile and elevator were just the opposite. As Frank Lloyd Wright put it at the turn of the century, the future shape of our cities will depend upon the outcome of the race shaping up between the elevator and the automobile. He also added that a wise person would place bets on the automobile.

Wright turned out to be right, of course. How such a visionary would view the matter in its current setting is, of course, a question that only the gods can answer. But there are many contemporary counterparts of Wright who believe more of the same is to be expected in the future. Modes of transportation that do not move over fixed paths and cover distances more quickly stand as means of transportation which will further reduce the benefits of geographic propinquity. An even more significant impetus for dispersion could be forthcoming from prospective communication developments. With means of communication that radically reduce the need for face-to-face or face-to-commodity contact, we would do away with what have been very important reasons for living in close geographic proximity. Shortly, perhaps all that will be holding the city together will be the systems of underground sewers and water mains we now have, and it is not outside the realm of possibility that future technology will dispose of the need for these things.

A Reversal of Dispersion?   While the technology is or will be there, which could foster urban dispersion of a magnitude that dwarfs anything we have seen to this point, technology still includes the elevator and other elements which could facilitate the development of a more compact city. Such cities would provide us with high density living, but would do so in ways that presumably maximize the benefits and minimize the costs that can accrue from such a living pattern.

There are visionaries who have provided us with fairly concrete descriptions of what such a city might entail. Typical of these is the city of skyscrapers, the upper portion of which is used for residential purposes. In such a complex of structures, the commute becomes vertical—say twenty or thirty stories—rather than horizontal and involving twenty to thirty miles. There would be interbuilding movement, of course, and this could be accomplished by aerial streets at every eight to ten stories involving a variety of transportation modes. These complexes are complete in the sense of providing opportunities for work, residential living and the total spectrum of recreational activities that one might engage in outside the home. One could live within such a city and hardly ever have need to step outside.

The appeal of such a setting lies, in part, in the fact that it minimizes the amount of time spent in transit between activities. It also fosters face-to-face communication, which some believe as essential to certain group decisions that must be made in many life situations.

How important these things are depends in part on the content of those life situations, which, in turn, are influenced by the "life styles" of the people who are a part of those situations. In this regard, recent talk of life style changes has bearing on the question of the kind of cities we will be living in in the future.

The apparent shift toward a clustered housing concept in much new construction is taken by some as an indication of a change in life styles. The housing demands of people are changing because of certain basic changes taking place in the way in which they want to live. People are now marrying later in life and having fewer children. And if we can judge from their complaints, they dislike increasingly their long commutes and the responsibilities of the ownership of a home on a large lot. Consequently, some builder-developers have found that their most successful ventures involve projects that revolve around some kind of clustered housing concept.

It is only a short step from statements like these to statements that assert the city of tomorrow will inevitably be of the skyscraper vintage. Recent indications of the possibility of substantially higher energy costs in the future which would increase considerably the cost of moving goods, people, and messages lends further credence to this argument.

But is it realistic to expect that our urban populations will come to settle in skyscraper cities?

The Best (or Worst?) of Both Worlds   A more realistic view of what is likely to happen to the density configuration of our cities in the future takes into account both dispersive and concentrative elements and does so in a way that provides proper weight to certain "realities" that are likely to be with us in the foreseeable future. One of these is the fixed site character of almost all of the urban plant which now houses most of our urban activities. While urban capital may ultimately become moveable over geographic space, that day is likely to be some time in coming. Sites with fixed capital investments will continue to be vested with important cost advantages which will work against any extensive dispersal of urban activities of the kind discussed above. The fact that the rate of growth in our urban population will slow down will also work to the advantage of areas with existing plant.

Given that what we have tends to perpetuate itself, at least for a while, also seems to rule out the possibility of the emergence of the skyscraper city. While clustered housing may well be the wave of the future, it is by no means clear how we can go from this conclusion to an urban society dominated by a skyscraper city. Much of what is coming onto the market that is dubbed as *clustered housing* is located well away from the core of the city. It has not resulted in much ultra-high density living for the purpose of being nearer to places of work. But this comes as no surprise, since employment in most of our cities, as noted above, has become dispersed in its location. What we want now in housing can apparently be accommodated in a setting that is a far cry from the skyscraper city.

Nor is it clear that the life styles of American households have really changed in ways that portend the demise of the automobile and all this entails with respect to residential housing patterns. The continued reliance on the auto despite the barrage of criticism it has received suggests the mobility it provides is of no small importance to the American household. Despite the fact that it provides a relatively expensive means of travel—especially in light of the recent and prospective increase in fuel costs—it apparently is the most effective way of meeting the mobility needs of many families, needs that must be very important to many.

Prosaic though it sounds, the American city is likely to continue on that path which leads to megalopolis, much like the one that has developed along the Atlantic seaboard. The metropolis of the future will be huge, highly diverse in its makeup, and made of many nodes or points of high density interspersed with zones of low density. What this says, in effect, is that our cities of tomorrow will, in certain important respects, be much the same as some of them are today.

Urban problems aside, the megalopolis of today is a reflection of not only the technology of the times, but a diversity in the response to that technology. There are people in most of our cities who want to live near "where the action is," there are people who want to live in more remote and isolated locations, and there are people who fall somewhere in between. There is also much diversity in the locational needs of producers, both in the private and public sectors of the economy. All this has given rise to a polynucleated structure which, despite its many unpleasant features, apparently serves our needs quite well.

What particular people do and why has changed and will continue to change. What is not likely to change is the variation in what each individual does and why. As we seek to cope with the problems of the city, the problems of energy, and other problems, there will be change that could reduce the importance of the automobile as a means of intraurban transportation. For reasons noted above, high speed forms of mass transit are likely to become more important, which implies some concentration. On the other hand, communication networks will develop in ways that will tend to disperse people. The response to all such developments will be varied. The outcome in its general shape or form should be much like the multiple node megalopolis that many people talk about. There will be "older" central cities as well as other, newer high density nodes in which different kinds of specialized activity will be found. Residential districts will be found in and around these nodes, and it may be that interspersed among all of this will be open space sufficient to maintain a viable ecology.

Overall, the density configuration is likely to flatten out further, although the change will not be as great as it has been over the past twenty-five years. Whether we get the best or worst features of what we now have depends on how we choose to address the contemporary problems of the city. About these matters, more will be said subsequently. For here, it is enough to say that our cities will continue to evolve in ways that provide an intermingling of both zones of low and high density and an average density that is slightly less than its contemporary counterpart.

REFERENCES

Bright, J., and Schoeman, M. *A Guide to Technological Forecasting.* Englewood Cliffs, N.J.: Prentice-Hall, 1973.

Chinitz, B., ed. *City and Suburb.* Englewood Cliffs, N.J.: Prentice-Hall, 1964.

Hoover, E. "The Evolving Form and Organization of the Metropolis." In *Issues in Urban Economics,* edited by H. Perloff and L. Wingo. Baltimore: The Johns Hopkins Press, 1968.

————, and Vernon, R. *Anatomy of a Metropolis.* Garden City, N.Y.: Anchor Books, Doubleday and Company, Inc., 1962.

Mills, E. *Studies in the Structure of the Urban Economy.* Baltimore: The Johns Hopkins Press, 1972.

Moses, L., and Williamson, H. "The Location of Economic Activity in Cities." *American Economic Review* 57 (1966): 211–22.

Muth, R. *Cities and Housing.* Chicago: University of Chicago Press, 1969.

Vernon, R. *Metropolis 1985.* Garden City, N.Y.: Anchor Books, Doubleday and Company, Inc., 1963.

Urban Poverty

SUMMARY

Poverty refers to living conditions in which the household fails to achieve some minimum standard of living. Available measures indicate those who live in poverty are concentrated among certain groups in the population. Poverty is most widespread among blacks, households headed by females, and the aged. The incidence of poverty is particularly high among blacks who are over sixty-five and black households with female heads.

Poverty is also a problem that knows no boundary. It is found in rural areas as well as the city, and within the city it is found in the suburbs as well as in the central city. Urban poverty, however, is concentrated in the inner core of our central cities. The urban ghetto is a fact and many of these places are where poor blacks live.

There are many causes of poverty. General economic instability is one. There are also factors that operate at the personal level, the most important of which are human capital deficiencies and racial discrimination.

Human capital has bearing on the skills people bring into work situations. The most important determinant of the human capital accumulated by people is education. Education can easily be shown to be an important part of the problem of the poor. The way in which education can be used to enhance the productive capacity of the poor is less certain.

Racial discrimination is believed by some to be an important cause of the poverty of blacks. The fact that blacks earn less than whites is not presumptive evidence of employment discrimination. A good part of that earnings differential is explained by human capital differences. Discrimination, however, plays a role in explaining these human capital differences.

We do have programs, both in the private and public sectors, that are aimed at helping the poor. Those in the public sector have the biggest impact, the most important of which are a part of our social security program. On balance—taking into account the structure of our taxes—these programs do redistribute income to the poor. We also do much, through government, in the area of education that has impact on the earnings capacity of some of the poor. There are some who argue, however, that our public concerns with the poor are unwieldy and ineffective and should be replaced with a generalized income assistance plan, such as the negative income tax.

Our concern with the poor has also raised the issue of what to do with the ghetto. Ghetto "enrichment," policies aimed at making the ghetto a better place to live, is one alternative. Integration, or opening up the suburbs to ghetto residents is another. Economic considerations weigh heavily in favor of a policy that fosters integration. It may be, however, that some enrichment activity in the ghetto in the sense of dealing with the problem of those who are alienated from society will contribute to the success of a strategy of integration over the long run.

Poverty refers to living conditions in which individuals or households fail to achieve a minimum standard of living. What conditions are these? There is little in urban economic theory that provides a basis for answering this question. That theory, of course, is concerned with outcomes that reflect the decisions made by economic beings. The concern is with outcomes that reflect rational, goal-oriented behavior, e.g., the maximization of utility. The outcome is a level of consumption that is the best possible given the circumstances. Whether it is *good enough* is a question that cannot be answered on the basis of the theory. Yet, if we believe there are people living in poverty, there must be consumption by some that is not good enough. What then do we mean by good enough?

WHAT IS POVERTY?

If poverty implies consumption that falls below some set of minimum consumption requirements, to know what poverty means implies that we have knowledge of the sense in which the consumption of some is deficient. Since consumption for most consists of many items, each of which can be valued differently by different people, the question of how we should conceive of the welfare of the person arises. What are the criteria that should be used in evaluating the impact of consumption on the welfare of persons? Are there objective criteria that can be used in defining what constitutes the conditions of minimum welfare?

A general statement of these criteria focuses on the "needs" of people. The problem is in defining what is meant by needs. People have biological needs and psychological needs. Most people think the biological needs are both important and easy to relate to what we mean by poverty. A careful consideration of the meaning of these needs, however, brings to the surface a number of problems.

One might argue that, at a minimum, the conditions of life should be such that people are kept from starving or freezing to death. Who could disagree with this? Yet when we consider carefully what is meant by starving to death, some problems arise. Everyone should have food, for if they don't, death will result in a relatively short period of time. No one believes in death by starvation, particularly if it happens quickly. But what if death comes more slowly? Suppose the problem is one of an inadequate diet which, if followed for an extended period of time, would reduce life expectancy of the person by 20 percent? Shouldn't everyone be allowed to live up to the limit of their life expectancy? Few would argue to the contrary. The problem is that it is by no means clear what the life expectancy of many people is. There is much variation, not all of which can be explained in terms of diet. There is also the issue of extending people's life expectancy with artificial kidneys or heart transplants. This can apparently be done, but it is presently very expensive. It is, nonetheless, a development which is beginning to have impact on the question of living and dying and hence seems relevant to the issue of the need to live.

We encounter even bigger problems if we try to incorporate notions of minimum psychological needs into the definition of poverty. The general concern of most who have tried to do this is with the conditions that lead to happiness. The problem is that happiness is a distressingly vague concept that for all mankind is related to just about everything. Even for individuals, it encompasses many things, the set of which apparently varies substantially from person to person.

To define poverty in practical terms is not easy. In such terms, poverty is, in the first instance, a lack of command over goods and services to meet the minimum needs of the person. That command, in a market economy, is determined by the income and the wealth of the person. The importance of income is evident. Whether we have to worry about a person's wealth is another question, in part because the wealth accumulations of people are strongly correlated with their incomes and vice versa. Still there are some who have low income, but sizeable amounts of wealth, e.g., the retired, who could, if necessary, "consume their wealth," as a means of staying alive and happy. Wealth seemingly should be taken into account when trying to evaluate the command a person has over goods and services. Yet, it cannot because there is no agency, either public or private, that collect very extensive data on the assets of individual households. Since the Census Bureau collects fairly reliable household income statistics, it is not surprising to find definitions of poverty expressed in terms of income.

Given income as the measure of the command over goods and services, the next step is to identify the level of income below which people can be said to be living in poverty. In the early 1960s, when attempts were made to calculate the number of poor in America, a cash income line was drawn at $3,000. The $3,000 figure was based on estimates by the Department of Agriculture for a low-cost budget permitting the minimum diet consistent with food preferences of the lowest third of the population and adequate enough to avoid basic nutritional difficulties. The concern was thus with diet, and an attempt was made to address the question of what the minimum nutritional needs of a family was. Other elements in that need were taken into account by applying a factor of three to these food costs. The reason was that food costs accounted for roughly one-third of the budget of moderate and low-income families.

The $3,000 figure applied indiscriminantly to all turned out to be unsatisfactory. The reason is evident. The income necessary to satisfy the basic nutritional and other needs of a family varies among familes. It obviously varies according to the size of the household; the food and shelter needs of a large family are greater than those of a small one. These needs also vary by location. Living costs differ by area; heating and clothing costs are less in Florida, for example, than they are in Maine. These differences should be taken into account as should those related to the health of people. Diabetics, for example, have to pay more for food and buy insulin as well.

As our poverty statistics are currently calculated, a range of income levels are provided that reflect the differences in family size, sex of the family head, number of children under eighteen, and farm versus nonfarm residence. These statistics are also adjusted to reflect cost of living indexes.

No one denies that there are arbitrary elements in the way in which these poverty statistics are derived. Yet, these statistics are not without a conceptual and logical foundation. What we have are numbers that do not allow us to delineate the number of people living in poverty with as much precision as we would like. They are, nonetheless, figures that serve us reasonably well in that they provide indications of orders of magnitude and how these are changing over time.

WHO ARE THE POOR?

With government figures that define the boundary lines of poverty, we can get reasonable benchmarks of the incidence of poverty. The facts are straightforward. Poverty is concentrated among certain groups in the population. It is most widespread among blacks, households headed by females, and the aged. In 1974, 11.6 percent of the nation's population had incomes that fell below the poverty level—see Table 9.1. While a little over two-thirds of these were white, this is a reflection of the number of the whites in the nation's population. The "incidence" of poverty in the sense of the proportion of people in a population group who are poor is much greater for blacks than whites. In 1974, only 8.9 percent of the white population lived in poverty. During the same year, close to one-third of the nation's black population had incomes that fell below the poverty line. This figure was even higher for households with female heads. The aged—persons sixty-five and over—show up as being less poverty-prone than blacks and households headed by females. Still, in 1974, close to 16 percent of this population had incomes that fell below the poverty line.

Further breakdowns of these data show additional points of concentration. For example, the incidence of poverty turns out to be particularly high among blacks who are over sixty-five and black households with female heads. The incidence of poverty is highest when the black households with female heads have three or more children.

The facts should not be particularly surprising. They are generally consistent with journalistic reports of poverty. The figures in Table 9.1, however, also reveal things that are less frequently the subject of these reports.

While there are still 24 million, or roughly one in nine Americans who are poor, the number is substantially less than it was twenty-five years ago. In 1959,

Table 9.1

Persons Below Low Income Level by Race, Sex of Head, and Age

	Number Below Low Income Level (Millions)				Percent Below Low Income Level			
	1959	1965	1970	1974	1959	1965	1970	1974
All Persons	39.5	33.2	25.4	24.3	22.4	17.3	12.6	11.6
White	28.5	22.5	17.5	16.3	18.1	13.3	9.9	8.9
Black and Other Races	11.0	10.7	7.9	8.0	56.2	47.1	32.0	29.5
Black	(NA)	(NA)	7.5	7.5	(NA)	(NA)	33.5	31.4
In Families with Male Head	29.1	22.1	14.3	12.5	18.7	13.2	8.2	7.1
In Families with Female Head	10.4	11.1	11.2	11.8	50.2	46.0	38.2	34.4
Persons 65+	5.4	5.0	4.8	3.3	35.2	32.0	24.6	15.7

Source: U.S. Bureau of the Census

there were 40 million poor people in America, or more than one out of five of the nation's citizens. This decline in poverty was evident among most groups where its incidence was relatively high, i.e., blacks, households with female heads, and the aged—see Table 9.1. The biggest decline was among the aged, a development that can be largely attributed to recent increases in social security payments. The incidence of poverty among families with female heads also declined substantially between 1959 and 1974. This was no doubt a reflection of the growing importance and acceptance of women in the work roles of American industry.

While a population of 24 million poor people indicates that we still have a poverty problem of some magnitude, the fact that the proportion of poor in the population is only half of what it was fifteen years ago suggests that we have made some progress in the war against poverty.

THE URBANIZATION OF POVERTY

Poverty is a problem that knows no boundary. As Table 9.2 makes clear, it is found both in our cities and in the countryside. The overall magnitude of the problem—measured in terms of number of poor people—is greater in the city than in rural America. Yet, this is a consequence of the fact that more people live in cities than in rural areas. Table 9.2 makes clear the fact that the incidence of poverty is greater in rural areas than it is in cities both for blacks and whites.

This is not really a surprising conclusion. As noted in chapter 2 and to be reaffirmed in chapter 13 when the subject of city size is taken up, people live in cities because they gain economic advantages by doing so. The nation's real productive might is found in its cities. Living standards that, on the average, are higher in cities than in rural areas are to be expected. If the productivity of what we do has anything to do with the presence or absence of poor people, as it does, we would expect more poor people to be in the countryside. The real question is: Why do we find poor people in cities?

The answer is found, in part, in the urbanization of America. As discussed in chapter 7, urbanization in this country was largely the result of a changing technology that provided incentives for people to live and work near one another. Two important aspects of this change, which helped to bring poor people to the city, were the technical revolution in southern agriculture and the technical change which reduced the demand for coal mined in the Appalachias. These developments created unemployment problems in the South. Some who suffered economic hardship as a consequence were enticed to northern cities by the job opportunities that developed during World War II. After World War II, the movement intensified because economic conditions grew worse in southern rural areas and much worse in the Appalachias. Now, southern blacks in the Mississippi Delta and southern whites in the Appalachias were pushed away by extreme poverty. Many had little to lose by moving to the "Promised Land"; and move many of them did. Their move was to cities, and, in most cases, to the center of these cities because here they were most likely to find housing accommodations

Table 9.2

Persons Below Low Income Level by Residence and Race

1973

	Persons Below Low Income Level			Percent Below Low Income Level		
	All Races	White	Black	All Races	White	Black
Metropolitan Areas	13,759	8,452	4,998	9.7	6.9	28.2
Inside Central Areas	8,594	4,305	4,062	14.0	9.3	29.6
Outside Central Cities	5,165	4,147	936	6.4	5.5	23.4
Nonmetropolitan Areas	9,214	6,690	2,390	14.0	11.2	41.1

Source: Bureau of the Census

177

plus an array of public services that many had never really known before. The move for most, in fact, turned out to be a profitable one. They were still poor, but for many, not quite as poor as they had been. Still, they lived in poverty as we define it, as do many of their children.

While some urban poor may have a long family heritage in the cities in which they live, the majority have roots in rural America. Their presence in cities is intimately tied up with the process of urbanization in the nation.

POVERTY WITHIN THE CITY: THE GHETTO

Popular reports of urban poverty indicate the poor live together in "ghettos" in the center of the city. There is an element of truth to such reports. Figures in Table 9.2 show close to two-thirds of the poor who live in our metropolitan areas live in the central cities of these areas. For poor blacks, this figure is over 80 percent.

There are also other measures that suggest the central city of the metropolis is where the very poor are. Poverty in the central city extends to educational attainment. The gap between those who live in the urban core and the suburbs is wide. The central city is also the primary urban location of blacks and other minorities, as well as the aged whose incomes are well below average. It is also the beneficiary of the bulk of the payments of the federal welfare programs.

That the poor are concentrated in central cities is largely a consequence of urbanization and the filtering that occurs in urban housing markets. Many of the city's poor, as just noted, have roots in the rural South. They came to live in the center of the city because this is where they found the housing they could afford. Middle and upper-income whites had, prior to their arrival, begun moving to the suburbs for a number of reasons including the automobile and rising real incomes—see chapter 8. In leaving the central city, they vacated relatively large dwellings which could be converted into multifamily dwellings at a relatively low cost. These units became a part of the supply of housing available for the poor. Those who moved into these dwellings were apparently willing to live in close proximity to one another. Theirs was a different culture from the established middle and upper-income white families of the city. They felt more comfortable among themselves, which made many middle and upper-income whites very happy. Some whites also did much to try to encourage this feeling. Residential discrimination was clearly a factor in the concentration of the urban poor in the center of American cities, about which more will be said in the next chapter.

Not all of the poor who moved into cities were assimilated in this way. Nor did all of those with city roots who became poor gravitate to the ghettos of the central cities. The fact that one-third of the urban poor live in the suburbs, as do 20 percent of the poor who are black, indicates the spatial distribution of poverty within cities cannot be fully explained by the urbanization and filtration process. Some of the rich live in central cities as do some of those in the middle-income classes, and some of the poor live in the suburbs. We do not really have good knowledge of precisely where the poor live in relation to the rich. In some cases, their residences abut one another. The data and techniques of analyzing that data, however, do not allow us to become very specific in discussing spatial patterns of poverty within cities. What we can say is: That while the poor are found in the suburbs, the poverty problems are concentrated in the inner core of our cities. It is also the case that the poor who live in the suburbs are not really integrated with the nonpoor. They live in clusters that are seemingly randomly distributed throughout the outer ring of the city.

CAUSES OF POVERTY

Studies of the cause of poverty have concentrated on factors which affect the wage and salary earnings of individuals. That earnings capacity, of course, not only depends on payments for labor services, but payments for the services of their property as well—at least for some. The wealth accumulations of people do have bearing on the incomes they earn, and there are substantial individual differences in the wealth holdings of the population. It seems, therefore, that statements about the causes of poverty should take factors that help explain the differences in wealth holding of individuals into account. The problem is that we know less about the cause of the wealth differences than we do about the cause of differences in the wage and salary earning capacities of individuals.

Fortunately, this gap in knowledge is not crucial to a consideration of the causes of poverty. The accumulation of wealth is not likely to be a direct path to a movement above the poverty line for most families. Wealth comes from inheritance, exappropriation, and income earned, which for the poor comes from payments for their labor services. Inherited wealth has little relevance to a consideration of why some people are poor. Exappropriation is much less important as a factor in explaining poverty in this country than it is in some others. In the main, the reason why people are poor in American cities has to do with factors that impinge on the payments people receive for the services of their labor. Thus, discussions of causes of poverty usually focus on factors that affect the wage and salary earning capabilities of the poor. These are ordinarily discussed under the heading of *macro* and *micro factors*.

Macro Factors

Macro factors are those factors that operate through the general economic environment. If poverty stems from the fact that some people do not have adequate command over enough goods and services, general economic factors that have impact on personal incomes have bearing on the problem of poverty. The ratio of the poor to the total population, for example, increased dramatically during the depression years of the 1930s. That we have apparently had less success in reducing their numbers since 1970 than we did during the 1950s and 1960s is, in part, attributable to macroeconomic problems in general and inflation in particular. When the overall economy suffers from periodic and recurring periods of inflation and recession, the problems of the poor and those who are near-poor will intensify. Economic stabilization is a necessary condition for the success of any effort to deal with the problem of poverty. A rapid pace of real economic growth will also contribute substantially to these efforts.

If we suppose that our stabilization efforts are successful and the nation's rate of economic growth is satisfactory, there may nevertheless be problems in particular regions or metropolitan areas. While the national economy may be getting good marks for its performance, there can be economic problems within the nation. Urban communities in eastern Kentucky, the Mississippi Delta, and the upper Midwest, among others, had economic troubles when the nation was moving along at a boomlike pace in the 1950s. Changes in technology, in the structure of demands, and in migration patterns, just to name a few, can alter the economic circumstances of a region in ways that cause problems in one place and generate economic booms in others. Differential movements in the regional economies are a fact, and they are a fact that helps to explain much of the regional differences that exist in the incidence of poverty. If we wish to address the problem of poverty, these differences must be reckoned with.

Micro Factors

Micro factors are those factors that operate through the person. If we suppose that the national economy is performing well and there are no special macro-economic difficulties in the city of concern, it is still likely that we will find poor people in that population. If we do, this must be a consequence of factors that operate through the person, or in social or environmental factors that are close by, but beyond the control of the person. As these things have been studied by economists and others interested in poverty problems, they generally fall under the headings of infirmity-sickness-motivation, human capital deficiencies, and discrimination with respect to employment.

Infirmity-Sickness-Motivation   While economists have little to say about income problems that stem from the fact that some people are too sick to work, some are too old and weak to work, and some people have real motivation problems, there are people who are poor for one of these three reasons. Those who are sick in the sense of being alcoholics, drug addicts, perverts, and the like are sometimes called the "disreputable poor." Their defects may be a consequence of the poverty as well as a cause. The point is that they will not be easily gotten back into the economic mainstream, and hence present a serious social problem, the solution of which may require income transfers.

Those who are sick or old and incapable of handling the demands of a workday life may be living in poverty that carries no disrepute. To bring them above the poverty line, however, will require income transfers.

These people constitute important parts of the "hard core" poverty problem and should not be forgotten. Much of our concern in recent years, however, has been with those who could move above the poverty line by entering the mainstream of the American economy. The problems of these people apparently stem from human capital deficiencies and racial discrimination.

Human Capital Deficiencies   The wage and salary component of the earnings of individuals is a reflection of their contribution to production in a market economy. Labor markets provide the valuations of that contribution. The demands for particular kinds of labor depend on the productivity of its use in production. The ordinary view of this productivity is that it declines out on the margin as more and more labor is used—see D_1D_1 in Figure 9.1.

Figure 9.1

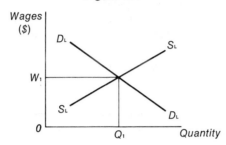

The supply of this kind of labor is a function of a number of demographic, social, and economic factors. Suppose these factors work themselves out so that the supply curve slopes upward and to the right—see S_1S_1 in Figure 9.1. This implies that more labor services will be made available at a higher wage and vice versa—not an unreasonable assumption.

The market interaction of supply and demand determines the wage—OW_1 in Figure 9.1—and the units of labor used at this wage—OQ_1 in Figure 9.1. The wage, of course, is the income earned by those who supply the labor service. High wages imply high incomes and low wages imply low incomes. If the wage is too low, the income of the wage-owners could fall below the poverty line. If this happens, it must have to do with demand and supply factors that come to bear on the wage.

The operations of most labor markets are, of course, influenced by monopoly elements that operate both through the demand side—firms—and the supply side —labor unions. Monopoly elements on the demand side can push the wage below the "worth" of the worker's contribution. Monopoly elements on the supply side can push it above that worth. In fact no one ever receives an income that is exactly equal to their contribution to production. Most Americans, however, receive an income that is approximately equal to the value of that contribution. If their wages are really low, the explanation is more likely to be found in the nature of their contribution rather than in monopolistic exploitation by the firms that use their labor services.

The primary reason why wages are low for some people has to do with low productivity. What they do for the firm is not valued very highly by that firm. Why is this? What determines the value of the contribution of an individual to production? In economics, much attention in recent years has centered on the notion of human capital. The productive contributions of people are believed to be a function of the work skills they have. These, in turn, are believed to depend mainly on the amount of human capital people have accumulated.

Obviously, when people are born, the limits to what they can do are set in terms of the genetic inheritance of their ancestry. This heritage does not determine exactly what they will do. What they learn is important and this is a function of their education. The term "education" is used here in the broadest sense, including the "environmental" experiences of the person prior to formal schooling, extracurricular activities while in school and postschool training. It is the education that is the investment that generates the human capital, which becomes manifest in the skills a person exhibits in production. Generally, the greater the accumulation of human capital, the higher the level of skills that will be exhibited and hence the greater the contributions of the person to production.

What kind of education experiences lead to the most rapid accumulations of human capital? While there are no conclusive answers, recent research of some economists suggests that formal schooling is important. Formal schooling in this case includes not only what goes on in our primary, secondary, and high schools, as well as higher educational institutions, it also includes formal postschool training of people.

To say that formal education is human capital investment, which determines what people will earn over the course of their working lives, is not to say that other things are unimportant. Nor is it to say that we can predict precisely what a person's lifetime income stream will be, given knowledge of his or her educational background. There still are those instances of Ph.D.'s who have very modest incomes and those persons with little formal education who become multimillionaires. These are the exceptions rather than the rule, however, and the exceptions are diminishing in importance.

The rationale of the positive correlation between formal education and earnings is that formal education becomes manifested in the skills a person brings to bear on the job. More formal education means, on the average, more skills, and higher skill levels mean greater contributions to production. In a system in which rewards are determined in competitive markets, greater contributions to production will be translated into higher awards.

Education is indeed a part of the problem of the poor. There is ample evidence that the nation's poor lag well behind others in formal schooling. They have human capital deficiencies, which hamper their abilities to contribute to production. Many, in fact, find it difficult to get work and when they do, the market does not value their labor services very highly.

To say that education is the answer to the problem of poverty, however, is not very helpful. We have to become specific about the kind of education that is necessary. When we try to do this, the complexities of the problem surface. People must have certain basic skills to deal with the problems that confront them in work situations. Some problems require greater levels of these "academic" skills than do others. Since we only have limited resources with which to deal with the problem of educating the masses, perhaps what we should do in the interest of maximizing the rate of return on our education resources is to establish a "two-track" system. In other words, let us set up a system in which some will concentrate on the academic, and others will concentrate on vocational pursuits.

We now get into issues that are controversial and unresolved. The presence of such issues, in turn, helps to explain why, in the face of evidence that education is both a cause and solution to the problem of poverty, we have had less success than anticipated from educational programs aimed at the poor.

Racial Discrimination   Discrimination in the sense of people displaying their preferences by discriminating between goods is the essence of economics. Some forms of discrimination, however, create problems. Racial discrimination with respect to employment is one of these. Such discrimination implies that the firm consciously takes into account the color of the skin of a prospective employee in its personnel decisions. The form it takes in urban America is that whites are considered differently—more favorably—than blacks and other minorities. This is reflected in the wage offers made to these two groups. Whites are offered more for the same kind of work and, more important, are provided with more opportunities for "upward movement" in the organization. The result is that whites earn much more than blacks, a fact that can be easily documented—see Table 9.3.

Table 9.3

Median Money Income of Families by Race
1959–1974

	1959	1970	1974
White	$5,928	$10,216	$13,271
Black	3,010	6,278	7,807
Black vs a Percent of White	50.8	61.5	58.8

Source: U.S. Bureau of the Census

This argument seems compelling. There is not only the evidence of the income differentials, but there is also the history of race relations in America, going back to the beginning, when blacks were treated as chattel or slaves. While slavery ended with the conclusion of the Civil War, blacks have apparently never been considered as equals in the eyes of many whites. Until the late 1950s, signs of differential treatment were in evidence in such places as schools, restrooms, buses, recreational facilities, and restaurants. There was differential treatment in the sense that most of the separate facilities available for whites and blacks were not equal. Since the facilities of blacks were generally inferior, this was taken as a reflection of racial discrimination, just as was the fact that there were few blacks in positions of responsibility in industry or government.

Since the latter part of the 1950s, many of these overt restrictions on blacks have been removed, and blacks now have more options with respect to how they spend their money, where they live, where they go to work, where they go to school, and where they take their vacations. Still, the income of blacks remains well below that of whites. Their unemployment rate is still much higher than that of whites, and the reports of whites discriminating against blacks have not diminished.

Few doubt that blacks and other minorities have been the victims of discrimination in American society that has adversely affected their economic position. Recent research of economists has done much to clarify the nature of this problem and warrants discussion here.

If incomes are largely the outcome of the operation of labor markets, demand and supply considerations should help explain the presence of racial differences in income.

With respect to supply, arguments have been advanced to the effect that blacks have lower productivity than whites. This is largely a consequence of differences in human capital. On the average, blacks have much less formal education, which is reflected in the level of skill they can bring to a work situation. Some studies have estimated that up to two-thirds of the income differential between blacks and whites is to be explained by human capital differences. This is substantial, and suggests that much of what some consider to be racial discrimination is economic discrimination of a kind we should endorse in the interests of economic efficiency. If people are not equipped to do a job, there will be added costs if they are allowed to do it.

To say this is not to say that racial discrimination has nothing to do with the black/white earnings differentials. Supply factors do not explain all of that differential. Demand is involved, and it is through labor demands that discrimination surfaces. White employers prejudiced against blacks do not have to hire them, or if they do, can pay blacks less. While firms are in business to make money—that is, to maximize profits—owners have discretion with respect to just how much profit to try to make. If the owners are white and have an aversion to associating with blacks, they can avoid using blacks, if they are willing to accept smaller profits. Discrimination in this sense has been said to be a reflection of tastes and preferences of the owner.

Can discrimination in this sense really exist? Some economists argue that it cannot in a system of competitive markets. In such markets, workers are paid an amount equal to the market valuation of their productivity. Firms will pay no more because they would be reducing their profits if they did. Presumably firms can pay no less because of competition among themselves for labor.

Suppose the firm has a choice among workers who are equally productive, some of whom are white and some of whom are black. Profits will be maximized if the firm picks indiscriminately among this group and pays the "going" wage. Suppose, however, that the owners of this firm have an aversion to associating with blacks. The firm may try to discriminate in its hiring practices; it may try to hire whites only. If it does, that firm may have to pay more. If others are pursuing the same policy, the price of white workers will be bid up and the price of black workers will fall. Note now that firms that hire only white workers will have higher labor costs and, therefore, lower profits. This gives the non-discriminatory firm a competitive edge.

If there are actual or potential employers who do not discriminate, the discriminating firm will, eventually, be forced to reconsider its hiring practices. To do so could be a matter of survival. This is why some economists argue that racial discrimination is impossible over the long run in competitive markets.

Until recently, of course, there were many firms, particularly small ones, that had no black employees, or if they had them, the blacks were only in menial positions. This could have been partly a reflection of discrimination because of the tastes and preferences of the owner. Yet, in recent years, employers have moved in directions that have reduced the amount of racial discrimination in employment practices. This stems, in part, from the rising political power of blacks and from increased social consciousness of whites. Both of these factors lie at the bottom of some of the legislation and governmental administrative actions taken which have fostered the hiring of blacks and other minorities. Despite this, the black/white income differentials persist, which suggests that supply factors are the predominant reason for these differentials. Racial discrimination has had impact on the incomes earned by blacks, and in some cases is a factor explaining why some blacks had incomes that fell below the poverty line. The extent to which this happened, however, has probably been overstated. If we could eradicate the racial prejudices of whites against blacks, we would reduce the black/white income differential, but that differential would remain because of black/white differences in human capital investments.

THE ECONOMICS OF
THE URBAN GHETTO

The urban ghetto is a widely used, if not well understood phrase. Everyone knows that there are ghettos in our cities. They are enclaves, populated mostly by minorities, located in the inner city of virtually every metropolitan area in America. Ghetto households live in very close proximity to one another under conditions of excessive density. They are households living in poverty, suffering all of the miseries associated with substandard levels of consumption.

This is, of course, the general view of an urban ghetto that most people have. While not unreasonable, since there are many places like this in many inner cities, it is not a totally satisfactory one. As noted above, the poor who live in the city consist of both blacks and whites—see Table 9.2. Second, as also noted above, while there are concentration points of poverty in the city, not all of the poor live in ghettos, nor are all of these ghettos in the inner city—see Table 9.2. The fact remains that there are ghettos in the inner cities of most metropolitan areas and the living conditions in these places strongly parallel the popular conception of life in an urban ghetto.

Why do we have ghettos? What economic factors are involved? Much that has been discussed above are elements in the answers to these questions.

If we assume that very few do so by choice—not an unreasonable assumption— the question of restrictions to the individual's freedom of choice arises. Why is it that people must live in ghettos? What are the restrictions on their choices and alternatives?

One important reason why some people live in ghettos is that they can afford nothing better. Low cost housing is available in the ghetto and most of those who live there can afford nothing else. For whatever reasons—discrimination, lack of education, poor motivation—these are people apparently caught in the web of poverty. Their salaries, when they are working, are so low that they must live in low cost housing, which they hope is at a location close to where they work.

The ghettos found in many northern cities, as noted above, have their roots in the waves of black migration from the South. Those who came up from the South lacked the education, training, and skills necessary for a full and productive participation in the urban economy. The employment opportunities of some were also restricted because they were black.

Blacks who came to the city also found restrictions on housing. For reasons to be discussed in the next chapter, blacks are effectively excluded from living in many parts of the city, particularly if their incomes are low. Many of the southern blacks—and whites—who moved to northern cities thus found the only housing they could afford—or where they were "welcomed"—in an inner city ghetto.

There are success stories. There have been those who either moved into or were born into these ghettos who made their way out, if only in the sense of moving up the income ladder. But most have lived out their lives in these ghettos, and many of these found their problems grew worse with time.

Employment problems for ghetto residents certainly intensified as business began to move to outlying locations. These moves, as indicated in chapter 8, were largely a consequence of technical change that increased the space requirements of business. This migration added considerably to the employment problems of ghetto residents, since it meant job opportunities were no longer so close at hand.

When jobs move away, one solution is to follow those jobs. Yet, this apparently was not really a feasible alternative for many blacks living in ghettos, in part because their housing opportunities were limited by what, in the final analysis, were the prejudices of whites—see chapter 10. Employment opportunities for blacks thus diminished, adding further to the poverty problems of those who remained in the ghettos.

The movement of industry away from the central city, by reducing the tax base, also created special problems for central city governments. It reduced the ability of these governments to provide public services to its citizens, at a time when the demand for such services was rapidly increasing because of the migration of blacks and others into inner city ghettos.

Conditions of abject poverty began to surface in many of the areas. The basic problem, particularly for blacks, was one of unemployment—see Table 9.4. This problem was compounded by the deterioration of public services and the physical environment. Lack of human capital investment and housing discrimination made it difficult for individuals to break out of these areas. This, in turn, intensified the problems confronting most ghetto residents, leading to various forms of antisocial behavior, e.g., drug abuse, crime, etc. Those who studied our urban ghettos began to talk about circular causation and the need to break into the cycle of poverty in order to address the problem. Those who lived or came to work in areas adjacent to or near these ghettos also began to talk about the

Table 9.4

Unemployment Rate by Race

1960–1975

(Unemployment as Percent of Labor Force)

Annual Averages	All Workers	White	Black
1960	5.5	4.9	10.2
1965	4.5	4.1	8.1
1969	3.5	3.1	6.4
1970	4.9	4.5	8.2
1971	5.9	5.4	9.9
1972	5.6	5.0	10.0
1973	4.9	4.3	8.9
1974	5.6	5.0	9.9
1975 (April)	8.6	7.9	13.8

Source: Bureau of Labor Statistics

need to address the problems of these areas. The primary concern of these people, however, was in the reestablishment of law and order in our central cities.

CURES FOR POVERTY

The problem of dealing with poverty, be it in the city or in rural areas, is, at one level, a problem of raising the consumption levels of a certain group of people. This can be done directly by providing them with consumption goods. It can be done by giving them money. It can also be done by undertaking measures that will influence their income earning capacity. The first two of these are presumably directed toward the aged, the sick, and others who are unable to provide for themselves. The solution to the poverty problems of this group will involve a redistribution of income, which will take the form of what are usually called *transfer payments*. Transfer payments also are a part of the short-run solution to the poverty problems of the able-bodied, who, for whatever reasons, are not really a part of the mainstream of American economic life. More important to this group over the long-run, however, are those measures that will help upgrade their earnings capacity.

We have, in fact, attacked the problems of poverty of both these groups through a burgeoning number of programs at all levels of government.

Redistributing Income and the Problems of the Poor

We do many things through government at all levels that redistribute income. We also do things privately—charities of various kinds—that redistribute income. With charity, the flow is from those with relatively high incomes to those with low incomes. The amounts involved in such giving are small, however, relative to the potential redistribution that can result as a consequence of the fiscal activities of the government.

Programs of Cash Transfer Payments   While all public expenditures of government can have direct repercussions on the consumption of the poor, those that have the most impact on the poor are those that make cash payments to individuals such as Social Security, veterans' pensions, and public assistance. These programs have their roots in the Great Depression, with its massive unemployment and sharp declines in earnings, which generated widespread destitution. It might be noted parenthetically that the economic stabilization programs of the federal government, at least until recently, are generally credited with doing much to alleviate poverty in the nation. Extended periods of economic slack keep unemployment too high and reduce real incomes, both of which can add significantly to the dimensions of the nation's poverty problem. If we have reduced the probability of their occurrence, we will have done much to deal with the poverty problem. Poverty will not be eradicated, however.

The programs of cash subsidies to individuals can be viewed as being addressed to this residual problem. The recent rapid growth in the importance of public assistance payments is shown in Table 9.5. The programs themselves are directed

Table 9.5

Public Assistance Payments

		Percent of Total Payments		
Payments Per Year		*Old Age Assistance*	*Aid to Dependent Children*	*Medical Assistance*
(Millions of Dollars)				
1950	$ 2,465	60.5	22.6	—
1955	2,748	58.4	23.0	—
1960	3,785	50.8	27.9	—
1965	5,476	37.4	33.0	—
1969	11,547	16.0	30.9	37.8
1970	14,467	12.9	33.6	38.1
1971	16,356	11.8	34.6	38.0
1972	20,005	9.5	35.1	43.5
1973	21,358	8.2	34.1	45.9
1974	20,660	N/A	N/A	N/A

Source: U.S. Social and Rehabilitation Service

towards a number of groups. The payments go to the aged and children who are in need because of the death or sustained absence of a parent. They also include payments for medical assistance, which have mushroomed in recent years.

Cash payments are also made to people who suffer an injury or contract a disease while working. These are payments that are a part of the workmen's compensation programs that have a long history in most states. More recently, they have received assistance from the federal government. There are also cash payments that are made to most of those who become unemployed.

Most of these programs have roots in our Social Security programs. There are, in addition, a number of other government programs in such areas as agriculture, housing, and social services, which transfer both cash and payments in kind to people, some of whom are poor.

An estimate of the dollar volume of these cash transfers and the number of beneficiaries is shown in Table 9.6, along with an estimate of the proportion of these payments that go to the poor. Significantly, there are differences in the proportions of the payments that go to the poor and in some cases the proportion is relatively small. This is not surprising, however; the current cash transfer system is not designed to provide every one with a minimum income. What we have, in fact, is a conglomeration of different programs which were enacted at various times for different purposes. The main beneficiaries who are poor are the aged and the sick and disabled.

Taxes   Do the poor really receive net benefits from cash transfer programs? To ask this question is to ask about the structure of the nation's taxes, for the receipt of net benefits implies that the benefits received are greater than the taxes paid. Do the poor receive net benefits in this sense? We must look at the question of the incidence of our taxes. In other words, we must inquire as to who really pays the tax bill.

While there are many kinds of taxes, the two most important categories as far as income redistribution is concerned are personal income and payroll (Social Security) taxes.

Most people believe that personal income taxes are progressive, and for good reason. The personal income tax rates are progressive, that is, the rate grows larger in the higher income brackets. Indeed, despite the tax "loopholes," estimates of the tax burden of individuals at different income levels show high-income people pay personal income taxes that are a higher proportion of their incomes than do low-income persons—see Table 9.7. This is offset to some extent, however, by the incidence of the payroll or Social Security taxes. Since these taxes are only applied to the first $12,000 of a person's income, they obviously fall more heavily on those with lower incomes. One estimate of the combined incidence of Social Security and personal income taxes indicates that the payroll tax completely offsets the tax advantages middle-income people have with respect to the personal income tax and substantially narrows the difference between low-income and high-income persons—see Table 9.7.

The net effect of the other taxes is more difficult to isolate. Property taxes and some sales taxes are regressive, but how regressive is unknown. Estate and gift taxes are progressive, but account for very little of the revenues of government. Corporate income taxes are more important and generally believed to be progressive, but by an unknown amount.

What this adds up to is subject to controversy and debate. Still, the prevailing opinion seems to be that we take relatively more away from the rich than we do from the poor. It is also believed by most that we give relatively more to the poor than we do the rich. The net effects of the fiscal policies of government are

Table 9.6

Government Transfer Programs: Dollars Transferred 1969; Beneficiaries 1970; Portion to the Poor 1965

Program	Dollars Transferred (Billions)	Number of Beneficiaries (Millions)	Portion to Poor
Old Age, Survivors Disability; Health Insurance			
Cash	$33.6	25.5	63%
Medicare	6.6		33%
Veterans' Pensions			
Cash	5.2	5.3	46%
Medical	1.6		
Unemployment Compensation	2.4	1.9	36%
Workmen's Compensation	2.6		
Temporary Disability Insurance	0.7		
Old Age Assistance	1.7	2.0	

Source: Alan Batchelder, *The Economics of Poverty*, New York: John Wiley and Sons, 1971, p. 146.

Table 9.7

*Federal Individual Income and Payroll Taxes
for a Four-Person Family with One Earner
1973*

Earnings and Tax Items	1973
$5,000 Earnings	
Income tax	$ 98
Payroll tax	585
Total Tax	683
Effective income tax rate	2.0%
Effective payroll tax rate	11.7
Total effective tax rate	13.7
$10,000 Earnings	
Income tax	$ 905
Payroll tax	1,170
Total tax	2,075
Effective income tax rate	9.0%
Effective payroll tax rate	11.7
Total effective tax rate	20.8
$25,000 Earnings	
Income tax	$3,890
Payroll tax	1,264
Total tax	5,154
Effective income tax rate	15.6%
Effective payroll tax rate	5.0
Total effective tax rate	20.6

Source: Edward Fried, et al., *Setting National Priorities:
The 1974 Budget,* Washington, D.C.: The Brookings Institution, 1973, p. 47.

thus to the benefit of low-income families. The fortunate are taxed to help those who are less fortunate. Whether this is enough help is another question.

Government Programs: Human Capital Investment and Racial Discrimination

Human Capital Deficiencies   Government has always been importantly involved in the production of education services. Education is, in the main, a public good. Our public concern with that good, however, began to intensify in the latter part of the 1950s with the "Sputnik" incident, and we became more concerned as public consciousness with respect to the human capital deficiencies of the poor was raised in the 1960s. As a consequence, much federal legislation was passed in the sixties, which provided additional federal assistance to all levels of formal education, including vocational education. This legislation also introduced educational programs which were designed to help children from poor families benefit more from their formal schooling. These included such programs as Head

Table 9.8

Federal Funds for Education and Related Activities

1965–1975

(In Millions)

	Total	Elementary-Secondary	Higher Education	Vocational	Loans	Other
1965	$ 3.909	$0.943	$2.053	$0.384	$529	$3.717
1970	9.222	3.212	3.913	1.589	508	3.429
1971	10.928	3.724	4.896	1.973	334	4.011
1972	11.771	3.857	5.172	2.343	349	4.527
1973	12.711	4.085	5.986	2.294	346	4.717
1974	13.954	4.599	6.585	2.389	381	5.425
1975	14.656	4.896	6.531	2.835	394	5.735

Source: U.S. National Center for Education

Start, the Neighborhood Youth Corps, and the Job Corps. Finally, more money was made available for a variety of programs concerned in one way or another with adult training. The focal point of much of this effort was to upgrade the skills of low-income persons.

The magnitude of this effort is clearly evident in Table 9.8. Federal funds for education and related activities increased almost fourfold between 1965 and 1974, with increases reflected in all of the major categories of education. Evaluations of the impact of this infusion of funds into the nation's education structures are only beginning to be made and the preliminary results are sketchy and controversial. We can say, however, that the nation, in recent years, has shown much concern for the human capital. Not all of this added concern was directed toward those who are poor, but much of it was.

Racial Discrimination   The nation has also shown a good deal of concern with the problem of racial discrimination with respect to employment. This began at the state level in 1945 when New York and New Jersey passed statutes that prohibited racial discrimination in employment. These became models for laws of other states and for municipal ordinances. By 1965, there were similar statutes in 34 states and ordinances in 50 cities covering employment in most of the states outside the South.

In 1964, Congress enacted legislation—Title VII of the Civil Rights Act of 1964—that laid down prohibititions similar to those contained in the state fair practices laws. In general, these laws have provided aggrieved individuals with the right to seek injunctions stopping discrimination. The Departments of Justice, both at the national and state levels, have authority to prosecute companies, unions, and employment agencies when there is discrimination on the basis of race, color, or national origin. This is a powerful tool that has been used infrequently. The threat of intervention combined with the pressures exerted by government in its employment and purchasing practices, however, have apparently had far-reaching effects on the employment practices of American business.

The real test of this legal foundation for action against discrimination may lie ahead. Until 1974, aggregate demands were strong and these are the kind of economic conditions in which blacks have a much better chance of finding and holding employment appropriate to their skills. There is little doubt, however, that the public is much more conscious of the problem of racial discrimination with respect to employment, and unless a serious "backlash" develops, the progress that has been made will be sustained and expanded.

PUBLIC POLICY ISSUES
IN URBAN POVERTY

Obviously, there are many policy issues that arise in our concern with urban poverty. One set of these concerns income maintenance policies; another concerns the ghetto and what we should do with it.

Income Maintenance Policies

As noted above, we have a wide assortment of government programs that provide cash and payment in kind (real goods and services) benefits to many people. Despite this, we seem to have grown increasingly dissatisfied with what we have. What we have, in the view of some, is a "welfare mess."

What we have, of course, are programs that provide assistance to many people for a number of different reasons. As noted above, not all of the cash and other payments that flow from government programs go to the poor. What we also have are government programs that vary considerably in terms of how they are structured. In some cases, the purposes of the program are well defined and the funds go to those who have an immediate interest in using them in ways that are consistent with those purposes. The education payments to the veterans of World War II are a case in point. This was a program, not coincidentally, that is generally considered as being one of the most successful. There are other programs, on the other hand, that have been given lower marks. The community action programs of the war on poverty, for example, became embroiled in controversy that greatly impaired their effectiveness. A close inspection of these programs, not surprisingly, reveals the lack of a clear statement of purpose in terms of some realizable goal or objective.

It is also sometimes difficult to say just what particular programs are supposed to accomplish after they have been around for a while. There is an initial statement of purpose in the enabling legislation that is often subsequently amended. While the intentions of these amendments may have been honorable, they often add substantially to the administrative costs of the program and in some cases make them virtually incomprehensible to potential beneficiaries.

As our experience with public welfare programs has deepened, however, we have come to understand better some of the general ingredients of programs that are likely to have a high probability of success in maintaining the incomes of some households above the poverty line.

As economists view these programs, the probability of success will be higher if they concentrate on raising the purchasing power of the poor. Much of what we now do to help the poor seems very paternalistic. While intentions may be honest and sincere, programs that impose standards of behavior on others, are, in the view of most economists, likely to be unsuccessful. If free choice is good for the rich, it should also be good for the poor. Hence, the argument is made that what we should do is to add to the purchasing power that the poor have and allow them to make their own decisions about what this should mean in terms of consumption.

Obviously, this point of view is subject to qualification. One need only ask, should we give generalized income assistance to a family, the head of which is an alcoholic? Yet, as economists see it, these are the exceptions. The evidence that the poor, in general, cannot spend their funds wisely is weak.

A second point is that income maintenance programs should contain incentives that encourage the beneficiaries to help themselves. Obviously, this cannot be a feature of any program designed to help the aged, sick, and disabled. But many of the poor are able-bodied and capable of entering the work force. While motivation is by no means the only problem confronting these people—indeed, in most cases it is probably a relatively small part of the problem—self-help should be considered as a part of any solution to their income problems and incentives are an important way of encouraging people to help themselves.

If we accept these as meaningful criteria, the interest by some economists in the negative income tax proposal is understandable. If the welfare mess is largely attributable to the fact that we have too many complicated programs with high administrative costs, no incentives, and too much paternalism, the thing to do is to wipe the slate clean and start with something new, something like the negative income tax.

The *negative income tax* is what its name implies. The government would "collect" a negative tax from those whose income falls below a certain level. It would also continue to collect positive income taxes from those whose incomes are above the level. The "collection" of a negative tax is, of course, a cash payment from the government to the person who "owes" that tax. The negative income tax is therefore a subsidy or generalized income assistance to those who are poor.

How much assistance will this be? This depends on where we draw the dividing line with respect to income and how the tax rates are set.

Suppose the poverty income of a family of five were set at $4,000 and a 50 percent negative income tax rate were used. Setting a floor of $4,000 and a negative tax rate of 50 percent implies that for each dollar that the income of the family falls short of $8,000, the family would receive a fifty cent subsidy. If the family had no income, it would receive a $4,000 cash payment. If it had $4,000 in income, it would receive a $2,000 cash payment and so forth.

Obviously, how we draw the line between poverty and nonpoverty income has bearing on the cash payment and the overall cost of the program, as does the tax rate we establish. That tax rate, however, also has bearing on the incentives that are built into the program. Higher rates mean less incentive and vice versa. If the rate were 100 percent, for example, those who earn income in the private sector of the economy would find that by doing so they simply substitute private dollars for public dollars. The most income they can earn is $4,000 if they are to receive help from the government. If this rate is lower, on the other hand, earnings in the private sector do not reduce the subsidy on a 1 to 1 basis. With a 50 percent tax rate, a person who made $2,000 in the private sector would get 50 percent of the difference between that amount and the $8,000 ceiling. His or her income would thus be $5,000. There is incentive to earn income in the private sector because it means a higher overall income.

The negative income tax has much appeal in terms of the criteria that economists apply to evaluating poverty programs. It is generalized income assistance which means there are no strings attached; the poor can spend it as they see fit. It also contains a mechanism, i.e., the tax rate, through which incentives can be built into the program. Finally, the costs of administering a negative income tax program should be relatively low. The bureaucracy to collect income taxes already exists, and there are reasons for believing that this system could implement a negative tax program with efficiency and dispatch.

The negative tax proposal is not without its problems, however. While such a program could be directed towards the poor in ways that provide them with incentives to add to their incomes through participation in the private sector, if it were successful, the costs of the program could become excessive. In the example above, if the family were making $7,000, it would receive a $500 negative tax payment. Since there are probably more families of five who have incomes of between $4,000 and $8,000 than there are below $4,000, a good deal of the subsidy would go to people who were not poor—that is, people who had incomes above $4,000. Building incentives into the program, if they do what they are supposed to, could thus make the program very expensive relative to the objective of bringing the income of all families up to some minimum level.

To say this is not to say that the negative income tax proposal has no merit. Most economists would argue that it compares favorably with the current hodge-podge of programs we have concerned with income maintenance. What it does suggest, however, is that the criteria we apply in evaluating public policies can come into conflict under certain conditions and we have to be prepared to make judgments about what we consider to be more important.

The Ghetto in a War on Poverty

There are important space dimensions to the problem of dealing with urban poverty. As noted above, urban poverty is concentrated in ghettos found, for the most part, in central cities. If we are to deal with the economic problems of the urban poor, our strategies, it seems, must take this fact into account. Yet, is the geography of urban poverty really important to the solution of the problem?

If our poverty concerns were restricted to cash transfer programs designed to bring the incomes of all people up to some predetermined minimum, we would have little need for concern with where the recipients lived. The important thing would be to get the right amount of cash to the right person.. Our concerns with poverty, however, have not been and probably never will be restricted to something like a negative income tax program. As a nation, we have a strong commitment to education, housing, and equal opportunities in employment. We have had and are likely to continue to have public policies that influence education, housing, and the hiring practices of firms, some of which will spill over into our concerns with the poor. This implies that we shall be implementing public policies that will have impact on the housing, education, jobs, and other opportunities of the poor.

If our approach to dealing with the problems of poverty is multipronged, the question of what to do with the urban ghetto becomes important. As this issue is typically discussed by urban economists, the alternatives are expressed as ghetto "enrichment" or the dispersal and integration of the ghetto population into the metropolitan area as a whole. The latter is sometimes called "opening up the suburbs."

Ghetto enrichment simply means concentrating the flow of money and other program benefits in the ghetto. The concern in this approach is with rebuilding the economic base of these communities along with upgrading the housing stock, education facilities, and other public services. An enrichment program is thus a program that is concerned with making ghetto communities better places to live.

Such a policy is not without appealing features, but most of them are not economic. Ghetto enrichment through subsidies that encourage black capitalism, renovate slum housing, and build better schools could turn out to be a very expensive solution to the problems of the ghetto poor. Those measures that would be taken to revive the economic base of the ghetto community are particularly suspect in this sense. Economic viability implies enterprise that is able to compete with others. Thoughts about developing industries in the ghetto that would supply the needs of ghetto residents turned out to be less promising than many believed initially. The problem was one of markets. The size of the ghetto, along with the relatively low incomes of its residents, meant purchasing power concentrations that, in many instances, were not sufficient to provide a market for production that reflected existing economies of scale. This meant that local production for local consumers was in many cases not really competitive with production outside, which did reflect those economies.

Certain kinds of firms operated by ghetto residents can flourish in the ghetto, such as small retail and service firms. These firms, however, are not the kind of firms that will solve the incomes and unemployment problems of the ghetto. They are, for the most part, low wage firms. Moreover, their number will never be large enough to provide the employment opportunities needed to deal with the unemployment problems in the ghettos.

Economic viability, in a market economy in which technology fosters specialization, means the scale of production must be relatively large to be able to reap the benefit of available scale economies. This means that ghetto enterprises, if they are to be successful, will have to compete with those outside the ghetto.

Now the problems begin to surface. Ghettos, while they have some appealing features—low-cost unskilled labor and proximity to markets—also have some unappealing features to many firms. One of these is the availability and cost of land. Ghettos are high density areas with relatively high land costs. In this sense, they cannot compete with most suburban locations for industry that has large site requirements. This means they cannot really compete for much of the industry that has become so important in the urban economy. The space requirements of a wide range of manufacturing and retailing firms have, as noted in the previous chapter, increased substantially, which is precisely why so many of them have moved to the suburbs.

It is by no means clear that firms with relatively large space requirements would be willing to come back to a central city location, unless the enticement in the form of a subsidy was substantial. Large subsidies, however, do not seem warranted on efficiency grounds. Firms moved away from the central cities because more profits were to be made in the suburbs. If markets were working properly, operation in the suburbs was an efficient use of the community's resources. To move back to the central city would probably add more to costs than revenues or benefits, which, according to the criteria of performance discussed in chapter 6, would be inefficient. To encourage them to do so would be to encourage inefficiency.

The alternative to ghetto enrichment is dispersal or integration of its people and economic activities with all other parts of the metropolitan area of which it is a part. This is seen by many as an alternative that corresponds most closely to the American ideal of equality of opportunity throughout the entire fabric of society. In light of the remarks just above, it also seems to have a higher probability of success. If jobs are an important part of the problem, jobs will be easier to find in suburban areas where employment opportunities are expanding more rapidly. Arguments have also been made to the effect that the problems of education, housing, and public services in the ghetto could be better solved by opening up the suburbs. To approach the problem in this way, however, will not yield quick results. Our difficulties with school desegregation make this fact abundantly clear, as has our experience with open housing laws and subsidies which fostered the construction of low-income housing in the suburbs.

Clearly, the solution of the problem of the urban ghetto involves more than just opening up the gates to the suburbs to the urban poor. Integration in the sense of a random distribution of the population can become a reality, as it has in some cases. It has not, however, when efforts have been made to integrate that part of the ghetto population out of which come juvenile delinquents, the violent, and the disturbed. What we know about city structure and the economic determinants of where people live and work suggests that any solution to the problem of urban poverty will involve some form of integration. Yet, so long as the alienated constitute a factor in the ghetto population, as do suburban whites who have strong prejudices against blacks, some ghetto enrichment measures will be called for and will probably be supported by blacks who have become conscious of certain political advantages that come with concentration.

While integration in the sense of random distribution within the community will be an important part of the long-run solution to the problem of the poor in our cities, interim measures which divert resources into ghettos may turn out to provide the quickest route to this idealized state of affairs.

REFERENCES

Becker, G. *Human Capital.* New York: Columbia University Press for the National Bureau of Economic Research, 1964.

Brimmer, A. and Terrell, H. "The Economic Potential of Black Capitalism." *Public Policy* 19 (1971): 290–308.

Chiswick, B. *Income Inequality.* New York: Columbia University Press for the National Bureau of Economic Research, 1974.

Downs, A. *Opening Up the Suburbs: An Urban Strategy for America.* New Haven: Yale University Press, 1973.

Myrdal, G. "An American Dilemma." New York: McGraw-Hill Publishing Company, 1964.

Ornati, O. "Poverty in Cities." In *Issues in Urban Economics,* edited by H. Perloff and L. Wingo. Baltimore: The Johns Hopkins Press, 1968, pp. 335–62.

Thurow, L. *Poverty and Discrimination.* Washington, D.C.: The Brookings Institution, 1969.

von Furstenberg, G.; Horowitz, A.; and Harrison, B. *Patterns of Racial Discrimination: Volume II, Employment and Income.* Lexington, Mass.: D. C. Heath and Company, Lexington Books, 1974.

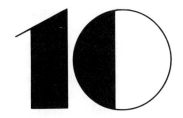

Urban Housing

SUMMARY

City residents have always been concerned with housing problems. While the urban housing problem is a composite of many problems, much emphasis recently has been given to the problems of inadequate housing and residential segregation and discrimination. These two problems provide the focal point of the discussion in this chapter.

Most studies of substandard housing suggest that the problem is largely a problem of housing the poor. The correlations show that most who live in substandard housing are poor and many who are poor live in crowded conditions and/or spend a relatively high proportion of their income on housing.

These correlations are not perfect. Not all of the poor live in substandard housing. There are also some who live in such housing who are not poor. Other factors are involved. Low-income families would benefit from more competition among rental property owners. Government policies also are a factor. There are, in addition, other market imperfections in the filtration process that cause problems, as do neighborhood effects, particularly as they impact on residential upkeep and maintenance.

Residential segregation by race is a well-documented fact in virtually every American city. Some of it is a consequence of a conspiracy among realtors, mortgage lenders and owners of rental properties, although the extent to which they conspire against blacks is usually greatly overstated. The income of black families, as low as it is, is another factor. Low incomes keep households in locations close to where there is employment, which implies that some of what we call racial residential segregation is really income residential segregation. The most important reason for racial residential segregation, however, is the prejudice whites have against blacks.

Some argue that because of racial residential segregation, blacks get less for their money in housing than whites do. Whether they do, in fact, is not a clear-cut matter. There are arguments pro and con, neither of which provide us with anything conclusive.

These problems—substandard housing and racial residential discrimination—are not new; neither is the concern we have with them. We have a long history of public concern with housing and a relatively unimpressive record of success. The question of housing policy is one that requires some decision with respect to how much income we should redistribute in order to be able to address our housing problems. After we make this decision, there are a number of other issues that have to be addressed, including that of generalized income assistance versus housing allowances, and if housing allowances, whether the focus should be on general versus direct subsidies. The optimal policy depends on many things, not the least of which is how well the housing market filters units down to low-income families.

Housing has long been a source of special interest to urban residents, probably because it provides for a basic need, i.e., shelter. Urbanites have also been long concerned about the adequacy—or inadequacy—of their housing. Such a concern is, of course, symptomatic of the presence of a problem—the urban housing problem.

While the urban housing problem is really a composite of many problems, as it was studied, diagnosed, discussed, and dealt with during the latter part of the 1960s and early 1970s, much emphasis was given to the issues of inadequate housing and residential segregation and discrimination. Since these are still the important elements of the housing problem in most cities, they provide the focal point of the discussion in this chapter.

INADEQUATE HOUSING

Virtually everyone agrees there are people living in inadequate housing in every city. There is less agreement about the nature and magnitude of the problem. To speak of it as a problem implies there are dwellings in the stock that do not measure up to some set of minimum standards. Looked at in this light, the general nature of the problem is clear. What is less evident are answers to important specific questions that can be raised. What standards? Just how many occupied units fail to meet the tests implicit in such standards? Where are they? Who lives in them? And why?

These are not easy questions to answer. The difficulty stems from the fact that it is by no means clear what is meant by a minimum standard of housing. This is partly due to the fact that housing consumption is not easy to define. Housing is, of course, a durable asset that provides a wide range of services to the occupant over an extended period of time. Housing can thus be considered both as a stock and a flow of services.

If our concern is with minimum standards of consumption, the flow of services is important. To focus on the flow of services, however, creates definition problems in that the dwelling provides a wide range of services that are not easily combined into an index of consumption.

Generally, the services provided by the dwelling flow from the physical facility itself, the site upon which that facility is situated, and the neighborhood in which the site is located. The physical structure is a number of elements, each of which provides a service to its occupant. These elements include sheltered living space or space for sleeping, food preparation, storage, and the like. They also include such things as water, solid waste, and heating and ventilating systems. The site of this structure encompasses dimensions of size, terrain, and location. The land space that makes up the site is used, of course, to house the physical structure. The space exterior to the dwelling can also serve for work and recreational purposes. How well it serves in this latter capacity depends on its size and certain topographical features, such as slope and foliage. The site also provides "locational services" to its occupant, not the least of which, as noted above, is access to the place of work of the head of the family. The housing services that flow from the neighborhood in which the site is located include, among other things, sewerage systems, water systems, refuse removal services, parking space, traffic safety, streets and roads, public transportation, and educational services.

Clearly, there are many elements in the package of housing services consumed, elements that vary considerably in terms of the particular need they serve. People do many things during the course of the day and different people do different things. Housing enters into these activities in that it assists people in what they are doing and does so in many different ways. How these many elements can be combined so as to be able to compare household satisfactions with housing consumption remains an unresolved problem.

Suppose, however, this problem could be solved. Others would remain, the most important of which is the equity question. What constitutes a minimum standard of housing consumption is not independent of what the community takes to be the "norms" or standards for human conduct.

Standards are, of course, relative. As it relates to housing, the point is easily illustrated. While most would consider dwellings without indoor plumbing facilities as unfit for human habitation, it was not always so. Not many dwellings in the 1850s had indoor plumbing, for example, yet most were considered to be habitable. What we consider as minimal standards of consumption can and have changed over time. Significantly, these changes have removed some of the links between what is necessary and overt indications of the physical well-being of the person. The needs to be satisfied are now partly psychological, some parts of which are not always recognized as being necessary. As this has happened, it has become more difficult to persuade people of the necessity of doing things that will increase the housing consumption of low-income families. The problem is: The efforts to upgrade the housing consumption of some in the community must necessarily reduce the consumption of others. Granted this, we are back to the problem of adding up the gains and losses from such redistributions and our inability to specify an income distribution that is "best." This stands as one important reason why there is so much controversy about minimum housing standards and little likelihood of reconciling the different points of view in the immediate future.

No matter how difficult the problem of definition, it is a fact that many people believe there are substandard dwellings in the urban housing stock and we have, through government, tried to deal with the problem in various ways. Actions that have been taken recently have been based largely on the results of studies that attempted to estimate the number of substandard households in terms of a) the condition of the unit, b) the ability of the household to afford the unit, and c) overcrowding. In the latter part of the 1960s, the Kaiser Committee (The President's Committee on Urban Housing) concluded there were six to eight million such units in the nation's housing stock. More recently an MIT-Harvard Joint Center for Urban Studies indicated there were more than 13 million such units. This difference stems from differences in the way in which these things were defined.

There is no need here to reconcile these differences. Whether we are talking about a problem that encompasses 6, 13 or 25 million households, it is not unreasonable to ask why it is that, in the world's wealthiest nation, there are families numbering in the millions that live in substandard housing.

Causes of Inadequate Housing

Why is it that some families are found living in inadequate housing in American cities? The housing accommodations that most American households have is largely the outcome of the operation of markets. That being so, an analysis of the causes of the problem of inadequate housing should focus on difficulties with the way in which housing markets operate and/or the equity or inequities of the outcomes these markets generated. The question of cause can thus be considered in terms of the efficiency and equity criteria discussed earlier.

Housing Markets, Budget Constraints and the Equity Criteria   Economic theory indicates household income has important bearing on the housing expendi-

---

Table 10.1

Estimates Housing Construction Needs

	Kaiser Committee 1968–1978	Urban Studies MIT-Harvard 1970–1980
Construction of New Units		
Units for New Households	13.4	14.4
Replacement for Net Removal of Standard Units	3.0	7.4
Allowance for Vacancies	1.6	1.6
	18.0	23.4
Replacement or Rehabilitation Units		
Units Becoming Substandard 1968–1978	2.0	
Replacement of Net Removals	2.0	13.1
Other Substandard Units in 1966	4.7	
	8.7	13.1
Total	26.7	36.5

Sources: The President's Committee on Urban Housing, *A Decent Home,* Washington, 1968; Joint Center for Urban Studies of the Massachusetts Institute of Technology and Harvard University, *America's Housing Needs: 1970 to 1980,* Cambridge, Massachusetts, 1973

tures of families. How income constrains housing consumption is a question that is ordinarily investigated in attempts to estimate the income elasticity of demand —i.e., the responsiveness of housing consumption to changes in income. The question of how important income is with respect to housing expenditures is one that, at first glance, seems easy. It is very important. Housing expenditures are the most important component of the family budget, accounting, on the average, for about 15 percent of the household's income. Yet, the fact that housing is so important is, by itself, not really very revealing of the way in which housing consumption is influenced by income. Families could spend large amounts of their income on housing because they prefer housing to all other kinds of consumption goods.

More insight into the impact of income on housing comes from knowledge of the household's consumption response to *changes* in income, i.e., knowledge of the income elasticity of housing consumption. One view of that knowledge (de Leeuw) suggests the income elasticity of housing demand to be unity, that is, changes in income lead to proportional changes in housing expenditure. When the household population is broken down into renter and owner-occupier classes, the response of renters is indicated to be a little stronger than the owner-occupiers.

How are we to interpret this information? Certainly, it indicates that households adjust their housing consumption to income change. Yet elasticity coefficients that indicate proportional changes in housing consumption to income change do not imply that housing expenditures are severely constrained by household income. These coefficients are averages, however, and averages can cover up. In fact, there are indications of much variation in the housing behavior of households. For example, de Leeuw reports the results of elasticity calculations that show marked differences in the income coefficients by size of the family, that is, the larger the family, the larger the coefficient or more responsive the household is in adjusting its housing consumption to income change. More important, there are also tabulations of Census and other data that strongly suggest families with low incomes have very large housing-income coefficients, which implies they are severely constrained in their housing consumption by their incomes.

What can we conclude from this? There is reason to believe that the bundle of housing services people consume becomes a burden to families with low income. This implies that a concern with the problem of housing the poor is a concern with something whose outcome depends, in part, on what is considered to be fair or equitable by those who are not poor. One can conceive of markets working properly, but, given certain distributions of income, generating outcomes that many do not like because it offends their sense of fairness. The problem of inadequate housing in our cities is partly a consequence of the way in which the nation's income is distributed. Our views of the magnitude of this problem thus depend on our views about income distribution or, in effect, our views about what is fair or equitable.

Efficiency Criteria: The Slumlord   City planners and others have for years pointed an accusing finger at the "slumlord." Slums are the primary locale of inadequate housing and we have slums because of the actions of "greedy" landlords who, in their quest for profits, have completely neglected the buildings they own. To argue this way, however, is to assume that landlords are capable of getting away with such neglect, which, in the context of the operation of a system of markets, implies some kind of monopoly power and hence market inefficiency. While competitive market conditions can exist within which landlords will choose a policy of little or no upkeep, competition does provide people with alternatives. When people have alternatives, landlords who seek to maximize profits by cutting back on upkeep might find it unprofitable to do so if their vacancies increase. If they were monopolists, they would not have to worry about vacancies. Since the number of owners of low-income housing is relatively large and there is no real evidence of extensive monopoly profits, it is by no means clear that they behave as slumlords.

The appeal of the slumlord explanation of slums lies in its simplicity and, for some, in its ideological overtones. The question is, does it contribute anything to the explanation of slums? The answer most economists give is no, even though more competition is always welcomed. There are simply too many facts not consistent with its economic implications. First, there is the fact that not all private dwellings that house low-income families are substandard. Second, there is the fact that the public ownership of some low-income housing has not done away with slums. If private owners were responsible, slums should disappear when we convert to public ownership. Finally, the existence of monopoly profits in this segment of the housing market has never been established. In fact, the recent increase in the abandonment of ownership by owners of residential properties in the poorer sections of some central cities suggests that profits may be below the competitive norm.

Supply factors are involved in the market processes through which slums are generated. For example, there is incentive built into some real estate tax laws to keep maintenance in some neighborhoods at very low levels. In some places, taxes on real property tend to impose a burden that is greater for those who own property in the central city. Under certain conditions, such taxes provide incentive for landlords to reduce upkeep and hence foster depreciation and deterioration at rates quickly leading to urban residential blight and slums.

Efficiency Criteria, Market Filtering and Market Imperfections   Residential filtering has been discussed above. As ordinarily conceived, filtering in the housing market is a process through which older units in the upper end of the income distribution filter down to those at the lower end. This, according to some, is how low-income families acquire housing that is consistent with a competitive market outcome. Others violently disagree.

For reasons noted in chapter 5, housing market outcomes are not really competitive market outcomes. The dwelling is anything but homogeneous. What is exchanged in the market place is highly differentiated. Such differentiation means not all units are competitive nor are all households in search of housing accommodations in competition with one another. Owners of thirty-room mansions do not really compete with those who own buildings filled with efficiency apartments. Nor do families earning in excess of $100,000 a year compete for dwellings with those who make less than $3,000. Market segmentation in this sense restricts competition and does so especially among sellers of low value property where there are likely to be few additions through new construction. This implies higher market prices which, if paid by those with low incomes, could reduce the amount of housing services these families can purchase. Some might be pushed into substandard housing as a result.

Is this an important possibility? The question is not easily answered. While it is a reasonable proposition, our empirical knowledge does not allow us to assert with certainty how much more, if at all, low-income families pay for housing of a given quality. Consequently, we cannot say very much about the impact of all this on their consumption of housing. Most urban economists believe, however, that filtering adds to the housing problems of black low-income families. About the housing problems of blacks, more will be said later.

Efficiency Criteria and Market Externalities   The facts are clear: housing has its share of market externalities. Much happens, both in the production and consumption of housing services, that spills over to households that are not directly involved, some of which has bearing on the problem of inadequate housing. Externalities that influence the upkeep decisions of homeowners and landlords are particularly important. What these are and their impact on upkeep decisions are usually discussed under the heading of neighborhood effects.

As noted above, neighborhood effects stem from the fact that neighborhoods are considered as a part of the housing service. As a consequence, what our neighbors do has impact on our satisfactions from housing consumption. This has important implications, one set of which, discussed earlier, concerns the incentives for undermaintenance that stem from neighborhood effects.

Since the value of residential property is related to the physical condition of neighboring properties, individual property owners have the incentive to "undermaintain" their property. The gains are most in a situation where there are no costs and positive spillovers from the actions of neighbors. This implies little or no upkeep by the property owner and, hopefully, a lot of upkeep by the neighbors. The problem is that the incentive is there for all. Thus, there is incentive for all property owners to undermaintain their properties. If each does what is in his or her own best interest, the result is an acceleration of the residential depreciation process leading quickly to residential decay and blight. Residential decay and blight, in turn, implies occupied dwellings which sooner or later will be judged as inadequate.

As noted above, this argument provides insights and is persuasive, but it does not constitute an explanation of urban residential depreciation. The problem, as noted earlier, is that in all communities there are neighborhoods that are deteriorating, some that are well maintained and some that are "mixed bags." If we are to account for maintenance in terms of neighborhood effects, we must be able to explain why these effects are strong in some neighborhoods, less so in others and perhaps absent in still others. But we have no theory that will allow us to do this.

Our explanations of residential maintenance and upkeep, as noted in chapter 5, must reckon with factors internal to the household that influence the upkeep decision. Studies of these factors have identified certain characteristics of the dwelling and its occupant that have impact on these decisions. One of these is occupant behavior that shows up in the way in which the property is used. When the property is subjected to "hard" use, for example, the costs of upkeep are high relative to any benefits that may be forthcoming to property owners from such upkeep. If these incremental costs cannot be imposed on those who are responsible, as they cannot when the income of the occupant is low, upkeep expenditures will become less profitable for the property owner, be it either a landlord or a homeowner. In such cases, the probability is high that the property will deteriorate rapidly in comparison with the circumstances in which the property is subject to more normal use.

If some households let their property depreciate more rapidly than others, this could spread quickly through a neighborhood because of neighborhood effects. Most urban scholars believe that neighborhood effects in this sense lead to urban residential blight and decay, and are to be regarded as a factor that contributes to the housing problems of the poor. Just how important these effects are, and under what sets of conditions they come into play, remain to be determined.

Other Factors: Tastes and Preferences   Tastes and preferences have impact on housing consumption, although seldom is this taken up in discussions of inadequate housing. Yet, it is certainly possible that some families, as a matter of personal choice, live in what others judge as substandard housing. The recluse who finds anonymity in such housing could be one of these. Poor people whose incomes have risen recently, but who still have strong neighborhood attachments may be another. There is also the household whose income just barely lies above the property line, a household headed up by one who does not have a strong taste for housing. Consumer behavior that maximizes satisfactions in this case could very easily lead to living in a substandard dwelling.

How many families or households like these are there? The number is probably small. Perhaps a more important matter is the personal choice that all households make with respect to how they use dwellings, a matter just discussed. "Hard" use can be shown to have logical links to the problem of residential deterioration. How important these links are is another question. It would be very easy to exaggerate the importance of this kind of behavior, just as the importance of the slumlord was blown out of proportion a few years back. Few deny, however, that there are differences in patterns of dwelling use, and it is generally recognized that the presence of these differences can greatly complicate the effort to deal with the problem of inadequate housing.

What's Really Important?   Most studies of substandard housing yield conclusions that strongly suggest the problem of inadequate housing is largely the problem of housing the poor. The correlations show most of those who live in substandard dwellings are poor and many of those who are poor show up as living in crowded conditions and/or spend a relatively high proportion of their income on housing.

But these correlations are not perfect. Not all of the poor live in substandard and/or overcrowded housing. There are also some who live in such housing who are not poor. These facts suggest other factors are involved. While the standard view of the slumlord is a caricature that contributes little to our explanation of slums, few deny that low-income families would benefit from more competition among rental property owners. Government taxing policies also contribute to the problem. In addition, there are market imperfections in the filtration process that cause problems as do market externalities, particularly those which impact on upkeep and maintenance decisions. Finally, there is the possibility that a very small part of the problem is self-imposed in the sense that it is a consequence of certain personal choices people make. ·

While there are limits to what can be said about the individual importance of each of these, we can say unequivocally that income distribution or the presence of poverty is the primary cause of the problem. Where these other elements become more noticeable is in our effort to help the poor with their housing problems. Most agree that we have not had a great deal of success with governmental programs aimed, both directly and indirectly, at the problem, some of which have transferred significant amounts of income or housing benefits to the poor. These programmatic experiences suggest there are other problems that have to be addressed. Perhaps the most important of these has been neglected to this point. It is now time to take up the problem of residential segregation and discrimination.

URBAN RESIDENTIAL SEGREGATION AND DISCRIMINATION

Residential segregation by race is a well-documented fact in practically every American city. Segregation indexes abound, all of which provide strong empirical evidence of racial segregation in the sense that blacks live in close geographic proximity to other blacks and whites live in close geographic proximity to other whites. In what stands as the most comprehensive study of the facts of the urban residential housing of blacks, the Taeubers have concluded that there is "strong and consistent evidence for the conclusion that Negroes are by far the most residentially segregated large minority in recent American history."

Much of what is observed now, particularly in northern cities, has roots in the waves of southern blacks migrating into northern cities in the middle part of this century. As this movement took place, blacks became housed in an increasingly segregated pattern. By 1960, the segregation indexes showed blacks living in highly segregated neighborhoods in all cities regardless of size, region, or the relative size of the local black population. This pattern has been largely maintained since then, despite some indications of recent growth in the number of integrated neighborhoods in America. While this may change in the coming years, it is not unreasonable to still continue to characterize the residential housing of blacks in our cities as highly segregated.

Most discussions of residential segregation by race assume that it is a problem. It doesn't have to be seen this way. It wouldn't be if segregated housing were simply a reflection of the exercise of free choice by American households. But is this the case?

It is certainly possible to conceive of a pattern of household tastes which leads to such an outcome. If whites preferred to live with whites and blacks preferred to live with blacks, for example, housing markets, working properly, could generate a racially segregated housing pattern. There are, in fact, "self-imposed or voluntary" theories of segregation, which, when examined carefully, are not found totally lacking in merit. There are also very persuasive arguments and a good deal of evidence that point to racial residential segregation as the outcome of market forces that have not come into play for black families in an impersonalized way. For various reasons and by various means, all the feasible housing alternatives have not been made available to blacks.

Urban economists generally believe that most racial residential segregation is the outcome of markets that have discriminated in the wrong way. Consequently, they are concerned with the problem. Not only does it stand in direct contradiction with important values of American society—equality of opportunity and freedom of choice—there are more practical and down-to-earth reasons for concern. If blacks are restricted in their housing choices, for example, they could be paying higher prices than whites for the same quality of housing. In addition to the inequity this implies, its budgetary impact could prove to be a real hardship to black families who have very low incomes. Confinement to a restricted number of residential areas could also create employment problems for those living there. The spreading out of the city, noted above, has come about in part because of the movement of industry away from the central city. With that industry gone, jobs that may have provided important employment opportunities to low-income blacks living in the central cities are gone also. If blacks are unable to follow these jobs because of housing restrictions, as noted in chapter 9, unemployment problems in the "ghettos" will arise. Housing restrictions are also believed to prevent blacks from taking full advantage of benefits that accrue to homeowners as a consequence of the structure of our income tax laws. There are home ownership benefits in these laws that cannot really be realized if there are restrictions on the ability of the family to move out to where land costs are low enough to make home ownership feasible.

This by no means ends the list of practical and down-to-earth unpleasant consequences of racial residential segregation. It is enough to make evident, however, the fact that racial residential segregation can impose serious costs upon those who are its victims.

Causes of Segregation

Conspiracy Theories   Much attention in popular discussions of racial residential segregation is focused on the aversion some members of the community have in dealing with blacks. At center stage are landlords, realtors, and mortgage lenders. Blacks are said to be effectively restricted from entry into certain parts of the housing market because landlords will not rent to them, or because realtors and mortgage lenders put up roadblocks to the purchase of a home in these neighborhoods. Case studies that illustrate particular instances of unfair treatment of the sort abound in social literature.

For this to happen, there would have to be a conspiracy. Some find it difficult to take the possibility of such a conspiracy seriously. If we suppose that blacks look for housing in a market that is populated with enterprising people who seek to maximize profits, there may be some difficulty in making such a conspiracy hold up. Certainly it is possible that there are some landlords, realtors, and mortgage lenders who have an aversion to dealing with blacks, along with some doctors, plumbers, social workers, and school teachers. Those who fail to deal with blacks, however, may find their vacancies rising and profits falling. These people might therefore consider it in their best interest to sell their residential income properties, real estate businesses, and mortgage lending businesses to those who do not have such an aversion. Yet, they might not. If they had strong feelings about blacks and their business, they might be willing to conspire against blacks and take the consequences in the form of lower profits. A conspiracy could be the outcome of a taste for discrimination.

In general, it is difficult to believe that such a conspiracy could hold up for very long, particularly in settings where there is a heterogenous population. The theory itself is also limited in the scope of its applicability. There are many forms of segregation, including that found in churches and fraternal organizations, as well as other forms found in housing such as income segregation. None of these others seem properly accounted for by some kind of a conspiracy. To assert this is not to deny the possibility that housing decisions of some black families have been influenced by people in the housing industry who have a personal animosity towards blacks. The bulk of what we observe, however, seems better accounted for by other things, including the incomes of families and the prejudices of many households against blacks.

Income While residential choice in cities was indicated earlier to be influenced by many things, journey to work was emphasized. The theory discussed postulated that households prefer sites that minimize the distance between residences and place of work. The importance of distance, however, varies by households, and income was indicated to have impact on the household's view about it. All of this, as discussed above, is reflected in the shapes of the bid rent curves of households. Households with high incomes were indicated to have bid rent curves that were gently sloped—see Figure 10.1. The reason for this difference

Figure 10.1

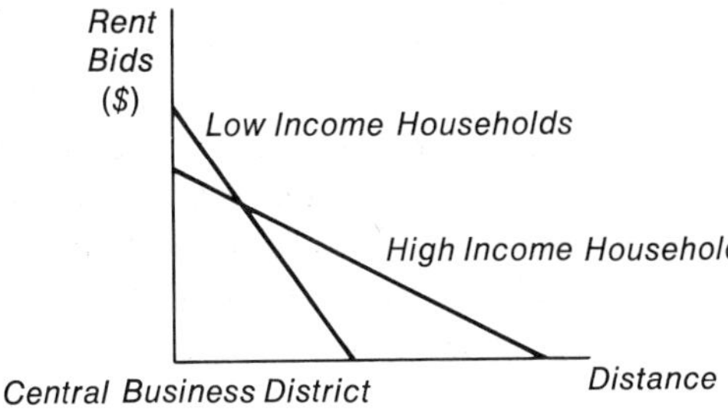

is the differential impact of commuting costs on the budgets of families with different incomes. Since the money costs of travel are roughly the same for all households, the burden of commuting costs is greater on families with low incomes. While this conclusion had to be qualified to take into account the fact that time spent in transit means more to families with high incomes, it was argued that Figure 10.1 represented a reasonable characterization of the differential importance of access to many of the rich and poor. Since there are indications that the rich tend to be spread out residentially all over the city and the poor are more concentrated in the central city, income was said to be a determinant of residential site choice in cities.

If income is important in this way, some of what we now call racial segregation could be income segregation. One thing we know is that the incomes of blacks are, on the average, lower than whites. If low incomes also restrict the residential site options of families to locations near places of work, blacks with their low incomes would tend to live near the primary center of employment. If this were the central business district, blacks could be expected to be living with other low-income families in areas in or adjacent to the central business district.

There are studies that show that income helps to explain the residential choice of blacks. Some of what we call racial residential segregation is indeed income segregation. If we were able to obliterate skin color differences, housing patterns might not change that much, so long as there were no significant changes in the distribution of income.

Yet racial residential segregation is by no means fully explained by the relatively low incomes of blacks. While low-income families tend to be concentrated in the central cities of our metropolitan areas, there are low-income families living in the suburbs, most of whom are white. There is, in addition, the fact that much industry has moved away from the center of our cities, industry that at one time provided a substantial number of employment opportunities for blacks. Increasingly, blacks, without moving, have come to live farther and farther away from their jobs, which suggests that income is not the only constraint in their housing choices.

Prejudice   Prior studies of the race question assign much importance to the attitudes of households. This comes through in two ways. One has already been noted above. People can, because of their attitudes, voluntarily segregate themselves from one another and do so on the basis of race. As it was put above, what we observe in segregation indexes could simply be a reflection of voluntary segregation.

Certainly, all groups, especially minority groups, tend to set themselves apart from others. They share a common culture and tradition that create bonds among them which, for some at least, make it easier to live together in close geographic proximity. They feel safer and more secure with those of their own kind. Such bonds, of course, are not a characteristic of blacks alone. They apply, to a greater or lesser extent, to all minority groups and undoubtedly account for some of the general class differentiation observable in housing patterns. It is not only blacks who are segregated, but Orientals, Indians, and Italians as well. There is enough evidence in our urban renewal experience to suggest that these bonds do have impact on residential choice.

These bonds also tend to weaken over time in the melting pot of experience, particularly in societies where there is a good deal of geographic and social mobility. Moreover, the degree of segregation among ethnic groups where these bonds are believed to be quite strong has been shown to be less than for blacks. To argue that racial residential segregation is a consequence of voluntary decisions made by both blacks and whites would, in light of such findings, require black separatist feeling to a degree that seems improbable. This improbability seems corroborated by survey research findings that show the great majority of blacks still prefer integrated to segregated housing. While the bonds of race, particularly in its current form of black separatism, may account for some of the racial segregation found in housing, it certainly does not appear to count for much.

More important are the attitudes of whites toward blacks. Much has been written about prejudice and white racism. Unfortunately, different authors often have different things in mind when discussing the problem and the meanings assigned are sometimes shaded by the value judgments of the author concerning these attitudes. The general concern, however, seems to be with a particular state of mind of whites towards blacks. This is a state that does not reflect a conscious and rational consideration of the facts concerning blacks. It is also a state of mind often manifested in an attitude of hostility. Black households, for example, who seek homes in a white residential neighborhood typically encounter hostility that has little to do with the facts which would emerge with integration. Why such hostility? When present, it no doubt reflects a number of things. For some, the color itself will be sufficient to generate hostility. For others, color conjures up a view of a household with total disregard for upkeep and maintenance. There are also those who become hostile because they think they see falling property values in the neighborhood.

When feelings of this sort have no foundation in fact, the attitude is appropriately classified as one of prejudice or bigotry. In many cases, the dim view that whites have of the consequences of a black living in their neighborhood is probably best characterized as prejudice or bigotry. In some cases, however, it may not be. Because of this possibility, investigators may encounter serious problems in attempting to deal with the issue of prejudice in scientific studies of racial residential segregation.

Suppose that through survey and attitudinal research, we were able to establish a scale of prejudice that could be applied to white households in an urban community. We could then construct a distribution of white households according to a prejudice scale, just as we construct household distributions according to scales of income, age, education, and life cycle. When viewed in this way, prejudice has impact on the household's valuation of particular residences, just as income, age, and education do. As a consequence, the impact of prejudice on residential housing patterns could be analyzed by linking its scale up to the basic elements of a residential housing model—access and amenities of the site and socioeconomic characteristics of the household—in much the same way we now do with income and age.

The point is the household attitude we characterize as prejudice or bigotry can be worked into the economic models used to study residential housing patterns. It would not be easily done for a number of reasons, not the least of which is the problem of scaling the attitude of prejudice. We can, however, conceive of racial residential segregation as the outcome of prejudice in a model that incorporates prejudice as a variable that influences the price or rent households are willing to pay for particular residences. The prejudice of whites against blacks would, in such a model, lead to racial residential segregation. If white families did not wish to live near blacks, they would be unwilling to pay very much for sites near where blacks lived. Correspondingly, their bids would be substantially higher for sites some distance away from blacks. The operation of the housing market in the face of such attitudes, combined with an income distribution that was skewed in favor of whites could be very easily shown to lead to a segregated housing market.

While these few statements do not begin to do justice to the complexities of the subject matter of how prejudice can be fitted into scientific analyses of the question of racial residential segregation, they do say enough to allow us to raise questions about what stands as a traditional view of the consequences of racial residential segregation. One of these is the view that blacks pay more than whites for the same quality housing.

Racial Price Discrimination in Housing Markets

There are data which, on the surface, show that black households get less for their money in housing than do whites—see Table 10.2. This is not surprising, however, if the housing opportunities of black families are restricted. Market restrictions can lead to market segmentation within which different prices for the same product or unit of service is possible. If there are price differentials stemming from market segmentation by race, they should not be to the advantage of those who are black. In a market which is segmented because of prejudice of whites, it is reasonable to expect blacks to pay more for housing of a given quality.

But is it so reasonable? If we consider the problem of race in housing as a problem that stems from the prejudices of whites against blacks, this interpretation can be challenged. Suppose that whites have a strong aversion to living among blacks; more so than blacks have to living among whites. With certain income distributions, it can be shown, as noted above, that a segregated housing market will emerge. Such a housing pattern means a housing frontier between blacks and whites. If so, and whites do have a greater aversion to being among blacks than blacks do among whites, whites would be less willing to live near that frontier than blacks. This implies that whites will move away from the frontier and blacks will move toward it, the effect of which will shift the frontier towards the white community. This adds to the supply of housing for blacks, and could continue until that supply is large enough, relative to black demands, so that housing prices within the black community are competitive with those on the frontier. This kind of market adjustment could, in fact, lead to outcomes in which blacks pay lower housing prices relative to those paid by whites.

How seriously should we take the conclusions of arguments of the sort? There are difficulties, the most important of which are the neglect of certain dynamic features of urban housing markets, as well as the attitudes of whites in their dealings with blacks in the housing market. The market dynamic is the growth of the urban black population. The number of blacks in segregated central city locations has increased both because of a high birth rate and heavy black migration into our urban centers. This means increased housing demand and hence upward pressure on the price of housing within areas in which the blacks are restricted. While this should encourage blacks to extend the frontier toward the white community, problems can arise. If whites near the current boundary line resist moving away from their homes, as appears to be the case from journalistic accounts, blacks will not be able to expand their housing supply to accommodate the increase in

Table 10.2

Characteristics of Renter-Occupied Housing Units:
Total and Non-white Inside SMSA's for
the United States: 1960

Monthly Gross Rent	Median Rent-Income Ratio		Percent Substandard		Median Number of Rooms	
	Total	Non-white	Total	Non-white	Total	Non-white
Total	24.9	26.1	20.7	41.2	3.8	3.2
less than $30	19.8	22.3	50.3	62.1	2.4	2.2
$30–39	20.8	24.2	42.9	56.3	2.7	2.4
$40–49	19.6	24.3	36.8	50.9	3.1	2.6
$50–59	19.0	23.9	29.3	44.5	3.4	3.0
$60–69	19.2	24.8	23.2	39.1	3.6	3.2
$70–79	19.8	24.8	17.8	33.9	3.8	3.4
$80–89	20.4	26.2	12.9	30.6	4.1	3.7
$110–115	21.8	28.1	8.6	27.4	4.3	4.1
$120 and over	22.1	29.4	4.5	23.9	4.6	4.7

Source: Chester Rapkin, "Price Discrimination Against Negroes in the Rental Housing Market," in *Essays in Urban Land Economics.* Berkeley: University of California, 1966 p. 336.

demands. If so, the market outcome will be one in which blacks pay more than whites for the same quality housing.

The facts in Table 10.2 might seem to support the second of these two arguments. Yet, these facts are not really expressed in ways that can confront the implications of these two arguments—they do not tell us about prices at or near the boundaries of the market segments relative to other places. Moreover, alternative arguments have been offered for these differences, some of which are focused on the housing measures themselves, which are alleged to include certain things for blacks that they do not for whites, e.g., utilities and furniture.

The issue of whether blacks pay more for the same housing than do whites is still shrouded with controversy. There are no conclusive answers. The fact of segregation, however, combined with overt expressions of residential integration as a goal by significant sections of the black community as well as a substantial number of journalistic reports of white resistance to the black "invasion," does suggest blacks do pay a premium.

CURES FOR HOUSING ILLS

What Has Been Done?

Our housing problems are not new; neither is the concern we have for them. Much has been done in the past, some of which has been action taken by private citizens working through the market place. When we consider cures for housing ills, however, the discussion typically focuses on government and public programs that have been and can be initiated to get the things done that markets don't. While we have had a long history of public programs aimed at housing, the scale of this activity has, until recently, been relatively small. Starting with the Depression years of the thirties, however, the government began to assume a much more active role in housing, particularly at the federal level.

When we look carefully at these programs, it is clear that much of what has been done was not aimed directly at the problems of inadequate housing or discrimination. While low-income families have received income benefits through the redistributional effects of certain government programs which helped some upgrade their housing consumption, most government housing programs have provided benefits to the nonpoor, at least until the latter part of the 1960s. Still, everything that benefits housing can be considered potentially beneficial to the poor. The notion of filtering suggests even that which benefits the rich leads to a release of housing that could filter down to those at the lower end of the income scale. It is thus not unreasonable, in a brief review of "what has been done," to consider most of what government does and has done in the area of housing.

Consider first those programs of the federal government. There are elements of the fiscal policies of the federal government that have had important impact on housing. While the federal government does not receive revenues in the form of residential real estate taxes, there have been and still are elements in the tax structure that have affected housing investment. The early stages of the recent apartment house boom were partly a consequence of a special depreciation provision in the tax law which encouraged the flow of equity money into apartment house construction projects. It is also the case that gains or losses from the sale of residential property are treated as capital gains or losses and hence taxed differently from regular income, a tax treatment generally believed to bestow special advantage on investments in multifamily residences. Then, there are those benefits provided to homeowners. All homeowners know that the interest costs on their home mortgages constitute a deduction for tax purposes. Fewer know that they are also exempt from making income tax payments on net imputed rents. That does not make it any less beneficial, however, and both of these benefits are believed to have a perceptible impact on the housing investment of many families.

More important are the federal programs directly concerned with housing. Much of what is now in force goes back to legislation enacted in the 1930s, when the Depression had such highly disruptive effects on the nation's residential mortgage market. Loan insurance through the Federal Housing Administration, the secondary mortgage market facilities of the Federal National Mortgage Association, and a liquidity pool for savings and loan associations in the Federal Home Loan Bank system are examples. In the 1940s, housing credit received another assist when the Veterans Administration was given authority to guarantee mortgage loans to veterans.

Throughout the 1950s and the first half of the 1960s, there was additional legislation that modified in various ways what the federal agencies could do. For example, the Federal Housing Administration was permitted to substantially liberalize the terms of the FHA-insured mortgage, as was the Veterans Administration. The special assistance programs of the Federal National Mortgage Association were also extended in various ways. Nothing really major happened in the area of residential finance until the latter part of the 1960s, however, when more serious financial difficulties arose at the time when the nation was becoming increasingly concerned with the low-income housing problem.

Congress responded with legislation that split up the secondary market and special assistance function of the Federal National Mortgage Association. The Federal National Mortgage Association, no longer recorded as a part of the federal budget, became an association that could now buy conventional as well as FHA and VA mortgages in its secondary market operations. A Government National Mortgage Association was also established that, in addition to assuming the special functions of the old Federal National Mortgage Association, was provided with the basis for creating a special financing instrument designed to tap sources of funds that had made only meager mortgage investments to that time, e.g., pension funds. As the same time, the Federal Home Loan Bank System was given the authority to establish a "secondary market" for conventional mortgages held by certain classes of lenders.

The federal government also initiated a series of programs concerned with urban renewal, which in their earlier stages contributed to the housing problems of the poor by removing a substantial amount of low-income housing from the stock without providing new housing. More recently, these programs have emphasized rehabilitation, and through the establishment of a Model Cities program, the scope of urban renewal was broadened to include other aspects of the total environment such as health, education, welfare, and recreation.

There are also federal government programs directly concerned with housing the poor, one of which has been in existence for some time. In 1937 the nation's public housing program was set up with the establishment of the Public Housing Authority, whose primary responsibility was the administering of such a program. The assistance provided by government in this program takes two major forms. One of these is in the form of financing aids in the construction of a public housing project. The other takes the form of a rent subsidy to those who are occupants in the completed housing projects.

Congress also authorized what are often called "Below Market Interest Rate Programs." These programs' primary purpose is reducing occupancy costs by providing financial assistance to reduce the mortgage interest costs of a low-income housing project. The initial programs were set up so that only nonprofit institutions could sponsor such projects and they were to be occupied primarily by persons who not only had low incomes, but were either elderly or handicapped as well. More recently, they have been expanded to include profit-oriented corporations and beneficiaries who need not be those who are elderly or in some way handicapped.

In addition to these, we have experimented recently with programs that have provided direct housing assistance to those with low incomes. For example, we have a rent supplement program under which tenant families pay 25 percent of their income toward rent. The assistance comes in the form of a direct payment by the federal government to the landlord, which is to make up the difference between the rent payment of the low-income family and the market rent.

There is another program designed to aid those with low incomes who wish to buy homes. Assistance is restricted to new or substantially rehabilitated housing units. Eligible buyers finance their purchases with FHA-insured market rate mortgages with private lenders. The federal government subsidy takes the form of paying part of the homeowner's monthly mortgage payment. With the maximum subsidy allowable, the homeowner's payment can be reduced to one that would apply if his or her purchase had been financed with a mortgage having a one percent interest rate.

Finally, there are those programs, admittedly small in magnitude, that provide subsidies to families which can only be used for rehabilitation. Much of this, however, is restricted to families living in what are designated as urban renewal areas. The subsidies themselves either take the form of a below market interest rate loan, or in some cases, come in the form of outright grants to the recipient.

State and local governments also influence housing investments and housing market activities, although there is much less in the way of programs designed to deal with specific housing problems. What has surfaced over the past five years or so are state house finance agencies, the purpose of which is to funnel money from the nation's money and capital markets into housing in the state. In the main, these funds are directed toward meeting the financing needs of these families in the lower and lower-middle end of the income distribution. The primary impact of state and local governments on housing, however, works through their fiscal policies. The revenue sources of such governmental units are particularly important because they depend so heavily upon real estate taxes, much of which comes from assessments made on residential properties. Obviously, the nature and magnitude of these taxes can have impact on residential investments in particular places. In some places, for example, real estate taxes are alleged to encourage homeownership and result in relatively high housing costs for those who rent. In other places, the reverse situation is said to prevail. And in most places, as noted above, it is argued that real estate taxes are such that they help to perpetuate the presence of slum housing in our cities.

Finally, the overall planning activities of cities, counties, multicounty regions, and states are believed to influence housing investment in particular places. For years, this influence was probably stimulative in its effects, as most regions were in active pursuit of the goal of economic and demographic growth. More recently, we have seemingly turned away from the goal of growth and, in fact, have been doing things that discourage growth in some places. We have also become more conscious of the environmental aspects of development and, through state and local government action, have added to development costs in ways that have influenced housing investment in some regions. The nature and extent of this influence, however, is not really understood very well. The only safe thing that can be said at this point is that it has grown and will continue to grow in the future.

What Should Be Done?

Even from this highly abbreviated description of public programs that have impact on housing, it is clear that we have tried much in terms of scope of effort. What have we tried to accomplish? A more careful examination of the background and content of each of these programs suggests that, until recently, our concern with housing has had its roots in a concern with the social welfare of the nation. While there have been many stated purposes for the programs legislated—to create jobs, to help the poor, to save the financial markets, to improve the tax base of cities, to do away with slums—underneath it all has been a concern with the housing welfare of some group or groups of people. The 1949 Housing Act formally articulated this concern for the first time. The most well-known of its many statements, of course, was the one that established the goal of a "decent home and suitable living environment for every American family." The concern in this statement is with those who do not live in decent homes or have suitable living environments and these are, for the most part, families with low incomes.

There is a paradox here. Much of what we did through government following the passage of the 1949 Housing Act—at least through the 1950s and 1960s—was not directly aimed at those living in inadequate housing. Yet, the ultimate rationale for most of this was linked to the goal of providing all American families with decent homes and a suitable living environment. More recently, we have become increasingly concerned with housing programs aimed at providing for the housing needs of the disadvantaged. At the same time, research concerned with housing policies has begun to focus more on efficiency questions as they come to bear on defining the role of government in housing. The tools of microeconomic theory have been applied increasingly, in ways that have deepened our understanding of the efficiency aspects of how to deal with the problem of inadequate housing. While there is still uncertainty and disagreement about what constitutes the proper elements of an effective program designed to deal with this problem, recent studies of housing policies and markets have brought to the surface important policy issues about which sensible things can be said.

These issues are, in the main, concerned with efficiency aspects of a housing program. The equity issue, in the sense of how much assistance, has never been resolved. It is still not possible to specify the redistributions necessary to achieve the consumption patterns—including housing—which will maximize the happiness coefficient of the population. While we may have personal views about the adequacy of the assistance given to those who have housing problems, it is difficult, if not impossible, to show that any given level of assistance has more scientific foundation than any other.

Suppose we take the amount of this assistance as given. The question then becomes one of putting together a program that will maximize the benefits derived from this expenditure—or as some would put it, we must get that program that gives us the most "bang for the buck."

There are alternative approaches. Indeed, there are a great many different things that could be done. Obviously, choices have to be made. But what choices? What are the decision rules?

The discussion of economic performance or welfare criteria above suggests we pay attention to the efficiency aspects of the program as well as equity in the sense of the vertical and horizontal equities involved in its implementation. As these matters have been studied in relation to housing, several issues have surfaced. One is the issue of generalized income assistance (e.g., a negative income tax) versus some kind of housing allowance. Another, when the focus is on housing allowances, is that of general versus direct subsidies. There has also been concern with the question of whether housing allowances should be aimed at the production of housing as opposed to consumption.

The issue of generalized income assistance versus assistance directed toward some specific type of expenditure such as housing has had a long history. It has reappeared recently as our concern with the poor intensified and economists brought the tools of microeconomics to bear more heavily on the efficiency aspects of programs that redistribute income from the "have" to the "have nots." Some, as a consequence of this study and research, now hold that generalized income supplements are a much more efficient way of dealing with the housing consumption problems of the poor. It can be shown, with the tools of microeconomic theory, that under a number of realizable sets of conditions, the consumption satisfactions of the poor will be maximized if they are permitted free choice in spending of the funds they receive.

This conclusion bothers many who are concerned with the problem of inadequate housing. Intuitively, it seems that less will be spent on housing if money is given directly to the poor and there are no restrictions on how that money can be spent. Indeed, it can be shown analytically that this will happen under most conditions. If our concern is with whether the program aimed at helping the poor is efficient, however, the consumption of a little more or less housing should make little difference in the evaluation of that program. What is important is the impact the program has on the satisfaction its beneficiaries receive. In a world in which freedom of choice is important, this can easily be shown to be a world in which generalized income transfers are the best means of redistributing income.

There are, however, difficulties with this conclusion. One is that it holds only in a world in which there are no externalities. Unfortunately, consumption externalities that operate to negate some of the benefits accruing from free choice are present in some cases. The money has to go to someone; presumably it goes to the household head. But what if that head has a drug problem or is an irresponsible alcoholic? The consumption habits of the head could impose negative benefits on other household members, which more than offset the positive aspects of increased consumption stemming from the income transfer.

The importance of this kind of negative externality is by no means clear. As noted in chapter 9, its importance is probably overstated. Yet it cannot be dismissed out of hand.

A second problem concerns the housing market itself. Assume there are no consumption externalities. There still could be problems. If new construction is geared towards those with relatively high incomes, the poor must make housing adjustments with units that were previously occupied. How they fare in such a market is thus linked to how the housing market filters units through to the poor.

How well do housing markets filter units down to the poor? As noted in chapter 5, this question is controversial; the evidence is not conclusive. Some argue that studies of chains of household moves indicate dwelling units do filter through the stock in ways that are consistent with the simple filtering notions, at least for white households. Others dispute this interpretation of these data and argue that, because of market imperfections, the poor are presented with few viable market alternatives. These differing viewpoints are difficult to reconcile, given the current state of our knowledge of the filtering process in housing.

That this question cannot be answered raises doubts about the potential effectiveness of generalized income supplements as a means of dealing with the problem of inadequate housing. This is not to say that income supplements will not contribute to the solution of our housing problems. Indeed, subsidies that take the form of general income supplements score well on grounds of vertical and horizontal equity; in that if properly conceived and administered, they can be directed to those with need and little will get lost along the way. At the present time, however, they are not generally considered as programs that can, by themselves, solve the problem of inadequate housing in our cities.

Suppose we consider measures that are aimed directly at housing. There are, of course, alternative ways in which funds can be pumped into housing. They need not go directly to the poor. In fact, our housing programs have, for the most part, had those in the middle and upper income strata as beneficiaries, at least until recently. Yet benefits to the poor can come through market filtering. The matter of filtering thus becomes important in evaluating the efficacy of a program that provides a general subsidy to housing.

Some argued that a filtering strategy of this kind has special benefits in the sense that it increases the number of families that can be helped with a given number of dollars. Since the amount of subsidy per household needed to put many low-income families into decent housing is relatively large, the number of households affected by any given sized public housing subsidy will be larger if the funds are used to encourage the construction of higher quality units, and units filter down the stock as there is movement into these newly constructed units. The difficulty with this argument is that such a strategy is likely to do very little to help the very poor, since their needs will be greater than that which will be made available to them through the filtering process.

If we are to deal with the housing problems of the very poor, it appears that some form of a housing allowance will be necessary. The next question is: What kind of allowance? Here a distinction is often made between those directed towards the production of new housing for the poor and those that go directly to the poor with the condition that they be used to increase housing consumption. We have had some experience with both, although not enough to provide a basis for a definitive evaluation. Both appear to have advantages and disadvantages. Production subsidies aimed at building low-income housing do add to the stock of units available to the poor. The problem with housing allowances of this kind is that they tend to generate inequities. Every dollar subsidy through builders, developers, and lenders may not reach the ultimate recipient in the form of increased housing consumption—the problem of vertical equity. It is also more likely that equals will not be treated as equals, (i.e., some may derive more benefits from such subsidies than do others), when subsidies are made in this way—the problem of horizontal equity.

A program of housing allowances that put money into the hands of the poor, if properly designed and implemented, will be much more equitable in this twofold sense. But programs that provide households with housing money may encounter difficulties because these households will, for the most part, find their housing alternatives are previously occupied dwellings. In light of our doubts about the filtering mechanism, it is by no means clear that increased demands in the lower income levels will set off a chain of price increases up these strata in ways that insure an increase in decent housing available to the poor. It could, but then again it might not.

The conclusion from the discussion thus far seems to be that no one program or policy will do if we are to deal effectively with the problem of inadequate housing. Each apparently has advantages and disadvantages and it is not clear which outweighs the other. These matters are further complicated by the issue of race as it comes to bear in our housing markets. Those who argue that housing markets tend to filter high quality units down to low-income families that provide them with units appropriate to their ability to pay, usually do not argue that this happens to low-income families who are black. While income is an important problem for many black families, it is, by no means, the only one. Racial prejudice and bigotry is another. While such prejudice may have subsided somewhat over the past five years, it still remains in the housing decisions of many households. To the extent that it does, blacks could continue to have difficulties in the sense of being unable to purchase units of housing service at a price equivalent to that paid by their white counterparts. It is at this point that we begin to hear, with increasing frequency from economists, the notion that some kind of subsidy scheme should be implemented as a means of fostering integration. Blacks, it is argued, should be provided with funds that can be used as a means of bribing whites to allow blacks to live among whites and these funds should also be given to some whites directly to encourage them to live among blacks. The public till would be used as the means of paying for the prejudice premium involved in market transactions involving both whites and blacks.

In the light of the discussion in this chapter, the attractiveness of such a proposal is seen to depend on several things. One is the question of whether those who seem to be bigoted in their housing activity are, in fact, bigoted. While most may be, it was suggested previously that some resistance to the movement of blacks into a neighborhood may not reflect prejudice. It is at this point the whole issue of the meaning of prejudice or bigotry reappears. Second, if there is to be a subsidy to cover the prejudice premium, we must know much more about the kind of outcomes our housing markets actually generate. The inconclusiveness of the statements that can be currently made about the market price of housing to blacks vis-a-vis the price of that same housing to white households would greatly complicate any effort to implement a program of subsidies designed to achieve integration.

If knowledge of the sort could accumulate, a program of subsidies designed to cover that prejudice premium might prove to be a highly interesting experiment, the success of which would depend on just how much economic behavior we find in the housing decisions of urban households.

REFERENCES

de Leeuw, F. "Demand for Housing." *Review of Economics and Statistics 53* (1971): 1–10.

Lansing, J.; Clifton, C.; Morgan, J. *New Homes and Poor People.* Ann Arbor, Mi.: Institute for Social Research, 1969.

MIT-Harvard Joint Center for Urban Studies. *American Housing Needs.* Cambridge, Mass.: The Joint Center for Urban Studies, 1973.

Muth, R. *Cities and Housing.* Chicago: University of Chicago Press, 1969.

Report of the President's Committee on Urban Housing. *A Decent Home.* Washington, D.C., 1968.

Taeuber, K., and Taeuber, A. *Negroes in Cities.* Chicago: Aldine Publishing Company, 1965.

United States Department of Housing and Urban Development. *Housing in the Seventies: A Report of the National Housing Policy Review.* Washington, D.C., 1974.

von Furstenburg, G.; Harrison, B.; and Horowitz, A. *Patterns of Racial Discrimination: Volume I: Housing.* Lexington, Mass.: Lexington Books, D. C. Heath and Company, 1974.

11

Urban Transportation

SUMMARY

The urban transportation problem breaks down into a number of problems. Some involve efficiency questions; others involve questions of equity.

The most visible and irritating of these problems is traffic congestion. Increased traffic flows slow down the average speed of movement, which can add significantly to the time costs of travel. These are cost additions that individual travelers usually do not take into account in their travel decisions. Traffic congestion is thus a consequence of the fact that the private costs of urban travel often do not reflect the full social costs of that movement. The solution lies in pricing policies that restrict use to the point where marginal social benefits and marginal social costs are equal, a point that may still generate some congestion.

There is also reason to believe that our pricing policies cause problems with urban transportation over the long run. We probably underprice the use of our transportation facilities, which implies we may have too much, rather than too little, transportation investments in our cities.

A long-run look at the urban transportation problem also raises the issue of mass transit. Rapid transit systems, particularly if they involve some form of rail transportation, have highly appealing features. The problem is that there are not many cities in which they are likely to be a viable alternative. They require density patterns of a kind not found in too many cities.

Questions about equity in the way in which our urban transportation networks meet the cities' transportation needs are frequently raised. The reduction in demands and hence in the service provided by urban public transit companies as the automobile became king and our cities spread out had a significant impact on the transportation choices of the poor. Just how much harm was inflicted on the poor is unknown. What is known is that reemphasis on mass transit systems that speed up the travel between the suburbs and the central business district will not solve the transportation problems of the poor. The primary difficulty we have in dealing with these problems now is that we lack real understanding of the transportation problems of the poor.

Urban transportation, as the term is ordinarily used, refers to all means of transporting goods and people in an urban setting. In its broadest sense, this includes transportation modes that move goods and people between as well as within cities. Most discussions of urban transportation, however, concentrate on the obstacles to movement within cities. Furthermore, the emphasis in these discussions is on the movement of people rather than goods and on the movement of people from their place of residence to their place of work.

Urban transportation is considered here in the sense of the movement of people within the boundaries of a city with particular emphasis on movement of people between places of residence and places of work. Urban transportation has already been considered above, in that the prevailing transportation network was shown to influence both residential and nonresidential location decisions within the city. Accessibility costs considered in chapter 5 were, in part, transportation costs. What transportation costs are between any two points in the city, of course, depends in part on the transportation network—the layout of transportation routes, the modes of travel over these routes. In chapter 5, transportation routes and modes of travel were taken as a constant. Considering routes and modes of travel as streets and highways, in a city dominated by the automobile, estimates could be made of transportation costs between various points in the city, given some assumptions about movement costs. Transportation costs, in this sense, were shown to have important bearing on the location choices of firms and households, and hence urban land use patterns.

The automobile, of course, was not the only form of transportation. People had transportation choices. The outcome of these transportation choices was, in turn, influenced by prevailing land-use patterns and all of those nontransportation things that helped to generate these patterns. That technology unfolded in ways that increased the space requirements of manufacturing firms, pushing them away from central cities, had important implications with respect to urban transportation investment decisions. The coming of the truck and the automobile made it possible for many firms to respond to this technology, taking full advantage of its potential. The fact that they could lower their production costs by moving to the suburbs also had important implications with respect to their response to the automobile and the truck.

The point is evident. Urban transportation investment decisions and urban location decisions are interdependent. The character of urban transportation investment has important bearing on the shape or form that our cities take. But, by the same token, the form of our cities has important bearing on the transportation investment decision we make.

Ideally, urban form and urban transportation should be considered jointly, within an analytic framework capable of handling this interdependence. In fact, the two are treated separately because we have no such framework. Of necessity, this is how these things must be dealt with here. Urban form and changes in that form have already been discussed—see chapter 8. Now it is time to discuss urban transportation.

URBAN TRANSPORTATION: WHAT'S THE PROBLEM?

Journalists often portray transportation in cities as one massive traffic jam. The culprit is the automobile. Traffic jams are described as lanes of cars, bumper to bumper, filled with highly agitated and frustrated people.

Like many stories in the popular press, there is some truth in this one. It also oversimplifies the problem and is misleading in certain respects.

The problem considered is that of the movement of people between place of work and place of residence. Over the years, there have been dramatic changes in the volume of such traffic and mode of transportation used. Precisely how much change is difficult to say. The pertinent statistics are not as they should be for comparative purposes. The use of the automobile is measured in terms of vehicle miles, that is, the number of miles driven in cities by passenger cars. Measures of the use of public transportation—railways, subways, trolleys, and buses—are the number of people using these vehicles. These figures nevertheless tell us a good deal.

Table 11.1 records these measures for selected years from 1940 through 1973.

Table 11.1

Urban Transportation: 1940–1973

	Passenger Cars	Public Transit Forms			
	(Billions of Vehicle miles)	(Millions of Passengers)			
		Buses	Trolleys	Railways	Subways
1940	130.3	4,239	534	5,943	2,383
1950	184.5	9,420	1,658	3,904	2,264
1955	226.4	7,240	1,202	1,207	1,874
1960	286.9	6,425	657	463	1,850
1965	380.4	5,814	305	276	1,858
1970	496.8	5,034	182	235	1,881
1973	569.7	4,642	97	207	1,714

Source: U.S. Federal Highway Administration, American Transit Association.

These figures indicate two things. One is a growing volume of traffic in our cities. While movement by public transit has been declining, this is more than offset by movement in the automobile. If we assume the average transit trip in our cities is five miles, as most metropolitan transportation studies suggest, and also assume that this figure applies both to the years 1940 and 1973, the amount of urban travel shows up as more than tripling over this period. That it does is not surprising, in view of the growth of our cities. The rate of growth of urban travel, however, was in excess of population growth. This suggests that individual trips increased both in number and distance, a fact consistent with rising income and the spreading out of the city. City residents with higher incomes could afford to travel more and, because of the spread city, were required to travel more.

These data also indicate the growing dominance of the automobile. If we assume again that the average urban transit trip is five miles, the automobile's share of the urban transit market is shown to rise from two-thirds in 1940 to 95 percent by 1973. Were more up-to-date information available, these gains might show signs of leveling off. Many cities have taken action recently to bolster the role of public transportation. In some cities, such as San Francisco, substantial investments in rail-type systems have been made. In most others, e.g., Cincinnati, the concern has been with moving more people on buses. Still, the automobile is king and is likely to maintain a dominant position in moving people in cities for some time to come.

What's wrong, if anything, in all of this?

Ask anyone—the politician, the planner, the man on the street. There are problems. The most visible and offensive in the minds of most is congestion. Movement in particular parts of our cities, especially during commuting hours, is not easy. Cars seem to come from every place, the flow of traffic slows to a snail's pace, people become edgy, tempers flare, and accidents seem to increase.

The problem of congestion is real. Whether it can be attributed to the growing importance of the automobile is another question. There was congestion in our cities long before the coming of the automobile. No matter how we travel, there is apparently a "peak load" problem, in that travel bunches up during certain times of the day. To be sure, the automobile is an important part of the problem as we experience it today. Yet there is reason to believe that urban congestion as we know it now may have passed its peak. The suburbanization of households and business firms has greatly dispersed the population in most of our cities. Dispersal of both the residential and business population in turn means a more dispersed pattern of trips within the city. The standard view of the congestion problem as one in which all cars converging on routes into and out of the central city during commuting hours no longer holds. While there are still many who commute from the suburbs to a place of work in the central city, that pattern of movement no longer dominates as it once did. Much of the commuting now involves movement crosstown—for example, around circumferential highways—rather than toward or away from the central business district.

To make this point is not to say there is no longer a problem of congestion. Indeed, there is. But the character and dimensions of the problem have been changing in ways that should be reckoned with in any discussion of its solution. Moreover, as we look more carefully at the problem, other questions surface. Are we really committing enough resources to urban transportation? Have we made the right choices with respect to urban transportation modes? Shouldn't we devote more of our resources to mass means of transportation within our cities?

When we begin to ask these questions, it becomes clear that our real concern is with performance. Our search is a quest for an efficient and equitable system of urban transportation. This is not an easy search. In most cities, the transportation systems we have reflect a mixture of public and private decision making that makes evaluation difficult. Still, we cannot avoid the concern with efficiency and equity.

In considering efficiency, it is helpful to separate the short run from the long run. In the short run, the primary problem is traffic congestion as it is popularly understood. This is the first matter of business. Over the long run, the problem takes on added dimensions. The most important of these is the possibility of more or less transportation investment and the related issue of transportation mode or what kind of investment. In popular discussions, these issues often get reduced to a concern with mass transportation. Will increased investment in mass transportation solve the cities' transportation problems? If so, what kind of transit should this be? Buses? Railroads?

If we suppose that we come up with some answers to these questions, the matter of equity remains. What groups, if any, will be most affected by any changes we make? What groups should be affected according to our equity criteria?

These, then, are the elements of urban transportation problems to be taken up in this chapter. Before doing so, however, it is helpful to outline briefly certain important aspects of the demand for and supply of urban transportation.

ELEMENTS OF URBAN
TRANSPORTATION DEMAND
AND SUPPLY

As noted above, the primary concern in this chapter is with transportation that moves people in cities, particularly between places of work and places of residence. Transportation to the commuter can be considered as a service "consumed" that competes with other items of consumption. So considered, there must be urban transportation demands and supplies, market elements that we should be able to analyze with the aid of basic notions of demand and supply in economics.

Demand

Demand in economics is a function of prices, incomes, tastes and preferences, and number of people or total population. The demand for transportation must therefore be some function of these things.

If our concern is with the aggregate number of commuting trips in an urban community, population factors can be important. Trip costs can conceivably influence the aggregate number of journey-to-work trips made in the city in the sense that if that cost is too high people will move away from the city. Still, within a certain range of costs, most people will make the trip to work no matter whether the actual cost is at the upper or lower end of that range. If the cost falls within that range, population has bearing on the total number of work trips made. A concern with travel demands then means a concern with population and the factors that affect the proportion of the population who commute.

To consider the question of the composition of these demands in terms of length and direction is inextricably linked up with the question of where people choose to live, work, and play. It is also a question that is influenced by price or transportation cost and the income of the traveler. Mixed up with these decisions is the question of mode, that is, the choice between the automobile, bus, and train. Price and income factors are particularly important determinants in choices made with respect to mode.

Price is important because these are substitute goods. All other things being equal, people will choose the cheapest mode. The question of which mode is cheapest, however, is more involved than it first seems. By way of illustrating the point, consider a commute of ten miles. To drive this distance costs fifteen cents per mile plus a one dollar parking charge, or four dollars per day. The bus covers the same route for fifty cents or one dollar per day. The automobile could, however, be the rational choice in this example.

Neglected so far are the time costs of this trip. As noted in chapter 5, price in the case of a transportation good includes not only the money outlay, but the income costs to the traveler of the time spent in transit. To illustrate the potential importance of this fact, suppose the commute by car is thirty minutes from door to door; by bus it is one hour. If the commuter makes ten dollars per hour and values the time spent in transit at 50 percent of his or her wage rate, the automobile begins to look better. The time cost for the car is five dollars; for the bus it is ten dollars. The total transportation bill by car is thus nine dollars; by bus it is eleven dollars.

The income of the person is obviously important and it cuts its impact on transit demands in two ways. Higher levels of income allow the person to absorb higher commuting costs if they so choose. But, by the same token, higher incomes raise the relative costs of the transit modes that require more time. If we suppose that the car costs more in the sense of money outlays but is quicker, higher incomes could push people towards the car. Not only could they withstand that money cost better because of their incomes, the overall cost of the use of the car relative to other modes would decline because of the impact of the income in the time costs of travel.

Finally, there is the matter of the commuters' tastes and preferences, the significant dimensions of which are convenience, comfort, and privacy. Convenience means flexibility in terms of time, which appears to be very important to some people. Comfort refers to the physical and psychic ease with which the actual trip is made. Ease is, of course, preferred to trips that are disabling physically and/or nerve shattering. Privacy refers to seclusion in travel; it is a state of travel highly valued by some.

While all these things are probably important—most urban economists argue that the important dimension of the commuting decisions is the time cost of travel. If people value their time in transit as much as some studies suggest—between one-third and one-half of their wage rate—it is easy to show the dominating effects of time through a hypothetical example. But is one-third to one-half the wage rate of a person an appropriate factor to apply when calculating the time cost of travel? This is a reasonable question. Most urban economists believes that it is, or at least believe that time costs are high enough to make a difference for most households.

Supply

Discussions of supply elements in urban transportation systems focus on the behavior of costs as the utilization of the capital required in a particular mode of transportation changes. Studies generally show cost variations between transportation models. The capital requirements for a bona fide rail system are huge, which implies that average costs or costs per passenger fall sharply with increasing utilization. The capital requirements of a bus system are also large, which means declining average costs with increased utilization. Costs estimates for both show declining unit costs, with those for the rail system falling below those for the bus system, at capacity utilization rates that imply very high density rates—see Figure 11.1. Before these densities, however, buses apparently provide a lower cost means of transportation.

Figure 11.1

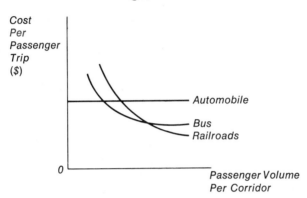

The distinguishing characteristic of the automobile is a cost curve that shows the cost per passenger mile to be relatively constant with increased utilization. This implies the automobile is a relatively inexpensive mode of transportation in cities where the major corridors run through areas of low population density and vice versa.

EFFICIENCY CONSIDERATIONS

The Short Run: The Problem of Traffic Congestion

Traffic congestion is long lines of traffic that appear in the major corridors of our cities while people are going to work in the morning and while they are going home in the evening. Saying we have traffic congestion problems because of the time schedule of industry does not tell us very much about the nature of this problem. While that schedule does create peak-load problems, we have peak-load problems elsewhere in the economy and they do not seem to cause as much difficulty as they do with traffic. More insights come from the application of urban economic concepts to the problem. What this shows is that traffic congestion is a condition that arises when certain travel costs are excluded from the costs explicitly considered by travelers when making travel decisions.

Technical Foundations   Any discussion of the economics of traffic congestion requires knowledge of technical aspects of the problem. The analysis of automobile traffic flows can be used to illustrate these aspects of the problem.

The concern is with the short run—that is, a time period in which the locations of the resident and business population are taken as fixed, as are the streets and highways that connect these locations. A travel corridor is assumed. At one end is the central business district or the place where the jobs are; at the other end is a residential neighborhood or the place where people live. The concern is with traffic flows from that neighborhood toward the central business district— the morning commute. Cars move toward the central business district over some network of urban highways. To simplify the discussion, assume there is only one highway, which has a specified number of lanes headed toward town. Given the distance to the central business district, the number of traffic lanes and the maximum permissible speed, we can make statements about the number of trips per some time unit that can be made over that highway and the average speed of those trips. Table 11.2 incorporates hypothetical data concerning traffic flows, traffic density and speed.

Table 11.2

Speed, Traffic Density, and Traffic Flow

Number of Trips on Freeway Per Hour Per Lane	Number of Cars on One Mile of Freeway at Any Instant of Time	Average Speed
2,000	40	50*
4,000	80	50
4,800	120	40
5,000	200	25
3,450	230	15
240**	240**	1**

* Maximum Speed
** Bumper to Bumper

The most important statement we can make is that as the traffic flow increases, i.e., we add to the number of cars that are moving between these two points on column two in Table 11.2, the number of people that move from the suburbs to the central business district per hour will increase—see column one in Table 11.2. A point is quickly reached, however, where the time required for any commuter to make the trip is increased—see column three in Table 11.2. Furthermore, with additional increases in the flow of traffic, a point will ultimately be reached where the number of people moved from the suburbs to the central business district per hour will decline—see column one in Table 11.2. Before this point is reached, the addition of more cars onto the highway will increase the number of people headed toward town proportionately more than it reduces the speed at which they travel to get there. But if we keep increasing the traffic flow, at some point the impact on these additions on the speed of movement will begin to offset the increase in the number of people on the road. When this point is reached, the number of people who can be moved from the suburbs to the central business district per hour declines.

Congestion, of course, emerges as the buildup of traffic begins. Those who are part of this process see it as the slowdown in their speed. Looked at in this way, the solution appears to be that of building additional highways which generate the capacity to handle the traffic at speeds consistent with what people want. To do this, however, can be a very expensive solution and one that for some cities might be impractical, in the sense that they would wind up as one big piece of paved highway.

Economic Foundations   Urban economics makes an important contribution to the discussion at this point. The problem of traffic congestion, as considered by the urban economist, stems from the fact that private costs of the movement of people from the suburbs to the central business district and back do not fully reflect the social costs of that movement. There are externalities that generate costs that are not reflected in the decisions people make about commuting to work.

The point is straightforward and simple. Recall that the cost of commuting includes both money outlays and the time cost of movement. The latter depends on the importance of time to commuters and the length of time of the commute. Money outlays when the automobile is used cover operating and parking costs, both of which are relatively insensitive to time.

Now note what happens to the time costs as the flow of traffic between the suburbs and the central business district is increased. Suppose we are at the point of utilization at which additional cars reduce travel speeds. Increasing the flow of traffic lowers travel speeds and hence increases the costs of travel for all those who commute this way. If this possibility is not reckoned with by those who make the decisions to commute to work by car over this highway, the social costs of movement will be above private costs at certain utilization rates.

Figure 11.2 provides a graphic illumination of this point.

Figure 11.2

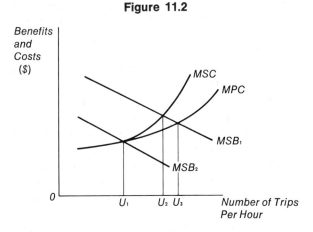

Traffic flows, as measured by the number of trips per hour, are represented on the horizontal axis and dollar costs or benefits are represented on the vertical axis. Since people want to come to the central business district, the trip bestows benefits. If we look at these benefits out on the margin—what happens to benefits with one more traveler on the road—they can be depicted by a marginal benefit curve. If we assume that all benefits accrue to people individually, as they travel, marginal private benefits will equal marginal social benefits. Two such benefit curves are depicted in Figure 11.2. MSB_1 represents an estimate of the marginal benefits of travel to the resident population during commute hours. MSB_2 represents an estimate of those benefits at other times. Not surprisingly, the travel benefits at commute times are valued more highly than they are at nonpeak times.

The marginal cost of travel—the increment to total travel costs occasioned by the addition of one more traveler—is represented by the *MSC* and *MPC* lines. Prior to point OU_1 they are the same; after this point they diverge. This divergence is what is meant by congestion. It stems from the fact that travel time slows beyond a certain utilization rate (OU_1), which adds to the cost of travel by increasing time costs. These additional costs are reflected in marginal social costs (*MSC*), but not in marginal private costs (*MPC*). Congestion is thus taken to mean utilization rates at which marginal social costs exceed marginal private costs.

Generally, most people are not aware of the fact that their use of streets and highways imposes costs on others in the form of slower travel speeds and hence higher time costs. Their commuting decisions are therefore based on comparisons of private benefits and private costs. If decisions are made on this basis, the number of trips per hour will be OU_3—see Figure 11.2. This is the utilization rate at which marginal private costs and marginal private benefits are equal. It is also a rate of utilization at which the marginal social costs of travel exceed the marginal private costs. This means congestion, which to the wary traveler is seen as slower travel speeds and all the aggravation that goes with these speeds.

From the viewpoint of society, OU_3 is also troublesome. It represents an inefficient use of this corridor. If marginal social costs are higher than marginal private costs at OU_3, marginal social costs will also be higher than marginal social benefits—see Figure 11.2. When added social costs are greater than added social benefits, our analysis from chapter 6 indicates the use of the resource—in this case the corridor—is too intensive. By using it less intensively, we would be taking less away from benefits than we would from costs. Efficient use, of course, is utilization at the point of equality between marginal social benefits and marginal social costs or point OU_2 in Figure 11.2.

Note now the meaning of efficiency implied by point OU_2. This is the point that represents the best of all possible worlds, given the constraints. It is also a world in which there is congestion. We know this because at the point OU_2, the marginal social cost of travel is greater than marginal private costs. We are still at a point at which the traffic flows at speeds below the maximum. This is not a matter of personal choice by individual drivers; rather it is a consequence of the magnitude of the traffic flows. Many drivers are forced to drive slower than they prefer, which in their eyes means there is congestion.

The point is an important one often lost sight of in discussions of the problem of congestion. The solution to this problem does not imply congestion-free travel. On the contrary, given the dimensions of the peak-load problem in moving people from their homes to their place of work, some congestion seems unavoidable. The resource requirements necessary to dispose of the problem completely could turn out to be staggering. To reduce congestion to zero could lead to a dramatic reduction in other items of that market basket full of goods we consume. Intelligent compromise is necessary. Point OU_2 is the outcome of such a compromise. It says, in effect, that all things considered, the community is willing to put up with this amount of congestion.

What actions might a community take to deal with its congestion problem? Recall that our concern is with the short-run. It is not possible to alter highway capacity as a means of reducing congestion. Long-term solutions to this and other parts of the urban transportation problems are taken up later. Now the concern is with what can be done about congestion today, next week, or over the next year or two.

Some effort could be made to stagger work hours and hence reduce the dimensions of the peak-load problem. Changes of this kind, however, even if they were appropriate, are likely to be very slow in coming. A more immediate solution would involve restrictions on the use of the highway to reduce its utilization to OU_2. This could conceivably be accomplished through the use of some kind of physical controls administered by some branch of government. We could, for example, set up road blocks at the points of access to our highway and make decisions at these checkpoints that would insure the flow of traffic did not exceed the optimum level. Such a solution may be inefficient, however, in that there could be problems in distinguishing between necessary and unnecessary trips. It is also likely to be found offensive in communities where people are accustomed to free choice exercised in a market setting. In such a setting, this is the problem of rationing a scarce resource—the highway—and hence its solution will involve pricing, since prices are the means through which rationing is accomplished in markets.

Inappropriate pricing, in fact, can be considered as the cause of the problem. The price of the transportation service, or the cost from the viewpoint of the commuter, does not reflect all components of the cost of providing that service. To be sure, commuters are held accountable for much of that cost. They must cover the operating and capital costs of the car, as well as the parking costs. They also pay for the capital and maintenance costs of the street and highway system through gasoline taxes. Commuters, however, are not held accountable for the time cost increments they can generate through their use of the corridor, and it is because they do not have to reckon with these costs that congestion arises and the resource is used inefficiently.

If pricing is the problem, the solution is evident. Prices should be adjusted so that highway users are made to pay for those increments to time costs that arise with use. In effect, there should be peak-load pricing, as there is in other parts of the economy where there are peak-load problems. Peak-load pricing in rationing highway use, however, is apparently not so simple as it seems. Some argue that the cost of administering a program that assesses drivers these costs would be greater than the benefits it yields. This argument has some validity if these costs could only be assessed through some scheme of toll booths. Recent technical advances, however, should make it possible to assess these charges without the installation of such a costly system. What might turn out to be more difficult is the matter of determining how much to charge, although since the problem is one of use exceeding capacity, it should be possible through experimentation to find a price that would adjust use toward an efficient level of utilization.

What is generally believed to be the most important obstacle to the implementation of such a program are political factors which, upon careful inspection, turn out to be consumer resistance. People have become accustomed to free highways, so the argument goes, and are not about to look kindly on any effort to make an explicit charge for their use. While this may be true, it does not follow that people can never be made to understand how assessing costs in this way will help them deal with the problem of congestion in the most effective way.

Efficiency Problems in Urban Transportation Over the Long Run   Suppose the pricing mechanism was used to address the problem of congestion in highway corridors between the suburbs and central business district, and the flow of traffic was reduced to a point where an efficient level of congestion was achieved—point OU_2 in Figure 11.2. This represents a short-run solution to the problem. It represents the best we can do, given current transportation capacity. Given enough time, however, we could adjust that capacity. If we consider this possibility, our time horizons are extended. We become concerned with the long-run, which means additional things enter into our concerns with urban transportation. It is no longer clear that the community will be satisfied with the congestion implicit in point OU_2. Even if they are, circumstances can change. There could be population growth and/or income increases that alter transportation demands in ways that require additions to capacity or more transportation investment.

Population and income increases are realistic presumptions for most cities. They, in fact, generate the kind of transportation problem that becomes the major preoccupation of transportation planners and other local government officials. If we take these things into account, the concern is greatly broadened. Not only must we decide how much additional investment, but we must also make decisions about the kind and site of the investment. We must think of the totality of the problem, that is, the community's transportation demands and transportation cost factors that operate through supply. In a market context, interactions between the suppliers and demanders in this market establish a price to which both suppliers and demanders adjust in making their transportation decisions. Out of these market interactions and adjustments come transportation investment decisions that provide the capacity necessary to transport people around within the city with congestion levels that are deemed appropriate, given tastes and preferences and economic constraints.

Such descriptions of urban transportation investment decisions, while they point us in the direction of things that have important bearing on outcomes, do not really tell us very much about how these decisions are made. Urban transportation is really a mixture of public and private activity. The public concerns are concentrated on the supply side. Because there are scale economies and ownership spillovers in the provision of the service, important parts of the supply have become a public responsibility. While the automobile is provided to us through the private market, streets and highways are constructed, maintained, and owned by government. Most public transit facilities such as buses, subways, and commuter trains are also either owned or very closely regulated by government.

Transportation demand, on the other hand, is largely a matter of dollar votes being cast by individuals in the transportation market. People can choose to walk, ride bikes, use their automobiles, or use some form of public transit. There are no rules or regulations that specify that one form of transportation must be used rather than another. There is free choice. Yet, the question frequently raised in discussions of the urban transportation problem is free choice with respect to what—to walk or drive a car.

There are a number of problems with the mechanisms we have within which free choice is exercised. Not all of the costs incurred by travel are assessed directly on the traveler. This is particularly true of the automobile. While the capital and operating costs of the automobile are directly assessed to the user, the capital and maintenance costs of the streets and highways are not. There are user fees, in the form of a gasoline tax, which are supposed to cover the costs of highway construction and maintenance. Popular opinion to the contrary, these taxes apparently do cover these costs. The automobile user is not fully assessed for the congestion and pollution costs that arise during peak periods of street and highway use.

The pricing of transportation services provided by public transit systems apparently do not cover all of their costs either. While there are no comprehensive data on the capital costs of transit systems, the estimates made of total costs suggest they exceed operating revenues by quite a bit. One estimate, in fact, has operating revenues at about 50 percent of total costs.

Evaluating the efficiency of our urban transportation system is clearly a difficult matter at best. The willingness of people to pay for the services is not easily discerned because not all costs are assessed directly. Nor are the nation's urban travelers assessed the full social costs of travel within the city.

The most common belief among urban economists is that urban transportation is, in general, underpriced. Underpricing implies a price that is below the social costs of transportation. Such a price can be interpreted as an indication of the fact that we are devoting too many resources to transportation. There are alternative uses for the resources that are now being committed to urban transportation. An unwillingness or inability to cover the costs of this use strongly suggests that we would prefer these resources be used in other ways. The efficiency implications of underpricing are thus that we should cut back the transportation services we currently supply and divert some of these resources to other uses. The first step would be to adjust the price of transportation upward so that people are permitted to show how they really feel about transportation relative to all other goods.

Note that if urban transportation is underpriced, economic analysis brings us to the curious position of arguing that measures should be taken that could restrict transportation investment in cities. This position is a curious one, in that it runs counter to the popular belief that what is needed to solve the urban transportation problem is more transportation investment.

Do we need massive infusions of investment in urban transportation? Or can we effectively deal with our transportation problems by finding better ways of pricing the transportation service? Certainly, better pricing would help. Whether it would be sufficient is another question. Some of the difficulty we would encounter in trying to address this question would stem from the fact that the urban transportation problem involves more than the issues of more or less transportation investment. There is, among other things, the question of transportation mode. Some students of urban transportation view this as a very important matter. Some, in fact, go so far as to argue that the urban transportation problem is not so much a matter of how much, but of what kind of urban transportation facilities are needed. It is at this point that the issue of mass transportation surfaces.

The Issue of Mass Transit

Many urban planners and city officials believe the cause of the urban transportation problem is the automobile. The car is the culprit because it cannot move nearly so many people at speeds anywhere close to mass forms of urban transportation. This kind of argument derives much of its force from capacity utilization figures. The automobile, for example, can be shown to move only up to 1,200 persons per lane per hour on city streets and only up to 4,000 on freeways. The capacity for buses is up to 4,500 persons per lane each hour on city streets and up to 18,000 on freeways. Rail rapid transit capacities are the largest, ranging from 21,000 persons per track each hour where six car trains are used with a three-minute time interval between trains, up to 72,000 persons where ten car trains are operating on the basis of ninety second intervals.

With these figures, it is easy to understand why many believe mass transit modes such as subways, trains, and buses are the answer to the transportation problems in our cities. The capacity figures for rail rapid transit are particularly impressive and probably account for the strong interest of many in rail transit forms. Capacity figures of this magnitude relative to those of the automobile imply a significant reduction in the problem of congestion if rail forms of mass transit were substituted for the automobile. Such substitution also implies less pollution, since the emission of pollutants from the automobile necessary to transport a given population to and from various points in the city is much greater than those released by a system of trains.

With advantages like these, why is it that rail transit is not only a relatively unimportant means of urban transportation, but has also declined dramatically as a form of travel in most cities? The problem with rail transit, of course, centers around the distribution of jobs and people within the city.

It is certainly possible to conceive of a rail transit system that attains higher speeds than the automobile in the city and moves around many more people as well. The question is: Will there be enough people to move?

This is a particularly important question for rail forms of transportation. Such transit is capital intensive, which implies a high fixed cost. High fixed costs, in turn, mean there must be many customers if the costs per customer are to be competitive with other forms of urban transportation. Will those customers be there?

There is reason for concern. A fixed route system with limited points of entry and departure on a narrow stretch of land going in a certain direction is limited in its ability to attract customers. It will attract customers, of course, if the routes go through high density residential areas, particularly if the potential ridership is distributed such that passenger volume is equal over all parts of those routes, and movement is toward one place, e.g. downtown. Where the density of the resident population is less, the viability of a rail transit system is questionable. While people can come from the east and west to catch that train headed north, the question of how far they are willing to come becomes important. Those who live within one-half mile from the station might be willing to walk. Beyond that, the time costs of walking from home to the train station and back will probably be too great. It is possible, of course, for the commuter to drive to the train station. "Ride and park" and "Ride and kiss" are important elements in the movement of people from their homes to their jobs in places where rail transit is important, such as New York. Bus service is also provided to train stations in some places.

Whether the movement of people to entry points and from departure points of a rail transit system can be accomplished in ways that add substantially to its customer base seems doubtful, excepting in the case of very large cities. "Park and ride" systems, for example, are expensive because they require an automobile to be used exclusively for that purpose. "Park and kiss" is less expensive in this sense, but can create costs in the sense of problems at home. A bus system that takes commuters to and from train stations is afflicted by neither of these difficulties. Yet, if the population it serves is dispersed, the bus collection and dispersion costs could be large. Changing from bus to train is also considered a nuisance by many.

The calculations of the comparative costs of travel on a rail system as opposed to buses and automobiles, as noted above, show the costs of the automobile to be the least expensive means of transportation when the traffic volume is light. Rail systems, taking into account the costs of getting to and from its entry and departure points, are less than the automobile when the traffic becomes heavier. Comparisons made of buses versus rail systems indicate the bus has unit costs that also decline with heavier traffic, though not as much as they do for rail transit forms.

This pattern of costs in the face of a city that has spread out goes a long way toward explaining why urban mass transit systems greatly diminished in importance over the past fifty years. The process of suburbanization, which was given a strong impetus by the coming of the automobile, itself made the automobile highly attractive as a means of transportation. The automobile, in fact, becomes the least costly method of moving on the low density routes that came with suburbanization. As a consequence, many households shifted from public transit to the automobile, giving rise to a massive investment in a system of urban streets and highways. Few would argue that this investment was unwarranted. Few would argue that our current urban transportation network is grossly inefficient. There are, however, inefficiencies reflected in the problems of congestion and pollution found in all the nation's metropolitan areas.

Some, in pondering these problems, ask: Shouldn't we begin to think about redressing the balance between the automobile and mass transit? While no general answer can be given, we do know that with respect to rail transit, two major conditions must be satisfied if such a system is to be workable. One is that the metropolitan area must be large. The traffic requirements are large and only likely to be fulfilled in places where there are a lot of people. Numbers are not enough, however. There must be concentrations of employment in the central business district so that there will be a sufficient amount of traffic along the routes established. Stated in this way, it is clear that rail transit systems will not be viable in smaller metropolitan areas. It is only in the bigger areas where rail rapid transit should be considered as an alternative. Yet, it may not even be a viable alternative in some of these. While New York, Chicago, Boston, and Philadelphia may have workable rail transit systems, Los Angeles does not. In the case of Los Angeles, it is not so much a matter of a lack of population base, but the way in which the metropolitan area is laid out. There is no real central business district where employment is concentrated.

Where the issue becomes difficult is in some of the nation's relatively large metropolitan areas such as Baltimore, Washington, D.C., Detroit, Seattle, and Cleveland. Since mass transit systems, of necessity, concentrate on the movement of people to and from central locations, the question of viability usually centers on the movement of people to and from jobs in the central business district. The movement of people to jobs in suburban locations is impractical because of the dispersion of those locations. The central question then becomes one of the traffic flows to and from the central business district that the system is likely to generate. Clearly, this will be influenced by the current distribution of residences and jobs in that metropolitan area. The more concentration, the higher the probability the traffic will be there. It can be easily shown, for example, that when there is a relatively high density pattern of residential living, most people will be found living near a rail line in a system of exactly spaced rail lines that radiate from the center of the city. This, of course, is why rail rapid transit is workable in cities like New York and Chicago.

Would rail transit be viable in Detroit? In Washington, D.C.? In Seattle? In Houston? The answer to these questions requires a good deal of detailed factual information about each of these cities. There are, nevertheless, several general observations that can be made.

The necessary conditions of high residential density and high hourly corridor volumes, for example, are most likely to be found in the large and old cities along the Eastern Seaboard and the Middle West. Thus, the probability that a rail transit system will be practicable is likely to be higher in Washington, D.C., than in Houston, Texas, or in Cleveland, Ohio, than in Phoenix, Arizona.

But will it be practicable in Cleveland? In fact, Cleveland has a rail rapid transit system whose capital costs can be regarded as sunk. Therefore, if the city has a transportation problem, improvements in its existing rail system would be one of the alternatives considered, if only because it would be a relatively inexpensive one. When the capital is there and is sunk, rail transit is more likely to be a part of the solution to a city's transportation problem. When the facilities are not there, the capital costs of constructing and putting such a system into operation loom as a real obstacle. This undoubtedly accounts for the fact that most cities without rail transit systems have chosen to address the problems of traffic congestion and pollution by adding to and strengthening their bus service.

How a city chooses to solve its transportation problems should also be influenced by the tastes and preferences of its residents. People do differ, for example, with respect to how they value time, in their needs for schedule flexibility, and in their concerns with convenience and comfort in travel. Some travelers like privacy, convenience and personal comfort; others don't really care much about these things. Some detest noise and congestion; others find the anonymity they value so highly in it.

Having said these things, it is still not clear whether the rail transit system should be developed further in Cleveland or started anew in Cincinnati or Miami. Obviously, our evaluations for particular cities require knowledge and information details that can only come from an investigation of the basic transportation facts in those cities. Speculations about the role of mass transit in particular cities are only reasonable when they are based on facts of the sort.

Is it the case then that nothing general can be said about the issue of mass transit? Must we always equivocate? Can we not take sides?

The nation's Urban Mass Transportation Assistance program provides a basis for making certain statements. In 1964, Congress passed the Urban Mass Transportation Act, which provides the basic statutory authority and the funds for the Urban Mass Transportation Assistance Program. The program itself has two major categories of expenditure—demonstration grants and capital grants. The demonstration grants are intended for experimentation with new uses of existing technology or for the development of a new technology. Capital grants are made for a variety of purposes, including the replacement of old buses with new ones and building or rebuilding rail transit systems.

The program has had its share of both success and failure. Demonstration grants were made for three general categories of programs, namely, bus, rail, and new or experimental systems. In the bus category, the one set of projects that turned out to be remarkably successful was the one which involved granting bus priority on freeways. Attempts to find ways of making rail lines more practicable apparently led to very little success, as did the effort to foster the development and application of new technology.

The capital grants were, in the main, made to support the building of rapid transit systems in Cleveland, Chicago, and Boston, among other places. The purpose of this support was to encourage the construction of rail transit facilities which would hopefully divert some freeway traffic flowing into central cities. While these lines apparently did just that immediately after they were opened, the pattern of growth in the use of freeways subsequently resumed.

While all evaluations made of this program to date do not come to the same conclusion, no one argues that it has been a smashing success. If its major aim was to foster the growth and development of mass transit, it has to be judged as unsuccessful. Ridership of mass transit systems, estimated to be a little over 8 billion riders per year in 1965, fell to an estimated 6.5 billion in 1973; and cities in which these transit forms were important continued to lose population.

Why has this program met with such little success so far? The problem could be that the program did not go far enough; that through it we have yet to make the commitment of resources necessary to turn the pendulum around in favor of mass transit. This argument is difficult to evaluate.

What does come through in an evaluation of this program is that its results are consistent with the view that mass transit demands are not affected very much by programs that alter the incomes of the users or the price of the transit service. Measures taken to lower the cost of using mass transit have been shown to exert relatively little influence on the behavior of many automobile users. What is more effective in influencing automobile use is a perceived increase in the cost of the use of a car. This undoubtedly explains why the Urban Mass Transportation Assistance program experimenting with allowing buses to operate on reserved lanes was successful. It imposed higher congestion costs on automobile users than on mass transit passengers.

The conclusion to be drawn from the experience of this program, tentative though it may be, is that mass transit as it is conventionally perceived—a fancy rail system—may not be the answer to the transportation problems of many cities, at least not now. Dispersion in some metropolitan areas has gone too far and the travelers in metropolitan areas seem to value the flexibility of the automobile very highly. The only conditions under which significant numbers of auto travelers might be enticed back to mass transit forms is if the cost of automobile use is increased perceptibly. Actions taken to crowd cars off the freeway through the establishment of bus lanes have met with some success precisely because they had impact on the costs of driving a car.

If this conclusion is reasonable, mass transit forms in general and buses in particular should gain greater acceptance in the coming years. The rapidly rising prices of cars, partly a consequence of the effort to deal with the problem of pollution, are adding substantially to the capital costs of using an automobile. Rapidly rising gasoline and oil prices are, at the same time, adding substantially to the cost of its operation. The cost of the automobile as a means of urban travel has thus risen relative to the costs of other forms of urban transportation. While it remains to be seen just how much impact this relative cost increase will have on transportation mode choice, it is likely that it will work to the advantage of mass transit forms.

EQUITY AND URBAN TRANSPORTATION

Our urban transportation systems have evolved in ways that many allege provide few, if any, benefits to the poor. The coming of the automobile greatly enhanced the mobility and locational options of a great many Americans. However, these benefits were not equally distributed. They were most readily available to those with relatively high incomes. Moving away from the center of the city increased out-of-pocket commuting costs in ways that would have strained the budgets of many low-income families if they moved into the suburbs. Moreover, commuting by car meant a capital outlay—the purchase of a car—which many of the poor were in no position to make.

That the poor could not exercise the option of commuting by car did not by itself mean they were being adversely affected by the automobile. Yet, their transportation and residential location choices were affected in the sense that growth in the importance of the car reduced the demands for the mass transit systems that provided for the bulk of the transportation needs of the poor. This decline in demand was important because it happened to an industry that operated with heavy fixed costs or a decreasing costs industry. A reduction in the demands of a decreasing costs industry, in turn, meant reduced service and higher fares. This clearly shows up in Figure 11.3. When demand shifts from D_1 to D_2, quantity is reduced from Q_1 to Q_2 and price is increased from P_1 to P_2.

Figure 11.3

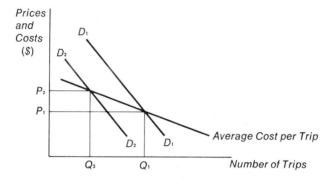

The flight to the suburbs thus had the effect of reducing the caliber of transportation service available to the poor and at the same time increased its costs in some places. The extent to which the well-being of low-income families was adversely affected is unknown. While automobile ownership is less frequent among the poor, there are many who do own a car, some of whom moved away from the central city. We do know, however, that blacks from all income groups suffered more than others, simply because their housing choices were restricted.

The impact of suburbanization on low-income families living in central cities was intensified because it included industry as well as residential users. A reduction in the quantity and quality of central city mass transit service would not have hurt as much if the poor had remained relatively close to their jobs. The movement of industry meant an increase in the distance between home and job for some of those who remained. More important than the increased distance, however, was the spatial dispersion of the jobs themselves. That they were no longer concentrated at a particular site made it difficult to use mass transit modes as a means of meeting transportation needs.

There is yet another aspect of the impact of the growing dominance of the automobile on the welfare of the poor. As streets and highways were constructed to serve the urban needs of the nation's automobiles, housing units were sometimes removed from the stock. This ordinarily did not happen with expansion on the periphery of the city—the suburbanization process. The urban component of the interstate highway system, on the other hand, did give rise to construction activity within the city, which was preceded by the removal of many low-quality units in the city. To the extent that this occurred, the poor suffered because of a reduction in the supply of dwellings that housed many of them.

From time to time, visible public concern for the transportation problems of the poor surfaces. Much of what is proposed as a solution to the overall problem of urban transportation, however, pays scant attention to these problems. Some proposals, in fact, would compound the difficulties of the poor. The grandiose plans of a rapid transit system that revolve around a rail system, for example, are plans that, if implemented, could redistribute income from the poor to the rich if subsidies were involved. Many designs put forward consist of radial lines that connect suburbs and central business districts. The benefits of these designs go primarily to middle-class suburbanites who work downtown. To the extent that subsidies are involved and the funds come out of the general revenues of government, these funds, in part, would be taken from those who do not have much and given to those who do. While this overstates the point, few would argue that the subsidizing of the suburban community is an appropriate way of dealing with our urban transportation problems.

The Demonstration Grant program of the Urban Mass Transportation Assistance program has provided funds designed to find solutions to the transportation problems of low-income residents of the nation's central cities. The program, among other things, established 83 routes in fifteen cities, intended to provide outward mobility for central city low-income residents to suburban factories or other places of employment. These projects were intended to provide a service that was not fully provided for in the existing routes of transit companies. All of them were apparently unsuccessful. A part of the problem was that many used the service to find a job and once they found one, bought a car and stopped riding the bus. That things like this happen throws into sharp focus the fact that little is known about the transportation needs of the poor. As we move to re-emphasize the role of mass transit in our cities—if only ever so slightly—it is likely that we shall concentrate our efforts on improving the movement of suburbanites into and away from the central business district. More emphasis should also be put on the transportation needs of ghetto residents, but it is not really clear what directions we should take in dealing with the problem. It could be that a re-emphasis on mass transit will create further problems for low-income families. It could be that the origins and destinations of ghetto residents commuting to suburban jobs are so diverse that some kind of automobile system would be best to solve their problems. If so, this should be incorporated into the plans developed as a means of dealing with the urban transportation problem.

All of this is highly speculative. What is paramount at this point is a need for a better understanding of the transportation needs of the poor.

REFERENCES

Hilton, G. W. "The Urban Mass Transportation Assistance Problem." In *Perspectives on Federal Transportation Policy,* edited by J. C. Miller. Washington, D.C.: American Enterprise Institute for Public Policy Research, 1975, pp. 131–44.

Meyer, J.; Kain, J.; and Wohl, M. *The Urban Transportation Problem.* Cambridge, Mass.: Harvard University Press, 1965.

Moses, I. and Williamson, H. F. "Value of Time, Choice of Mode and the Subsidy Issue in Urban Transportation." *Journal of Political Economy.* 71 (1963): 247–64.

Owens, W. *The Metropolitan Transportation Problem.* Washington, D.C.: The Brookings Institution, 1966.

Quandt, R., Ed. *The Demand for Travel: Theory and Measurement.* Lexington, Mass.: Lexington Books, D. C. Heath, 1974.

Smerk, G. M. *Urban Mass Transportation.* Bloomington: Indiana University Press, 1974.

Vikrey, W. S. "Pricing in Urban and Suburban Transport." *American Economic Review: Papers and Proceedings.* 3 (May 1963): 452–65.

Walters, A. A. "The Theory and Measurement of Private and Social Costs of Highway Congestion." *Econometrica.* 29 (1961): 676–99.

12

Problems in the Urban Public Economy

SUMMARY

Urban government, in the sense of municipal governments, provides an important package of public services to city residents. The political units through which these services are provided are also highly fragmented.

Fragmentation of municipal government is decried by many. It is not only considered to be inefficient, but it is also believed to be a source of a number of important problems in our cities. Careful examination of the efficiency argument indicates it to be less persuasive than its proponents believe. In fact, fragmented government makes some sense on efficiency grounds if it is viewed as the outcome of a process that enables people to articulate their demands for public goods better. Political fragmentation, however, does make it difficult to redistribute incomes in the city.

The fiscal problems of central cities are both highly publicized and very real. The budget stresses are greater in the central city, because proportionately more of the community's poor have come to live there. This both increases the demand for public services and, at the same time, given local government fragmentation, reduces the ability to pay for them. These demands have been bolstered further by the growing effectiveness of the poor to articulate their needs. Cost pressures stemming from a technology that does not provide much basis for productivity increases in supplying services have also added to the problems of central city governments. So have the growing militancy of city government employees and the increased effectiveness in bargaining for higher wages and other benefits.

The issue of equity in considering the fiscal problems of the central city is important. Many believe that because people can move away from central cities, a question of equity arises. If the poor remain, who is to help shoulder the burden of their public needs? Some suggest the solution to this problem is political consolidation. Most people believe this is not a good solution. The assistance to central city governments has come primarily through intergovernmental transfers.

The problem with introducing equity into this debate is that we really don't know what to do with it. Our activities through government are not really linked to some coherent plan which is designed to achieve some set of equity goals. This is not surprising, if only because of the difficulties encountered in attempting to define what equity means. The evidence seems to suggest that the poor do receive net benefits from the activities of government. Yet, we do not really know the magnitude of these benefits or whether their distribution helps to alleviate what many believe to be the inequities between central cities and suburbs.

The public economy is important in the United States for reasons touched upon in chapter 6. One of these concerns is the provision of public goods. Public goods were indicated earlier to be an extreme case of an externality. They are goods that can be consumed by one person without diminishing the consumption of others. National defense was cited as an illustration. At the local level, the administration of justice is another.

Of course, governments do more than this. At the local level, they are involved in the provision of educational, recreational and hospital services. Careful inspection of these services, however, raises questions about the "publicness" of what is being provided. Some education, for example, is provided through the private sector, as is much of the recreation we consume in cities. There are, in fact, some government scholars who have serious doubts about the utility of much of what is done through government.

The question of the role of government in the economy does not have a clearcut answer. Some of what government does is purely public; but much of it is not. Education, for example, is not a pure public good. Many believe, however, that it has enough benefits that are external to its consumers to warrant some kind of government assistance. The same can be said about many of the other things governments do. The problem is that whether governments do too much or too little in any or all of these areas is by no means clear.

Publicness is certainly a part of the criteria to be used in making such judgments if we have any concern with efficiency. Many argue that equity should also be a part of those criteria. Governments can do many things that redistribute income and wealth. The question of what they should do is not easily answered, for reasons that were discussed in some length in chapter 6. There is also a question in the minds of some as to whether government is the most efficient means of redistributing the nation's income and wealth to achieve some set of equity goals. Most government scholars, however, believe redistribution is a legitimate function of government and it is often held to be an explanation of why governments do certain things.

Government in the United States, of course, provides its services and carries out its redistribution activities through three levels, namely federal, state, and local governments. Since most of the nation's population lives in cities, much of what is done at all levels of government can be construed as being urban. Most of the public services made directly available to people living in cities, however, are provided through local government in the sense of city, county, metropolitan areas, and special district governments. It is through such governmental units that we provide such things as public education, police and fire protection, public health and welfare programs, public transportation, and water supply and sanitation.

Because of the importance of these activities and because they are provided through local government, discussions of the urban public economy tend to center on the activities of government at the city level. While the activities of government at the federal and state levels impact importantly on local government and hence cannot be ignored when considering the urban public economy, it is not unreasonable when considering that economy to focus on the activities of local government.

The concern in this chapter is with the activities of municipal government, which, in many instances, span a political subdivision that is only a part of the metropolitan area of which it is a part. Much of the discussion will therefore center on activities of government in cities—cities in the sense of being legal entities as opposed to a metropolitan area that encompasses a labor market. Not all of the discussion will be concerned with cities in this sense, however. The discussion of economies of scale in local government will be concerned with government operations that span the boundaries of a labor market or metropolitan area. The meaning of *cities* in this chapter, more so than in any other chapter, will depend on the context of its use.

SALIENT CHARACTERISTICS OF LOCAL GOVERNMENT

According to the United States Constitution, sovereign power is shared by the state and federal governments. The roots of local government are not found in the constitution; rather these governmental units have been created by state government. That they are the creatures of 50 state governments may help explain the large number and seemingly bewildering variety of units created. In 1972, for example, there were 78,218 local government units, including 3,044 counties, 18,517 municipalities, 16,991 townships, 15,781 school districts, and 23,885 special districts. While this number is smaller than it was twenty-five years ago, largely as a consequence of the consolidation of school districts, it is large by any standard.

The county, local and municipal governments have limited and varied powers to level taxes and spend the funds collected. School districts have the power to levy property taxes to support public education. Special districts have been created for special purposes, the most important of which are water supply and waste disposal.

That there are so many local governmental units doing so many different things suggests complexity and problems. This possibility is highlighted by the composition of local government in many of the nation's largest metropolitan areas. The number of such units in Chicago or New York, for example, is in excess of 1,000, giving rise to what many perceive as serious problems of overlapping jurisdictions, confusion, inefficiency, and unhealthy competition. These, in turn, are problems that constitute important elements in the major problems in the urban public economy, namely, fragmentation, fiscal crises, and fiscal inequities.

Local Governments: What Do They Do?

Local governments, as noted above, collect taxes, receive funds from both state and federal government, and generate revenues from various charges made on some of the services they provide. They, in turn, spend these funds on a number of activities.

The majority of the funds that local government receives come from taxes—close to one-half—and the bulk of the tax receipts come from property taxes—see Table 12.1. The fact that intergovernmental transfer payments account for over one-third of the funds received indicates the importance of the urban interests and activities of state and federal government to local government. Still, taxes yield the bulk of their revenues and the property tax is the predominant form of tax revenue. Many do have a sales tax and some a payroll tax, but in the aggregate, these taxes do not produce nearly as much revenue as does the property tax—see Table 12.1.

Local governments also raise revenues from public service enterprises such as water, electric power, gas, and public transit and user charges for noncommercial services provided in such areas as health, housing, and sanitation.

The bulk of the funds provided to local government by other levels of government—intergovernmental transfers—come from state government. While this has changed somewhat recently with the implementation of a revenue-sharing program by the federal government, the dollar magnitude of the funds going from state to local government still exceeds the flow of federal dollars.

The majority of the funds received by local governments both from tax and nontax sources are spent on education. Over 45 percent of their budgets is devoted to education—see Table 12.2. The remainder is spread fairly evenly over a relatively large number of expenditure categories, including transportation, public welfare, health and hospitals, police and fire protection, housing and urban renewal, parks, sewage and sanitation, utilities and government administration—see Table 12.2.

These proportions undoubtedly vary by individual government units, although given available data, it is difficult to make many concrete statements about the nature of these differences. There are "spillovers" of expenses and tax revenues between the various governmental units that complicate the interpretation of available figures. Studies of individual cities and journalistic reports, however, do suggest considerable variation in what different local governmental units do, although education is the dominant expenditure in most cases.

The overall magnitude of spending by local government has increased dramatically since the end of World War II. Expenditures of state and local government reflected in the national income accounts increased twentyfold from 1946 through 1974, which is substantially in excess of the increases that occurred in the other major categories of spending—see Table 12.3. This increase in state and local government spending is also reflected in all major spending categories, with the largest gains in education and public welfare—see Table 12.4.

Table 12.1

Government Revenue Sources
1972
(Millions of Dollars)

	Total	% of Total	Fed	% of Total	State	% of Total	Local	% of Total
Total Revenue	381,849	—	223,378		112,309		113,162	—
Intergovernmental Revenues	—		—		27,981	24.9	39,017	34.5
Taxes	262,534	68.7	153,733	68.8	59,870	53.3	48,930	43.2
Property	42,133	11.0	—		1,257	1.1	40,876	36.1
Industrial Income	109,974	28.8	94,737	42.4	12,966	11.5	}	
Corporation Income	36,582	9.6	32,166	14.4	4,416	3.9	2,241	2.0
Sales and Gross Receipts	57,589	15.1	20,101	9.0	33,250	29.6	4,238	3.7
Death and Gift	6,730	1.8	5,436	2.4	1,294	1.2	—	—
Other General Revenues (Charges)	44,688	11.7	18,389	8.2	10,780	9.6	15,519	13.7
Other Revenues	74,629	19.5	51,256	23.0	13,677	12.2	9,696	8.6

Source: U.S. Bureau of the Census: Governmental Finances in 1971–72

Table 12.2

General Governmental Expenditures
(Direct and Intergovernmental)
1972
(Millions of Dollars)

	All Government	% of Total	Federal	% of Total	State	% of Total	Local	% of Total
Total	321,389	100.0	188,100	100.0	98,810	100.0	105,393	100.0
National Defense	79,258	24.7	79,258	42.1	—	—	—	—
Space Research	3,369	1.1	3,369	1.8	—	—	—	—
Postal Service	9,366	2.9	9,366	5.0	—	—	—	—
Education	69,990	21.8	13,045	6.9	38,348	38.8	47,786	45.3
Highway	19,442	6.0	5,540	2.9	15,380	15.6	6,303	6.0
National Resources	14,215	4.4	15,739	6.2	2,595	2.6	649	0.6
Health & Hospitals	17,033	5.3	5,478	2.9	6,963	7.0	6,983	6.6
Public Welfare	23,558	7.3	14,739	8.4	19,191	19.4	9,012	8.6
Housing & Urban Renewal	5,411	1.7	4,611	2.5	149	0.2	2,748	2.6
Air Transportation	3,575	1.1	2,538	1.3	178	0.2	1,013	1.0
Employment Security Administration	2,291	0.7	1,911	1.0	1,133	1.1	3	—
Interest on General Debt	23,077	7.2	17,114	9.1	2,135	2.2	3,827	3.6
Other	50,805	15.8	18,402	9.8	12,738	12.9	27,068	25.7

Source: U.S. Bureau of the Census: Governmental Finances in 1971–72

Table 12.3

Gross National Product
by Type of Spending
1946–1974
(Billions of Dollars)

	Total Gross National Product	Personal Consumption	Gross Private Domestic Investment	Net Exports of Goods and Services	Government Purchase	State and Local Government Purchase
1946	208.5	143.4	30.6	7.5	27.0	9.8
1950	284.8	191.0	54.1	1.8	37.9	19.5
1955	398.0	254.4	67.4	2.0	74.2	30.1
1960	503.7	325.2	74.8	4.0	99.6	46.1
1965	684.9	432.8	108.1	6.9	137.0	70.1
1970	977.1	617.6	136.3	3.6	219.5	123.3
1974	1,396.7	877.0	208.9	2.0	308.8	192.4

Source: U.S. Department of Commerce

Table 12.4

State and Local Government
Spending by Function
1946–1973
(Billions of Dollars)

	Education	Highways	Public Welfare	All Other
1946	3.4	1.7	1.4	4.6
1950	7.2	3.8	2.9	8.9
1955	11.9	6.5	3.2	12.2
1960	18.7	9.4	4.4	19.3
1965	28.6	12.2	6.3	27.4
1970	52.7	16.4	14.7	47.6
1973	69.6	18.6	23.6	69.3

Source: U.S. Department of Commerce

The revenues used to finance this increased spending came from the traditional sources, such as property and sales taxes. They also came from income taxes and from the federal government and other nontax sources, all of which have grown rapidly in importance in recent years—see Table 12.5.

Table 12.5

State and Local Government
Revenues by Source
1946–1973
(Billions of Dollars)

	Property Tax	Sales and Gross Receipts	Income Taxes	Revenue from Federal Government	All Other Revenues
1946	5.0	3.0	0.9	0.9	2.7
1950	7.3	5.1	1.4	2.5	4.5
1955	10.7	7.6	2.0	3.1	7.5
1960	16.4	11.8	3.6	7.0	11.6
1965	22.6	17.1	6.0	11.0	17.3
1970	34.1	30.3	14.6	21.9	30.0
1973	45.2	42.0	23.4	39.3	40.2

Source: U.S. Department of Commerce

Since the end of World War II, expenditures have exceeded receipts in the general accounts of state and local government, but in many years, this deficit was more than made up for by a surplus in the governments' trust fund accounts. The result was some years of very moderate overall deficits and some years of very moderate surpluses, at least until the 1970s, when revenue sharing funds temporarily helped swell receipts and led to relatively large budget surpluses. These surpluses have diminished over the past year or two, but some current forecasts suggest they will reappear again as the educational needs of the nation decline due to the falling birth rate.

Forecasts of surpluses in state and local government sound unreal in the face of reports of fiscal crises in many of our cities. The two can be reconciled, however. While there may be balance among the aggregates, there can be imbalances among political subdivisions that make up the whole, as indeed there appear to be. These imbalances in turn are problems that many believe are with us because of the fragmentation of local government.

POLITICAL FRAGMENTATION

The fragmentation of local government was noted above. Within the boundaries of our metropolitan areas, local government functions are carried out in a relatively large number of politically distinct and geographically separable units. Many believe this to be an inefficient way of running local government and argue that city governments should be restructured so as to integrate their operations over an entire metropolitan area. "Consolidation of local governments" is a banner that has been waved for some time now. To many, it stands as a solution to most of our urban problems. Not all agree, however.

Political fragmentation, or consolidation, is apparently both an important and controversial issue in the minds of many urban scholars. To discuss it seriously requires knowledge of the reasons local government has become so fragmented. While this is a political phenomenon, it has economic roots that warrant discussion.

Articulation of Demand

Political reformers often decry the selfishness of those who live in the suburbs and refuse links to the central city through annexation. Economists usually have less difficulty with self-interest and, consequently, look differently at the political decisions some suburbanites make. In fact, the political fragmentation does not seem so outrageous to one concerned with the economic aspects of political behavior, particularly the demand aspects of that behavior.

Demand is, of course, a crucial element in the determination of the level and composition of activity in the private sector of a free market economy. Yet, as noted earlier, there are demands that cannot be expressed in the market place, i.e., public goods demands. Some of these demands are satisfied through activities of the federal government; some through the activities of state government. Much of what we demand from government, however, comes to us through the activities of local government.

What do people want from local government? There can be problems in articulating household demands for public goods if the local government unit that provides them is too large. Problems will arise when there are variations in household preferences and incomes.

Recall that a public good is one that, when made available, becomes available to all. No one can be excluded from its consumption. Consider now some difficulties that confront local government as it attempts to provide an efficient quantity of such a good. Suppose the concern is with fire protection. A specific commitment has to be made. The capital equipment must be purchased, people must be hired and, in some cases, trained, and procedures must be established. If we suppose that the scope of this operation covers the entire metropolitan area and is set up in such a way that each person or neighborhood receives equal treatment, it is possible that the service will be inefficiently provided.

Suppose people differ in their needs, desires, or ability to pay for public goods. Suppose, because of their life styles, there are some who expose themselves to more fire hazards than do others. To meet their fire protection needs would be to provide a service that would probably be in excess of what many others require. To provide less service would fail to meet the needs of these particular families.

The point warrants amplification. Suppose that there are two groups of people in the community who differ in the amount of public goods they want. Assume that group X wants $500 per capita per year and group Y wants $250 per capita per year. This difference could be due to differences in incomes and/or tastes and preferences. If people from groups X and Y are mixed together and these public goods are provided by one governing body, no amount of public goods production will be best from the viewpoint of both groups. Providing production in the neighborhood of $500 per capita per year will make more goods available to those in group Y than they want. To reduce it to $250 will make less goods available than the people in group X want. To put the amount somewhere in between will make both groups unhappy. If each group, however, is brought together in a separate jurisdiction and public goods are provided by separate governmental units responding to the collective demands in each of the jurisdictional units, public goods production can be made to satisfy their demands.

Political fragmentation can indeed bring about improvements in the use of our public resources. While central city mayors may complain about their inability to raise taxes to pay for needed services, the real problem may be that they provide too many unwanted services to some parts of the population. People who feel they are not getting their money's worth and can live wherever they may choose may move. If they move to another city or unincorporated place in the same metropolitan area and get what they want, that move can be interpreted as one that improves the efficiency of the provision of public goods by local government. Since people have been doing this in our cities for some time, it is not unreasonable to argue that local political structures are consistent with the criteria of efficiency in the provision of public goods.

The argument is persuasive; whether it is correct is another question. There are problems with it. Fragmentation would not be efficient if we failed to realize economies of scale in government because of it. It would also not be efficient if there were spillovers. People may move to the suburbs because they can get the mix of taxes and expenditures they want *and* other services free from the central city. Finally, there are questions of equity involved in political fragmentation that should be considered.

Economies of Scale

Most of those who favor some form of consolidated government rely heavily on notions of economies of scale in their arguments. Many believe that political fragmentation leads to inefficiencies in the sense of duplication of effort and a failure to take full advantage of the economies of scale in the production of many public goods. The argument, on the surface, is appealing.

The concept of a scale economy was discussed at length in chapter 2. The parts of that discussion relevant here are scale economies internal to the firm. These economies come into play when there are indivisibilities in the production process. Higher levels of output permit the use of technologies that foster more specialization, which enhances productivity.

Fragmented government could frustrate efforts to realize such economies. Governmental units that serve the section of the metropolitan area of which they are a part may not be able to push output up to the threshold levels at which economies internal to the scale of operation within the firm come into play. Is this, in fact, the case?

The question of economies of scale in local government has been investigated and the results are ambiguous. With respect to some services, there are economies of scale; for others, there are not. Hirsch, in summarizing the results of various investigations of production costs in the provision of local public services, classifies them according to whether they are "horizontally" or "vertically" integrated. *Horizontally integrated services* are those services provided by government, the control of which is over a number of units providing essentially the same service, e.g., police protection, primary and secondary education, refuse collection, hospitals, and fire protection. A *vertically integrated service* is one in which the government controls a number of different operations involved in the production of one service provided to the community. Water, sewage, and electricity are illustrations of this kind of operation.

According to Hirsch, the production of horizontally integrated services experiences little in the way of economies as the scale of a city in the sense of a metropolitan area increases. Vertically integrated services, on the other hand, are subject to internal economies of scale. Thus, there are some public services that are best provided on a small scale and others on a larger scale. This suggests that the services provided by local government fit a hierarchical pattern. Since the population served is dispersed, the location of the capital facilities involved in providing the service depends on the costs of getting it to the consumer—or the consumer to the service—relative to the economies of scale realized in providing the service. Apparently, there are differences among services. For some—Hirsch's horizontally integrated services—market areas are small because movement costs are relatively high and there are no appreciable economies of scales realized in the production of that service. Efficiency considerations require that the fixed plant involved in providing these services be widely dispersed throughout the community. For others —Hirsch's vertically integrated services—economies of scale are important relative to movement costs. Spatially concentrated production is appropriate.

When public goods provided by local governments are viewed in this way, the complaints about duplication because of political fragmentation in the provision of these services begin to lose some of their force. There are a great many police and fire stations and school buildings scattered throughout most metropolitan areas, not so much because of political fragmentation, but because it makes good sense economically. Whether these spatial distributions are the best distributions is another question. There certainly is reason to believe, however, that duplication in the provision of some services through local government is not so serious a matter as some people think.

There are, of course, public goods in which economies of scale are realized, e.g., the provision of water and sewage services, which implies a centralized location and a span of operations that could conceivably cover the entire metropolitan area. Public goods of this kind stand as an argument in favor of consolidated government. The fact that public goods of this kind stand as few among many, however, reduces the force of this argument. Moreover, the provision of these public services does not require total consolidation. They can be provided in other ways. Special districts, for example, are a means of coping with this problem. If production and distribution require a large-scale operation, sponsoring governmental units that have jurisdiction over an area necessary to achieve that scale of operation makes sense. If that service is only one of many and most of the others do not require large-scale operations, setting up a governmental arrangement that is restricted in the scope of its activity, e.g., a special district, also makes sense. Another way of dealing with this problem would be to concentrate the activity in one political jurisdiction. The service could then be provided directly to customers throughout the entire metropolitan area by dealing directly with other public bodies in that metropolis.

The issues involved in evaluating these types of arrangements are not so simple as these few remarks suggest. They range well beyond the subject matter of economics in general and economies of scale in particular. Still, the continued presence of such arrangements does suggest that economies of scale provide less warrant for consolidation of the many political units in our metropolitan areas than some political reformers believe.

Spillovers

Political fragmentation can lead to inefficient outcomes if "spillovers" are present. *Spillover* is a term ordinarily used when the benefits of a public good—or bad—accrue to those who live outside the political jurisdiction in which that good is produced. The spillover occurs if the beneficiary from another political jurisdiction contributes nothing to cover the cost of product—pays no taxes or user's fees.

How can this be? It can very easily happen if there is political fragmentation. The number of public goods whose consumption cannot be confined to residents of the political jurisdiction in which they are being produced is not small. Law enforcement, for example, is a public service that generates benefits that can spill over on those living in other political jurisdictions. Safe streets in a central city creates benefits for anyone who shops or finds entertainment there, whether they live in or outside that city. When nonresidents enjoy these benefits, there will be spillovers in the sense that they get something for nothing.

Or consider the case of the people within a city, nestled within some metropolitan area, that provides its residents with a public "bad" in the sense of a totally inadequate public health program. If this failure breeds disease and the carriers, in interacting with others outside the city, pass this disease on, there are spillovers.

Some public activities produce spillovers that are complex and extraordinarily difficult, if not impossible, to measure. Education is a good example. Education is generally believed to have benefits that are both internal and external to the person. Its internal benefits are the direct satisfaction from consumption of the educational services and the long-term income benefits associated with the human capital increments. The external benefits are those that accrue to individual communities and society as a whole because our democratic process works better if the population is educated. If these social benefits improve the functioning of local government, there will be spillovers if the population is mobile. The community beneficiaries of public education expenditures may not be those who provide the educational services. People can move away and take their education investments with them just as those with little education can move into the community.

No one doubts that there are education spillovers in cities. How important they are is unknown, in part, because of difficulties of measurement. While most, though not all, would agree that an educated citizenry makes democracy work better, just how much education contributes to the effectiveness of the way in which local government functions is a controversial question.

If spillovers exist in a metropolitan community with fragmented government, as they do, must we be concerned? We must if we are concerned with efficiency, since spillovers have efficiency implications.

Consider, by way of illustration, the provision of law enforcement services in a central city that is surrounded by a great number of politically distinct neighboring communities. If the benefits accrue to those living in other political jurisdictions, the marginal metropolitan area benefits of the service will exceed the marginal city benefits—see Figure 12.1.

Figure 12.1

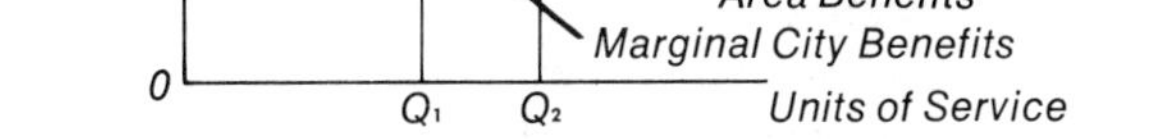

Suppose the city has knowledge of the marginal city benefit curve. In acting rationally, it will provide OQ_1 units of law enforcement. This may be enough for the city. It will not be for the metropolitan area of which the city is a part. The efficient solution for the entire area is OQ_2—see Figure 12.1. The spillover has created an inefficiency in the sense that not enough of the service is provided for the residents of the metropolitan area as a whole.

Or consider the city that provides for the power needs of its residents and does so in ways that create pollution which spills over into other communities. Pollution arises when marginal social costs of production exceed the marginal private costs —see Figure 12.2. Properly treating the wastes from production incurs costs that the city does not consider. Hence, the waste is not treated properly and pollution that spills over into neighboring communities is the result. This result is inefficient. Output is taken to OQ_1 when the city decides on the basis of its estimates of marginal social or private benefits and marginal private costs. Were it confronted with the social costs of its production, output would be OQ_2. Too much is produced. Pollution results and spills over onto neighboring communities.

Figure 12.2

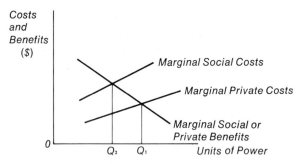

A part of the problem of spillovers could be dealt with by charging user fees. If the city provides certain cultural services that attract residents from other communities within the metropolitan area, for example, their share of the costs can be recouped by an admission charge. In some cases this is feasible; in others, such as law enforcement, it is not. When it is not possible and spillovers exist, there are grounds for advocating the enlargement of local government jurisdictions to include the area within which there are beneficiaries. This is not the only solution to the problem, however.

If the spillovers involve people who work within the city, but live elsewhere, they can be assessed for the public benefits they consume through taxation and, indeed, in many cases they are. The problem can also be resolved by transferring the public service in question to another level of government. Or the function can remain at the local level but be financed, in part at least, by transfers from state and federal government—intergovernmental transfers. In fact, some local government activities involve federal and state government in this way.

The difficulty in attempting to evaluate the significance of spillovers is that many cities try to deal with the problems they create by user fees, various forms of taxation imposed on those who do not live in the city, and intergovernmental transfers. The problem is not that cities do these things, but in the measurement of the outcome of their efforts. Many elements are involved that cannot be easily disentangled. The fact that local governments do rely on user fees, impose taxation on those who live elsewhere, and are the recipients of intergovermental transfers, however, does reduce the force of the spillover argument in favor of political consolidation.

Redistribution and Political Fragmentation

Political fragmentation can have important repercussions with respect to the ability of local government to redistribute income through its taxing and expenditure powers. If there are many political jurisdictions within the metropolis and if people are free to move from one to the other, cities in the sense of legal cities in large metropolitan areas will be restricted in the extent to which they can redistribute income through the exercise of their fiscal power.

The point can be easily illustrated. Suppose a city that is one of a number of cities in some metropolitan area decides to embark on a program designed to upgrade the housing of its low-income residents. To do so will require money, which is not likely to be forthcoming from the beneficiaries. Assume the financing, if this project is to be undertaken, has to come from the city's more affluent citizens. This can be done by raising taxes. If taxes are raised, however, and the additional revenues are used to finance what may be considered by some as unwanted activities, some residents might move. Those who do, of course, will be those who could afford to give up some of their incomes to finance programs that would benefit others.

If the population of the city consists of people who only get limited satisfaction from giving to others, if people are free to live wherever they choose, and if there are options in the sense of a number of cities or political jurisdictions within the metropolitan area the city is located, that city will be restricted in the extent to which it can do things that will redistribute the incomes of its residents. Whether this is a problem depends on the extent to which a city chooses to use its fiscal powers to redistribute incomes. This, in turn, depends on such things as the distribution of incomes in the city and its political power structure.

Cities that have large disparities in the incomes of their residents are more likely to try to redistribute income through the fiscal powers of local government than are those where income is more evenly distributed. The poor have more needs that require public assistance and are less able to contribute to the financing of activities that satisfy these needs. Where the poor are large in number, one would expect more agitation for income redistribution. Whether political action will be taken which redistributes income, however, depends on what the political scientist calls the power structure of the city. A city can have a large low-income population with needs that imply much public assistance, but the politics of local government might be such that these needs will not be met through local government. In other cases they might.

Over the past decade, political factors have apparently been working in ways that are more accommodating to the needs of low-income households. Because the economic problems of redistributing income in cities have not changed, the fiscal problems of many cities have intensified. They have also come more into public view and warrant more detailed discussion.

FISCAL PROBLEMS OF CENTRAL CITIES

All cities and unincorporated places in our metropolitan areas have fiscal problems. Public demands forever seem to be far in excess of public revenues and budgets are difficult to bring into balance, both in central cities and in the cities and villages in the suburbs. In an economic world, this fact is not surprising; it is to be expected when resources are scarce in relation to needs. Budgetary problems are more severe in some cities than in others, however. They are in fact most severe in the central cities of our major metropolitan areas.

While facts concerning the fiscal problems of central cities are not available in abundance, earlier studies confirm that these cities do suffer more fiscal stress than suburban cities and villages. Per capita expenditures are higher in central cities—see Table 12.6. Per capita taxes also are higher—see Table 12.6. That the

Table 12.6

Local Government per capita Expenditure and Taxes
Inside and Outside Central Cities
in 37 Largest SMSA's
(1964–65)

	Inside Central City	Outside Central City
Total Per Capita Expenditure	$ 332	$ 278
Total Per Capita Taxes	200	152
Per Capita Income	2,607	2,732

Source: Advisory Commission on Intergovernmental Relations: *Fiscal Balance in the American System (1967)*

absolute tax burden is higher is particularly significant in view of the fact that incomes are lower in the central city—see Tables 12.6 and 12.7. More revenues are needed to finance the package of services central city government provides; yet the tax base from which this level of spending would be more comfortably financed if it were financed is in the suburbs. This constitutes a fiscal imbalance in the eyes of many students of the city.

Things were not always this way. In fact, it is only since the end of World War II that we have begun to pay much attention to these fiscal problems, and for good reason. These problems began to build in the 1950s, seemingly reached a peak in the latter part of the 1960s, only to go on to another succession of peaks in the 1970s, culminating in the crises of the city of New York.

Reasons for the Fiscal Problems of Central Cities

At one level, the fiscal problems of central cities stem from an inability to pay for the local government services the public wishes to consume. The difficulty arises from the fact that public demands for the services provided by local governments have been accelerating at a time when the revenue base from which such demands might be met has been eroding. Why is that central city government spending has been increasing so rapidly? What has been happening to the revenue base?

Many things have happened that help to explain the recent trends in local government spending and receipts. This list would include the great migrations of the 1950s and 1960s, rapidly rising demands for public services, reliance on the property tax as a source of revenue, the rising political power of public

Table 12.7

*Income Distribution in
Metropolitan Areas by
Location and Race
1972
(Percent Distributions)*

	White		Black	
	Inside Central City	*Outside Central City*	*Inside Central City*	*Outside Central City*
Under $2,000	2.5%	1.9%	8.2%	6.9%
$2,000–2,999	3.1	2.1	9.3	4.1
$3,000–3,999	4.3	2.6	8.9	7.3
$4,000–4,999	4.9	3.2	8.8	6.4
$5,000–6,999	9.8	7.7	14.5	11.6
$7,000–8,999	11.0	9.3	10.8	14.3
$9,000–11,999	17.4	16.8	14.6	14.4
$12,000–14,999	15.3	16.4	9.9	13.5
$15,000–24,999	23.2	29.7	12.9	17.8
$25,000 and over	8.2	10.4	2.1	3.8

Source: U.S. Bureau of the Census

employees, the structure of technological progress, and the growing fragmentation of local government and the problem of spillovers.

Migration and the Changing Socioeconomic Composition of Central Cities
The flight of business firms and middle and upper-income white households to the suburbs in the 1950s and 1960s was discussed at length in chapter 8. Changing transportation and production technology, rising incomes, and population growth precipitated the movement of a great many households and business firms to outlying locations in the suburbs. This movement slowed, and, in some cases, even reversed the population growth of the central city. These cities did not become ghost towns, however. There was movement into these cities that offset the movement out.

As noted in chapters 8 and 9, economic change in southern agriculture and the economic decline of the coal industry in the Appalachians precipitated the movement of a great many low-income blacks and low-income whites from the South to northern cities. The pattern of this movement, significantly, was from the rural South to the central parts of many northern cities. As the middle and upper-income whites moved to the suburbs, many of the units they vacated were converted from single to multifamily units, making them more suitable to the housing needs of low-income families. The low-income migrant was thus pulled toward the center of the city in part because of the availability of housing.

The outcome of this pattern of migration was the emergence of a substantially different structure of residents and industry in our central cities. Low-income whites and blacks replaced middle and upper-income whites who moved to the suburbs. Relatively small high risk firms replaced the larger and less risky manufacturing and retailing firms that moved away. One important consequence of this change was a relative decline in the income and wealth base of the central city. Per capita incomes, which had been at their highest levels in and around the center of our cities, fell below those in suburban cities. Property values in the central city also fell relative to those in the suburbs. The low-income household and marginal firm bid less for land space than did the previous occupants. This, coupled with the overall slowdown in the growth of central city populations, restrained the upward movement in real estate values relative to what was happening in the suburbs.

This relative decline in income and wealth had important implications with respect to central city government revenues. Both the tax and nontax revenues of local government depend importantly on the income and wealth base of the community. If that base declines or fails to grow as rapidly as it has, the ability of the community to pay for public services will be restricted. If the service level is to be maintained or even increased, the tax burden on local residents will increase. This, indeed, apparently happened in our central cities. Per capita taxes are shown to be higher in central cities than in the suburbs, in spite of the fact that incomes are higher in the latter compared with the former—see Table 12.7.

Replacing middle and upper-income families with low-income families from rural areas also had impact on central city public expenditures. Some classes of spending were pushed up, the most important of which was public assistance. The public assistance needs of low-income families are, in general, much greater than those of middle and upper-income families. The difference is even greater if the low-income families are migrants who have assimilation problems, as did blacks when they moved North. The demand for certain kinds of services such as education, in contrast, probably declined as the low-income family replaced the more affluent families who were leaving the city. Expenditures of this kind tend to be very sensitive to income in that the higher the income the greater the expenditure and vice versa.

The question of which of these two was more important is an empirical question that is not easily answered. Both, however, would be a part of any explanation of the current fiscal difficulties of the central cities.

Rapidly Growing Demands for Public Services   Services, as an item of consumption in the national economy, have grown rapidly. The nation has, in fact, moved into the postindustrial era, which is to say that the majority of production and hence consumption now consists of services, rather than manufactured products. For a number of reasons, we have chosen to consume more and more services as we have become more affluent. Services have turned out to be a superior good, that is, a good whose demand increases rapidly as incomes rise.

While many of these services are provided through the private sector of the economy, more than a few are made available through government, particularly at the local level. Public demands for the kinds of things local governments ordinarily do are thus accelerated as we become more affluent.

Much of this increased demand was concentrated in the rapidly growing suburbs that surround the central cities. Incomes rose more rapidly in the outlying areas because of their settlement by the city's more affluent residents and business firms. The demand for services like education and transportation rose sharply in places where incomes were growing rapidly. Some of these income gains spilled over into the central city, generating moderate increases in the overall demand for public services. What happened to central city incomes, however, had less impact on public service demands there than did certain attitude changes that took place both within the central city and its suburbs.

Society has, for a number of reasons, become more aware of the hardships of being poor and has apparently become more sympathetic with the problems of the poor. As a consequence, we have become increasingly willing to devote resources to satisfy the needs of the poor. One concrete manifestation of this lies in the rapid growth of intergovernmental grants to central cities to help meet the needs of the poor.

The attitudes of the poor have also changed. No longer do Americans seem to be ashamed of misfortune and attempt to conceal it. Rather, more and more of the nation's poor seem to view public assistance as a right of any American citizen. The poor have also worked more vigorously to get a more effective expression of their views in the nation's political system. The demands for public services in our central cities have thus increased because the demands of the poor have been better articulated and the public as a whole has become more sympathetic to their needs.

The Structure of Technology and Technical Progress   One easily documented fact is that the price of services has been increasing more rapidly than the price of commodities. By way of illustration, the services component of the consumer price index increased 92 percent between the years of 1950 and 1970, compared with a 37 percent increase in the commodity component of that index. This fact has obvious implications with respect to the expenditures component of the budget of central city governments; these expenditures are, for the most part, made to provide residents with a bundle of services. If the costs of providing that bundle are rising relative to the costs of doing other things, it can be argued that government expenditures have risen to the levels they have partly because of cost factors.

Why have service costs increased so rapidly? Technology is involved. Productivity gains are less likely in the provision of a service than they are in the production of commodities. This is so because the substitution of capital for labor is highly limited in providing services in general and the services provided by urban governments in particular. Thus, productivity increases in the operation of government are difficult to come by. The technology applicable to the production of a service does not lend itself to changes that result in productivity increases. Consequently, a rigidity is built into the process through which services are provided by government. This rigidity tends to lead to substantial and cumulative increases in the real costs incurred in supplying them. One writer has taken careful note of this fact, and has concluded that this technological structure accounts for a good deal of the fiscal problems of central cities in the past and will continue to do so in the future.

The Wages of Public Employees   The failure to achieve significant productivity gains in the public sector need not cause any stress in the budget, if the wage increases granted by the city are kept within the bounds of productivity increases taking place. The problem is that this seldom happens. There is, in the first place, the city charter, which often includes specific stipulations to the effect that city employees must be paid a competitive wage. This means a wage similar to those paid employees in comparable positions in the private sector. Since productivity improvements tend to be greater in the private sector, if only because commodities constitute a part of production in this sector, attempts to remain competitive with the private sector will help to push up the unit costs of local government more than those of the rest of the economy.

More recently, the wages paid to public employees have been increasingly influenced by their efforts to organize and bargain with the city about wages and other matters. Municipal employees have, in fact, become an important power group in many central cities. While organization and collective bargaining provides city workers with countervailing power to protect their interests in dealing with an entity that has monopoly power, it can also create problems. Even though there are legal uncertainties surrounding some of the sanctions applied in the bargaining process, e.g., strikes, the potential economic consequences of success are certainly clear. With productivity increases in central city governments that are smaller than in the private sector, success in keeping pace with the wage gains achieved in private industry will lead to cost increases. This, in turn, will up the ante necessary to provide the community with a given bundle of services.

Property Taxes   Property taxes, as noted above, are the primary source of tax revenues for municipal governments. Many believe this is the source of some of the difficulties of central cities. While the property tax has provided a stable source of income for most cities, it has not served them well in meeting their expanding needs, so the argument goes.

The tax is generally believed to be unresponsive to income. Progressive income taxes, of course, are the most responsive. As incomes rise, many find themselves in a higher tax bracket, which means their tax bill goes up both absolutely and relatively. Property taxes, on the other hand, are widely believed to be regressive with respect to income, that is, the lower the income the greater the tax burden. While recent studies raise doubts about just how regressive the property tax is, it is still regarded as being the least responsive to income change. Thus, if expenditure growth is to be financed by property taxes, there may be problems. Rising incomes in the community will not help very much; the only way to finance a sizeable increase in expenditures will be to increase the rate applied to the base. Certainly, this has happened in many of our cities. It is no accident that taxes per capita in central cities are higher than those in the suburbs—see Table 12.6.

How much of the revenue difficulties of central cities can be attributed to the fact that they raise the bulk of their tax revenues through the property tax is by no means clear, however. Even if cities had the power to collect a progressive income tax, it is doubtful that their tax revenues would have been all that much greater. The primary taxing problem of the central city has been the eroding tax base. The movement of households and business firms to the suburbs and their partial replacement by low-income households and marginal firms had adverse effects on the value of property in the city. This, in turn, had adverse effects on the receipts from property tax collections. The same thing would have occurred, however, if tax revenues came from the income tax, since the income tax base would also have been adversely affected by these developments.

Local Government Fragmentation, Spillovers, and Budget Problems   Local government fragmentation and the problem of spillovers was discussed above. The spillovers that stem from the fact that a sizeable proportion of the suburban community commutes into the central city to work has led to the development of the *central city exploitation hypothesis*. This hypothesis, in effect, argues that some of the fiscal problems of the central city stem from suburban exploitation. The residents of the suburbs who work in the central city benefit from the services provided by government but do not provide the city with any compensation for the benefits received.

According to the discussion of spillover above, when spillovers take the form of uncompensated benefits, the production will be restricted to levels that are below optimum. This is important to those concerned with the question of efficiency. The presence of such spillovers, if they involve the consumption of services provided by central city government, will also raise the cost of that consumption above the level that would prevail in their absence. It is in this latter sense that commuter spillovers can be said to add to the budget problems of the central city. But do they? Just how important are they?

The evidence is mixed. Some claim to have found that the revenue flows to the central cities from the activities of commuters fail, by a considerable margin, to compensate those cities for benefits that flow outside the city. Others, looking at the same question, come to exactly the opposite conclusion. The focus in these studies is usually on the impact of the commuter on central city personal income and nonresidential real property tax revenues. Unfortunately, we have no way of reconciling the difference or drawing firm conclusions about spillovers.

What's Really Important?

All the things discussed to this point contributed to the fiscal problems of the central cities; some more than others. Which ones contributed more than others is, with one exception, a difficult question. The exception, of course, is the changing socioeconomic composition of the city. Central cities became the residence of many low-income blacks and whites and the home of many marginal firms. This change both increased the demands for public services and at the same time, given local government fragmentation, reduced the ability to pay for them. These demands were bolstered further by the growing effectiveness of the poor to articulate their needs. There were cost pressures stemming from a technology that does not provide much basis for productivity increases in supplying services. These cost pressures added to the problems of central city municipal governments. The growing militancy of city government employees and the increased effectiveness in bargaining for higher wages and benefits also added to the cost pressures.

Central cities obviously have problems. They are the locus of proportionately more of the urban poor, or people who generally have a greater need for public assistance. Yet, because they live in the central city, they restrict that city's ability to meet those needs. Not surprisingly, then, much of the heated discussion of the "fiscal plight of the central cities" focuses on the inequity of it all.

EQUITY PROBLEMS IN THE URBAN PUBLIC ECONOMY

Are There Equity Problems?

The issue of equity was discussed at some length in chapter 6. In contrast with efficiency, there are no explicit criteria in economics that tell us whether a particular economic outcome is equitable or not. Most economists believe that economic events that do not alter income distribution or lead to less income inequality are better than those that lead to more inequality. There is no way, in terms of economic analysis, of demonstrating that one distribution of income is better than any other.

People do make judgments, however, about fairness in the distribution of the nation's income and wealth. How these individual judgments can be aggregated and considered in the sense of a whole is by no means clear. Yet we do get some indication of what the collective attitude is through the actions of government. In recent years that attitude appears to be shifting to one of more concern with inequality.

Data on the distribution of income between central cities and suburbs do not show the striking contrast that some people would have us believe exists. Incomes are lower in the central cities, but they are not that much lower—see Tables 12.6 and 12.7. The big difference is between urban and rural areas.

Still, there are disparities in consumption between residents of central cities and residents of suburbs and more of those at the lower end of the consumption scale live in central cities. The needs for public assistance expenditures are thus greater in central cities and the ability to pay for that assistance is less. This creates a problem, the solution to which, in the eyes of many, will involve income redistribution.

Suppose some redistribution of income is called for. With fragmented government and free choice in residential location, this will not be easy if it is to be done through the spending and taxation policies of local government. Only if the rich received satisfaction from giving to the poor could redistribution be easily carried out.

Suppose the normal instinct of people living in the central city were to favor less, rather than more taxes—not an unrealistic assumption. Redistribution through local government would be difficult if that government were fragmented. Taxation that hit heavily at the rich and a pattern of expenditures that distributed most of the benefits to the poor would redistribute income. But if a municipality had the legal authority to impose taxes which "soaked the rich," the rich would probably not bear that burden for long. They would move elsewhere in the metropolitan area. The only way to meet the public assistance needs of the poor in this city would be to tax the poor.

The point is exaggerated. To put it this way, however, highlights the essential difficulty confronting central city governments that attempt to redistribute income through the use of the budget. If the more affluent members of its community are in no mood to give some of their income to others, it will be difficult to make them do so. Those with the means have the ultimate weapon, that is, the freedom to live where they choose.

Until recently, we have tried to deal with this problem through consolidation of local government and/or intergovernmental transfers.

Consolidated City Government

While the advocates of consolidated city government have been highly vocal, there are very few instances of successful consolidations. The consolidation of city with county governments has occurred in Miami, Jacksonville, Nashville, and a few other places. Our metropolitan areas, however, number in the hundreds and cities in the thousands. Moreover, even when city and county governments have been consolidated, growth of the consolidated city has spilled over into adjacent counties. When this happens, fragmentation in local government reappears.

Annexation is a means of consolidation. Annexation is political activity that ordinarily leads to "small scale" consolidation when it is successful. That success, however, has also been greatly limited. By and large, the most success we have had in extending the geographic boundaries of local government has been with particular governmental functions, i.e., the establishment of special districts. The number of special districts, however, suggests that the boundaries of these districts by no means span those of the metropolitan areas of which they are a part.

That we have had such little success in the consolidation of local government is not surprising. The efficiency arguments in favor of consolidation, as noted above, are not as persuasive as the advocates believe. While there may be economies of scale in some of the things city governments do, they are not as important as many believe. Nor are spillovers—which do exist—as important as they are sometimes made out to be.

The important problem created by political fragmentation is the obstacles it puts in the way of income distribution. These obstacles, in turn, are the production of behavior that reflects self-interest. People prefer more to less. This is why they move when municipalities seek to redistribute income by raising taxes and using the additional tax receipts to finance programs that distribute benefits to the poor. Once they have moved, they can, for this reason, be expected to resist any attempt to consolidate municipal governments in the overall metropolitan area. And resist they have.

The issue of consolidation burns less brightly today, probably because of a recognition of this basic fact of political life. Redistribution efforts have been more successful through a program of intergovernmental transfers that has evolved over the years.

Intergovernmental Transfers

Intergovernmental transfers are funds that move from one tier of government to another. This movement in the United States has been primarily from the federal government to state and local governments and from state governments to local governments. Significantly, local governments are the primary beneficiary of these movements, funds that in recent years have accounted for over one-third of their total revenues—see Table 12.1.

Some History   The origins of intergovernmental transfers go way back. Certain functions of government implemented at the state and local level, such as road construction and education, have been partly financed with federal government funds for years. Back in 1802, Congress stipulated that 5 percent of the proceeds from the sale of public lands should go to the construction of roads by state governments. In 1818, Congress also provided that states be given 5 percent of the net proceeds of land sales within their boundaries with a proviso that 3 percent be used for education. This was the beginning of the development of a program of "categorical" grants—fund transfers that were tied to a specific function—made by the federal government to state government, which were gradually expanded to include public assistance and other categories of government activity. The form of these grants also changed over time, becoming increasingly more sophisticated with respect to allocation formulas and matching requirements.

The grant-in-aids going directly from the federal government to local governments originated during the Depression. These funds were, in the main, associated with emergency programs concerned with getting the nation out of the Depression and were administered by ad hoc agencies, such as the Public Works Administration and the Works Progress Administration. More recently Congress has seen fit to authorize programs aimed at direct aid to local governments in such areas as education, housing and community redevelopment, airport construction, and waste treatment and sewage disposal facilities.

Funds coming from state government to local government have been of two basic types. One is shared taxes, such as gasoline and motor vehicle taxes. The other is grants of appropriated funds used to support specific functions such as education, highways, and welfare. In the earlier stages in the development of the grant program, education was the primary beneficiary. In recent years, more and more of the state government aid to local governments has gone to finance public welfare expenditures.

More recently, some of the funds from federal government to both state and local governments have taken the form of unrestricted grants, that is, they have been tied to no specific function. In the popular press, this has been called *revenue sharing.*

Revenue sharing has its roots in the notion of the use of the federal government budget surplus that was anticipated in the 1960s to help state and local governments with their financial problems. When the federal budget surplus failed to materialize because of Vietnam and the expansion of the domestic programs of federal government, the idea of revenue sharing remained. Its appeal to some now was in the promise it held for loosening the controls the federal government had on state and local government activities. For others, it was the promise of more funds.

In 1972, the Congress enacted legislation that authorized $30 billion of federal funds for revenue sharing, to be paid out in a series of installments covering 5 years. While this program has by no means replaced assistance given through the federal government's program of categorical grants, the amounts involved are not insignificant. They are close to one-fourth of the total received by state and local governments in the year preceding the enactment of the enabling legislation.

While the future of revenue sharing is still uncertain, it has had an auspicious start and could turn out to be an important element in the fiscal affairs of local governments for some time to come.

Income Distribution Consequences of Intergovernmental Transfers   The bulk of the funds for intergovernmental transfers come from the general fund of government, which, at the federal level, is largely derived from taxes. The funds transferred, until revenue sharing, are generally assigned to specific tasks or functions. The income distribution effects of these transactions depend on who bears the burden of the taxes and who receives the benefits from the expenditures.

The question of the incidence of taxation—who bears the burden of the taxes —is unsettled and surrounded by controversy. We cannot really tell by looking at those on whom the taxes are assessed. Taxes can be shifted from one to another in ways that are not easily measured. In general, it is believed that taxes at the federal government level are progressive, or fall more heavily on high-income people. This is less so at the state level. In local government, because of its heavy reliance on property taxes, the tax structure is believed to be regressive, or fall more heavily on low-income people. While the validity of these beliefs has yet to be fully verified, they are widely accepted. Suppose we accept them.

That we take from a fund to which high-income people are the heaviest contributors does not necessarily mean income is being redistributed. Those funds could be returned to high-income people by the expenditures of government. Assume, however, these expenditures were made in ways that bestowed the major benefits on the poor, e.g., through school luncheon subsidies to schools in central cities. It is by no means clear that the benefits are restricted to the poor. Subsequent actions of the poor could bestow benefits on the not-so-poor. These outcomes are uncertain. We, in fact, know less about the incidence of public expenditures than we do about the incidence of taxation.

Nevertheless, recent estimates made of the impact of government budget on the economic well-being of the poor suggest that they receive net benefits. There is some redistribution through the activities of government, and some of that redistribution comes about as a consequence of the mechanism of intergovernment transfers to local government, both from the federal and state government. These transfers have helped local government deal with what many consider to be some serious inequities in the distribution of income that cannot be dealt with in central cities because of political fragmentation. Just how much help these programs have provided, however, is by no means clear.

Revenue sharing could alter the distribution of the benefits from these transfers. Some believe that a redistribution has taken place only because these transfers took the form of categorical grants. Decisions about use, made at some distance from the political process in which the self-interests of particular groups in the community are expressed, are more likely to be decisions that direct benefits to the poor. But do they? This is a political question, the answer to which seems uncertain. If it were a reasonable proposition, however, the movement from a program of categorical grants to one of revenue sharing could alter the pattern of benefits in ways that lessen the redistribution of income associated with intergovernmental transfers.

It is by no means clear that this is happening, at least in our larger cities. Most of the funds are apparently being absorbed in the operating budgets, which implies these funds are being used pretty much as they have been. New programs and new directions would involve a greater diversion of these funds to the capital budget.

As more and more of the revenue sharing monies are spent and the results are put carefully under the economic microscope, our notions of what revenue sharing does in the redistribution activities of local government should be clarified.

Conclusions

The issue of equity considered in the "fiscal plight of the central city" is controversial. Most people have sympathy for the hardships of others. Most are willing to support measures taken to deal with these hardships, so long as they do not seriously interfere with their perceptions of what society owes them. The problem with this, of course, is that most of us apparently believe that society owes us a lot.

Charity is a part of our world, but it in no way measures up to the task of redistributing incomes in ways that reduce economic hardship to acceptable levels. If this does not come about through voluntary actions, we think of accomplishing our equity aims through government. If we choose to do so, the problem of specifying what equity means can be sidestepped by assuming that we move toward a more equitable solution if inequality is reduced. Many economists do this. Even so, it is by no means clear that the way in which we seek to achieve this form of equity through government is successful. Intergovernmental transfers have been a major way of providing help to central cities. A cursory look at this program suggests it may be helping to achieve equity in the sense of reducing some of the disparities that exist between central cities and suburbs. A more careful look at the program and the difficulties we have in attempting to trace the incidence of its costs and benefits suggests, however, that our success may be less than we believe.

We are still pretty much in the dark with respect to the issue of equity in the use of our public resources. Our activities through government are not really linked to some coherent plan which is designed to achieve some set of equity goals. This is not surprising, if only because of the difficulties involved in attempting to define what equity means. Nevertheless, the evidence seems to suggest that the poor do receive net benefits and their distribution is helping to alleviate what many believe to be the inequities of the current relationship between central cities and suburbs.

REFERENCES

Advisory Commission on Intergovernmental Relations. *Fiscal Balance in the American System*. Washington, D.C.: American Enterprise Institute, 1967.

Baumol, W. "Macroeconomics of Unbalanced Growth: The Anatomy of Urban Crisis." *American Economic Review*. 57 (1967): 414–26.

*Hirsch, W. *The Economics of State and Local Government*. New York: McGraw-Hill, 1970.

*Maxwell, J. *Financing State and Local Government*. Washington, D.C.: The Brookings Institution, 1969.

Neehan, W. *Political Economy of Urban Areas*. Skokie, Ill.: Markham Publishing Company, 1972.

Netzer, R. *Economics of the Property Tax*. Washington, D.C.: The Brookings Institution, 1967.

Ott, D.; Ott, A.; Maxwell, J.; and Aronson, J. *State-Local Finances in the Last Half of the 1970's*. Washington, D.C.: American Enterprise Institute for Public Policy Research, 1975.

*Tiebout, C. "A Pure Theory of Local Expenditures." *Journal of Political Economy*. 64 (1956): 416–24.

---

* This chapter draws heavily from the writings of Hirsch, Maxwell, and Tiebout.

13

City Size

SUMMARY

City size is an important issue in popular discussions of the city and its problems. The issue of city size, however, only makes sense in the context of a discussion of a hierarchy of cities. There is no one best size, but rather a hierarchy of ideal sizes. The one appropriately applied to any given city depends on how that city fits into the urban hierarchy.

The size of cities in the urban hierarchy depends on how market and cost factors come into play and work themselves out in the system of markets that generates the hierarchy. Population growth, technology, transportation, spatial variations in input costs, urbanization economies, and location preferences are considered, as they have impact on the hierarchy. While some elements of size in the hierarchy can be linked to these, we do not have a full understanding of why particular cities fall into certain size classes.

The question of whether cities are too big is often raised and considered without proper recognition of the productivity of our cities. The diseconomies of scale, said to give rise to problems, do not turn out to be so important after all when put carefully under the economic microscope. The real cause of most important urban problems is negative market externalities, and these do not seem to be strongly associated with city size.

The issue of a national urban size policy, upon careful inspection, turns out to be less important than usually believed. The problems of cities, in general, and big cities, in particular, are real; but they are not problems that are likely to be resolved by measures taken to reduce the size of cities, as some would have us do. Under certain conditions, a policy that seeks to adjust the size of some cities in certain ways might make sense. For the United States, however, it probably makes more sense to direct our efforts to the problems within the city and let size take care of itself.

As noted earlier, people have come to live in cities for a number of reasons, not the least of which is economic advantage. Real incomes are generally higher for city residents than for those who live in a rural setting. In recent years, however, much has been said about the stress and strain of urban living, particularly in larger metropolitan areas. Somehow, things seem to have gotten out of hand. Many a compact city of an earlier era has grown into a metropolitan area that has reached a size that lies well beyond the optimum. Thus, the time has come to develop some kind of urban population policy that will address itself to the problems of cities that are too large. The time has come to put into effect the measures through which a redistribution of population will be brought about that will allow people to live in optimum size cities.

Such arguments seem persuasive and compelling. But are they valid arguments? Are the premises upon which they are based reasonable? While the contemporary city has its problems, not all agree that city size is one of the most important of these problems. Many do, however, and argue that what we need are measures that divert our urban population into smaller urban centers. Who are we to believe? How can we address ourselves to the basic issue involved?

These are questions about which the urban economist should be able to make sensible statements. The basic issue is which size is best. Population redistribution to remove people from the urban stress in large urban centers implies that cities are now too large. But what size is to be considered the optimum size? 10,000? 100,000? 250,000? 1,000,000? What can we say about the issue of city size? In fact, most of the discussion to this point has relevance to the issue of city size, cities being considered in the sense of those whose boundaries define a labor market.

CITY SIZE IN A SYSTEM OF CITIES

It is clear from chapter 3 that the issue of city size cannot be considered independent of the notion of a system of cities. It, therefore, makes little sense to talk of an ideal city size. If urban society organizes itself into a hierarchical pattern in which there is differentiation with respect to size, there can be no one best size. Rather, there must be a hierarchy of ideal sizes and the one appropriately applied to any given city depends upon how that city fits into the urban hierarchy. What can be said about city size in this setting?

Determinants of City Size: Market Factors

Recall from chapter 3 that by assuming costs do not figure importantly in the location decisions of firms and that firms sell in spatial markets, markets can be shown to organize production into a hierarchy of urban centers. By abstracting further from these circumstances, it also was shown that a simple system of cities model can be constructed. Finally, on the basis of the assignment of certain values to the parameters of this model, outcomes were simulated that provided numbers denoting city size and the proportion of the city population found at each size designation—see Table 3.5 in chapter 3.

Simple inspection of the numbers in this table indicates a range of sizes are permissible in this system, including some very large ones. On the face of it, this table suggests that bigness, smallness, and that which lies in between is not necessarily bad. This result is seen as something that can be interpreted as the outcome of the way in which markets, operating efficiently, organize production in geographic space. Is this a reasonable interpretation of these simulated results?

The question is not easily answered. One way of addressing it is to focus on elements that determine the way in which markets organize production in a central place model, namely population, technology, and the transportation networks. These are elements denoted as having impact initially on the market areas of firms which, in turn, is subsequently reflected in the urban hierarchy patterns established. If what emerges in a simple system of cities model depends on population, technology, and transportation costs, we should learn something by taking a more careful look at the links between these variables and the outcomes generated by a simple system of cities model.

Population and the Urban Hierarchy   Ordinarily, little interest centers on the question of population in discussions of a simple system of cities models. The concern instead is with rural populations in the hinterland of first order urban centers, the relationship between market areas served by centers of different orders, and the proportion of the population served by a center living in that center. Once we assign values to these parameters, the hierarchy can be constructed. The number of layers in that hierarchy and the city size classes can be as many as we choose. It depends upon the parameter values. Looked at in this way, total population is given once values are assigned to the parameters. Those that underlie the simulations in Table 3.5, for example, indicate a total population of 65,536,000 and an urban population of 64,512,000.

This procedure can be reversed. We can specify a given population and make statements about city size on the basis of this model. When this is done, the size of the city in any given order is seen to depend on parameter values, that is, the proportion of the population assigned to particular centers (k) and the relationship specified between market areas or populations served by centers of different orders. If the value of k is high, for example, cities in all orders will be large in relation to the population they serve. The converse will be true when k is low. If the value of s is high, the population of the higher order cities will be larger than it would be if s were low. But given k and s, how large will the largest of these be in absolute terms? In a simple system of cities model, this depends on total population.

Suppose that population increases. Increased population, we know, means increased demand. Excess profits will emerge for firms serving customers in the lowest order market areas, which will cause new firms to enter. The size of the lowest order market area will shrink as a consequence, which means the number of first order urban centers will increase and will be located closer together. When this happens, a simple system of cities model predicts an increase in the number of higher order centers. The number of higher order centers in this model is determined by the number of lower order centers because of the assumption that a fixed number of lower order centers come to nest in the hinterland of the higher order centers. Any increase in the number of lower order centers must, therefore, result in an increase in the number of higher order centers. When the number of higher order centers increases, this model predicts an additional city will be added to the urban hierarchy. This additional layer will, of course, take the form of an area that has an urban center that is of the highest order in the system. Population growth in a simple system of cities model is thus seen as a force that both increases the number of centers in all orders of the system and adds higher order centers to the hierarchy, which implies that the big get bigger with overall growth in the population.

Technology and the Urban Hierarchy   Technology can have impact on the market areas served by firms. Suppose, for example, technology yields significant internal economies of scale in production. The market areas of firms that benefit from these economies tend to be large. Higher levels of output lower costs, and if these cost savings are passed on to the consumer in the form of lower prices, the perimeters of the market served by such firms will be larger than if no such scale economies were present. This implies fewness in the number of firms serving the population, which, in turn, means concentrated production. The conclusion seems to be that the system of urban centers that emerges will consist of fewer cities that are both larger in size and farther apart from one another than would be the case in the absence of technology.

This is not an unreasonable conclusion. Firms that experience internal economies of scale as they expand output should find they can sell in other markets for less than smaller firms, in spite of the greater distances from the plant to the customer. Firms that benefit from such technological change, therefore, extend the perimeters of their market areas. If demand is constant, this means some firms will be forced out of business; hence, there will be fewer firms serving the market.

Whether the number of centers will decline, however, cannot really be predicted, due to the absence of more detailed information about the impact of the technical change on production requirements in general and the labor requirements in particular. It could be, for example, that the labor requirement per unit of output will decline. If so, the proportion of the population served by these firms who live in the urban center where production takes place will decline. If total population does not decline, however, either the number of cities somewhere in the hierarchy and/or the rural population will have to increase according to a simple system of cities model. Since the reasonableness of this conclusion is in doubt, questions can be raised about the usefulness of statements that can be made about technology and the urban hierarchy on the basis of these models.

Still, there are certain statements that can be made. For example, if technology does induce significant internal economies of scale in production, lower order urban centers will suffer economically. Firms with small scale operations will now be at a competitive disadvantage. Since these firms stand at the core of the economy in lower order centers, such centers will begin to experience economic difficulties. This, in fact, stands as an important part of the explanation of the economic plight of the nation's many small towns and villages. Technical developments have had impact on product and service characteristics in ways that have made the traditional kinds of services provided by these centers less attractive to consumers. The regional shopping center emerged and, as a consequence, the demands for the services provided by retail outlets in small towns declined.

Transportation and the Urban Hierarchy   Transportation costs in a theoretical system with dispersed customers and a transportation surface affect the geographic distribution of firms because they are a cost and hence affect profits. As noted in chapter 3, raising transportation costs in such a system causes firms to disperse because dispersed production will keep transportation costs at a minimum. As a corollary, it would seem that lowering transportation costs will lead to more concentration of production and people, or larger cities. This conclusion does not necessarily follow from a system of cities model, however.

Consider, by way of illustration, a technical change that reduced the costs of transportation nationally. We know from above that a reduction in these costs will, in the first instance, lower the delivered price of goods to all excepting households living at sites adjacent to points of production. If this happens, quantity demanded will increase, generating excess profits. If these profits are large enough, new firms will enter the industry which, through competition, will reduce the spatial extent of the market areas of firms. This means more firms selling to populations served by first order centers and hence means more first order centers. According to a simple system of cities model, if the number of first order centers increases, the number of second order centers also increases, as do third order places and so on. If the total population remains constant, the total number of orders in the system must be reduced. In other words, the largest city in the system will now be smaller.

How seriously should we take conclusions like this one? Certainly, there are reasons to be skeptical. There is historical evidence, for example, that supports the notion that major cost reducing changes in the nation's transportation system are followed by periods in which relatively more production has come to be located in the nation's largest cities. This is not a very surprising conclusion, however, for it is consistent with what comes out of a system of cities model, when the assumption of a transportation surface is dropped. When there is a transportation network, the benefits of any reduction in transportation costs are passed on to those who locate along or near the routes and junctions in that network. Since the routes connect urban centers and these centers are, in fact, the locus of the major junctions in that network, transportation cost reductions bestow special advantages on those who are located or will locate at these major points. By doing so, they generate more urban concentration.

Yet, this need not be the result. Much depends on the spatial configuration of the transportation cost changes. That change, for example, might benefit sites not served very well prior to the change. If so, the result could be a dispersal of production.

Conclusions   When urban society is conceived of as a system of cities, it becomes possible to interpret some of the bigness, smallness, and that which lies in between as the result of the way in which markets organize people and their resources in an urban setting. Starting with certain basic economic notions, it is possible to construct system of cities models that generate city size distributions that fit certain facts reasonably well. It can therefore be argued that the existence of a New York, a Phoenix, or a Bakersfield should not be an unsettling experience, since we find cities of these sizes in simulations from system of cities models that tell us something about ideal arrangements.

How seriously should arguments of the sort be taken? There are obvious difficulties. The discussion above makes it clear that the combinations of r's, k's, and s's as considered in chapter 3 do not really provide much insight into why the city size distributions turn out to have the shapes that they do. While grounded in economic notions, such systems of cities models are derived in ways that involve heroic assumptions. This implies it is difficult to link model outcomes up to "casual" facts. When we considered the implications of technical change or transportation cost changes, for example, the outcomes were uncertain. While it is possible to link up technical change to certain hierarchical outcomes, the links between cause and overall effects cannot be made clear-cut. Even so, this should not obscure the fact one of the variables—population growth—was shown to generate outcomes that are consistent with certain facts about the systems of cities, that is, an increase in the number and size of cities.

While it is clear that we cannot fully rationalize size in terms of a system of cities model, the fact that we find cities of different sizes should come as no surprise to anyone who has even a limited understanding of that system. Moreover, the fact that the urban outcome of population growth is, in some respects, con- sistent with the predictions of a simple system of cities model suggests there is a presumptive case for some bigness in that system. Or at a minimum, it can be taken to suggest that the burden of proof for arguments to the contrary lie with those who make such arguments. Our view of the system of cities to this point, however, is truncated. It fails to take cognizance of the fact noted earlier that the system of cities is really a number of systems. In addition to markets, cost factors have to be considered explicitly.

Determinants of City Size—Cost Factors

Spatial Variations in Input Costs   The urban hierarchy derived from central place notions is based on the assumption of ubiquitous resources, which makes demand the key factor in determining the location of firms in the central place models. As noted in chapter 3, this is a shaky assumption. There are localized resources, that is, resources found only in certain places. In many cases, these resources can be transported to other sites and become incorporated in the production process there. To do this, however, incurs a cost, which means spatial cost differences in these inputs. This, of course, is reflected in such facts as a higher cost of iron ore for use in steel-making in the states of Arizona or Florida, compared to the states of Minnesota or Illinois. There is also the fact that labor and/or land costs are less in many urban centers throughout the South than they are in the large metropolitan centers in the North. Finally, the costs of providing the facilities for certain kinds of recreation services, such as shorelines for surfing and mountains for skiing, are obviously more in the heart of Kansas than they are in California or Colorado.

As noted in chapter 3, cost factors of this sort generate spatial distributions of economic activity that differ from those generated by a central place model.

Central place notions do not provide much insight into the location of the steel industry, the aerospace industry, or parts of the nation's rapidly growing recreation industry. Nor do they provide much insight into the growth of urban centers in such states as California, Arizona, Texas, and Florida. Spatial input cost differences are important and must be accounted for if we are to explain in any detail the emerging urban settlement pattern.

Can this be done? There are, to my knowledge, no formal models that establish the interconnections between cost and revenue factors in ways that allow us to extend the range of facts that can be linked up to the number, size, spacing, and functions of cities. The best we can do now is to take such cost elements into account as this was done in chapter 7. In other words, we can make a series of informal statements that suggest certain urban implications of those input cost factors known to have impact on the location decisions of firms.

Places like Pittsburgh, Buffalo, Chattanooga, and Chicago, for example, can be said to have reached the size thresholds they have, in part, because of their strategic location with respect to certain kinds of inputs that figure importantly in the production processes of some firms. Places like Miami, Phoenix, and Los Angeles have also grown to their present size partly because they have an abundance of such amenities as mild climate and propinquity to water, which influence the costs of certain classes of firms.

To point to such facts and interpret them in this way is not unreasonable in light of our understanding of location theory. Moreover, having knowledge of such facts helps us evaluate better the circumstances surrounding the issue of the best size of particular cities as they are considered in the context of the urban hierarchy. We are not, however, in a position to judge precisely how important these facts are, particularly as they stand in relation to other facts that have bearing on the size and geographical location of particular urban communities.

Urbanization Economics   Scale economies are fundamental to an understanding of city size and the urban hierarchy. Statements have been made about how some of these economies—internal economies of scale—influence the number, size, and spacing of cities in a system of cities through interaction with transportation costs—see chapters 2 and 3. Much of what we observe in the urban hierarchy, however, cannot be explained by the interaction of transportation costs and internal economies of scale. Even in firms where internal scale economies have been fully exploited, employees only number in the thousands, whereas many of today's cities and metropolitan areas number in the hundreds of thousands and millions.

The economic rationale of the existence of New York, Chicago, and Los Angeles must be found in other economies, and much attention in studies of the economic structure of these places centers on urbanization economies. Such economies, as discussed above, are a product of a technology that promotes firm specialization. To realize the benefits from such specialization often requires operations not only in relatively large markets, but spatially concentrated ones as well. How large and how much concentration depends on the nature of the product or service being provided, and in discussions of these things, a distinction is usually made between publicly and privately produced goods and services.

Public or quasi-public goods include the energy and communications services discussed briefly above, as well as a relatively wide range of goods provided by local governments such as police protection, fire protection, refuse collection, and education. The efficient scale of output in this class of activity has important bearing on the question of city size. If significant economies of scale are realized which require spatially concentrated markets, cities will grow larger.

As noted in chapter 12, studies of costs in such areas of activity show varying results. In the case of horizontally integrated services, e.g., primary and secondary education and police protection, there is no evidence of economies of scale. In the case of vertically integrated services, e.g., water sewage and electricity, there is. In no case, however, does it appear that cities of one million or more are necessary in order to realize these economies. Scale economies of this kind may contribute to the explanation of why many cities in the sense of metropolises achieve economic viability when they reach, say, 250,000. If our concern is with New York and Chicago, however, we must look to other things.

What other things? Chapter 2 provides clues, the most important of which is the business services industry found in most cities. This industry, it will be recalled, consists of service-oriented firms that require much face-to-face contact in their operations and at the same time require a relatively large market for profitable operations. Law, accounting, printing and publishing, engineering, and economic consulting firms are important illustrations. They are also the kind of firms found in abundance in large cities. Firms that consume their services are also found in large numbers in large cities.

Activity that has links to the other urbanization economies discussed in chapter 2 are also found in our larger cities. For example, there are indications that larger cities spawn much new industry, presumably as a consequence of the inventive and innovative activities they foster.

Urbanization economies exist. This much we know from studies made of the economic structure of metropolitan areas like New York. Such economies help to explain the size of larger cities, but just how much of that size is attributable to such economies is another question. Our knowledge has not developed to the point where we can make precise statements about the proportion of the productivity of cities that is attributable to urbanization economies.

Determinants of City Size: Locational Preferences

While the market and costs factors just discussed are key elements in economic explanations of city size, there are other aspects of consumption to consider. Much consumption, of course, has to be close to places of work. Residential locations that are far away from the workplace are impractical because of prohibitive commuting costs. So long as there are significant productivity gains associated with spatially concentrated production, there will be cities in the sense of spatially concentrated residences. Consumption, however, has more direct bearing on the existence and growth of cities.

While profitability depends both on cost and revenue factors and revenue factors are influenced by patterns of consumption, if people are unwilling to consume what can be produced in cities at savings in costs, spatially concentrated production will not be profitable. That people live in cities suggests that they are willing to consume the market basket of goods and services produced in cities. In fact, there are some demands that are best satisfied in our large metropolitan areas. Services such as specialized medical and legal services, theaters, symphonies, and night clubs—services that have become an increasingly important component of consumption—fall into this category. They are services that are characteristically difficult to transport from one place to another. They are also services that have profit threshold levels that require high levels of demand to support. Profitability thus implies a need for a central location in areas of high population density.

Much of what we consume today, however, can be just as easily consumed in a rural setting. Moreover, while population density may create the setting necessary for the consumption of some things, it also has its troublesome aspects. Some argue that attitudes with respect to density are changing, that people no longer like living close to one another. Unfortunately, much of this discussion tends to mix things up in ways that add little to our understanding of the role of locational preferences in the growth of cities.

Much emphasis in discussions of locational preferences concentrates on the problems of traffic congestion, noise and air pollution, and high crime rates, problems that make cities a less attractive place to live for many. If people move away from cities because of these problems, however, such a move does not reflect a change in locational preference. If the problems were dealt with, living in the city would become more expensive in terms of money costs. This might cause some people to move away; yet, these would not be moves that stemmed from changes in the preference for city living. While it might help to know something about the attachments of people to the city to be able to forecast how they will react to the higher living costs, the outcome could not be considered a consequence of changing location preferences.

A change in preferences for city living implies a change in attitudes of households toward a particular life style, the life style that city living is all about. Those who decide, for whatever reasons, to search out a more "natural" life in a rural setting, either in some kind of communal arrangement or by themselves, are people who undergo a change in location preferences. The number of these appeared to be on the increase in the latter part of the 1960s and the early 1970s; yet there is no indication that the number who moved away from cities or moved from larger cities to smaller cities has reached a sizeable proportion of the population.

While people may be less comfortable living in cities now than they were twenty years ago, it appears to be more a consequence of what has happened in our cities, rather than any fundamental change in attitude regarding life in the big city.

ARE CITIES TOO BIG?

The problem of defining a city, discussed in chapter 1, comes into sharp focus in considering the question of city size. Cities are multidimensional structures. Some have large populations with low per capita incomes, and others have small populations with high per capita incomes, e.g., Asian cities compared with American cities. It is therefore conceivable that some cities with small populations would rank higher when the scale of measurement was income compared with those that had larger populations. Which of these criteria should we employ? Population? Income?

Population is used most frequently in studies of city size and is the one used here. There is, in fact, a good deal that can be said about city size by considering population within some defined boundary as the measure of city size. These boundaries, as noted above, are taken to be those which delineate labor market; hence the concern is with metropolises.

Diseconomies of Scale and City Size

The concept of diseconomies of scale was discussed in chapter 2. According to this concept, there are certain threshold levels of activity in the city beyond which average costs of production will increase. Since cities are not infinitely large, it seems plausible to argue that diseconomies of scale exist and they help to explain the limits to the size of our cities.

Studies of diseconomies in cities have, in the main, stressed the costs of providing public services. Some of these services, as noted in chapter 12, are subject to economies of scale. If viewed collectively, these costs are probably U-shaped with the bottom of the curve occurring in cities that have populations in the neighborhood of 250,000—see Figure 13.1.

Figure 13.1

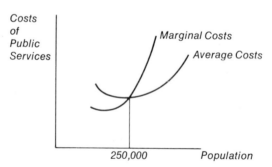

If we take minimum costs as the criterion for judging the size of cities and the cost of providing public services as the costs we wish to minimize, the implication of Figure 13.1 is clear. What we want are medium sized cities; in fact the 250,000 figure has appeared with some frequency in discussions of the optimum size of a city.

How seriously should we take the assertion that small to medium-sized cities are best? There are problems with this assertion. In the first place, the conclusions of the studies of the costs of public services are not without weakness. Most of them use expenditure figures in the calculations made, which is a point of weakness. Rising levels of expenditures might denote the consumption of more services rather than increased expensiveness, and it is not clear that this possibility has been dealt with adequately in these studies.

Secondly, there are problems in making intercity comparisons because the mix of services provided through the public sector of the economy differs among cities. In some cities, for example, the automobile is king, while in others, public transit plays a more important role. There are also intercity differences, as between the public and private production and distribution of utilities. Whether these differences, which have obvious bearing on the comparisons made, have been properly accounted for in these studies, is by no means clear.

Nor does this end the list of difficulties encountered in studies of public costs. At a minimum, they raise questions about the validity of the conclusion that small cities are better than large cities because they provide their residents with lower cost public services. Even if smaller cities did provide their residents with lower cost public services, however, it does not follow that people should be living in smaller cities. The consumption of public services is only a part of total consumption and not the most important part at that.

People live in cities because incomes are higher, and incomes are higher because of scale economies in the private sector. Those who think cities are too big often argue that diseconomies come into play in the private sector after certain size threshold levels are reached which dissipate the earlier gains. While the argument seems reasonable, a more careful look suggests that it has little supportive evidence or analysis.

The realization of diseconomies of scale within a plant, if indeed it happens, has no bearing on the issue. When the point is approached within the plant at which long-run average costs begin to rise, the firm has the option of building another plant. The presence of multiplant firms, in fact, indicates decisions were made that placed limits on the size of plants in cities and elsewhere. Bigness in cities cannot mean higher consumption costs because of internal diseconomies of scale realized in urban plants.

The concept of industry diseconomies also provides little reason for believing costs will rise as city size increases. While industries may experience rising costs after achieving a certain size, as noted in chapter 2, there is little evidence of it.

The concept of urbanization diseconomies seems more promising. City size is, after all, the concern, and urbanization diseconomies presumably come into play when the city reaches a certain size threshold. Yet, as observed in chapter 2, there are difficulties with the concept. The cost of many firms in the private sector does increase as city size increases. What happens, however, seems to be more a consequence of changes in the proportion of inputs used rather than arising from changes in the scale of activity. With land fixed in supply, increased use bids up the price of that land and hence the costs of its use. Land costs are higher in big cities than in small ones for this reason. Yet, this does not mean that our cities should be smaller. That land costs rose with the growth of our cities is, as noted in chapter 8, one of the reasons why our cities spread out. The firms and households who moved away from the central city still remained in the city, if city is taken to mean the metropolitan area of which the central city is a part.

Studies of costs in the private sector of the economy of our cities, although few in number, generally do not indicate any significant differences in production costs by city size. While most people appear to believe that big cities are more expensive places to live, this does not show up in cost studies, although these studies admittedly do not yield conclusive results. What does appear to vary are the expectations of residents in cities. With larger cities, the range of consumption goods is larger, which for many means a higher level of overall consumption. Those who argue that living costs are higher in big cities could be confusing the costs of overall consumption with the costs of a comparable market basket of goods and services. While it is by no means certain that consumer costs are the same in cities of all sizes, neither is it clear that they vary by size as much as the American public appears to believe.

Negative Market Externalities and City Size

Most serious arguments concerned with the excessive size of large cities focus on the negative market externalities of large cities. If increases in the population of a city, say, through net in-migration imposes costs on residents that are not fully taken into account by the in-migrant, the city can become too large. The migrant presumably decides to move to the city because it is in his or her best interest. This implies the benefits of doing so are greater than the costs. If the move imposes costs on others, however, which the migrant does not take into account, there will be problems. The social cost of the move will exceed private costs or those costs that enter into the calculations of the movers. That too many moves will be made can be easily seen from Figure 13.2. OM_2 is the proper

Figure 13.2

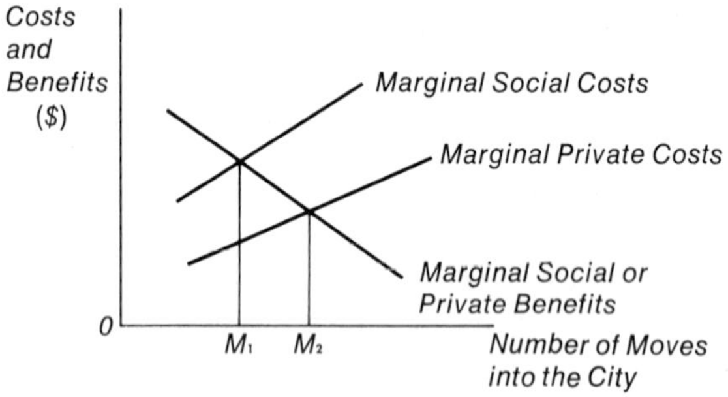

quantity of moves, given marginal social benefits and costs, but OM_1 moves are made.

It is easy to jump from this argument to the conclusion that city populations are too large. When we begin to raise the practical questions of how many people should be moved out of what city to where, or who should be kept from moving to what city, it becomes clear that the argument does not say enough. What costs are being imposed on whom becomes important. Is size involved? To answer this question, we must consider the problems that size is supposed to precipitate. The most important of these in discussions of city size are congestion and pollution.

Consider the problem of congestion first. As noted in chapter 11, congestion results from the fact that travel speeds on a given transportation network decline as traffic on the network increases beyond some volume. If we start with some congestion, an increase in population that adds to the traffic volume on that transportation network will intensify the problem. It adds to the number of travelers, which reduces the speeds that all can travel.

Those who believe cities are too large argue that the best way to deal with this problem is to move people out of large cities into smaller ones. Estimates have been made of the impact of this solution on congestion, and some show substantial cost reductions. Careful inspection of the calculations leading to this conclusion, however, reveal serious flaws in the analysis which underlies the calculations. The analysis assumes, in effect, that the productivity of a trip is the same for a small city as it is for a large city. This is most certainly not the case. Large cities, as just noted, became large because of the productivity of using land intensively. To fail to reckon with this fact is to understate the impact of the movement away from our larger cities on overall production and hence to overstate the reduction in congestion costs.

The efficient level of congestion in large cities can be expected to be higher than in small cities because higher productivity implies a more intensive use of land for buildings and for transportation facilities. A more intensive use of land, in turn, implies more congestion.

The level of congestion in most large cities is, of course, not efficient. This is because of the way in which we price our transportation services. The marginal social costs of travel are not fully paid by those who use our streets, highways, subways, and commuter trains. The proper way to address this problem is through pricing, such as congestion fees for the use of city streets and higher peak-hour fares for public transit, or through means that foster a greater use of mass transit forms, such as the reservation of expressway lanes for buses. All of this was discussed in detail in chapter 11. By resorting to such measures, because of their potential impact on transportation costs, the population of the large city might be reduced. More than likely, proper pricing would simply reallocate the population in the sense of moving them from the central city to the suburbs. To try to deal with the problem of congestion by limiting the city's population growth would probably only have the effect of reducing the growth of population and employment in the suburbs. Congestion in and around the central business district would undoubtedly remain.

The impact of population restrictions on the pollution problem in cities would probably have much the same effect if nothing were done to address the basic problem, that is, costs that confront producers and automobile owners that do not reflect the costs of properly discharging the wastes from production and use. Restricting population would probably also have little effect on the problems of crime, disease, housing, and poverty in our cities for precisely the same reason—population growth is not the sole or perhaps even the most important cause of the problem.

All of this is not to suggest that increasing size does not add to or intensify these problems. What is clear, however, is that much of what concerns people about large cities turns out to be problems that cannot really be addressed effectively by trying to reduce the size of those cities. In fact, it could even make things worse. To attempt to deal with the problems of pollution and congestion by moving people from large cities to smaller ones, might reduce the dimensions of these problems somewhat, but would do so in a way that reduced the nation's real consumption. If large cities, in fact, are sites of high productivity, and there is no reason to believe that they are not, moving people out of large cities into smaller ones will reduce the nation's productivity and, hence, real consumption.

National Urban Size Policy

Sensible discussions of the issue of city size from the perspective of the nation as a whole recognize the basic fact that the size of each city depends, in part, on the size and location of all other cities. All that we know about the hierarchy of cities is an important input into policy discussions concerned with city size.

The most important thing we know about this hierarchy is its permanence. All data concerning the size distribution of cities indicate there are a relatively small number of large cities and a relatively large number of small cities in all nations. Second, these data also indicate that if these distributions change, they do so only very slowly. Finally, these facts show that the characteristics of the size distribution of particular nations vary. In some, a few large cities dominate; in others, the largest cities are not so large, but there are more of them.

What these facts suggest is that public policy measures, unless they are of massive proportions, are likely to have only very modest effects on city size distributions and hence the size of particular cities. The impact of such policies will depend partly on the stage of development of the country in which they are being applied. The countries that are in early stages of economic development and are about to undergo a period of rapid economic and demographic growth are countries likely to have more success in altering the size of cities, compared with the mature and more slowly growing countries that have highly developed systems of urban physical investments, along with a population that has deeply embedded location preferences.

England is most often cited as an example of the latter. The official policy in England has been to discourage the growth of London and the southeastern part of the country, while revitalizing the relatively large nineteenth century metropolises of northern England and southern Scotland. This policy has not met with a great deal of success because of the maturity of the nation and its deeply ingrained commitments in the form of existing urban investments and the locational preferences of its citizens.

Canada, on the other hand, is a country in a relatively early stage of economic development, with anticipated strong upward trends in income and population. Much of its population is now concentrated in a few large metropolitan centers. The likely direction of future economic expansion will revolve heavily around the exploitation of its rich and relatively unexploited natural resources, which are widely dispersed throughout the nation. This suggests some dispersion in the nation's population is desirable. That the physical plant necessary to accommodate this expansion is not yet in place and that some of the necessary population may have to be "imported" suggests conditions under which efforts to modify size distribution of its cities might achieve some degree of success—assuming that Canada chooses to exploit its natural resources in ways that foster economic and demographic growth.

Israel is an example of a country that has pursued a policy of population dispersal with some success. With large-scale public ownership of land and complete national control over construction, the Israeli government has met with some success in its efforts to slow the growth of Tel Aviv and concentrate on the rapid growth of population in new towns and smaller existing cities. The rapid growth of population through migration, the rapid growth in the economy, and the cultural setting in which this growth has taken place provided a setting in which the forceful measures taken by the government have succeeded.

Would the pursuit of such a policy in the United States lead to similar success? Certainly, the basic underlying conditions differ from those of Canada and Israel. While we have not reached the stage of economic maturity of many European countries, neither are we at an early threshold of economic development. Moreover, while more urban growth is anticipated, that growth, relative to the current population, will be less than it has been. Finally, the nation's urban transportation, utility, and other public investments are large relative to future requirements. All these things suggest that the pursuit of a policy of population dispersal will be more difficult in the United States than in countries like Israel and Canada. It would indeed appear to require more massive intervention in areas of private decision-making than the federal government has been willing to consider to date.

The difficulties aside, shouldn't our policy be one of a dispersal of our population? Or should it? What should be the goals of policies concerned with city size?

Many students of the subject argue that these goals are the same as those of other national policies, e.g., efficiency, equity, growth stability, and participation. The question then becomes one of: What size will help us achieve this composite of goals?

If we equate the goals of national urban size policy with those of the nation's socioeconomic system considered as a whole, there are problems. Under certain realizable conditions, these goals are not totally consistent with one another. What may be equitable, such as providing aid to poverty-stricken regions or cities, may turn out to be an inefficient use of resources and will reduce the growth potential of the nation. Illustrations like this one come easy. The conclusion they lead to is that there is no unambiguous goal or set of goals to which a national policy on urban size can be addressed. It may be that we want to disperse the population to achieve what is equitable in the minds of some; yet, if population is dispersed to achieve this goal, it may impair economy efficiency and hence reduce real income and consumption.

In a book on urban economics, the primary concern is with efficiency questions. If we take efficiency as the goal in considering the question of urban size, a policy of population dispersal begins to lose some of its appeal. The population is already dispersed into a hierarchy of cities, which has been indicated to be an efficient system for the utilization of the nation's economic resources. Arguments to reduce the size of cities can certainly be questioned in light of our knowledge of that hierarchy, although that knowledge does not really indicate which of the many alternative forms of this hierarchy might be best.

The United States is highly urbanized, although no more so than other highly industrialized nations. It is also a nation that is less dominated by larger metropolitan areas than other industrialized countries. Do we have the proper arrangement of cities? Should we have fewer big cities or more? These questions are not easily answered. What does appear to be the case is that the large metropolitan area is beginning to occupy a slightly smaller role in the United States' hierarchy of cities. Census data show a downward trend in the relative importance of the nation's largest population over the past thirty-five years. This fact does not necessarily mean some of our cities are too large. Such cities as New York, Chicago, and Los Angeles have not grown smaller; rather, more urban growth is being accommodated in the nation's smaller metropolitan areas. While metropolitan New York may be too big in terms of efficiency criteria, the fact that its growth rate has slowed does not constitute proof that it is.

As noted above, most of the concern about the excessive size of the nation's largest cities is focused on problems such as pollution and congestion. While size may be involved in these problems, it is by no means a very important part. Measures taken to reduce the size of cities will not be very effective in dealing with these problems, for reasons just discussed. The proper way of dealing with the city's problems of congestion, pollution, crime, and the like is to address these problems directly. A more sensible urban policy is one that concentrates on improving urban environment *within* the city. In doing so, the cost and benefits of living in cities might be rearranged in ways to slow the growth of some cities and even reduce the size of others. If so, this would come about as a consequence of thousands of decisions made by private people and firms experimenting to find the best location for themselves, given their own individual circumstances. Undoubtedly, mistakes are made in this process. Our experience to date with efforts to alter city size gives us little reason to believe that in nations like the United States the outcome will be improved very much by direct measures taken by the federal government, unless we are willing to undertake drastic action.

REFERENCES

*Alonso, W. "The Economics of Urban Size." *Papers and Proceedings of the Regional Science Association*. 26 (1971): 67–83.

Baumol, W. "Macro Economics of Unbalance Growth: The Anatomy of Urban Crisis." *American Economic Review*. 57 (1967): 415–20.

Hansen, N. *Rural Poverty and the Urban Crises*. Bloomington, Ind.: Indiana University Press, 1970.

Hoch, I. "Income and City Size." *Urban Studies*. 9 (1973): 299–328.

Hoover, E., and Vernon, R. *Anatomy of a Metropolis*. Cambridge, Mass.: Harvard University Press, 1959.

Lichtenberg, R. M. *One Tenth of a Nation*. Cambridge, Mass.: Harvard University Press, 1960.

*Richardson, H. W. *The Economics of Urban Size*. Lexington, Mass.: Saxon House jointly with Lexington Books, D. C. Heath and Co., 1973.

Tolley, G. S. "The Welfare Economics of City Bigness." From *Urban Economics Report No. 31*, Chicago: University of Chicago, 1969.

---

* This chapter draws heavily from the writings of Alonso and Richardson.

14

Urban Planning

SUMMARY

Urban planning consists of a number of activities, one of the most important of which concerns land-use controls. While land-use controls have a long history in the United States, they have only come into widespread use over the past thirty years. Now most municipalities have some form of zoning activity, although what they do through zoning varies substantially.

The economic foundation of zoning is land use patterns, which generate negative ownership externalities. The unwarranted intrusions many property owners worry about can be considered as negative ownership externalities, and zoning is the means of dealing with this problem. Zoning in this sense is called *externality zoning.* Zoning has also been used to achieve other purposes. *Fiscal zoning,* as it is often called, has been used extensively by suburban communities as a means of excluding certain types of land use.

The use of zoning is the outcome of a political process influenced by economic factors. Economic and demographic change may give rise to market forces which, if left unfettered, would change a community's pattern of land use. If the emerging pattern is not consistent with the community's zonal classifications, political pressure to change those classifications will arise. The outcome, if we assume representative government, will depend partly on the location of the property—whether it is located from urban development, in a partially developed urban area, or in a fully developed urban area. In the latter case, the composition of the neighborhood surrounding the property—for example, whether they are renters or owner-occupiers—will have bearing on the outcome.

The impact of our use of land use controls on the efficiency and equity of urban land market outcomes is uncertain. Charges of *overzoning*—the provision of a higher level of land use than would maximize the social benefit from that use—have been made. The available evidence suggests that some communities have overzoned through the use of minimal lot size ordinances. The extent to which cities have overzoned, however, is by no means clear. *Underzoning*—the allowance of land use that generates uncompensated negative externalities, which lead to a lower use of that land—is also believed to be important. Underzoning does occur. The extent to which it leads to lower uses of land, however, is uncertain.

The current concern with environment will undoubtedly expand the scope of our concerns with land use controls. It is also possible that we shall concentrate more of this control at higher levels of government as the boader environmental concerns become more important.

Urban planning means many things to many people. Its meaning has also changed over time. This makes it a difficult subject to deal with in a book on urban economics, which no doubt explains why it is seldom taken up explicitly.

The general concept of planning is easy enough to understand. Dictionaries define it as a scheme of program for making, doing, or arranging something. If that something is economic activity, *urban planning* is activity involved in organizing the use of economic resources in cities or urban space. In a free market economy, planning is carried out within the private producing and consuming units of that economy. In such a world, economic activity is the outcome of market decisions that reflect the interaction of private demanders and suppliers in the urban market place. Planning, as defined above, is clearly a part of such a world; it is done in the private sector. Yet, this view of planning does not coincide with what most people mean when they talk about city planning. Urban planning is, in the minds of most, identified with the activities of some public body or bodies.

These two views are not necessarily inconsistent. The rationale for government in economics is found in market failure—see chapters 6 and 12. To the extent that markets do not work effectively—e.g., there are ownership externalities—there is reason for public intervention and control. A rational use of public resources through the public sector implies planning, which is, of course, what many consider urban planning to be.

Precisely what kinds of activities are these? Traditionally, city planning activity has been taken to mean activity concerned with physical planning. To most, this means a concern with the way in which land is being used, with particular emphasis on the physical features of that use. This concern, in turn, has encompassed many different types of activity, including establishing the pattern of city streets and the setting aside and development of land for public purposes, such as parks, museums, and the like. In the United States, this kind of activity has been in the domain of local government under powers delegated by the states.

More recently, the scope, if not the effectiveness, of the activities of the urban planner has been broadened. Urban planning is now taken by many to include not only land-use planning and control, but planning associated with all activities of urban government. This implies a spectrum of activities ranging from waste collection and disposal to running day care centers and administering justice. It includes the regulatory, revenue generating, and investment activities of urban public bodies and is not restricted to a concern with spatial aspects of this activity.

Urban planning so conceived is a concern with the planning involved in the activities of urban government.

The meaning of urban government has also begun to change. Both the state and federal government have come to play a more important role in urban planning. Through an assortment of subsidies, they have helped steer local government into more planning activities. Many planners also believe that the state and federal will, in time, assume a more direct and important role in urban planning.

Planning in this sense is easy to grasp conceptually. What it means in terms of the planning actually done in urban government is another matter. Since this is not a book about the economics of planning in urban government, a more restrictive view of the activities of urban planning is appropriate. The primary concern in this book is with land-use controls. While only a part of what most people mean by urban planning, they are an important part.

LAND-USE CONTROLS IN THE UNITED STATES

Government has always had a role in the layout and construction of American cities. In colonial America, for example, government took the initiative in urban development by designating sites for development, establishing methods of land acquisition, and, in some cases, by actually developing the layout of the city. In the nineteenth century, however, government played a more passive role, in part because of its attempts to encourage westward economic development through the provision of land to its citizens. The government's role during this period was largely restricted to providing grids of street layouts upon which the force of the market came into play. Construction flourished and cities were built and grew. But the outcome was by no means satisfying to many. Tenements, health problems, and a decline in the quality of particular neighborhoods that stemmed from some "unwarranted" change became concerns to many, giving rise to various kinds of government actions which imposed certain forms of restrictions on markets. Land zoning, including subdivision activity, was one of these. Public health measures also began to be used in ways that influenced private urban development, e.g., specifying standards for sources of water supply. Building and housing codes were another form of public control that came into use. The acquisition of land for public purposes also began to grow in importance.

While all of these are parts of the planning activities of urban government that have had impact on the course of urban development, the most important to date has been land zoning, including land subdivision activity. This kind of activity has roots that go way back; yet, it did not really take hold until a court decision in the 1920s dissipated any legal doubts about it. Since then, all fifty states have provided legislative authorization for zoning regulations to be implemented at the local government level, and more than 10,000 local governments have developed some kind of land-use control program.

Zoning is often a part of an overall community plan. Typically, that plan will contain economic, social, and demographic information and analysis about the city, as well as maps which indicate the present structure of land use. It also includes a statement of goals and objectives and a program of actions designed to achieve these goals. Zoning comes into play at this point. It lies at the heart of the process of implementing the plan. If we wish to achieve certain goals with respect to our use of land in the city, we must have rules that guide behavior into channels that lead to the desired result. Zoning, including land subdivision activity, is really a shorthand way of talking about a set of ordinances that establish these rules.

The formulation and implementation of the plan are carried out by a citizen's board—the planning board—usually appointed by the mayor or city council. This board, in turn, hires a staff that is ordinarily intimately involved with all aspects of the planning process. Often, though not always, this board will be charged with the responsibility for both formulating and implementing the plan. Sometimes there are two separate boards—one for planning and one for zoning. In this case, coordinating problems can arise. But no matter whether these functions are separately or jointly performed, land use zoning stands at the core of what we try to do to achieve the goals and objectives set forth in the plan.

What are those zoning ordinances that establish the rules of the game? The rules of what game?

Traditionally, zoning ordinances have been "settlement" rules. They have been concerned with particular parcels of land and how they were to be used. The concern was with type of use (e.g., residential versus nonresidential), population density at the site, and the size and bulk of buildings. Zoning maps were constructed, which delineated zones or districts in which particular types of "harmonious" uses were to be permitted. With such maps, zoning was believed to be "self-executing" in the sense that to carry out the intent of the zoning ordinance, it was only necessary to have a building official determine whether the proposed construction was in conformance with the requirement of the ordinance.

It all sounded so simple; yet it turned out to be anything but that. As these regulations were initially implemented through local government, the primary concern was with inappropriate development. The initial protection provided against "incompatible intrusions," however, was inadequate. Things were not well enough defined. Particular decisions often raised issues that were not easily disposed of. What came to be recognized was the fact of "varying circumstances," which led to the provision of appeal, amendment, and "variance" procedures in the zoning regulations of most cities. It also led to the tightening up of these controls through a more explicit specification of types of use permitted in particular places. Zoning in the United States became a complex process as the number of zones increased and the stipulations that applied in each of these zones expanded.

It also became a process that achieved its greatest success in what many believe to be a highly questionable area. If exclusion was the aim, its most successfull achievements came in suburban cities that sought to keep out low-income households using such means as minimum lot size stipulation.

This approach to controlling the use of land soon revealed its shortcomings. More detailed specifications did not necessarily deal with the problem of fuzziness in the meaning or inharmonious uses. The self-execution of a more elaborate set of rules still seemed to call for more exceptions. While concern remained about the abuse that could stem from a failure to specify the meaning of inharmonious use, we apparently came to believe that a highly detailed set of specifications of what went where in the city was not the answer. The pace of change in most cities apparently made it very risky to consider such things as "set in concrete."

The thrust of zoning began to shift again. More administrative discretion was inserted into land use decisions. The zoning process began to evolve in ways characterized by some as the "developer proposes and the municipality disposes." Planned Unit Development, which has come into widespread use over the past ten years, represented a vigorous attempt to move the zoning process in this direction and to do so in ways that provide what is now believed to be the flexibility required for an orderly development process. Yet, Planned Unit Development has come under attack recently and there are those who argue that we may be headed back toward the use of rules that specify particular uses for particular parcels of land.

We come back to the basic questions. What uses for what land? Why do we worry about it? What can urban economics contribute to our understanding of the issues involved in land-use controls?

WHY ZONING RESTRICTIONS?

Externality Zoning

Why might a community take political actions that sanction urban land market restrictions in the form of zoning? We know there is journalistic evidence that suggests that many urban property owners believe some form of zoning restrictions is necessary. Many have a serious and genuine concern about the prospect of "unwarranted intrusions" in their neighborhoods. In a world of growth and change, of course, the possibility of neighborhood change is very real. It is also conceivable that some of this change might not work to the advantage of property owners in the neighborhoods where it takes place. Consider, for example, property owners in a residential neighborhood. Certainly, to any one of these owners, the chemical factory, a go-go bar, or even a service station would be considered undesirable. Were a chemical factory to locate down the street, clean air would become a thing of the past, as would a number of other amenities in the neighborhood.

Do people who worry about unwarranted intrusions have a legitimate concern, or are they just paranoid? Certainly, there is reason enough in location theory for believing that the service station might find the heart of a residential district a profitable location. Moreover, given the dynamics of the city, it is not only the service station that many residential home owners have a right to fear. The shopping center, certain kinds of industry, and even certain types of residential users could become threats to some residential property owners as the city spreads out or begins to renew itself. While some complaints of urban property owners about unwarranted intrusion may have no real substance, a number of them do. When there is substance to the complaint, it becomes an important matter. It, in fact, becomes important enough to lead to agitation for some kinds of restriction against the intruder. As these things have worked themselves out in most American communities, the restrictions have taken the form of zoning ordinances.

This explanation can be easily converted into an economics explanation. Unwarranted intrusions can be considered as ownership externalities. The service station that moves into the neighborhood site generates third party effects. The noise, dirt, congestion, and ugliness it creates are factors external to the transactions that make that location profitable, e.g., the sale of gasoline. But they are factors affecting the use of property in surrounding sites in negative ways. In the language of chapter 6, they are negative ownership externalities.

Zoning, which represents a community response to problems created by negative ownership externalities, constitutes action directed at the problem of efficiency. Should that service station be built at a certain intersection in the neighborhood? Suppose the location was a profitable one. Yet, suppose also that it imposes congestion and pollution costs on its neighbors for which it is not held accountable. The private costs of its operation will not fully reflect the social costs. If the firm were held accountable for social costs, it might not find that location profitable enough to warrant operation there. If the firm operates at this location without being held accountable for the pollution and congestion it creates, its operations would be economically inefficient.

It is worth noting at this point that not all external effects that stem from the pattern of urban land use generated by the urban land markets are negative. Some may be beneficial. For example, someone could build an expensive home in a modest neighborhood, adding to the value of homes already there.

There are also a number of adjacent uses that generate external benefits and costs that do not cause problems. One set of these are adjacent activities that create mutual benefits or external economies. An obvious example is the retail firm that locates adjacent to other retail firms and by doing so helps generate traffic flows that are mutually beneficial. Obviously, we want to encourage this kind of propinquity, and markets, in fact, do. If such benefits exist, they will be reflected in lower money costs and/or higher revenues, which means profits will be highest at adjacent locations. These benefits are really a part of what is meant by scale economies—see chapter 2.

Adjacent use that generates mutual harm will also be reckoned with through the operations of markets. Hospitals are seldom found located next to large discount stores, because adjacent locations would add to the operating costs of both. Mutual harm means higher costs and/or lower revenues and hence lower profits.

Adjacent use creates problems when one user generates an external cost and the other does not—A creates an external cost for B and the impact of B's use on A is either neutral or positive. When the service station moves into a residential neighborhood, it creates external costs for which it makes no compensation. It comes because it encounters no harm, only benefits. Its move into the neighborhood, however, creates problems. The private costs of operation are less than the social costs by an amount equal to the negative spillovers—congestion, noise, and pollution—created. Its operations are thus economically inefficient; marginal social costs exceed marginal social benefits.

This inefficiency will not go unnoticed. Those who are its victims—the residents —will be keenly aware of what's happening and will be justified in their efforts to do something about it. Zoning ordinances could be the result, but they need not be.

Do We Really Need Externality Zoning?

Just because some property owners are adversely affected by what their neighbors do, by itself, does not justify interference with the market mechanism. The desired result could be achieved by resorting to some form of voluntary compensating payment between those involved in the dispute.

By way of illustrating the point, suppose that Jones buys property next to Smith. Smith's property is used for residential purposes, as was the property that Jones purchased. Jones now decides a change in land use is in order. As a consequence of an exhaustive investigation, Jones comes to the conclusion that a service station could be profitably operated on his property. Smith objects. If Jones were to build and operate a service station on his property, the noise, congestion, and pollution generated would have the effect of lowering the value of Smith's property. Jones wants to do it because of his belief that a successful operation will increase the value of his property. It is clear that a service station in the neighborhood will bring both gains and losses.

Suppose that Smith's losses exceed Jones' gains. The service station entry could be prevented through voluntary actions by Smith and Jones. If Smith and Jones want to maximize their wealth, Smith could offer to compensate Jones by an amount greater than the increase in the value of Jones' property that would come with the service station. Smith would only make this offer if Jones agreed to use his property for residential purposes only. If both agreed, a transaction would take place that would make both Smith and Jones better off. The potential problem of unwarranted intrusion would be averted without recourse to zoning ordinances; it would be averted because of the use of a compensation scheme, which in this case was simply a payment made from Smith to Jones.

But will this happen? Clearly, Smith would prefer the problem be resolved in other ways. For example, to prevent Jones from operating a service station through a zoning ordinance would be less costly to Smith. Whether, as a consequence, Smith will be able to get the zoning ordinance to keep Jones and others from using adjacent land in adverse ways is a matter to be discussed below. This is a matter of political economy.

Wealth effects aside, there are economic reasons for believing that voluntary transactions involving compensation payments are not a very practicable way of minimizing negative ownership externalities in land use. The problem is a variant of the free rider problem. If Jones builds and operates a service station on his property, Smith is not the only one likely to be affected. There are others close by who will suffer from the noise, congestion, and pollution created by that service station. The value of their property will be reduced as well.

Since the worth of that service station to the neighborhood depends on the property value gains to its owner relative to the property value losses of all those who suffer losses, the total loss must be considered as a sum of what could very well turn out to be a relatively large number of individual losses. Each of those who would incur a loss will gain if Jones' property were restricted to residential use. The individual gain, however, will be at a maximum if each loser could avoid making payment to Jones and let his or her neighbors do it. If this is how potential losers view the matter, it is unlikely that a collective offer will be made to Jones, which will get him to alter his plans. The land use pattern in that neighborhood is not likely to be the right one unless there is a restriction of property rights, which could come about through zoning ordinances.

Fiscal Zoning

Fiscal zoning is zoning that seeks to create a pattern of land use for purposes other than economic efficiency. The use of zoning ordinances to deal with an externality that arises when land is used in certain ways is an attempt to improve the efficiency of the urban land market. Much of what has been done in the area of zoning, however, cannot be considered as a concern with the problem of efficiency.

The practice of large lot zoning by suburban communities was mentioned above. Such a practice is aimed at the exclusion of low-income households from these communities. While there are a number of reasons why such communities might want to exclude low-income households, the most important of these is what their presence would mean with respect to the composition and cost of public services. As noted in chapter 12, the public service needs of low-income families are high and their ability to pay is restricted. Their movement into a suburban community populated with high-income people would thus change the character of local public services and increase the costs to current residents. It would, in effect, redistribute income from current residents to those who move into the community.

Zoning vacant land into large lots for high-value single family homes is one way to keep this from happening. While the vacant land might be better suited to apartment development, the community may decide that vacant land is better. Apartment development could give rise to migration, which would create fiscal problems for them. The objective of minimizing these problems will give rise to fiscal zoning.

There are other reasons for fiscal zoning. Yet no matter what the reason, the outcome is the same—fiscal zoning leads to a different land use pattern than if the zoning is aimed at economic efficiency.

THE POLITICAL ECONOMY OF ZONING

Zoning is a series of ordinances, a set of administrative procedures, and a number of people making decisions in light of these ordinances within the framework of these administrative procedures. What kind of ordinances? What kind of administrative procedures? What kind of people making what decisions? The answers to these questions are found in political terrain. Zoning is political activity, but it is political activity that arises because of a perceived need that has strong economic roots. If we want to understand zoning outcomes, we must have some understanding of the political economy of the zoning process.

Zoning Under the Benevolent Dictator

Suppose our concern is with zoning as a means of dealing with efficiency problems created by the presence of external diseconomies in the current pattern of land use. Suppose, further, that our political system revolves around the actions of a dictator who has absolute power. This is also a dictator who is all wise and beneficent and one who takes into account the wants and ability of his or her subjects to pay, in making economic decisions. Finally, suppose that there are negative ownership externalities because of the current pattern of land use. The dictator's job is to do away with these externalities by reassigning the use of land. What land? Reassigned to what uses?

The negative ownership externalities generated by the current pattern of land use depend on technical factors as they come to bear on the conditions of production and tastes and incomes of individuals as they come to bear on consumption patterns. That a chemical factory generates negative ownership externalities to its neighbors is partly a function of the fact that conditions of production create pollution, which spills over into adjacent locations. That these spillovers create problems is due, in part, to the fact that pollution is not viewed favorably by nearby households.

Situations like this have to be identified, boundaries established, and corrective actions set forth. Suppose the industry polluters are located in the center of the city and we can establish the boundaries within which the negative ownership externalities occur—see Figure 14.1. This boundary can be reduced if these

Figure 14.1

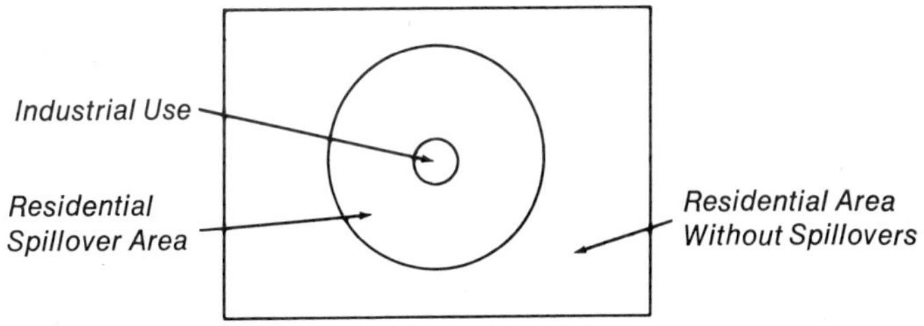

Industrial Use

Residential
Spillover Area

Residential Area
Without Spillovers

industries are moved out to the urban periphery where much of the spillover would be in rural areas—see Figure 14.2.

Figure 14.2

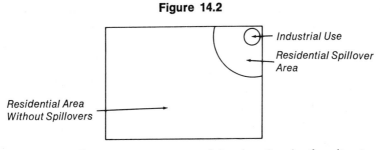

Industrial Use

Residential Spillover
Area

Residential Area
Without Spillovers

When industry polluters move to an outlying location in the city, transportation costs could be increased. This possibility has to be considered in evaluating the efficiency aspects of such a move. Suppose, however, the gains to residential users exceed the additional transportation costs occasioned by the move. Rearrangement from Figure 14.1 to Figure 14.2 is warranted. The dictator should issue a decree to move the industry polluters away from residential users.

Looked at in terms of this example, the job of rearranging land use to minimize ownership externalities looks easy. In fact, it is anything but that. Many activities in cities spill over into others, often in very subtle ways. There is a great deal of interdependence in the urban economy that has an important geographic dimension. The problem is that up and beyond the obvious cases, activities that generate negative ownership externalities in adjacent areas are often not easy to identify. The job of the dictator, if he or she were concerned with what people wanted, would be a difficult one.

Suppose the dictator were omniscient. The general outline of what would have to be done is easily described. Given a knowledge of the characteristics of the activities that generate negative ownership externalities when located next to one another, boundaries could be established into which certain kinds of activity fit. There would be decrees that segregate out of particular places those uses that impose negative ownership externalities on the activities assigned to those places. Rearranging land use in this way should generate a pattern of use that minimizes negative ownership externalities. The question is: Could we expect this pattern to emerge in a democratic political setting?

Representative Government and Zoning Decisions

Suppose the power to enact a zoning ordinance rested with the legislative body of a city—that is, the city council. Suppose this body was composed of people who were responsive to those who elected them, and each person was allotted one vote in the political system. The concern is with the economic factors affecting the decisions of the council when enacting or revising zoning ordinances in a political system of one person—one vote representative government. In considering these decisions, it is helpful to make several distinctions. One distinction to be made is between action taken by council in isolation from all other political bodies in the metropolitan region of which it is a part, and action taken considered in the context of this region. The second distinction is to distinguish between actions taken in a situation where there is no urban development, one in which there is partial development, and one in which there is total development.

Municipality Decisions Considered in Isolation   Consider first the decision made affecting areas where there is no urban development. Suppose our general concern is with the enactment of a set of regulations that spell out the ways in which land is to be developed. The specific concern is with economic factors that generate the political pressures brought to bear on council members.

Suppose both commercial and residential uses are planned and that some planned commercial use will generate negative ownership externalities when it is located adjacent to certain classes of residential users.

What kind of political pressure will be brought to bear on council? The nature of this pressure will depend on the location of the land to be developed in the region of which it is a part. Suppose, for example, this land is in a remote location. If the transportation costs to and from that location are prohibitive, there will be little political pressure brought to bear on council members. If the land lacks economic value, the council can do whatever it wants and not adversely affect the economic interests of anyone.

Suppose the undeveloped land to come under zoning regulation is located in accessible places and is capable of being developed in other respects. Assume the demand for this land is heaviest among residential users, which implies some demand by businesses that provide certain kinds of services to residents. Neither the future residential nor commercial user is likely to be represented in the council's initial deliberations. It is the builder-developer who seeks to influence the council as to the way in which this land should be zoned and subdivided. Assume that some form of segregation is used by the council at the outset, e.g., residential use must be segregated from all others. The builder can present a plan adhering to this principle and that will be that. But suppose that the builder-developer has a different view of what kind of land use will generate maximum profit. Suppose he believes a mixture of certain kinds of commercial activity along with the residential use would maximize his profits. The builder-developer, in these circumstances, has economic incentive to try to influence the decisions of the council. In the absence of residents in the area with a vested interest in how the property is developed, if the city council is responsive to the political influence of interested persons, the builder-developer will probably have his way.

If the builder-developer prevails, this need not lead to a loss in the economic welfare of the community. In fact, it could bring added benefits to those who ultimately become residents of the area. A centrally located shopping center should, if properly developed, bring benefits to those who live in the neighborhood. These benefits are reflected in the profitability of operations at some location in this intended residential neighborhood. The problem is that profits from such commercial operations might turn out to be greater for the firm that generates negative ownership externalities. Less concern with parking facilities—which would create congestion—would mean lower development costs, as would less concern with the ecology of the area in the design and construction of the structures that house this activity. This possibility generates incentives for the builder-developer to bring political pressure that leads to "underzoning." Underzoning, in this case, means allowing uses that generate negative externalities to users in adjacent locations without any means of compensation.

Suppose we consider the case where the land to be developed is a part of an area that is partially developed. Now we deal with circumstances in which there are those who will be directly affected by the zoning ordinance. If the developed area consists of single-family residential users and the area to be developed is zoned as single-family residential, the present residents probably will have no objections to future development if it conforms to the segregation principle implicit in this zoning ordinance. They might object to certain kinds of single-family residential development, however. Many middle-income people, for example, would probably object if future development paved the way for movement of low-income families into the neighborhood. This could give rise to political pressure for a type of zoning ordinance that would exclude certain kinds of residential users.

What will the outcome be? An analysis of economic factors alone is not likely to give us the answer. Certain sets of conditions as they are reflected through economic behavior, however, will have impact on the council's decisions. One of these is the tenure arrangement of the residents in the existing neighborhood. If they are renters, one result might be expected. If they are owner-occupiers, the result could be different. Renters are much more mobile than homeowners and hence are apt to be less vocal and intense in their resistance to developments that might be construed as unwarranted intrusions. Homeowners, on the other hand, are more likely to act with vigor and dispatch. If the city council were responsive to majorities in their political decisions, and if one person counted as one vote, homeowners, if they were a majority, could have it their way in these decisions. In partially developed suburban neighborhoods, where the number of home-owning residents is relatively large, homeowners would exert the dominant political influence and could push their advantage to the point where fiscal zoning, or what some call overzoning, occurs. If successful, they will have generated ordinances with restrictions on property that relegate it to a use that is "higher" than that which would occur through the operation of a competitive market—for example, ordinances that specify large lot sizes with single-family homes.

Consider finally the case of the council grappling with the problems of urban transition and redevelopment. In an urban area that grows, ages, and is subjected to various kinds of technical and social change, there is likely to be change in the pattern of land use. The spreading out of the American city, discussed above at some length, brought with it profound changes in the pattern of urban land use. As it occurred, there were shifts and changes in use relations both within and on the periphery of urban development. With some notable exceptions, there was movement towards a desegration of land use in our cities. Zoning ordinances that embodied a segregation principle came under attack. Zoning boards in fully developed cities became very busy public bodies. They made decisions which in some instances altered the segregation principle and in other instances did not.

The success of developers in seeking to change patterns of land use in fully developed areas has obviously varied. Where they seek to exert political pressure in cities with representative government, the outcome will, as in the partially developed case, depend, in part, on the composition of the population who could be affected by it. If the community is primarily residential, this will have bearing on the degree of resistance to the change. To the extent that segregation is a principle believed to minimize negative ownership externalities—to the home owner a principle that will keep property value from falling—zoning variances leading to more nonresidential use of the land will be resisted. How much resistance will depend on such resident characteristics as the tenure status. If proportionately more of the residents are homeowners, the resistance will be greater than if they are renters, for reasons just noted. In general, zoning decisions resulting in land use changes are likely to meet with more resistance in areas that are fully developed because there are more people who will be directly affected by the change.

Municipal Zoning in a Regional Context   Metropolitan areas, as noted earlier, usually consist of a number of municipalities or separate governments. This political fragmentation, as noted in chapter 12, is not so irrational as some believe. Not only are there areas of cooperation reflected in such things as special districts, but competition among government units has not been without benefits. There are also areas in which political fragmentation is believed to cause problems, one of which is municipal zoning.

What impact, if any, is political fragmentation likely to have on the zoning decisions of particular municipalities? Is there any reason to believe that zoning decisions of municipality A will generate negative spillovers into other municipalities in metropolitan area X? If so, will decision makers in A take these things into account in their deliberations?

Much of the zoning in A is not likely to generate significant spillovers on other nearby municipalities. There are, however, some zoning decisions which could. One way to minimize the pollution and congestion created by certain kinds of industry is to pass a zoning ordinance excluding them from the city. If these industries, as a consequence, choose to locate in an adjacent city, that decision would be partly the result of zoning activity in A.

We cannot really say whether this zoning decision made life better in A and caused problems elsewhere without a great deal of additional information about the characteristics of these industries, tastes and preferences of the affected populations, and the economic structure of the cities involved. Suppose, however, that the movement elsewhere did make life better in A and caused problems elsewhere. Is this a fact that would be taken into account in the zoning decisions made in A?

It might if the residents in A were renters. The protection of rental property in A relative to other places would, in time, increase its capital value and ultimately increase the rents charged. If this is perceived by the renting residents of A, they will have an interest in "protecting" property throughout the entire metropolitan area. After all, they don't want their rents raised. To argue this way, however, assumes that renters are mobile and experience no significant restrictions on their housing opportunities throughout the entire metropolitan area. It is to assume, in effect, that they are living in units best for them, given their incomes, tastes and preferences, and the available stock of housing units. While this may be true for many, it is not true for all.

Communities populated with homeowners who make the same decisions will not have this incentive. Any increase in the capital values of the property in these communities because of zoning ordinances that cause problems elsewhere will accrue to these homeowners. Communities filled with homeowners may thus have incentive to push for ordinances imposing costs on neighboring communities. In this case, there may be justification for placing a metropolitan area representative on the zoning board in A or making provision for some kind of metropolitan area review of the zoning decisions in A.

Unrepresentative Government and Zoning Decisions

Considered in a setting in which there is representative government making decisions in response to a careful reading of the votes of the electorate—each of whom has one vote—certain statements can be made about how economic factors will influence political decisions made in the zoning process. However, the assumption of representative government may be unrealistic. To some political scientists, this view of the political decision-making process is naive at best and its application can lead to conclusions that are misleading and perhaps even wrong. What this kind of model neglects is explicit consideration of the question of the distribution of power in general and economic power in particular. Inequality in the distribution of economic power is believed to have significant impact on the political process, which includes outcomes generated by zoning boards.

It is difficult not to believe that the distribution of economic power has impact on zoning. The problem is that we don't know very much about the causes and consequences of economic power. There are few economic models that provide insight into how economic inequality affects the distribution of political power. We can say that concentrations of economic wealth make it easier to exert political pressure. Widely dispersed economic wealth requires the coalescence of a relatively large number of people in a political action. In this case, numbers add substantially to the complexities of the problem of generating political action. The precise impact of a concentration of wealth in the community cannot be predicted without a great deal of information about the extent of the concentration and the nature of the interests of the wealthy. Even if we had this information, there are limits to what we could do with it.

All is not darkness, however. The concentration of economic wealth in many cities is not so great as to preclude the use of the notions of representative government and zoning decisions as a framework within which the facts about zoning can be given an insightful interpretation.

ZONING OUTCOMES

Unfortunately, there is little scientific research concerned with municipal land use controls, probably because the phenomenon itself is so complicated. This complexity is partly a matter of scope and partly a matter of variation in subject matter. According to a study by the National Commission on Urban Problems made during the latter part of the 1960s, there were over 5,200 political jurisdictions that had zoning restrictions. This study also uncovered widespread variation in the aims, techniques, subject matter of concern, and accomplishments of those governmental bodies concerned with land-use control. The precise nature of this variation, however, is not easy to pinpoint. The evidence, when carefully examined, turns out to be largely anecdotal. Data concerned with actual land-use control practices and outcomes are indeed in short supply. Broad sweeping conclusions about zoning outcomes are thus not possible. There are, nevertheless, a number of sensible statements that can be made about certain aspects of these outcomes.

Overzoning   *Overzoning,* as noted above, implies zoning ordinances that provide for a higher level of land use than would maximize the social benefits from that use. Large lot zoning that keeps land from being used for apartments or nonresidential uses could be overzoning. Other forms of potential overzoning activity include the exclusion of multiple dwellings and minimum housing requirements.

Surveys commissioned by the National Commission on Urban Problems indicated this kind of zoning was widespread. The data collected show that 25 percent of the metropolitan municipalities of 5,000 and above permitted no single family houses on lots of less than one-half acre. Of these governments, 11 percent had two acre zoning; 20 percent had one to two acre zoning; 33 percent had one-half to one acre zoning; and more than 50 percent had one-fourth to one-half acre zoning. The Commission data also showed about 35 percent of these municipalities had zoning ordinances specifying minimum floor space requirements.

That a municipality has large lots and minimum housing size zoning ordinances does not, by itself, indicate overzoning. The zoning ordinance simply could be a ratification of existing demands in these communities, i.e., people in fact want large lots upon which to build large houses. Yet, that there are so many communities with this kind of zoning and a relatively small number of people who could afford such homes strongly suggests that much of it is overzoning.

Fiscal zoning in this sense does not really make the world a better place to live. Considering the metropolitan area as a whole, overzoning of this kind probably leads to inefficient and inequitable market outcomes. The restriction of some land to a limited set of uses is likely to affect the price of that land. That price will probably be lower than if the zoning ordinances allowed more bidders to compete for it. If so, there is reason to argue that it will not be assigned to its "highest and best" use, that is, it will not be used efficiently.

Inequities could stem from what happens to the price of land elsewhere in the metropolitan area of which this community is a part. Overzoning restricts the options of some outside the community. They could, as a consequence, bid up the price of land elsewhere to levels that are higher than they would have been in the absence of this restriction. If so, those who pay this higher price will receive less benefit. Overzoning thus has redistribution effects, the equity of which could be questioned.

Underzoning   *Underzoning,* as noted above, is the allowance of land use that generates uncompensated negative externalities which lead to "lower" uses of that land. Since zoning is supposed to be a way of preventing such patterns of land use, underzoning implies that the zoning effort is unsuccessful.

Evidence of underzoning is not easily assembled. Even where the uncompensated costs imposed by one user on the other are clearly visible, they are not easily measured in most instances. It seems clear that a residential household suffers from congestion and pollution created by the newly located service station down the street. Just how much suffering occurs for given amounts of congestion and pollution is a much more difficult question. The value of the property of the residential owner will be reduced, but it is not easy to disentangle the effects of this set of negative externalities from all other factors influencing property values.

In addressing the question of the extent to which underzoning is a problem, the best we can do now is examine some general arguments that have links to indirect evidence. One of these is the argument that zoning has not really accomplished very much, which is to suggest that there has been a great deal of underzoning. All we have to do is to look at what has happened to our cities over the past fifty years. Suppose we start with a view of the city as an ideal construct. What everybody wants is the city beautiful, something that is laid out and developed in accordance with certain aesthetic and engineering principles. Yet, look around and what do you see—cities that have grown into sprawling metropolitan complexes falling far short of these principles. All this, not coincidentally, took place during a period in which the use of zoning by municipalities spread rapidly throughout the nation.

The evidence that cities have become sprawling metropolises is compelling. It was discussed at length in chapter 8. It reflects in rent, price, and density gradients that show up as becoming more gently sloped. Chapter 8 also presented evidence that urban development over the past fifty years violated the segregation principle that some considered to be sacrosanct. Our cities have grown in ways that led to a greater mixture of residential and nonresidential land use. Whether all this implies underzoning is less certain.

It is certainly not what most city planners wanted. Nor does it seem to come very close to the ideal city that most people have in mind when asked to describe what is in their dreams. Yet, few things in this world measure up to what's in our dreams. Given our strong preference for the mobility provided by the automobile, it was inevitable that our cities would spread out. Did they spread out in ways that created negative ownership externalities that imposed uncompensated costs on a large number of people? The question is not easily answered. Suppose they did. Was zoning involved? If so, was the result under-zoning in the sense of a lower level of land use than otherwise would have occurred? These are also not easy questions to answer.

One thing is clear. The fact that our cities do not now measure up to someone's conception of the city beautiful does not stand as evidence that we have under-zoned. Given economic constraints, i.e., the limits to what we can do, we could have the best of all possible worlds if the automobile is to play an important role in that world. While this is probably not so, the case against what we have now cannot be established on the basis of general arguments against urban sprawl. Moreover, the fact that we seem to get the same result, i.e., urban sprawl, irrespective of whether development is being guided by land use controls or not, suggests that underzoning may be less important than some believe. There are metropolitan areas like Houston, for example, which have had little guidance with land use controls which are much like any other rapidly growing city that had extensive zoning ordinances oftentimes aimed at the achievement of some kind of "master plan."

Another line of argument that, on the surface, implies underzoning focuses on zoning variances and the corruptibility of officials who make and administer our zoning ordinances. A striking feature of the administration of a system of land use controls is that little is viewed as being set in concrete. After World War II, many cities developed master plans or plans that involved detailed zoning specifications as guides for future development. What followed after the adoption of these plans was their dilution through zoning variance procedures. Many exceptions were granted through a variance, and before long some plans became virtually unrecognizable from what they were initially.

Why were there variances, which in some cases substantially altered the initial plan? Some argue that this was a consequence of the corruptibility of those who administered the controls.

This is a broad-gauged charge, the truth or falsity of which is not easily demonstrated. One observation is worth making, however. There is reason to believe that there has been, is now, and forever will be, attempts to influence political bodies responsible for a program of urban land use controls. If decisions concerning the use of our economic resources are made largely by individuals in markets, and zoning ordinances constrain market participants in ways that are not consistent with their perception of what's most profitable, those participants will try to influence the officials who promulgate and administer these ordinances. Those who find their way blocked to what they perceive as profitable development projects by particular zoning ordinances can be expected to take actions that alter these ordinances in ways that allow such development. If the process of political change is such that "under-the-table" payments or bribes are necessary to bring about such change, such payments will probably be made.

Illegal payments to city council members or members of a zoning board to get some parcel of land "rezoned" are generally believed to result in underzoning. Certainly, this could be the case. Putting a service station in the heart of a residential neighborhood could turn out to be a very profitable venture if the firm did not have to compensate the nearby residents for the congestion and pollution costs they would experience. That profitability, in turn, provides the incentive for someone to bend or break the law. The result will be underzoning or a pattern of land use that reduces the value of some property owners within the neighborhood.

It appears as though evidence of bribery can be taken to indicate the presence of underzoning. But can it? There are circumstances in which under-the-table payments to members of the city council or zoning board could improve the pattern of land use within the city. Cities with static master plans are cities where this is most likely to happen.

Most cities are dynamic and growing organisms. Through zoning ordinances, we can try to circumscribe that growth in certain ways. If those ways are inconsistent with market outcomes, the incentive to bribe some public official could be there. To illustrate, suppose in the private sector of the central city that commercial redevelopment was the most profitable form of redevelopment. Suppose also that zoning ordinances in the city specified that redevelopment, when it occurs, has to involve both residential and nonresidential elements. If we assume that nobody really wants to live in the central city, the incentive for bribery is there. The zoning ordinance is out of tune with the realities of the market. It stands in the way of profitable commercial development in the central city. If this development does not result in underzoning, that it cannot take place means land within the city is not being used efficiently. Suppose that under-the-table payments were the means by which this ordinance was changed. Because of a zoning variance, commercial development alone can take place. Without condoning such an illegal act, that act would lead to a socially useful result. The act is illegal and distributes the gains from such a change in ways that few would approve. Still, corruption in this case cannot be equated with underzoning.

The presence of zoning variances and corrupt public officials thus cannot be taken as evidence per se of underzoning. In some cases it might; in others it will not. Undoubtedly there is underzoning in most cities; its importance, however, is an open question.

THE SEEDS OF CHANGE?

An Expanding Scope of Action?

The growing national concern with environment has implications with respect to land-use controls. The concerns of the environmentalist are far-reaching and extend well beyond the boundaries of our cities. What we do in cities, however, has environmental implications, which, in turn, have implications with respect to urban development.

These concerns have been reinforced by recent legislation. Federal and state legislation enacted in the late 1960s and early 1970s provided for certain forms of environmental protection. At the federal level this includes the National Environmental Policy Act of 1969, the Clean Air Act Amendments of 1970, and the Federal Water Pollution Control Act of 1972. The state legislation varies considerably. It ranges from specifying the requirements for environmental impact analysis to legislation prescribing diverse forms of environmental land use planning laws.

Municipalities have also begun to show concern for environmental preservation, partly in response to the provisions of the federal environmental regulatory acts. This concern is manifested in the development of an environmental policy, which, in the case of larger cities, often includes setting up an environmental agency to provide advice and help implement the programs adopted.

What a growing concern with environment implies with respect to land use controls exercised by the city is by no means fully clear at this point. Environment is an all-encompassing term. Much of what we have been trying to accomplish for years through land use controls can be construed as a concern with environment. Some of our recent concern with environment can be considered as a growing disgruntlement with the outcomes of that effort. In other words, it could be argued that we are despoiling our environment by virtue of the way in which we use land, e.g., mixing up incompatible uses, permitting spotty development, failing to take into account the full range of the needs of the community in particular projects, and inadequate provision for spillovers in development projects. Certainly, this seems reflected in the fact that environment planning in cities has, in its initial stages, emphasized the inclusion of environmental impact statements as a part of urban development plans submitted to the appropriate public body for approval.

Our environmental concerns extend beyond a concern with traditional land use subject matter, however. We have become greatly concerned with the quality of our air and water, along with the preservation of areas of scenic beauty or ecological sensitivity. These are concerns that have land use implications; yet we really don't know very much about these implications. Air pollution is associated with population density, but the degree of the problem depends on such things as patterns of industry and transportation within the city.

In the main, the solutions we have proposed to deal with pollution problems have not had a great deal to do with land use patterns. They have involved such things as the installation of smog abatement equipment on automobiles and the requirement of the use of fuel oil with low sulfur content for use in heating and energy-producing plants. Alterations in the way in which we use land, however, could contribute to the resolution of the problem. The concentration of people and economic activity in a relatively small area puts much stress on the environment of that area. Dispersion of the population would provide an urban environment capable of assimilating a greater amount of effluents or wastes that are by-products of the production or consumption activities in the economy. It could be that the rearrangement of activity within the city, e.g., moving certain kinds of industry out on the urban periphery, would help moderate the problem. We are, however, only beginning to assemble knowledge of the links between the problem of pollution control and the way in which we use land.

As that knowledge grows, the scope of the action taken by public bodies concerned with controlling land use patterns will grow. This will be reflected in an extension of the criteria used in evaluating particular situations. Environmental impact studies made by urban developers will someday take into account in a meaningful way the quality of air and water, ecological sensitivity, and aesthetic criteria. When they do, the geographic jurisdiction of the governing bodies may be expanded considerably. We will be moving into areas of concern in which the geographic scope of the problem is larger. Industrial waste that gets into our atmosphere, for example, often spreads out over relatively large geographic areas, paying little attention to legal boundaries.

States have been moving vigorously into land-use planning activities recently, usually for the purpose of preserving areas of scenic beauty or ecological sensitivity, such as coastal areas, wetlands, mountain wilderness upland areas, and flood plains. These states may be providing the foundation for future land-use activities, whose scope will be significantly expanded.

It is probably premature to speculate about the nature and the location of the land-use controls that shall be applied in subsequent generations. While it is possible that the scope of what we do with these controls will be broadened substantially and their implementation will be concentrated in the hands of higher levels of government, this is by no means a certainty. The knowledge we have about ecology, assuming that it is adequate, has yet to be effectively integrated with our economic knowledge of urban land markets. We do not, in other words, have a good enough handle on how the problems of environment and land use are linked together to be able to assert with confidence that the solution to these problems will involve more or less land-use controls at higher or lower levels of government.

Auction Methods of Zoning

Zoning decisions made by political bodies, as noted above, can lead to both inefficient and inequitable results. The inefficiencies arise when the group being adversely affected is large in number and each member of the group perceives the potential loss of any change as being too small to devote much effort to influence the outcome. If this group is pitted against a single person or a few persons who see important gains coming out of the change, it will exert the less dominant influence and hence lose out. Change, in this case, may generate benefits that are less than the costs imposed on those whose interests are adversely affected, that is, it will generate inefficiencies. This will happen because, in terms of political pressure, the resistance to change is understated when the incidence of that change is widely diffused over a large group of people.

Suppose the benefits from change are greater than the costs. In this case, change would lead to efficient results. Yet, we might argue against the change on grounds of equity. To illustrate, suppose that when the service station moved into a residential neighborhood, it generated benefits that were in excess of the costs it imposed. Changing the zonal classifications to allow commercial use of the property in dispute makes sense on efficiency grounds. But it will also impose costs on some neighborhood residents. The lion's share of the benefits would flow to the station owners if the zoning board simply decreed this zoning change. Or some of the benefits could flow to zoning board members if payment was necessary to get them to recognize the efficiency implications of the change. In both cases, costs would be imposed on residents. Questions could therefore be raised about the equity of the distribution of the net gains when there is change that makes society better off. Since there will be gainers and losers, why isn't it possible to ease the pain of the losers by compensating them in some way? Indeed, considerations of equity strongly suggest that some form of compensation is warranted.

In view of these difficulties with zoning procedures as they are commonly practiced, other procedures are frequently discussed. Urban economists most frequently discuss the auction method of zoning. With such a method, competitive bidding among the affected parties would determine the outcome.

To illustrate how zonal classifications could be sold or auctioned off, consider the case of the investors who wish to locate a service station on property that is is in a residential neighborhood and is now classified as residential. The issue of whether this property can be rezoned commercial with the auction method will be determined by a competitive bidding process. This bidding process could involve the submission of sealed bids which indicate the amounts bidders are willing to pay for the change or are willing to pay for no change. Who are the bidders? They are presumably persons who will be affected by the change—the potential investors and the residents in close proximity to that property. Each person will cast a vote which will be, in effect, a dollar vote. If the total sum of the dollars voted in favor of the change exceed the amount in favor of no change, the residential property will be rezoned commercial. If the dollars in favor of no change exceed those in favor of change, the property will remain zoned as residential.

This decision rule is a simple one and should be an effective one with respect to insuring efficiency in land use. The process itself should deal with the problems arising when we rely on market forces or political bodies to assign land to alternative uses. The problem with markets is market externalities; the problem with political bodies is underrepresentation of some interested parties. Auctions deal with both these problems. Third parties who are affected by the transaction, no matter how small, can easily express their views about the change in recognizable and influential ways. If those views are such that the change would yield an efficient outcome, this should be reflected in the dollar votes they cast.

What now of the distribution of the benefits from the change, that is, the money accumulated through the submission of bids? Suppose the dollars in favor of change exceeded those voting for no change. The losing bidders would be returned their bids. The information contained in these bids, in turn, would provide a basis for compensating them for their losses. The necessary compensation would be measured as the amount of their bid to prevent the change. Thus, they would receive cash in an amount equal to twice the amount of their bids. The cash would be there to make these payments. Those who won submitted bids, the dollar sum of which was in excess of the amount bid by the losers. The difference between these two bids would cover the administrative costs of the auction and whatever else was deemed appropriate.

Suppose the sum of the change bids were greater than the bids for change. This would be taken to mean that there will be no change in the zonal classification of the property for some specified time. The bids of the losers in this case—the advocates of change—would be returned, as would the bids of the winners.

The equity aspects of such a distribution scheme—others are possible—are appealing. It provides a mechanism for compensating individuals who would suffer losses as a consequence of a zoning change. It would thus deal with an important aspect of the problem of resistance to change. Those who are going to be hurt by change resist it. If we can insure that they will be properly compensated for the damage inflicted upon them, resistance to change that improves the efficiency of the economic system would be reduced.

The auction method sounds so simple. If, in addition, it is as effective as it appears to be, you wonder why it is not in use. There are, of course, potential problems with its use. One is the possibility of gambling that could distort outcomes. Since no change decision would result in doubling the amount bid, there is the possibility that there will be no change bids by some who have no connection with the change whatsoever, simply because of the potentially attractive pay-off. If gambling of the sort becomes important, it could forestall any change, be it good or bad. This could be a serious problem. It is also a problem that can be overcome. In the most hotly contested zoning decisions, the ones where auctions might contribute to the resolution of the problem, the protagonists are readily identifiable and in close proximity to the property being contested. The bids by gamblers could therefore be controlled by restricting those who can make bids on the basis of proximity to the property under consideration.

There are other potential problems with equally as effective potential solutions. That we do not use some kind of auction in zoning decisions seems more a consequence of the normal obstacles to the adoption of something that stands as a radical departure from current practice. The sheer volume of rezoning decisions would preclude its use in all cases. But there are some important zoning decisions, the parties to which exert unequal influence on the political decision-making process and decisions of which involve a clearly defined wealth conflict that might be better arbitrated by use of an auction process. At least, there are reasons to believe that the auction method has considerable promise compared with what we have now.

REFERENCES

*Clawson, M., and Hall, P. *Planning and Urban Growing*. Baltimore: The Johns Hopkins University Press, 1973.

——————————. "Why Not Sell Zoning? (Legally That Is)." *Cry California* (Winter, 1966–67): 9–39.

Coase, R. H. "The Problem of Social Cost." *Journal of Law and Economics*. 3 (1960): 1–44.

*Davis, O. A. "Economic Elements in Municipal Zoning Decisions." *Land Economics*. 39 (1963): 375–86.

National Commission on Urban Problems. *Building the American City*, Washington, D.C.: U.S. Government Printing Office, 1968.

*Ohls, J. C., and Weisberg, R. C. "The Effect of Zoning on Land Values." *Journal of Urban Economics*. 1 (1974): 428–44.

Scott, M. *American City Planning*. Berkeley: University of California Press, 1969.

Siegan, B. H. "Nonzoning in Houston." *Journal of Law and Economics*. 8 (1970): 71–147.

---

* This chapter draws heavily from the writings of Clawson, Davis, and Ohls.

15

Models of City Growth

SUMMARY

Macroeconomic modelling and forecasting of metropolitan areas means a concern with economic base and input-output models, as well as econometric models and models that revolve around some technique of allocating national totals to urban regions.

Economic base models are the most frequently used method of forecasting city growth. Base models range from naive base-service formulations to regression models that structure the economy in ways that take the interindustry segment of the economy into account.

Three sets of problems are encountered when making forecasts with an economic base model. First there is the problem of identifying the export sector of the economy. Some firms in an urban community both export and sell in the local market, and there is no easy way to distinguish between their exports and local sales.

The second problem stems from the need to make an independent forecast of the city's economic base. "Shift and share" techniques are often used because with their use we can take advantage of available nationwide industry forecasts. In the short-run, shift and share provides reasonably good results; over the long-run, it is less satisfactory.

The third problem is that the urban base multiplier, which is used as a means of calculating the impact of exports on the nonbasic sector of the economy, tends to be unstable.

The ad hoc adjustments forecasters frequently make in the base multiplier are best made with knowledge of the interindustry structure of the city that comes with input-output information. We can, in fact, derive forecasting models from an input-output transaction table. Input-output forecasting models suffer from many of the problems of economic base, including the requirement of an independent forecast of exports and the potential instability of the internal structure of the model.

Econometric model building as a means of studying and forecasting the growth of an urban region is only in its infancy. Nevertheless, there have been efforts to build econometric models of the economy of some of our larger metropolitan areas and to use these models as a means of forecasting economic growth.

Urban econometric models are not without problems, the most severe of which are data problems. Still, these models are looked upon as having potentially productive applications in forecasting macroeconomic change in urban areas.

Finally, there are the models that look at sources of growth first as they influence the national economy. Then these national figures are allocated among the regions or urban areas of the nation according to techniques that emphasize either demand or supply factors.

If we use the modelling in the sense of a systematic investigation, modelling and forecasting economic aggregates of cities such as employment and income go back a few years. The earlier efforts stemmed largely from forecasting needs, particularly by city planners and federal government officials concerned with implementing urban housing programs. The emphasis in these earlier modelling efforts was largely on notions of economic base, the applications were relatively simple, and the results, more often than not, were off target. Economic base notions nevertheless persist and are currently found at the heart of many regional or urban economic projections.

Disenchantment with the outcome of base studies, however, leads the city economic model builder in different directions. Input-output extensions of the economic base model are one direction. The development of regional econometric models patterned after the national models is another. The latter, in particular, have become important in recent years and at this point are seen by some as the wave of the future as far as forecasting economic magnitudes in cities is concerned. We have had, on the other hand, very little success to date in constructing supply-oriented models of city growth.

These few remarks suggest that a concern with macroeconomic modelling and forecasting of urban or metropolitan areas is a concern with applications of the notions of economic base and input-output discussed in chapter 4 and the applications of econometric model building techniques that have emerged in our studies of the national economy. Forecasting city growth can also be approached from a national perspective.

ECONOMIC BASE MODELS

The Question of Data

Economic base, as it was discussed earlier, is a crucial part of an economic process that generates income and output in an urban community. It would seem, therefore, that the focus in economic base studies and predictions should be on measures of aggregate income or output. Most economic base models, however, use employment as the unit of measurement. The primary reason is that employment figures are readily available. Income data, when we go below the state level, are either incomplete or available only for the nation's larger metropolitan areas with a very long time lag. State employment agencies, as well as the nation's Department of Labor, make wage and salary data available for employers covered by unemployment insurance laws on a timely basis. These data, however, exclude important components of income, such as property and proprietors income.

Suppose employment data are used in that the parameters and variables of the model are expressed in terms of employment, as are the forecasts. The use of employment data could cause problems in several ways. One problem stems from the fact that there are often geographic wage differences within the same industry. For example, retail employees probably make more in Detroit or New York than they do in Birmingham, Alabama. The expansionary effects of adding a retail employee to Detroit then differs from that in Birmingham. Second, by using employment data, we fail to reckon with changes in the physical productivity of the worker. Productivity increases do occur and can generate expansionary effects which will not be accounted for when employment is the unit of measurement in an economic base model.

As a practical matter, in making forecasts, we work with the tools and data that are at hand. Since employment data are the easiest to access when making economic forecasts of cities, they are most often used. Their use is not entirely a matter of availability, however. Employment data are broken down in ways that facilitate segregating the economy into its base and nonbasic components. For reasons that will be touched on shortly, this is a matter of importance when using an economic base framework in making a forecast. Employment numbers, however, do exclude elements in the economy that have impact on its growth path. Consequently, care must be taken in the interpretation of forecasts in which they are used as the unit of measurement.

Earlier Models: The Base-Service Ratio

Earlier forecasting applications of the notion of economic base focused on the base-service ratio. The local economy, according to economic base, is structured into basic and nonbasic or service components. The basic component is activity, the output of which is exported. Nonbasic or service output is that consumed by local residents.

Suppose by working with employment data for some community, it is possible to find out how many people work in basic industries and how many work in service industries. Assume total employment of 100,000, of which 25,000 is basic and 75,000 is nonbasic or service. With this information it is possible to calculate a basic service employment ratio and what has come to be called the *urban base employment multiplier*.

The base-service ratio is defined as

$$\frac{E_s}{E_b} \tag{15.1}$$

where E_s is service or nonbasic employment and E_b is basic employment. The urban base multiplier is defined as

$$\frac{E_t}{E_b} \tag{15.2}$$

where E_t is total employment. So defined, the base-service employment ratio for our hypothetical community is

$$\frac{75,000}{25,000} = 3$$

The urban base employment multiplier is

$$\frac{100,000}{25,000} = 4$$

In fact, both calculations figured prominently in many economic projections made of particular cities or metropolitan areas a few years back. Employment data were readily available. All that needed to be done was to separate these data into their basic and nonbasic components and then calculate the base-service or urban base multiplier.

These two ratios or multipliers can be used in a simple and straightforward way of making forecasts of employment. Take metropolitan Cincinnati, by way of illustration. Total employment in Cincinnati in 1970 was approximately 525,000, of which roughly 175,000 were in basic industries. This implies a base-service ratio of two and an urban base multiplier of three.

Suppose we were given a forecast indicating employment in the city's basic industries would be 210,000 in 1980. A total employment forecast would be derived in one of the following two ways:

I

a. Base-Service Ratio $= \dfrac{\text{Nonbasic Employment}_{1980}}{\text{Basic Employment}_{1980}}$

    Base-Service Ratio $= 2$
    Basic Employment$_{1980}$ $= 210,000$
    Non-Basic Employment$_{1980} = E_s$

b. $2 = \dfrac{E_s}{210,000}$

    $E_s = 210,000 \times 2$
    $E_s = 420,000$

c. Total Employment$_{1980}$ = Base Employment$_{1980}$ + Nonbasic Employment$_{1980}$
    Total Employment$_{1980}$ = 210,000 + 420,000 = 630,000

II

a. Urban Base Multiplier $= \dfrac{\text{Total Employment}_{1980}}{\text{Basic Employment}_{1980}}$

    Urban Base Multiplier $= 3$
    Basic Employment$_{1980}$ $= 210,000$
    Total Employment$_{1980}$ $= E_t$

b. $3 = \dfrac{E_t}{210,000}$

    $E_t = 210,000 \times 3$
    Total Employment$_{1980}$ = 630,000

If basic employment reaches 210,000 and the urban base multiplier is stable, total employment in metropolitan Cincinnati should be 630,000, or it should increase by 20 percent between 1970 and 1980.

Economic Base: More Recent Versions

Recent models of economic base often take the form of a regression equation or systems of regression equations. Base theory, in effect, postulates a positive causal relationship between basic employment and total employment. The causation runs from basic employment to total employment. Suppose this relationship were adequately described by the equation for a straight line, that is

$$y = a + bx \tag{15.3}$$

y is the dependent variable in this equation; x is the independent variable. Causation, in other words, runs from x to y. Given this interpretation of equation 15.3, we can substitute E_t (total employment) for y and E_b (basic employment) for x and get

$$E_t = a + bE_b \tag{15.4}$$

Given actual data for E_t and E_b over some finite time interval, we can estimate the parameters of this equation through regression analysis; that is, we can estimate the values of a and b.

Doing this for metropolitan Cincinnati, we arrive at the following:

$$E_t = 95,000 + 2.5 \ E_b$$

If we suppose that base employment in Cincinnati in 1970 is 175,000, according to this equation, total employment will be 532,500.

$$E_t = 95,000 + 2.5 \ (175,000)$$
$$E_t = 532,500$$

All this is easy to see. It is also easy to see how this equation can be used to make forecasts. If we have a forecast of basic employment (E_b), it can be fed into this equation and the outcome will be forecast of total employment (E_t). Suppose we take the 210,000 figure above as a forecast of basic employment in metropolitan Cincinnati in 1980. Plugging this figure into the equation yields a total employment figure of 620,000 or

$$E_t = 95,000 + 2.5 \ (210,000)$$
$$E_t = 620,000$$

There is, of course, a strong similarity between the ratio approach set forth in equations 15.1 and 15.2 and the regression approach in equation 15.4. Activity in the basic sector must be forecast independently. It is an input that is fed into the model. Both models then apply a multiplier to that figure to arrive at the forecast. The difference is in the form this multiplier takes. In one case, it is simply a coefficient; in the other, it is a coefficient plus a constant term, which is added to the product of the multiplying operation.

Another dimension can be added to the structure of the economy the base model represents by taking into account the fact that sales to local customers include sales of both final and intermediate products. The economy can now be represented in the following way:

$$E_t = E_b + E_{sf} + E_{si} \qquad (15.5)$$

where E_{sf} is employment generated by firms producing final products which are sold to local residents and E_{si} is employment generated by the sale of intermediate products to local business firms.

What now of the determinants of E_b, E_{sf}, E_{si}? Disaggregation is possible at this point. Specifically, we can break these three major groups down into industry components. For example, we could break exports down by industries that sell most of their output to government, e.g., aerospace, and all other. Employment generated by the production and sale of final goods to local residents might be broken down into a number of groups, including retail trade and services. The possibilities with respect to the intermediate goods groups are numerous.

Why would we choose to disaggregate in this way? If the dominant factors that influence particular industries vary, as they seem to, disaggregating industry into more homogeneous groups will bring substantial benefits. With disaggregation, we have a much better chance of linking the determinants to the employment being generated. These links might be established in a number of ways, including the use of regression analysis involving equations such as

$$\bullet \quad E_i = a + bX \qquad (15.6)$$

where E_i is the employment generated by the ith industry and X is the major determinant of the employment. The ith industry might be retailing, for example, and X might be total employment taken as a proxy for household income.

Since the employment generated in any one industry could be taken as a major determinant of the employment of another, there is likely to be interdependence in the system of equations constructed. This means some kind of simultaneous solution procedure will be necessary to estimate the coefficients of these equations. We now begin to move into the terrain of econometric model building. It is possible, however, to move in this direction in ways that emphasize economic base notions and the outcome can still be construed as an economic base model. If this model, in turn, is structured in a certain way, it can be thought of as a forecasting model.

Problems in Making Forecasts with Economic Base Models

Identifying the Economic Base   To make forecasts with an economic base model requires that the economy be sectored into its basic and nonbasic components. This is more difficult than it seems at first glance. From simple inspection of the classifications of industry, it is by no means evident which industries export and which ones sell to local residents. One complication is that many firms both export and sell to local residents. There are also many industries that include firms that export and firms that sell locally. This latter problem can be addressed in part by working with more disaggregated industry data. For example, instead of working with the category manufacturing, we might be better served by breaking down the manufacturing sector into certain components, such as primary metals and food processing. To the extent that firms in the primary metals group export their output and the firms in the food processing group sell theirs locally, disaggregation will deal with the problem. Yet, it is unlikely that all firms in the food processing industry will sell their output in the local market. Firms that both export and sell locally are the most important part of this problem, and they are not effectively dealt with by industry disaggregation.

A frequent approach to the problem of identifying the base involves the use of a segregation principle or technique. The most important of these is the location quotient.

The *location quotient* is defined as the ratio between the proportion of the city's total employment in a specific industry and the proportion of the nation's employment in that industry. Symbolically, the location quotient is

$$L_{qi} = \frac{\dfrac{cE_i}{cE_t}}{\dfrac{nE_i}{nE_t}} \tag{15.7}$$

where L_{qi} is the location quotient of the ith industry, cE_i is the employment generated by the ith industry in the city, cE_t is total employment in the city, nE_i is the employment generated by the ith industry nationwide, and nE_t is total employment in the nation.

Just what kind of information do we get from a location quotient? Suppose we calculate a location quotient for the primary metals industry located in greater Cleveland and find it takes on a value in excess of 1. This implies the primary metals industry is more important in Cleveland than it is in the nation as a whole. If we assume consumer tastes and the conditions of production in this industry are the same all over, a coefficient in excess of 1 implies that this industry in its Cleveland location exports some, much, or perhaps even all of its output. We can, in fact, derive formulas from equation 15.7 which allow us to calculate the export employment of this industry. By doing this for all industries, we get an estimate of total export employment.

How reasonable will this example be? In many instances, it could be off target. The problem is the regional or metropolitan area differences in consumer tastes and the conditions of production. In terms of location quotients, metropolitan San Francisco may show up to be an exporter of certain kinds of services, e.g., music. In fact, it exports very little of these services. The people of San Francisco apparently love their music and are more than willing to consume all that is produced locally. As a consequence, they consume a greater than average amount of music. A coefficient that evaluated the exports of this industry in this community in terms of how it compares with the national average will provide misleading information.

A recognition of this problem has given rise to modifications of the calculating procedures. Rather than comparing a particular city or metropolitan area to the nation, attempts have been made to compare that city with other urban areas that are similar with respect to size, industrial composition, consumer tastes, etc. It is assumed that the one in this group that has the smallest share of production of a given product is neither an importer nor an exporter. Given this assumption, the share of that city or metropolitan area is interpreted as a "minimum" requirement. Any employment above this minimum requirement is considered as exports.

The minimum requirements approach stands as an improvement over the location quotient. How much the estimates of exports are improved with the use of this technique is another question. It is one thing to say that comparisons should be made between cities that are similar with respect to size, industrial composition, and consumer tastes. It is quite another to be able to group cities in this way.

Survey research techniques have also been applied as means of generating information which provides the basis for classifying economic activity in the city with more precision. If we need to know how much output firms sell locally and how much they export, what could be simpler than to ask them? This has been done, but with only limited success. The problems encountered are twofold. One has to do with the problems that some firms, such as retail establishments, have in determining whether they are selling to local residents or someone who lives outside the city. The second has to do with "indirect" exports, the intermediate sale by local firms to other local firms that incorporate these products into commodities that are exported. Simply asking firms about the geographic destination of their sales will not uncover these sales. There are ways of generating this kind of information through survey research techniques, but to do so substantially raises the costs of the survey.

At this point, there is no completely satisfactory and relatively inexpensive way of determining with precision the economic base of a metropolitan community. In many instances, however, we can get a reasonable approximation of that base without incurring too much expense.

Forecasting the Economic Base   Suppose we were able to segment the economy into its basic and nonbasic components. We could then get an empirical estimate of the urban base multiplier, which is necessary for making forecasts. To use the urban base multiplier, however, we must forecast basic employment. The base is external or exogenous to the model; that is, it is not determined by the internal mechanism that constitutes the model. It has to be fed into the model independently. This creates problems.

We are not without methods of forecasting the economic base. The one most frequently used is called "shift and share." This technique is designed to take advantage of the nationwide industry forecasts that are made. Our interest in industry forecasting is a long-standing one, and some fairly sophisticated and refined analytical techniques have been developed recently, e.g., input-output, which have greatly improved our industry forecasts.

Shift and share analysis is a way of both describing and forecasting long-term change in such macro variables as income and employment for subnational areas such as Census regions, states, counties, and urban areas. As a descriptive device, the shift and share framework partitions macro change in income or employment into three components, namely, 1) that which stems from general growth in the economy, 2) that which stems from the particular industrial mix of the regional economy, and 3) that which stems from the competitive advantage or disadvantage of an urban region. One and two are often combined so that shift and share discussions are typically focused on the industry mix and competitive components of economic growth.

Consider employment growth in metropolitan area A. Suppose employment grew 100,000 over the past five years. This growth had to be reflected in some industries in the area. Perhaps it was reflected in all industries. Suppose we made industry-by-industry calculations and found the employment growth in each industry. We could also make the same calculations for the same set of industries considered nationally. With this information, along with shift and share notions, we could begin to make some statements about the "sources" of growth in A.

If industry X grows nationally and X has production facilities in A, X should grow in A, all other things being equal. What happens in A then is seen to depend upon the kind of industries A has. If the industry composition of A exactly matches that of the nation, the growth in A should match that of the nation, all other things being equal. If A has fast-growing industries, its growth rates should be in excess of that of the nation, all other things being equal. If, on the other hand, A has slow-growing industries, its growth rate should be less than that of the nation, all other things being equal.

The growth that stems from the industry composition of A is, of course, the industry mix component of growth. Formal calculations of that component are possible, and it can be easily projected if we have industry forecasts for the nation. All that has to be done to make such a forecast is to apply A's share of particular industries to the income or employment of those industries anticipated at some future date. If we sum up these results, we have a forecast of industry growth in A that can be said to reflect its industry mix.

How good will this forecast be? It would be a good one if all other things remained constant. It is at this point that the competitive element comes into play. The share of X that A has may change. A's competitive advantage with respect to producing X may improve or deteriorate.

This is important. A, for example, could be the site of much industry that was mature and slow-growing nationally, which suggests A will be a slow-growing metropolitan community in the future. But it is also possible for A to develop a competitive advantage with respect to those industries. If so, its share of production might increase. In fact, A could grow rapidly because of a shift of its share of certain industries. Or it could be the reverse—A grows slowly because it loses industry that is growing rapidly nationally.

These are matters that in shift and share analysis are considered to be a part of the competitive element of growth. They are also matters the earlier discussion of location theory in chapter 3 indicated to be important. While the fixed site character of plant and equipment imparts some locational stability to industry, that industry grows and must replace some of its used plant and equipment from time to time gives rise to the possibility of locational shifts. Our history, indeed, suggests that many firms take advantage of this possibility in that industry shares of particular urban regions change or shift over time. When this happens, it complicates the use of a shift and share framework in attempting to forecast the exports of an urban region. If the competitive element were stable, projecting basic income or employment could be done easily in the manner described above.

If the competitive position of metropolitan areas changes over time, however, this must be taken into account.

Studies that have been made of both the logic and the performance of shift and share frameworks as forecasting devices suggest there are obstacles to dealing effectively with the competitive component. Not only is it not stable over long periods of time, but the way in which it moves about does not appear to be associated with the factors generally believed to determine the competitive position of an urban region. Shift and share has been used with success when the concern is with aggregate regional change over relatively short periods of time, e.g., five years or so. If the concern is with longer time periods, e.g., ten years or more, that success diminishes. It represents a way of using certain sets of information, i.e., industry forecasts, that usually lead to results that are better than those that come from the use of some kind of naive extrapolation technique. When we have a lengthy time horizon, however, these results do not measure up to the absolute standards of accuracy most decision makers apply.

The Instability of the Urban Base Multiplier   Suppose the obstacles of identifying and forecasting the economic base were resolved. Problems would still remain. The forecast procedure entails applying the urban base multiplier to the forecast of the community's economic base. The multiplier is the internal or endogenous mechanism of the model. Its application in a forecasting context—as has been done above—assumes stability in that multiplying coefficient. We estimate the urban base multiplier on the basis of historical data and then project that estimate into the future as a part of the forecasting procedure. It is because we believe this relationship—the multiplier—is stable that we use economic base models in making forecasts of city growth. The problem is that this multiplier may not be very stable.

There is evidence that indicates urban base multipliers are not stable over long periods of time, or even in short time periods, in some cases. This evidence is believable in part because there are good reasons for expecting them to change, particularly in communities that experience sustained economic growth over extended periods of time. Long periods of sustained growth imply growing markets. Such markets tend to jump to levels that support certain kinds of activity which they previously did not. Growth, for example, could ultimately lead to a population large enough to support a symphony, major league baseball team, or specialty clothing shops. This process is often called *import substitution* and, as it occurs in most cities, the imports most frequently substituted for are intermediate goods. This is, in no small measure, the reason for the interest of many urban economists in input-output analysis, since the input-output framework concentrates heavily on the purchase and sale of intermediate goods.

If our concern is with accurate forecasts, adjustments will probably have to be made to the urban base multipliers used in the forecast. These adjustments, in turn, will have to be done on the basis of the best judgment of the forecaster, which implies that forecasting city growth with the aid of an economic base model is more of an art than a science. But this holds true for economic forecasting in general.

INPUT-OUTPUT MODELS

Input-output models developed to study aggregate economic change are much like economic base models in some respects. They differ sharply in others. The base model can be capsulized in the following equation:

$$Y = \frac{1}{(1 - b) + m} \, \overline{X} \qquad\qquad (15.8)$$

where Y is income, $1/(1 - b) + m$, is the urban base multiplier, and $\overline{X}$ is exports and is taken to be external or exogenous to the model.

An input-output model can be expressed in an equation that has much the same structure, that is

$$O = \frac{1}{1 - A} \, \overline{Y} \qquad\qquad (15.9)$$

where O is the sum of the output or sales of all industries and $\overline{Y}$ is the sum of the final output or income generated by all industries. $1/(1 - A)$ requires more explanation. Technically, it is a set of coefficients, arranged in an orderly manner in a matrix, where each vertical array or column describes the technical structure of the particular industry to which the column refers. These coefficients are, of course, the input-output coefficients discussed earlier—see Table 4.2. They tell us something about the purchases per dollar of sales of the ith industry from the jth industry. The term A refers to Table 4.2; it is simply a shorthand expression of it.

Where does $1/(1 - A)$ come from? It is derived from the equation

$$O - AO = \overline{Y} \qquad\qquad (15.10)$$

which simply asserts that total output (O), less intermediate goods production (AO), is equal to final output or income $(\overline{Y})$. It will be recalled from chapter 4 that, with information on total sales of all industries and a matrix of input-output coefficients, we can calculate intermediate production. By factoring equation 15.10 and solving for O, we get

$$O(1 - A) = \overline{Y} \qquad\qquad (15.11)$$

or

$$O = \frac{1}{1 - A} \, \overline{Y} \qquad\qquad (15.12)$$

It is clear from a simple visual comparison of equations 15.8 and 15.9 that there are structural similarities. The focus is on some economic activity (Y, O) which is considered to be a function of a value or set of values assigned to the exogenous or independent variable $(\overline{X}, \overline{Y})$. Furthermore, there is a multiplier in each $(1/(1 - b) + m, 1/(1 - A))$.

The differences surface when we interpret these equations in light of the earlier discussions of both base theory and input-output analysis. Economic base theory implies causation from the base $(\overline{X})$ to total income $(\overline{Y})$. Input-output, on the other hand, is not so much concerned with causation, but consistency and simultaneity of relationship. In other words, the concern is with what elements in O, given $1/(1 - A)$, are consistent with the elements given in $\overline{Y}$.

The input-output model clearly brings into the foreground the importance of interdependence in the economy, something that is suppressed in the economic base model. Yet, input-output models are much less comprehensive in another sense. In fact, as expressed in equation 15.9, it is totally devoid in any way of dealing with the question of income generation within an urban community. What this equation says is that if you give us your estimate of total urban income broken down by relevant industry categories, we can tell you what set of industry outputs are consistent with those income figures. The internal or endogenous mechanism in the input-output model is focused on intermediate goods sales and purchases. In this form, the external or exogenous element is the thing we want to forecast.

Stated in this way, the task of those who wish to build a forecasting model using an input-output framework is clear. The endogenous mechanism of that model must be extended to comprehend additional elements of reality. In input-output terminology, this says that the processing sector must be closed with respect to certain elements in the final demand sector.

Recall briefly the format of an input-output transaction table—see Table 4.1. The task in terms of this table is to transfer something from that part denoted as the final demand sector to that part indicated as the interindustry or processing sector. What might this be?

Economic base theory usually comes into play at this point. Suppose we assume exports are the exogenous element in this model; that is, they are the driving force that underlies any growth that might take place in this community. When this assumption is made, the columns designating households, business, and local government are moved into the processing sector. When this happens, the model is said to be closed with respect to these sectors. Final demand is now shown to consist only of exports and the processing sector now including households, business, and local government, in addition to the industry component of the economy.

The recalculation of the input-output coefficients from this revised transactions table will yield a table of coefficients that differ from those in Table 4.2. The reasons for this are clear enough. The internal structure of the model now includes the "induced" effects of industry sales. Prior to closing the processing sector with respect to households, local business, and local government, one dollar's worth of sales to a final demand sector had impact on the processing sector only to the extent that intermediate goods were used in production. Other inputs, such as labor and capital, were obviously a part of the production process, but we had no need to worry about them in calculating technical coefficients because they were not included as a part of the processing sector. By including households and local government and local business in this sector, this no longer holds. The impact of and payment to labor and capital are now a part of the processing sector, which means that what the laborer and capitalist do with the income they earn feeds back into the sales and purchases of the industry in the community. The spending of that income, in effect, induces further increases in the industrial output of the community. The inclusion of these induced effects thus implies that the output requirements of the ith industry from the jth industry for each dollar's worth of its exports will be higher. In calculating the industry effects of one dollar's worth of sales to an exogenous sector we must now not only take into account the output requirements that stem from the fact that intermediate goods are used in production, but also the output requirements that result from local sales of final goods to households, businesses, and government because of the income generated by that initial sale.

The derivation of a forecasting model from the basic input-output transactions table can be accomplished in several ways. The fundamental elements in any such model, however, are generally the same.

If we rely on economic base notions in structuring the model, those elements might look something like

$$X_i = \sum_{i=1}^{n} r_{ij} X_j + Y_i \qquad i = 1, \ldots . n \qquad (15.13)$$

where X_i represents total output of the ith industry, $r_{ij} X_j$ is the output of the ith industry which goes to the jth industry, and Y_i is the output of the ith industry which goes to the final demand sectors.

This equation indicates a major task in building an input-output forecasting model is to identify the interindustry and final demand sectors in the economy. If we accept the notions of economic base that postulate exports as the driving force in the economy, the final demand sector in the model will be exports or

$$Y_i = \sum_{p=1}^{m} (Y^p i) \qquad \begin{matrix} i = 1, \ldots . n \\ p = 1, \ldots . m \end{matrix} \qquad (15.14)$$

where Y_i is the output of the ith industry which goes to the final demand sector and (Y^{pi}) is the pth market to which that output goes. These markets are export markets and to talk of the pth market is to distinguish markets such as sales to the federal government, sales to certain other regions, etc. The output of the industries that export to these markets must be forecast independently.

After these forecasts are made, the total output of the remaining sectors are forecast as follows

$$X = {}^t \frac{1}{{}_i 1 - A} Y p_{it} \qquad \begin{matrix} i = 1, \ldots n \\ p = 1, \ldots m \end{matrix} \qquad (15.15)$$

where the superscript t denotes the forecast year. This equation says, in effect, that the forecasts of exports must be fed into a computer program that can solve for the output requirements of industry in this community given this level of exports.

This solution would include a forecast of final output as well as a battery of forecasts of components of the economy, including outputs of those industries that are a part of the processing sector of the model. Obviously, the forecasts of an input-output model are rich in the details they provide about future movements in the economy. The input-output forecasting model is also a very expensive solution to the forecasting problem, the biggest part of which stems from generating the numbers that make up the input-output transactions table. Since there are no quick and easy ways of accumulating sales and purchases data, the construction of an input-output transactions table is expensive.

Even if costs are no problem, input-output analysis may still be impractical in that costs still outweigh the benefits they provide to those who use it. The real benefits from input-output lie in the detail it provides about the industry structure of the community. In smaller communities, this is not likely to be of much value. There isn't much economic structure in a small city, simply because its size does not justify much local production. The collection of interindustry sales and purchases data in these circumstances will not yield very much useful information.

Suppose we are concerned with large metropolitan areas, where the economic structure warrants the collection of interindustry facts. There are still obstacles to overcome in converting these facts into a model that will forecast major economic aggregates. Input-output, as a framework for making regional forecasts of income and employment, suffers from many of the same shortcomings as does economic base. In its implementation to date, for example, the driving force is the export sector in the economy. The input-output forecasting model is thus a variant of an economic base model and hence is subject to many of the problems touched upon in the discussion of economic base models. While a properly constructed input-output table will generate information that should allow us to identify those industries that export, the sales of those industries have to be forecast independently. Forecasting exports was indicated above in the discussion of economic base to be a difficult task. It is no less so when it is a requirement associated with forecasting with an input-output model.

The problem of instability in the multiplier mechanism of the model is also just as real with input-output as it is with economic base. Input-output forecasting models, as they have been developed to date, are static representations of the economy. Hence, they are like economic base models in the sense that they cannot handle directly such important dynamic possibilities as technical change, import substitution, and relative price changes. All these things can affect the basic structure of the economy and its response to change coming through an external or exogenous force like exports. If the basic structure of the economy changes as it grows, this will not be captured in $1/(1-A)$ unless there is some ad hoc provision made for it by those using the model to make forecasts.

It is in this exercise of judgment that input-output does provide an advantage over economic base. The ability to make ad hoc adjustments in the internal mechanism to reflect anticipated structural changes in the economy is an important matter, which can be more effectively dealt with when input-output information is at hand. Knowledge of the interindustry structure of an urban region is knowledge that can help in attempting to decide judgmentally how much import substitution is likely to occur. What might be produced locally that is now imported obviously depends on what is not being produced locally and hence is being imported. Knowledge of local industry structure means knowledge of the gaps where import substitution can occur. The local impact of technical change and change in relative prices can also be evaluated more effectively with knowledge of the structure of the economy which an input-output table provides.

ECONOMETRIC FORECASTING MODELS

Econometrics is an amalgamation of economic theory, mathematics, and statistics. It emerged as a discipline as economists sought to subject their theories to more rigorous tests. Its role in economics accelerated dramatically with the coming of the computer. Calculations could now be made that were never dreamed of just a short while ago. Computer modelling became an important research tool, and some of the models developed were forecasting models.

Most computer-oriented econometric modelling building concerned with forecasting has focused on forecasting national aggregates such as national income, gross national product, and total employment. More recently, econometricians have turned their attention to regional or urban forecasting problems and have developed regional econometric models, primarily for states. Econometric models of metropolitan areas, however, are now beginning to surface and are likely to become an increasingly important way of addressing the problem of forecasting urban income and employment.

Econometric Forecasting Models: The General Structure

The initial task in constructing an econometric model is to construct a mathematical model that replicates the salient aspects of that part of the economic world being studied. Suppose our concern is with national income or output. Traditional macroeconomic theory provides a basis for constructing a model that replicates a system generating the nation's income.

As noted in chapter 4, this theory indicates income to be determined by aggregate demand or spending. In a world in which there is no government or contacts with the rest of the world, this relationship is indicated by

$$Y = C + I \qquad (15.16)$$

where Y is national income, C is consumption spending, and I is investment spending.

The theory postulates that consumption (C) is determined by income (Y) or in a very simplified form,

$$C = bY \qquad (15.17)$$

If we take investment to be determined by forces outside the economic system represented by this model then

$$I = \bar{I} \qquad (15.18)$$

where $\bar{I}$ is given.

This model, as shown in chapter 4, can be solved for Y or

$$Y = C + I \qquad (15.19)$$

$$C = bY \qquad (15.20)$$

$$I = \bar{I} \qquad (15.21)$$

$$Y = bY + \bar{I} \qquad (15.22)$$

$$Y - bY = \overline{I} \tag{15.23}$$

$$Y(1 - b) = \overline{I} \tag{15.24}$$

$$Y = \frac{1}{1 - b}\overline{I} \tag{15.25}$$

Equation 15.25 can be construed as a forecasting equation. If we have an estimate of b, we can calculate the multiplier $1/(1 - b)$. Given the multiplier and independent forecasts of investment, Y can be forecast. That forecast, however, is not likely to be very good. Too much of the economy that has bearing on income has been left out. The model must be extended to account for these additional variables. The model should also incorporate a lag structure that adequately takes into account the fact that the economy does not react instantaneously to change.

The additional variables should incorporate the other elements of demand, namely, government $(G - T)$ and the rest of the world or net exports $(X - M)$, supply factors such as employment (E), capital (K), and technology (t), and financial factors such as money demand (M_d) and money supply (M_s). The model should also include price variables such as product prices (p), interest rates (i), and wage rates (w), as well as capacity and utilization measures like labor force (L) and unemployment (Un).

The basic structure of a model which takes these additional things into account might look as follows:

$$C = f(Y, i) \tag{15.26}$$

$$I = f(Y, i) \tag{15.27}$$

$$C + I + (G - T) + (X - M) = Y \tag{15.28}$$

$$Y = f(E, K, t) \tag{15.29}$$

$$\frac{\Delta Y}{\Delta E} = \frac{w}{p} \text{ or } p = \frac{w}{\dfrac{\Delta Y}{\Delta E}} \tag{15.30}$$

$$\Delta w = f(\Delta p, Un) \tag{15.31}$$

$$M_s = M_d = f(Y, p, i) \tag{15.32}$$

$$Un = L - E \tag{15.33}$$

This model links spending to income and financial variables. It links income or output to labor and capital inputs and the state of technology. It relates money demand to income, prices, and the interest rate and has prices with determinants that have been derived from relationships that are a part of economic theory.

This model is important because it has been the basis for most large-scale econometric models that have been built. It has been expanded to incorporate additional variables and more complicated lag structures. The end result is a system of equations that have parameters, e.g., $1/(1 - b)$ in the equation $Y = 1/(1 - b)\overline{I}$ that must be estimated. The problems of estimation are both important and difficult. But estimates are made and forecasting models are derived. To use these models, however, we must have a method of calculating a solution—the solution algorithm. Such algorithms are available. Given the algorithm, the forecast can be made. To do so, values of the external or exogenous variables in the model, e.g., $\bar{I}$ in $Y = 1\,(1 - b)\,\bar{I}$, must be specified and fed into the program solving the model for the values of its internal or endogenous variables, e.g., Y in $Y = 1/(1 - b)\,\bar{I}$, over the forecast period.

The problems encountered in developing and implementing an econometric model are difficult, and in some instances, unresolved. Because of this, the use of econometric models as a means of making forecasts does not remove the element of personal judgment from the forecast. Moreover, the forecasting record of these models has been something less than spectacular, since we began to use them in a serious way a little over ten years ago. But that record has been improving. Moreover, a carefully constructed econometric model represents the best way devised to date to account systematically for the many variables we believe to have bearing on what happens to the national economy.

Econometric Models of Regions and Urban Areas

The growth in regional econometric model building, as noted above, was related to the progress made in the development of econometric models concerned with the national economy. This, in turn, is an outgrowth of the fact that most urban and regional economists hold to the belief that what happens outside a region has important bearing on what happens within—economic base theory. Since what is happening outside is ordinarily capsulized reasonably well in what is happening within the national economy, what better way to make a regional forecast than to use as the driving force in the region the output from a model that forecasts the national economy. As it turns out, this is a model that forecasts a number of important component parts of the national economy, such as housing, plant and equipment, and interest rates. This could be activity that is more directly related to what happens in a region—plant and equipment spending, for example, as it has bearing on industrial output in the state of Ohio.

This belief in the importance of what goes on outside the economy has given rise to a generation of what are sometimes called *satellite models*. These are models that specify a structure for the region and then link that structure to the output of an econometric model for the nation as a whole. The concern, then, is with the structure of the regional economy and its links to the nation.

To reduce it to its most elementary level, assume economic base notions provide the model with its basic structure. The concern is with the economic growth path of some metropolitan area, and the structure of the economy that is growing is given by the following set of equations.

$$Y = C + I + (X - M) \tag{15.34}$$

$$C = bY \tag{15.35}$$

$$M = mY \tag{15.36}$$

$$I = nY \tag{15.37}$$

$$X = \overline{X} \tag{15.38}$$

by substitution

$$Y = bY + nY + \overline{X} - mY \tag{15.39}$$

$$Y - bY - nY + mY = \overline{X} \tag{15.40}$$

$$Y(1 - b - n + m) = \overline{X} \tag{15.41}$$

$$Y = \frac{1}{1 - b - n + m}\overline{X} \tag{15.42}$$

where $1/(1 - b) - n + m$ is the urban base multiplier. To implement this model, we must estimate this parameter. Is it 2.5? 3.75? 1.60? Or what? Suppose we get an empirical estimate. This estimate along with a forecast of exports will yield a forecast of the income of this metropolitan area.

This, of course, looks very much like the forecast procedure followed above when talking about economic base. There is a difference, however. The external or exogenous variable of this model—$\overline{X}$ or exports—would be tied to the forecasts made from some econometric model for the nation as a whole. If we assume that exports from metropolitan areas to other parts of the nation are sensitive to income conditions elsewhere, it would be reasonable to establish the links to forecasts of the nation's gross income or Gross National Product. Or if these exports are highly sensitive to a certain component of spending, such as plant and equipment, and this component is one of the forecasted outputs of an econometric model of the national economy, it would be sensible to establish links to the forecasts of this component of spending.

There are other differences. The most important of these is that econometric models constructed for regions such as states or metropolitan areas will be represented by a much more elaborate set of equations than will economic base. Regional econometric models are much like their national counterparts in some respects, but different in others. The big difference is in the emphasis given to production or output in the model of a region. In the national models, expenditure variables lie at the heart of the structure of the model. Expenditures are assumed to determine income and production, and most of the equations of the model are concerned with the links between them.

Expenditures play a less prominent role in regional econometric models, simply because data for major segments of the expenditures side are missing at the regional level. Econometric model builders focusing on regions or urban areas have had to concentrate instead on output and income measures. In a typical regional model, the economy is broken down into several producing sectors such as 1) Exports (X), 2) Trade (T), 3) Other Services—private (S), 4) Government (G).

Exports are linked to some national economic aggregate such as *GNP* or

$$X = f(\overline{GNP}) \tag{15.43}$$

Trade is taken to be a function of retail sales (C) in the region or

$$T = f(C) \tag{15.44}$$

Other services are usually considered to be a function of personal income (PY) of the region or

$$S = f(PY) \qquad\qquad (15.45)$$

Government is also linked to personal income (PY), the tax rate (TR), and intergovernmental transfers (IT) or

$$G = f(PY, \overline{TR}, \overline{IT}) \qquad\qquad (15.46)$$

Employment variables are included in such models and are usually taken to be functions of output and unemployment

$$E = f(PY, Un) \qquad\qquad (15.47)$$

Employment, wages, and the nonwage component of income are typically linked together to generate personal income (PY). Finally, personal income (PY) and prices (p) are usually assumed to determine retail sales (C).

The precise details of these linkages as they are built into any given model vary. The end results, as it is in the case of the model for the nation, is a system of equations, the parameters of which must be estimated. The problems of estimation are no less difficult at the regional level, but solutions are possible and a forecasting model can be derived along with the necessary solution algorithm. In other words, regional or metropolitan area econometric forecasts are possible. The forecasting performance of these models is uncertain, in part because they have not been used for a sufficiently long period. There are also special data problems associated with the implementation of such models stemming from the fact that there are very long lags in the release of information about some of the important variables included in the model. There are, in addition, data problems in the sense that some variables that should be included as a part of the model cannot be included because there are no data providing adequate measures of them. While this is true of the national models, it is more of a problem for regions and metropolitan areas.

Despite these difficulties, econometric model building is generally looked upon as having potentially productive applications in forecasting macroeconomic change in metropolitan areas. It deals with certain problems better than economic base models and provides the user with more details about the future course of the economy. Its advantage over input-output relate principally to costs. The data requirements are less stringent and hence less costly, and it is by no means clear at this point that we get better forecasts from the more expensive way.

FORECASTING CITY GROWTH FROM A NATIONAL PERSPECTIVE

As noted in several different ways in the discussion to this point, forces external to the city have important bearing on its pace of economic growth. Decisions made in Washington, D.C., concerning the nation's defense budget are crucial to metropolitan areas with heavy concentrations of defense-space-oriented industry. The demand generated by the rapid pace of growth in the Southwest can spill over into northeastern cities that produce commodities that fit the growing consumption needs of those in the Southwest. A fertility increase in the Mississippi Delta can have impact on population growth in New York. And a technological break-through in Los Angeles can influence the productive capacity in Boston or Seattle.

With the exception of what the federal government does, none of these things can be said to be national in the sense that they have no regional origin. Yet many are national "variables," in that their consequences are potentially nation-wide. This is important because it means that the impact of an event, e.g., increasing fertility in the Mississippi Delta, on a particular city, e.g., New York, will depend, in part, on what's happening in many other cities. One way of handling this problem is to consider the question of city growth from a national perspective. This means that the sources of growth in an urban economy, such as fertility, technology, federal government policies, industrial organization, migration, and social attitudes, should be considered first for the nation as a whole as they influence the national economy. After doing this, then the geographic implications can be considered.

To look at the problem of forecasting in this way has a number of advantages, the most important of which is that it forces the forecaster to come to grips with the fact of interdependence in the economic system. Through the technique of allocating national totals to urban regions, one is forced to consider these inter-dependencies, since the sum of the individual allocations cannot be greater or less than the total amount allocated.

Conceptually, there are two general methods of allocating national totals among regions or urban regions. One focuses on the structure of the nation's demands for the output it produces. The other focuses more on location or supply factors as they affect the decisions firms make with respect to locating the new investment that adds to the nation's capacity to produce.

The demand-oriented method of allocation is the most frequently used projection procedure (Bureau of Economic Analysis). This method begins with projections of national totals such as Gross National Product, personal income and earnings, and employment. Given these projections, the next step is to allocate these totals among the nation's industries. The level at which industry is to be disaggregated has to be selected. These disaggregation decisions often depend on the number of industries at the local level for which trend data are available. Once these decisions are made, an allocation procedure must be established. Ordinarily, trends in each industry's share of the total are identified, investigated, and, in the first instance, extrapolated. These extrapolations are likely to be modified on the basis of judgments made by those making the projections, to take into account any anticipated changes in technology or the structure of demands that could alter past relationships.

Given the industry totals, the remaining problem is to allocate these totals to the nation's regions and urban regions. The most common way of doing this is to structure the regional economies into their basic and nonbasic components and apply some variant of shift and share analysis in making actual allocations.

This division of the regional economy into its basic and nonbasic components is, as noted above, not an easy task. When it is to be done for all of the nation's cities, simplifications are necessary. Typically, location quotients are used as a means of deriving the export base of the community. The output of industries that function as a part of the base and nonbasic sectors of the economy have to be broken down into those basic and nonbasic components. The basic or export components of that industry must then be allocated among regions. It is at this point that some form of shift and share analysis usually comes into play.

Urban areas that have certain industries can be expected to share in any growth projected for these industries. If we assume they all hold onto their current share of the market and no more, the current figures of their share of total industry output could be projected into the future and used as a basis of calculating the future output of these industries in these areas.

For many, however, that share is likely to shift. The comparative advantages or disadvantages of city sites may change and affect the ability of the city to compete for industry. The competitive factor has to be taken into account. When dealing with a large number of areas over which allocations are to be made, the problem of dealing with the competitive factor can become unmanageable unless certain simplifying procedures are adopted. Ordinarily, an analysis of trends in the share these areas have of different industries is made. Trend extrapolation is one way of dealing with the question of the competitive factor. This is often done initially. Then these extrapolations are modified according to the best judgment of the forecaster after taking into account all those things which could have impact on the competitive factor in ways not reflected in past trends. There are checks on these judgments in the sense that no more or less than the output projected can be allocated.

Nonbasic industry output is usually allocated in much the same way as that of basic industry. The focus is on shares of the national output of industries whose product is consumed locally. These are usually projected on the basis of trend analysis and judgmental modifications made of those trends by the forecaster.

The limitations of addressing the question of forecasting city growth with a model that focuses first on the nation and then on the problem of allocating national totals to subareas, stems from the fact that much of the detail we know about supply and demand factors which could influence the outcome in particular areas cannot be handled. The question of the competitive element in the share of the industry that any one subarea has is dealt with in a very crude fashion. Much is missed in the way in which this is done.

There is power in this approach to forecasting, however. There is a total to which the sum of each of the individual parts must add up. This gives us a perspective that we do not have when focusing on individual areas. It forces us to reckon with the interdependencies in our economic system. As we look at individual subareas, we can very easily over or underestimate the impact of an expected external development. The checks against over and underestimation with a forecasting model that encompasses the nation lie in the summation of the figures for the individual parts and comparison with the national totals. Given the allocations techniques usually applied in these models, consistency of the sort cannot insure accurate forecasts. But it is a useful attribute, the importance of which will grow as our forecasting techniques improve.

Models that have roots in supply factors are less common (Harris). There are similarities with demand-oriented models in the sense that projections of national aggregates such as Gross National Product, income, and employment provide a basic input into the model. These aggregate projections are also broken down by some industry grouping. What we start with in the allocations to be made are projected industry outputs for the nation as a whole. The differences lie mainly in the techniques of allocation.

In supply-oriented models, the emphasis is on factors influencing the decisions of firms in these industries to locate a plant within particular subareas or regions. If we assume that access of a location to markets and/or the location of materials has important bearing on the profits of the firm, transportation costs will be a crucial element in that location decision. Locations with access to both materials and markets are locations where the transportation bill is at a minimum. If we can get information about transportation costs, a model can be constructed which will allocate the location of anticipated production among regions or urban areas according to the comparative advantage these areas have with respect to accessibility to markets and materials.

There is, of course, more to the comparative advantage of a location than its accessibility to markets and materials. The presence or absence of agglomeration economies, and high or low labor costs, to mention just two, are supply elements that can have impact on the locational attractiveness of a site. How all these things might be incorporated in a supply-oriented model which allocated industry output among regions is by no means clear. The methodology with respect to supply-oriented allocations is much less well developed. It is nevertheless possible to conceive of making these allocations on the basis of such a model done with control totals that would insure consistency in the changes among subareas. We have achieved less success in approaching the problem in this way, however.

REFERENCES

*Bolton, R. *Defense Purchases and Regional Growth*. Washington, D.C.: The Brookings Institution, 1966.

Bureau of Economic Analysis, U.S. Department of Commerce. *Area Economic Projections: 1990*. Washington, D.C.: U.S. Government Printing Office, 1974.

Federal Reserve. "The Employment Multiplier in Wichita." *Monthly Economic Review*. Federal Reserve Bank of Kansas City 37 (1952): 1–7.

*Glickman, N. "An Econometric Model of the Philadelphia Region." *Journal of Regional Science* 11 (1971): 15–32.

Hall, O., and Licari, J. "Building Small Region Econometric Models." *Journal of Regional Science* 14 (1974): 337–53.

Harris, C. *The Urban Economies: 1985*. Lexington, Mass.: D. C. Heath and Company, 1973.

Pfouts, R. "An Empirical Testing of the Economic Base Theory." *Journal of the American Institute of Planners* 23 (1957): 64–69.

*Tiebout, C. "An Empirical Regional Input-output Projection Model of the State of Washington." *Review of Economies and Statistics* 51 (1969): 334–40.

---

* This chapter draws heavily from the writings of Bolton, Glickman, and Tiebout.

16

Urban Simulation

SUMMARY

Urban simulation means a concern with computer models that replicate some part of the city. As they have developed to date, this has been largely a concern with building models that simulate residential locations or residential land use patterns in the city.

Several of the earliest of these models focus on the question of residential extension. The links to economic theory in these models were minimal. Instead, the concern was with developing a computer algorithm or calculating procedure that would match up households and sites. One way in which this was done was to calculate indexes of attractiveness for each site and to develop computer routines that would evaluate these indexes and make "development decisions" according to a set of criteria put into the computer program.

More recently, computer simulation models concerned with matching households and sites within cities have been built to incorporate market factors such as price. Since residential development in most cities is largely the outcome of the operation of urban housing markets, it makes good sense to do this.

Several housing simulation models with "economic roots" are discussed. The problem addressed in these models is the same; we have households, residential sites and structures, and new construction. The sites have a geographic dimension that is important because accessibility is assumed to be important to households. The concern is with the development of a computer program that will match up households with sites in a realistic way. The difference now is in our view of the world in which these things come about. Now the concern is with a world that is populated with people that behave economically in making decisions.

More grandiose model designs have been attempted. The most widely known of these is the one constructed by Jay Forrester. Forrester was concerned with the city in the sense of the central city of a metropolis. He focused on the household and business population in that city. Employment and unemployment, labor's geographic and occupational mobility, public expenditure and tax policies, the housing stock, new construction, and filtering were all a part of a model that Forrester believes make explicit the functional aspects of the urban interactions between these two.

The Forrester-type model pays close attention to interdependence in the urban economy, which may argue is its* real source of strength. It also has a number of serious flaws which are discussed.

Simulation is a term used in a very specific way in urban analysis. The dictionary definition of feigning or pretending has little to do with what urban simulation is all about. Simulation in an urban context is closely linked with urban theory and modelling.

Since the primary concern of this book has been with urban economic theory and its applications, urban simulation is very much concerned with the subject matter of this book. Urban simulation with economic roots would draw heavily from both the theory and applications portion of this book. In fact, some of what was done in the applications chapters can be considered simulation, although it is not what most urban scholars have in mind when they talk about urban simulation. The point warrants amplification.

Consider the question of where people live in cities. Recall that the theory of residential location developed in chapter 5 provided the foundation for the discussion in chapter 8 of why families moved to the suburbs. This discussion was, in effect, a discussion concerned with residential choice in geographic space. The theory developed in chapter 5 highlighted certain important economic elements in these decisions that influence outcomes. In chapter 8, certain kinds of change were postulated, e.g., the coming of the automobile, rising real income. The implication of this change was then considered in terms of the microeconomic model of decision making developed in chapter 5. In terms of this model, the automobile led to suburbanization as did rising per capita income because both caused the bid rent curves of households to become more gently sloped.

This discussion involved simulation. The sequence of statements made that led to the conclusion that people would move to the suburbs can be considered a manipulation of the model of residential choice developed in chapter 5. The response of households to the automobile was simulated with a decision-making model. This was done with a string of ordinary language statements and some simple, two-dimensional geometry. This model, however, could have been expressed in the form of a string of mathematical equations, which is what many people have in mind when talking about urban simulation.

To the urban scientist, the model of a city is a model that has a logical structure expressed in mathematical form. The models discussed in the previous chapter can be used to illustrate the point. The simplest of these was a system of linear equations that could be solved "analytically."

$$Y = C + I \qquad\qquad (16.1)$$

$$C = 0.8Y \qquad\qquad (16.2)$$

$$I = \bar{I} \qquad\qquad (16.3)$$

These equations, it will be recalled, were taken to represent the economy. If we specify that $\bar{I}$ equals 10, we can solve this system of equations for income or Y.

$$Y = 0.8Y + 10$$
$$Y - 0.8Y = 10$$
$$0.2Y = 10$$
$$Y = 50$$

With these equations, we can also simulate the effects of different levels of investment $(\bar{I})$ on income (Y). For example, if $\bar{I}$ rises to 20, according to this model it can be shown that the level of income (Y) will increase to 100.

Do simulations like this provide useful insights into the real world? The answer clearly depends on whether the system of equations from which such conclusions are derived provide adequate representations of reality. According to the discussion of urban econometric models in the previous chapter, this set of equations is not an adequate representation of the macro economy. In fact, simple systems of linear equations apparently seldom provide an adequate representation of economic reality when the concern is with urban phenomena. When a geographic dimension is added to an economic model, the scope and complexity of the reality of concern is greatly increased. Many believe that the relationships between urban variables are nonlinear and involve feedbacks that are not easily dealt with by the calculus of economic theory.

The development of the large-scale computer has provided the urban scientist with the opportunity to cope more effectively with these difficulties. With the computer has come the development of a new analytical tool, the computer simulation model, which is what most people now mean when they talk about urban simulation.

The computer simulation model is, in its raw form, a system of mathematical equations, which means it is similar to the system of equations represented by equations 16.1 through 16.3 in one important respect. The basic structure of the model is expressed in mathematical form. There are significant differences, however. The computer model, because it is capable of "brute-force" solutions—iterations or recomputations that converge towards a solution—can incorporate much more of the world's complexities. In the language of the mathematician, this means a model that can incorporate nonlinear relationships and interdependencies or feedbacks.

Earlier attempts at the development of urban computer simulation models were very much concerned with constructing complex systems which took full account of these nonlinearities and interdependencies. More recently, urban economists have begun to try to incorporate more of our economic knowledge of the urban world into the simulation model. While the urban world is indeed complex, most economists believe that we can come to understand this complexity better if we consider it in context of a model with roots in economic theory.

The subject matter of urban simulation is vast, complex, and, most significantly, only in its infancy. There are, nonetheless, a number of sensible things that can be said about its development to date which can be easily grasped. In what follows, the structures of several kinds of models are discussed. The primary problem of concern in this discussion is the question of where people live in cities. Simulation modelling, as it is discussed in general terms, promises much more. To deliver what it promises, however, usually requires a housing model, and much of the computer modelling done to date has been concerned with residential location.

Simulation Models of Residential Extension

One early concern in urban computer simulation modelling was the question of residential growth or extension. The focus was on the question of where within the city future residents would live. The concern was with the residential development process and how it was addressed in the earlier models. This was a question of where within the city new residential development would take place. To the east? The west? The south? Would a "leapfrog" pattern develop? What were the probable densities of the new development?

The task was to develop a computer model that represented the residential development process. The links to economic theory in most of the earlier models were minimal. Typically, the focus was on some conception of the decision-making process involved in residential development, which emphasized the role of the builder-developer. If the builder-developer was assigned a key role, to model the residential extension process meant the construction of a model that replicated the decisions made by builder-developers in this process.

In earlier attempts at modelling the residential extension process, the primary concern was with factors external to builder-developers that had impact on development decisions. A frequent assumption was that population growth provided the impetus for new residential construction and population was taken to be exogenous to the model. Those who used these models had to stipulate the amount of population growth expected during the simulation period, and by doing so they, in effect, stipulated the aggregate amount of residential development to take place.

To exclude population from the model meant the exclusion of a variable that is important to many of the concerns we have with cities. To do so, however, simplified the problems of model construction. The task was now one of constructing a model concerned with analyzing and predicting where residential development would take place within the city.

The general structure of the earlier models concerned with residential extension in this sense revolved around an algorithm or calculating procedure, which "matched" households with parcels of land in the city. This matching process involved comparing the characteristics of households with site demands with the characteristics of the available sites. Households were assumed to be attracted to certain sites, and certain characteristics of the household were taken to provide indications of the features of the site they found attractive. The site characteristics selected were those believed to be important to households. Accessibility was, not surprisingly, considered to be the most important of these.

If accessibility was important, geographic delineation of the city became important. The model builder had to be able to pinpoint the geographic location of potential sites for residential development. Geographical delineation, in this sense, meant defining the areal units of the model. There are, after all, an infinite number of points in the geographic space encompassed by a city. Computers can only deal with finite quantities and there are limits to the number of these they can handle. These points have to be aggregated, and we must be able to distinguish the resulting areal units from one another in a meaningful way.

What is involved in making geographic distinctions is by itself easy to see. It is simply a matter of dividing up the city into units of areal extension such as in Figure 16.1. Presumably, the geographic locations of each of the squares in this grid can be identified by some system of geographic coordinates, or in terms of distance and direction from some point, e.g., a central point or the central business district.

Figure 16.1

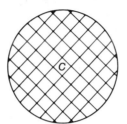

With the city so considered, we can begin to build a simulation model. Some assumptions are necessary. Suppose accessibility to place of work is the only thing about the site that matters to households. Suppose we also specify the location of the workplace in advance—one central place such as C in Figure 16.1—and assume that all households have the same need for accessibility and the same ability to pay for it. To make these assumptions means that we have no systematic basis for assigning users to particular sites. The bid rent curves of all households are the same. Even so, a simulation model that assigned users to sites could be constructed. The question of where people live, given these assumptions, could be decided by a calculating procedure that involved a random selection process. Assignments would be made on a random basis.

Such a model could be easily constructed, but it probably wouldn't provide very interesting results. Both the theory and applications sections in this book provide reasons for believing that residential location is not the outcome of a random process. Differences in income and tastes and preferences give rise to differences in accessibility demands, which should have impact on where people live. It is also the case that nonaccessibility features of the site, e.g., neighborhood, lot size, size of the house, etc., are important to many households. If these things are somehow taken into account, the process of matching households to residences should become systematic, at least in part.

There are, of course, many ways in which these things might be handled. One approach developed by Chapin, Weiss, and others back in the latter half of the 1960s focused on an assortment of characteristics of the site indicated by prior investigation to have bearing on urban residential development. Their list included, among others, 1) marginal land not in use, 2) accessibility to work areas, 3) assessed value, 4) travel distance to the nearest major street, 5) distance to the nearest elementary school, 6) residential amenity, and 7) availability of sewer facilities.

These characteristics can be considered as criteria in terms of which the relative attractiveness of sites in the city can be determined. To do this, the city has to be divided into areal units as in Figure 16.1. This is often done by using Census tract or enumeration district units because Census has most of the data required to construct indexes of attraction. In the Chapin, Weiss, et al. study, smaller areal units were used, partly because primary data were generated to construct these indexes.

Given the grid of areal units and these data, values for the indexes of attraction were calculated and assigned to these units. A computer algorithm was developed that was to distribute households residentially throughout the city. This program had the computer examine each areal unit or grid square and note the index of attractiveness it was assigned. Whether or not the areal units were to be developed as a consequence of this inspection was determined by a procedure that took the attractiveness measures into account as some fraction between 0 and 1. This fraction was taken to represent the probability of that unit being developed if one unit in the city were to be developed. Development was programmed to occur when this probability was highest.

This was done for a specified number of households on the first computer pass. After this pass was finished, the unused land was reassessed and the attractiveness indexes were recalculated. The computer then made a second pass, distributed additional household groups, and the remaining land was again reassessed and the attractiveness indexes recalculated. This process was repeated until the forecast date was reached and all households were distributed residentially throughout the city.

This model and others like it are not so simplistic as these few remarks might suggest. The equations that constitute these models represent, in the mind of those who have built them, important parts of the reality of the residential development process. Yet, there is also much that is missing from these models, the most important of which are market factors such as price and income. Residential development in most cities, while influenced by public policy, is largely the outcome of the operation of urban housing markets, where such things as prices, profits, incomes, tastes, and preferences are important. Since they are so important, we have good reason to argue that they should be incorporated in the structure of the model that seeks to simulate these outcomes. This, in fact, has been the concern of a good deal of recent research by urban economists.

Housing Simulation Models with Economic Roots: Simpler Versions

Suppose our concern is essentially the same; we want to build a model that will simulate residential housing in cities. Now, however, our concern is with these housing outcomes as they come about through the operation of urban housing markets. The basic problem is still the same; we have households, residential sites and structures, and construction. The sites still have a geographic dimension that is important and the accessibility, or lack of, this geography implies is important to households. We also still want a computer program that will match households up with sites in a realistic way.

The difference now is in how we view the world in which these things come about. Now our concern is with an economic world in which markets are the primary means through which the use of the nation's resources, including housing, is organized. Now we are dealing with groups of people that behave in a prescribed way when they make certain kinds of decisions. Their concern is with maximizing something. To the households, this is maximizing satisfactions from consumption, which includes satisfactions from the consumption of housing. To the owner of residential properties, this is maximizing the profits from investment. To the builder, it is maximizing the profits from building new dwellings. These are groups of people functioning as economic beings in the housing market. If people do behave as economic beings, that economic behavior must be modeled properly if we are to understand where they live.

Demanders   Demand in the residential housing market is the sum of the individual demands of households. At the individual level, as noted in chapter 5, these demands are a function of the tastes and preferences of the household, its income, the price of housing, and the price of all other goods. When the spatial dimension of housing is recognized, accessibility also has to be taken into account, as it reflects through both the tastes and preferences and income of the household. Finally, there are, as noted earlier, neighborhood effects in the consumption of housing which, because of the tastes and preferences of households, have bearing on the evaluations many make of particular dwellings.

Given the tastes and preferences and incomes of the household, the price of housing, and the price of all other goods, we should be able to make reasonable statements about housing demands. One of these is that for most this demand can be reasonably characterized by the conventional demand curve.

Figure 16.2

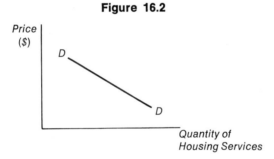

This means that most households are willing to consume more when prices are lower or will pay more for lower levels of housing consumption. As discussed in chapter 5, most households are also willing to pay more when that consumption is at a site accessible to places of work, shopping, and recreation. They will also pay more when that site is in a neighborhood that has an abundance of residential amenities.

To incorporate the housing demand of households in a simulation model of the housing market requires an equation or system of equations with parameters that link housing consumption to the variables that influence satisfactions from housing consumption. This means links to such things as household's tastes and preferences and incomes as well as house prices.

De Leeuw and others, while developing a housing simulation model at the Urban Institute, derived a system of equations that established these links and made estimates of the parameters of these equations for a number of metropolitan areas. The evaluation of each household of each dwelling in the Urban Institute model is done through equations that link the satisfactions from housing consumption to four parameters.

The basic demand equation in the Institute model is

$$U_{ij} = H, X, Z_1, Z_2, Z_3 \qquad (16.4)$$

where U_{ij} is the utility of dwelling j to household i; H is the utility of the housing services consumed; X is the utility of nonhousing goods; and Z_1, Z_2, and Z_3 are characteristics of the zone in which the dwelling is located. Z_1 refers to accessibility characteristics, Z_2 to wealth characteristics of the neighborhood in which the dwelling is located, and Z_3 is the racial composition of that neighborhood. Each of these three is taken to have bearing on the utility from consumption.

Additional equations are specified, which link the satisfactions derived from each element in equation 16.4 to other variables. The links are the four basic parameters. One expresses the strength of the household's preferences for housing versus other goods and services. As it is measured in the model, it is the ratio of housing expense to income and it is estimated for the following groups: white nonelderly families, white elderly/single person households, black nonelderly families, and black elderly/single person households. The other three parameters measure the strength of household responses to housing price changes and household responses to differences in the wealth and racial composition of the neighborhood in which the dwelling is located.

Empirical estimates of the parameters are necessary. Once made, these parameters are combined into a single equation—the utility function—which is the equation in the model that represents the means by which households evaluate dwellings. If we have information about the income, race, and age characteristics of a household as well as the price of a dwelling and the racial and wealth characteristics of the neighborhood in which that dwelling is located, this equation will estimate the "worth" of that dwelling to the household.

Suppliers.   As noted in chapter 5, the durability of the dwelling means that most housing needs are met by units in the existing stock, that is, units that were built at some earlier date. These units are owned by someone. Some are owned by the occupants; some are owned by those who rent them to others. Those who own properties that are rented or used by others are usually called *landlords.*

Ordinarily, all dwelling owners are considered as landlords in economic analyses of supply in urban housing markets. This means a concern with maximizing profits from the ownership of residential property or a concern with

$$\Pi = R - C \qquad (16.5)$$

where Π is profits, R is revenue derived from rents, and C is costs, including capital and operating costs.

If the urban housing market is assumed to be competitive, landlords will take rents as given and try to maximize profits by adjusting the supply of housing they offer. In analyzing how landlords behave as suppliers, the quantity of housing supply is usually taken to mean a standardized unit of the many housing services that flow from the dwelling. This is necessary because, as noted in chapter 5, dwellings are highly differentiated. The total quantity of housing services provided by individual dwellings varies. The quantity provided by the large expensive house set in a spacious estate in an attractive suburban location in the city, for example, is much greater than that provided by the one-room flat located in a ghetto in the city. To be able to compare and aggregate supplies requires some standardized unit of measurement.

How do landlords behave as suppliers? If our concern is with the long-run—say five years or longer—landlord behavior can be characterized by the supply curve denoted in Figure 16.3.

Figure 16.3

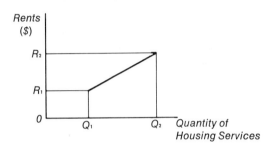

Note there is a minimum quantity offered, that is, OQ_1. This is a consequence of the fact that housing services flow from dwellings that are indivisible. If a dwelling comes on the market, a certain minimum quantity of housing services will be made available. Since dwellings are differentiated, what quantity OQ_1 will be depends on the dwelling. It will be relatively large for some dwellings, less so for others. No matter what the minimum is, however, there will be some rent OR_1 below which owners will withdraw their dwellings from the market.

Above OR_1, Figure 16.3 indicates that landlords increase the quantity of housing services they offer in response to higher rents. They can do this by improvement and addition expenditures. These expenditures enhance the services provided by a dwelling and hence increase the quantity of standardized units of housing services it provides. Higher rents enable landlords to overcome the additional capital and operating costs incurred in making these improvements. If they add to their profits when doing so, they will add to the supply of housing services as rents rise beyond OR_1.

According to Figure 16.3, there is apparently also a limit to the addition and improvement expenditures a landlord will make—OQ_2 in Figure 16.3. This limit is imposed, in part, by the possibility of additions to the stock of housing and hence flow of housing services through new construction. Builders are an important group on the supply side of the urban housing market. They stand ready to add new units to the stock if it is profitable to do so. Builder profitability depends on dwelling prices or rents and the costs of construction. The links between the price of new and existing dwelling are particularly important. Since the new and the previously occupied dwellings are considered as substitutes by most households, the revenues derived from the sale of a new unit is importantly influenced by rents on existing units. If these rents are low relative to the rent level that would be needed to make the construction and sale of a new unit profitable, there will be no new construction. Even so, supply can be increased by enhancements through additions and improvement—Q_1 through Q_2 in Figure 16.3.

Suppose now that when rents reach OR_2, the revenues from ownership become such that it is now profitable to construct new dwellings. When this happens, landlords of existing dwellings could find it is no longer profitable to add to the supply of housing services by improvements and additions. That supply will now be increased, however, by new construction.

The behavior of owners of existing dwellings in the Urban Institute model is expressed in equations that have strong roots in microeconomic theory and bear a resemblance to the structure implicit in the discussion just above. The equation incorporated into the simulation model is derived from assumption of maximization of expected profits, an expression for expected profits, and a production function for housing services. That equation constitutes the supply curve for existing dwellings and is specified as follows:

$$Q_j = B_1 + B_2 \left(\frac{2}{3}\right) \left(\frac{P_j - P_o}{P_c}\right) Q_o \qquad (16.6)$$

Q_j is the level of housing services currently provided by dwelling j, Q_o is the level of housing services provided by dwelling j ten years ago, P_j is the price per unit of service offered by dwelling j, P_o is operating costs per units of service, and P_c is capital costs per unit of services for a new dwelling. B_1 and B_2 are the parameters to be determined empirically. B_1 is interpreted as the depreciation rate, and B_2 is interpreted as the price elasticity of supply.

The dependent variable in this equation can be looked at as the quantity of housing services offered for sale at the end of the simulation period. This quantity is a function of the quantity now assumed to be forthcoming from dwelling j at the beginning of this period, the rate of depreciation over the forecast period and the supply response of owners to changes in the price of the dwelling—the elasticity of supply. Values for the depreciation rate and the elasticity of supply must be estimated from the data for the city which the model is applied. Given these parameter estimates, along with figures on the quantity of housing services that flow from the dwelling at the beginning of the simulation period, quantities supplied at alternative prices at the end of the period can be calculated. In other words, supply curves can be calculated. What those curves will look like depends on the rate of depreciation and supply adjustments made by owners in response to price changes.

Builders are given a more passive role in the Urban Institute model. The building industry is simply assumed to offer new dwellings at a price proportional to the level of services the dwelling provides. This price is inserted into the model. It is a price that approximates the cost of new dwelling construction in the city to which the model is applied.

Simulated Market Outcomes   The concern remains with the question of what type of household will be living where. Now, however, this comes about as a consequence of the operation of urban housing markets in which housing prices or rents play a key role. In such a setting, we have demanders searching for a place to live and suppliers responding with offers of previously occupied dwellings and newly constructed units. The market solution is a matching of households with new or existing dwellings. The match-up constituting the solution is one in which no one can improve their position without imposing a loss on someone else. Households have maximized their satisfactions, given their tastes and budget constraints. Builders and landlords have maximized their profits. In the language of chapter 6, what we want is an efficient solution of market outcome.

The algorithm computers use in finding efficient market outcomes is often discussed in general terms as a *game*. Initial stipulations have to be made as to how the geography of the city will be handled or, in effect, how the units of areal extension will be defined. Population and income change during the period of the simulation have to be specified. It is also necessary to have estimates of the parameters that define the response of households, landlords, and builders to the market conditions that may arise.

The game consists of each market participant searching for something. For landlords, it is the price and quantity at which they can rent their property at a maximum profit. For households, it is a place to live at which their satisfactions are maximized, given their tastes and budget constraints. For builders, it is maximum profits from construction. These groups interact in this search. The initial outcome may not provide each participant with the best result possible. Some landlords may have set their price too high and hence may have vacant units. There may also be two or more households that have selected the same dwelling.

Suppose after the first pass through the computer, there are vacant units and more than one household bidding for a number of units. The computer algorithm must insure that this type of outcome will lead to another pass through the computer. There must be routines denoting the responses of landlords, builders, and households when they have not obtained the objective of their search, and these must be responses that move the market in the direction of an efficient solution. For example, if some landlords have vacancies because they set the price too high, that price should be lower during the next pass through the computer.

If the response of the participants to existing market conditions cannot be captured in a system of linear equations, which is typically the case, a computer program will have to be written that iterates or recalculates solutions which converge on a result that satisfied the solution crieria. No market participant can be made better off by change without imposing a loss on another participant. Unlike most games, when this point is reached, there are no winners or losers. Rather, there is a series of statistics that indicate where what groups of people live where along with indications of prices, levels of housing consumption, and vacancies are at these locations.

This is precisely the outcome of a solution in the Urban Institute model. The Institute model, compared to other urban simulation models, is small. It consists of only a few dozen households and dwellings, each of which is taken to represent thousands of households and dwellings. Smallness, in this sense, creates problems for those concerned with the geographic distribution of residents in cities, since it does not provide for detailed distinctions in characterizing the way in which these residential patterns can change. Models of this kind, however, can be easily manipulated and, as a consequence, make it possible to simulate the process through which house prices and quantities are determined, and link this process to residential location.

The Urban Institute model divides a metropolitan area into five zones, four of which contain previously occupied dwellings. The boundaries of these zones are drawn so as to separate the central city from the suburbs. Each of these two is split into two groups on the basis of racial composition, accessibility, and house values. Each of these zones is assigned a number of dwelling units which provide a specified flow of housing services.

Households with given levels of income and of a specified type are introduced, as is the builder.

In the beginning, the algorithm has each owner or landlord choose a price per unit of housing services. The equation for the supply curve then determines the flow of housing services that will be provided at that price. The landlords begin by choosing a price that is slightly higher than the price of new construction.

Households evaluate the quantities offered for sale at the prices chosen by the landlords and the price set for the builder. This evaluation is made in terms of the utility equation. Given the price, the housing services offered at that price, the accessibility of the dwelling, and the characteristics of the neighborhood in which it is located, the utility equation can be used as a means of determining which dwelling provides maximum satisfaction for each household.

Given the initial price set by landlords, which is arbitrary, it is only by chance that households and dwellings will be matched up in what corresponds to an efficient market solution. If landlords initially set the price above the new construction price, every household will choose a newly constructed dwelling. Owners of previously occupied dwellings will find their units vacant. At this point, the program has owners moving down their supply curves, which implies a lower price and a smaller quantity of housing services offered for sale at that price. Households, in light of these price and quantity adjustments, then reevaluate these dwellings. As a consequence, some begin to shift from newly constructed units to previously occupied dwellings. In the course of doing so, some owners may lower prices to the point of taking households away from other landlords. Some may find themselves with two or more households bidding for the dwellings they own.

This process will continue in the sense of additional passes through the computer until no landlord or household has any reason to change the variables under his or her control. For landlords, this is a situation in which the unit is not vacant or being demanded by more than one household. For households, this is the situation in which landlords are no longer changing their prices and service levels.

The solution or efficient market outcome of this model consists of information on the level of housing services, prices paid, the location of each household, and the occupancy status of each dwelling in the sense of whether it is new, existing-occupied, or existing-vacant.

This model generates outcomes that show residence by geographic area. The areal distributions, however, are very broad and general. As noted above, the results show geographic dstributions for, at most, five subareas in any metropolitan area. While this may be of benefit in investigating certain kinds of questions that concern changing urban residential structures, for many others it will not. The strength of the Urban Institute model is in its ability to simulate the housing market in ways that allow us to consider a broad range of policy questions that concern the housing problems of those with low incomes.

Residential Simulation Models with Economic Roots: More Ambitious Versions

More ambitious attempts are underway to construct residential simulation models. One of these was developed under the sponsorship of the National Bureau of Economic Research, in the early 1970s. Whereas the Urban Institute model only deals with a few household and dwellings types, has only five residential zones, and has economic activity concentrated in the central business district, the National Bureau of Economic Research model incorporates twenty-seven dwelling types, seventy-two household groups, nineteen work places, and forty-four residential zones. By disaggregating in this way, the number of possibilities with respect to outcomes are greatly increased. Among other things, this means a much greater computational burden in finding market solutions. This, in turn, has important impact on how the model is put together.

The National Bureau of Economic Research model is the outcome of a massive research undertaking. It is a very big and complicated model that is not easily described if the concern is with details. More general statements about the elements and makeup of the model can be made easily enough, however.

The National Bureau model encompasses the application of much of the urban economics concerned with city structure. It is a housing market model. Factors that have bearing on aggregate housing demand, such as population and employment growth, are taken as given. The user of the model must specify the change in employment to occur during the simulation period and must specify the work sites at which this change takes place. If these are additions, this implies additions to the household population. The user in this case must indicate the income and educational attainments of these additions so they can be classified by household type.

The model itself is broken down into a number of submodels concerned with demand and supply elements in the market, as well as one that provides for a way of clearing the market.

The demand side of the market is taken into account in two ways. One is a model that indicates the number of moves that will be made during each simulation period. Empirical studies of the mobility behavior of households provide a basis for deriving equations that "select" those households who will move during the simulation period. This model also specifies the work place locations for the mover. The movers include both households who are added to the work force during the simulation period and households who are already employed in the city. All of those who are added to the work force are included. The movers from those already employed in the city include only those equations of this submodel indicated to have a high probability of moving, e.g., families where the age of the head is relatively young, etc.

After the number of moves to be made is determined, the second model, a demand allocation submodel determines the kind of housing these movers will look for. In the National Bureau model, this depends on both accessibility and nonaccessibility factors. The nonaccessibility factors are dealt with, in part, in the decisions that were made with respect to household type. The income of the household as it has bearing on its housing consumption is also important. All these characteristics are linked housing types to determine the type of housing that will be demanded.

Given the type of housing demanded at a work place location, the demand for a site in the commuting area of that location is considered to be influenced by the price of housing at those locations and travel costs, which includes the value of commuting time to the household.

On the supply side, there are three submodels that determine the number and kind of units that come into the market during the forecast period. One of these is the vacancy submodel. Established households within the city who move during the simulation period vacate dwellings. The vacancy submodel is the means by which the National Bureau model adds these units, denoted by housing type and work place location, to the available supply during the simulation period.

There is also a filtering submodel, which is concerned with quality changes in the existing stock. In matching households with housing, given the large number of households and housing types, it is possible that situations of excess supply or demand will emerge in the simulation. The filtering submodel provides a basis for altering the quality of certain units in the stock on the basis of market information. If quality premiums show up in the calculated market prices, for example, there is a routine that compares these premiums with the costs of upgrading the dwelling. The outcome could be a change in the quality of some of the housing in the city.

The supply submodel provides for housing construction and conversions. It is a routine that compares the demand for and supply of housing by types and work-place location. On the basis of these comparisons, "need" is identified. The construction industry can respond to this need. Whether it does or not depends in the model on whether it is profitable. This is determined by comparisons of the market prices generated by the model with construction and conversion cost information that has to be introduced into the model.

Given these supply and demand elements, the overall model has an algorithm that "clears" the market—the market clearing submodel. Given moving households who have chosen the housing types they want, and the filtering, vacancy, and supply submodels that revise the housing available to meet the demands of the mover, we have figures that provide the constraints in a cost-minimizing linear programming model that forms the core of the market clearing submodel. The solution of this model locates moving households classified by work place location, house type, and income to available housing classified by location and type.

The National Bureau model is the most ambitious attempt, to date, to construct a simulation model of an urban housing market. It is ambitious in the sense of attempting to incorporate much more detail about market participants than other models, and in attempting to bring to bear as much of the economic knowledge as we have accumulated about urban housing into the basic structure of the model. Limitations of the computer and that knowledge are the source of limitations in this model. Among other things, it is not easy to "use." Still, much has been learned, both about urban housing markets and urban simulation, from the research that was a part of this work. Moreover, it has been developed in a flexible way. With additional research that paves the way for incorporating a job and population growth submodel as well as a job location model, the National Bureau model should be capable of being developed into a general urban model. It would not be the first of these, however.

Urban Simulation Models: The Grand Design

One of the earlier of the urban simulation models aimed at broader concerns was the Jay Forrester model, published in *Urban Dynamics*. The Forrester model attracted much attention in the early 1970s, partly because of the scope of the modelling effort, partly because of the methodology underlying the model, and partly because of the "counter-intuitive" or surprising conclusions forthcoming from his simulations.

While there is much economic content to the Forrester model, there is little in the way of economics in it. Forrester was concerned with the city in the sense of the central city of a metropolis. He was concerned with the household and business populations in that city. Employment and unemployment, labor's geographic and occupational mobility, public expenditure and tax policies, the housing stock, new construction, and filtering are all a part of a model that Forrester believes makes explicit the functional aspects of urban interactions between these two populations.

The output of the Forrester model is expressed in terms of the size and mix of the household and business population, the mix and occupancy of the city's housing stock, the local government tax rate, and the employment, skill, and mobility records of its population.

The basic distinctions made among the household workers are 1) managerial-professional, 2) worker, 3) underemployed or unskilled. The basic distinctions among businesses are 1) new, 2) mature, 3) declining. The distinctions among units in the housing stack are 1) premium, 2) worker, 3) declining. The basic distinctions among business plants are 1) new, 2) mature, 3) declining.

The city in Forrester's model is treated as an independent system. It receives impulses from outside, which have impact on what happens to it. Change in the city, however, is assumed to have no impact on the rest of the world.

The level of economic activity changes in the city with the in-migration of new firms. Firms entering never leave; rather they trace out a life cycle going from new to mature to declining. The distinctions are significant because Forrester assumes different levels of activity for each stage in the life cycle of the firm. New firms are taken to be larger and use relatively more managerial and professional labor than mature or declining firms. Declining firms, on the other hand, use the least amount of labor and proportionately more of what they use is the unskilled type. Mature firms lie somewhere in between these two, both with respect to size and composition. According to Forrester, each life cycle stage lasts for a specified number of years; then the firm moves on to the next one.

The significance of these assumptions with respect to the firm is that it makes both the history and the features of the city that attract new firms key determinants of future levels of activity. If the city does not attract new firms, what happens to it in the immediate future will depend on how many firms it attracted in the past and when. If new firms do not continue to migrate into the city, it will, in time, wither away.

A key feature of the city, then, is its attractiveness to firms, relative to the "rest of the world." According to Forrester, this attractiveness depends largely on the mix of population in the city and the tax rate on property.

The mix of the population has bearing on the kind of labor inputs available for business. A relatively large managerial-professional component in the population tends to attract new industry because new industry uses a relatively large proportion of this type of labor. Population mix also influences new firm location in cities through its impact on social environment and the tax rate. High rates of unemployment and/or underemployment, for example, are assumed to be unattractive features to business because of what they imply with respect to social environment. A predominance of this kind of population also discourages new firms from coming to the city, by their impact on the city's tax rate. Since the unemployed and underemployed generally require more public welfare expenditures, their presence implies higher taxes to be able to pay for these taxes.

The tax rate is also assumed to be influenced by the size of the tax base. That base, in the Forrester model, depends on the mix of uses between business and housing, and within the housing sector on the mix of housing between premium, worker, and underemployed groups. Since assessed valuation of property is assumed to be highest for business, the tax rate shows up as being lowest when business is an important part of the overall mix of the population. They will be highest when housing of the underemployed is most important.

Household populations are not constant. They are attracted to and away from cities. The units of attractiveness to households are job availability, taxes, and housing availability. The importance of these things is assumed to vary by household type. Taxes, for example, discourage the managerial-professional type from coming to a city. On the other hand, they encourage the underemployed to come because they are assumed to indicate the size of the public expenditures in the city. If we assume the underemployed shares disproportionately in expenditures that contribute less to taxes, they would be attracted to places of high taxes. The underemployed are also assumed to be very sensitive to housing availability.

Finally, housing in the Forrester model is treated as a highly structured market. Premium housing is used by the managerial-professional class, worker housing by the worker class, and so on. Units are added to the stock through new construction through the premium and worker housing classes. Units come into the underemployed class only through filtering.

All these relationships are fitted together in a model that, despite its oversimplification, is highly complicated. It is a model that pays very close attention to the interdependence in internal and external developments, which many argue is its real source of strength. It is also a model that has generated policy prescriptions that run counter to conventional wisdom, the most well-known of which is the regeneration of a city by the demolition of slum housing and its replacement by industry.

Most urban economists have problems with models like Forrester's. These problems should be evident to anyone who has come this far in this book. They relate to things that have been both included and excluded from the model. The exclusions are evident. Focusing solely on the question of the aggregate income determination, little of what was discussed in chapters 2, 3, and 4, which has bearing on the growth and/or decline of a city, is included in the model. There is no attempt to reckon with matters of access and transportation, economies of scale, changes in the national and international demands for ouput exported from the city, export base multipliers, and exogenous population movements.

The internal problems most economists have with the model relate primarily to the way in which the parameters of the model were estimated. For the most part, this was done in an arbitrary fashion with results that many economists would argue do not conform very closely to what our current economic knowledge suggests to be the truth. The assumption about the predictability of the level of activity of business firms on the basis of their age is a case in point. There is, in fact, no evidence to suggest this is the case. There is also the assumption that housing availability in the city is important to the underemployed. The fact is that much migration of the poor to our cities has been to cities that had a tight housing market at the time the movement occurred. Nor does this end the list of assumptions that seem to run counter to what we know about the urban economy.

The Forrester model is indeed an attractive one to policy makers, because it is put together in ways that facilitate consideration of public policies. It is also attractive because it is operational; it can, in fact, simulate what it says it will simulate. How seriously that output should be taken, however, is another question.

Urban Simulation Models with Economic Roots: The Grand Design of the Future?

Future urban simulation models with economic roots are likely to be combinations of the nonspatial models of income, employment, and structural change discussed in the previous chapter and the land use models discussed in this chapter.

Today's econometric model of urban regions will find an important place in tomorrow's urban simulation model. These models will continue to link aggregate city income and employment to its major industries. The income and employment of these industries will continue to be functionally related to selected income, price, and locational variables. All of this, however, is likely to be supplemented with equations or submodels that allow the model builder to take supply variables in general, and migration variables in particular, explicitly into account. This will, very likely, mean the introduction of measures of geographic differentials of such quantities as wages, land costs, and taxes, which have bearing on labor and capital migration decisions both within and outside the city. As noted in the previous chapter, while there is much that remains to be learned about the channels through which supply factors influence aggregate income and employment in the city, they are important if our concern is with the long-run. This means they will inevitably become a more important part of these simulation models.

Another addition to this part of the model will be equations that enable us to make statements about the distribution of incomes in the city. What kind of equations will be introduced as a means of doing this is by no means clear, largely because our knowledge of factors affecting income distribution is limited. Since what happens to this distribution is important to any analysis of change in residential land use patterns, this is an area that will be researched much more extensively. Coming out of this research should be knowledge that allows us to add equations concerned with income distribution to the model.

That portion of the model concerned with land use or the spatial allocation of households and businesses will have a structure that is much like that of models of the National Bureau of Economic Research and the Urban Institute discussed above. There will be demand equations, supply equations, and market clearing equations. In the residential sector, more will be done with neighborhood effects as they influence household valuations of residences at particular sites. To incorporate income distribution as a part of the model will also strengthen the residential sector of the model, given the importance of income in residential choice.

The big improvements, if they are forthcoming, however, will be in the incorporation of more of the choice mechanism of businesses as they select a site within the city. In most urban simulation models constructed to date, the sites of business firms are taken as a variable. As discussed in chapter 5, this may not be an unreasonable thing to do with basic firms, unless there is technical change which substantially alters their space requirements. Where the nonbasic firms locate, on the other hand, is more sensitive to locational factors, e.g., where its customers are, that come into play within the city.

Given the expected evolution of computer technology and the likely state of our knowledge of the city, the general approach of future generations of urban simulation models will be much like some of those just discussed. The city or metropolitan area will be divided into zones. Land users will be classified into types, as will both the residential and nonresidential structures. The difference with future models will be that aggregate economic activity in the city will be linked to what is happening in the urban real estate market. The movement of business and households into the city, adding to its population, will, in future models, depend in part on valuations made which take account of, among other things, wage, land cost, and tax differentials between the city and the rest of the world. These things, in turn, will be influenced by the factors that come into play in the city's real estate markets as they respond to the change and requirements of the macroeconomic change taking place.

It is much easier to talk about likely simulation developments and outcomes in a very general way, than it is to be specific. It is easy to lose sight of the forest if we become concerned with the trees, particularly if our concern is with something that has its share of problems. That computer simulation modelling has had its share of problems is reflected in the fact that such modelling has had its ups and downs during its comparatively short life span. The downs are usually associated with disappointment that stems from unrealistic expectations. Despite the complexities we have built into some of these models, they are still very naive in many respects. Because of this they don't answer the kind of questions that many believe they should. Few urban economists doubt, however, that over the long-run, computer simulation models will come to occupy an increasingly important role in the decision-making process through which the fate of our cities is largely determined.

REFERENCES

Alonso, W. *Location and Land Use*. Cambridge, Mass.: Harvard University Press, 1964.

Chapin, F., and Weiss, S. "A Probabilistic Model for Residential Growth." *Transportation Research* 2 (1968): 375–90.

de Leeuw, F. "The Distribution of Housing Services." *The Urban Institute* 6 (1971): 208–16.

———; Struyk, R.; and Marshall, S. "The Urban Institute Housing Model: Second Year Report." *The Urban Institute* 6 (1973): 208–18.

Forrester, J. *Urban Dynamics*. Cambridge, Mass.: The MIT Press, 1969.

Herbert, D., and Stevens, B. "A Model for the Distribution of Residential Activity in Urban Areas." *Journal of Regional Science* 2 (1960): 21–36.

Ingram, C.; Kain, J.; and Ginn, R. *The Detroit Prototype of the NBER Urban Simulation Model*. New York: University of Columbia Press. National Bureau of Economic Research, 1972.

Little, A. "Model of San Francisco Housing Market." *San Francisco Community Renewal Program* C65400 (1966).

EPILOGUE

This is a book whose primary concern has been with showing students how urban economics, considered as a scientific language, can be applied to help us understand the economic facts of urban life. In my view, this is the proper way to present the subject. To present it in this way, however, is to provide the student with insights into what may seem to be fragments of urban life, even though some of those fragments are quite large. It therefore seems appropriate at the end to try to pull some of these threads together and look at the economic aspects of cities on a broader scale.

Books about cities written in the latter part of the 1960s and early 1970s were very much concerned with the big picture. Many of them painted a very dismal picture of urban life and generally held out little hope for any improvement in the future. Significantly, cities have not withered away. Urbanization continues, albeit at a slower pace. On the other hand, neither have the problems of the city disappeared. Slum housing remains; the pollution count rises in the summer; city streets are still congested at certain times of the day; and central city public officials still complain about fiscal strangulation. Nevertheless, life goes on in our cities with seemingly far fewer complaints than were heard back at the turn of the 1970s.

That people complain less is not necessarily an indication that things are better. The urban riots of the 1960s were not chance events; the problems that gave rise to them were real. Is it the case that we are now sitting on a keg of urban dynamite that could go off with the slightest unexpected provocation?

Without attempting to minimize the current problems in cities, in my view, a more reasonable interpretation is that things really weren't so bad as we used to believe they were just a short while ago. Certainly it is clear from the earlier discussion of scale economies, transportation costs, and the issue of urban size that the nation's productivity is linked to life in cities. Our living standards are as high as they are because of our technical know-how, and, significantly, we must live and work in close proximity to one another to take full advantage of this technology. To move apart would, in all probability, mean a substantial reduction in our living standards, which, in my view, few would be willing to accept.

Life in cities is, of course, not all sweetness and happiness. We pay a price for the productivity of our cities. Propinquity or nearness means congestion and pollution and a good deal of congestion and pollution when our markets don't work very well. Yet, we have apparently passed the peak of the congestion problem in many cities and have been making progress in dealing with the pollution problem in some cities. These improvements are due in part to the fact that cities, through the operation of the marketplace, have spread out. The circulation of traffic in our metropolitan areas follows a more dispersed pattern, which reduces the amount of congestion. Dispersion has also contributed to our efforts to deal with the problem of pollution. Both problems remain in most cities. City residents, however, are not being strangled by long lines of traffic and polluted air as some earlier authors had forecast. We have, in fact, reduced the dimensions of these problems slightly.

The poor remain in cities, many of whom still live in substandard housing. Yet both the number and proportion of poor people in our cities have declined and continue to decline when the economy is at full employment. The number of families living in substandard housing has also been reduced. Moreover, a reading of urban history suggests that some earlier authors did not really put the issues of urban poverty and urban housing in perspective. Many of the urban poor who came from the rural South and the Appalachias came because they lived in abject poverty in these places. The move to the city led to improved living standards for many.

These things aside, there are still poor people living in cities and many live in slum housing. It is also the case that much of this problem is still concentrated in urban ghettos whose residents are primarily black. While the economic miseries of those living in the urban ghettos have eased through the broad range of public assistance programs that have been initiated, poverty in cities, particularly in central cities, remains in ways that are not without some potentially explosive elements. As we see these problems today, however, they are primarily reflected in the fiscal problems of central city governments.

Central city mayors have complained for years about the fiscal strangulation of the central city by its suburbs. The discussion of these complaints in chapter 12 indicated these fiscal problems to be very real, but that they exist for reasons other than those put forth by the mayors. While there may be some exploitation of central cities by their suburbs in the sense of spillovers that benefit the latter at the expense of the former, a more important part of the problem stems from the growing inability of central city governments to meet the public needs of the poor through measures that redistribute income.

The spreading out of the city and the fragmentation of government this has brought about makes it extraordinarily difficult for central cities to do things that redistribute income from those who have it to those who do not. Efforts to do so encourage the high-income families to move away. The fact that people have the freedom to live where they please is the root cause of the fiscal problems of a central city that wishes to do a lot for its low-income residents.

Consolidated government is one answer to this problem; intergovernmental transfers are another. Our experiments with consolidated government thus far have not borne much fruit. Intergovernmental transfers, on the other hand, have turned out to be a reasonably successful way of getting funds from the suburbs to the central cities. Whether these transfers have helped deal effectively with the problems of the poor in central cities, however, is another question.

The problem with intergovernmental transfers is that in their initial stages, there is usually little recognition, by both those who give and receive, of what is happening and why. The taxes necessary to fund the initial programs may impose little visible burden on the suburban community. If those programs are expanded, however, these tax burdens increase and become more visible. This happened in most American cities recently at a time when the problem of *inflation and recession* was reducing the real incomes of the suburban resident. As a consequence, suburban taxpayers began to resist measures that expanded or even sustained public assistance programs. Some central cities tried to keep what they had through an assortment of short-term and temporary financing measures. In some instances, these financing palliatives led to a financial crisis. New York City underwent such a crisis in 1975.

The short-term resolution of these fiscal problems has centered around belt-tightening measures, which mean cutting back on some of the programs designed to aid the poor. Efforts to help the urban poor by redistributing income through intergovernmental transfers thus turned out to be less successful than we had judged them to be initially. This, in turn, raises questions about how successful we have been in dealing with the problems of the poor in our central cities.

A more fundamental question, yet to be answered, is how much is enough. If income redistribution is necessary to deal with the problems of the poor in central cities, just how much redistribution should there be? This is a very important question in a world in which most people place self-interest above their concerns for others. It is also a question about which the urban economist—or any other urban scientist for that matter—has little to say. Questions of equity are involved and, for reasons discussed in chapter 6, these are difficult questions.

The problem of equity in the distribution of income is, of course, given a political solution. We do, in fact, redistribute income through the activities of government. This is important, for if there is a preference for current political structures and little likelihood of turning back from the spread city, it suggests that the fiscal problems of central cities will persist so long as the poor remain concentrated in these cities.

Is opening up the suburbs the answer to these problems? Given the spread city, certainly much of the housing and economic opportunities suited to the needs of the central city poor is in the suburbs. This suggests that a part of the solution to the fiscal problems of central cities and hence the problem of the urban poor is to integrate the central city poor with suburbanites out in the suburbs.

This will not be easy for reasons that were discussed at some length in the chapters concerned with urban poverty and urban housing. The primary obstacle is racial discrimination, with respect to both employment and housing. While some progress has been made dealing with the problem of racial discrimination, it still remains as an important fact of urban life. Suburbanites have and will continue to resist the movement of low-income blacks into their neighborhoods. Most of this resistance stems from unwarranted prejudice; some of it stems from a warranted concern with spillovers that would arise by bringing the alienated poor into the suburbs. The question of how to deal with unwarranted prejudice is a difficult one. Perhaps subsidies that allow blacks to bid their ways into suburban neighborhoods, as suggested in chapter 10, is a part of the answer. Dealing with the problem of the alienated who live in central cities, as discussed in chapter 9, might be best addressed by "ghetto enrichment" measures, which tried to deal with the personal problems of the alienated in their present locations.

The problem of discrimination aside, whether integration in the sense of opening up the suburbs is a workable solution to these problems depends on the future shape and form of our cities. As this question was discussed in chapters 7 and 8, what cities of the future will look like depends on what happens to our communications, transportation, and materials technology, as well as the attitudes of the people about these technologies and city living. The viewpoint presented in these chapters was that cities will change, but only very slowly. The New Yorks, San Franciscos, and Bostons will not disappear. Cities as we know them will be with us because of the restraints to change built into the urban system by the fixed-site character of our urban investments. While impending technical changes suggest that we may be confronted with transportation, communications, and materials options that provide strong incentive to disperse, the probabilities of a radical departure of what we now know as a system of cities or urban hierarchy is very slight.

These dispersive factors are more likely to come into play within the city. Modes of transportation that increase the speed and reduce the cost of travel, along with modes of communications that reduce the need for face-to-face or face-to-commodity contact, will make dispersed living on more spacious sites more attractive than it already is. If the past contains clues to the future, many households and business firms will respond to this incentive. A further spreading out of the city is thus likely. The extent to which the density gradients of our cities are further flattened will be limited, however, by the fixed-site character of the plant housing our urban activities. Sites with fixed capital investments will continue to be vested with important cost advantages, which will work against the dispersal of activity in cities. The trend of rising energy costs, if it continues, will also tend to limit future dispersion.

What we are likely to see in the future are cities that are spread out more than they are today, although the change will be less than it has been over the past twenty-five years. Our cities will continue along the path leading to megalopolis, which means they will be large, highly diverse in make-up, and constituted of many nodes or points of high density, interspersed with zones of low density. Our cities of tomorrow will be similar to cities of today. This implies that measures designed to open up the suburbs to the central city poor will, within limits, continue to be a viable strategy to deal with the problems of the urban poor.

Cities are an important part of the human condition and are likely to remain so in the foreseeable future. Cities have problems that will not disappear so long as problems are a part of the human condition. Since problems appear to be an integral part of life, they have to be addressed. Hopefully, what we know about the economic roots of our urban activities will help us cope more effectively with these problems as they become manifest in cities.

Index

Accessibility:
  journey-to-school and, 86–87
  journey-to-shopping and, 87
  journey-to work and, 83–85, 346–47
  (*See also* Distance frictions, mobility, residential location)
Allocative efficiency:
  applications of criteria
    city size, 288–92
    externality zoning, 299–301
    housing, 219–23
    political fragmentation, 258, 260–62
    transportation, 236–37
  benefits, 107–9
  competitive markets, 109–10
  conditions of, 108–9
  contrast with engineering efficiency, 106–7
  costs, 107–9
  market failure
    free rider problem, 113
    ownership spillovers, 110–12
    public goods, 112–14
    technical difficulties, 110
  (*See also* competition, costs, demand, externalities, markets, public goods, revenues, welfare economics)
Appalachias, 132, 176, 265, 363
Arizona, 73, 132, 136, 283

Bakersfield, 282
Baltimore, 2, 129, 135, 147–48, 242
Base-service ratio, 321–23
Bid rent curves:
  applications, 149–52, 154–58, 211
  definition of, 85
  (*See also* nonresidential location, residential location)
Birmingham, 321
Black capitalism, 196–97
Boston, 129, 132, 135, 142, 147–48, 242, 365
Buffalo, 132, 136, 147–48, 283

California, 72, 73, 132–33, 136, 282–83
Central place theory:
  applications, 135–37

market areas, 47
market nets, 47
networks of market nets, 47
(*See also* location decisions, location economics, markets, urban hierarchy)
Chapin, S., 347–48
Charleston, 129–30
Chattanooga, 283
Chesapeake Bay, 111
Chicago, 74, 132, 136, 140, 147–48, 242, 251, 283–84, 292
Cincinnati, 131, 147, 322–23
Cities:
  definition of, 5–8
  fiscal problems of, 263–70
  future of, 137–42, 160–67
    communication changes, 161
    population growth, 161–62
    scenarios, 164–67
    social values, 162–64
    transportation changes, 160–61
  growth of, 64–66, 69, 73–75
  numbers of, in U.S., 32
  size of, 286–92
    diseconomies, 286–88
    negative market externalities, 288–90
    policy issues, 290–92
  spreading out of, 146–48
  structure of, 80
City building, 12, 27–28
City size in a hierarchy:
  determinants
    input cost variation, 282–83
    population growth, 278–79
    technology, 280–81
    transportation, 281
    urbanization economies, 283–84
Civil Rights Act of 1964, 193
Cleveland, 132, 136, 147–48, 242, 325
Colorado, 282
Communications, 161
Compensation payments, 301–2
Competition:
  efficiency and, 109–10
  firms and, 13
  markets, 14
  racial discrimination and, 184–85

Urban simulation:
definition of, 344–46
grand design models, 357–59
housing models, 348–57
models of the future, 359–60
models of residential extension, 346–48
(*See also* nonresidential location, residential location)
Urban sprawl:
definition of, 146–48
issue of, 159
(*See also* spread city)

Vertical integrated services, 259
Veterans Administration, 217

Washington, D.C., 1, 147–48, 247
Watts, 1
Weiss, S., 347–48
Welfare economics:
costs and benefits, 107–9

definition of, 106
(*See also* allocative efficiency, externalities, public goods)
West, 133, 136
Works Progress Administration, 272

Zoning:
auction methods of, 313–15
environmental aspects of, 312–13
externality zoning, 299–301
fiscal zoning, 302
history, 297–99
political economy of
under benevolent dictator, 303–4
under representative government, 304–6
under unrepresentative government, 307–8
outcomes
overzoning, 308–9
political corruption, 311–12
underzoning, 309–12